Games, Learning, and Society

This volume is the first reader on games and learning of its kind. Covering game design, game culture, and games as twenty-first-century pedagogy, it demonstrates the depth and breadth of scholarship on games and learning to date. The contributors represent some of the most influential thinkers, designers, and writers in the emerging field of games and learning – including James Paul Gee, Soren Johnson, Eric Klopfer, Colleen Macklin, Thomas Malaby, Bonnie Nardi, and David Sirlin. Together, their work functions both as an excellent introduction to the field of games and learning and as a powerful argument for the use of games in formal and informal learning environments in a digital age.

Constance Steinkuehler is an assistant professor of educational communications and technology at the University of Wisconsin-Madison. She is currently on leave to serve as a senior policy analyst in the Office of Science and Technology Policy in the Executive Office of the President to advise on national initiatives related to games and learning.

Kurt Squire is an associate professor of educational communications and technology at the University of Wisconsin-Madison. He is the director of the Educational Research Integration Area at the Morgridge Institute for Research, a design and research lab that makes scientific discovery visible through the development of games and simulations for public understanding.

Sasha Barab is a professor in the Teachers College at Arizona State University, where he also holds the Pinnacle West Presidential Chair and is a founding senior scientist and scholar of the Learning Sciences Institute.

D0556655

LEARNING IN DOING: SOCIAL, COGNITIVE, AND COMPUTATIONAL PERSPECTIVES

SERIES EDITOR EMERITUS
John Seely Brown, *Xerox Palo Alto Research Center*

GENERAL EDITORS
Roy Pea, *Professor of Education and the Learning Sciences and Director, Stanford Center for Innovations in Learning, Stanford University*

Christian Heath, *The Management Centre, King's College, London*

Lucy A. Suchman, *Centre for Science Studies and Department of Sociology, Lancaster University, UK*

BOOKS IN THE SERIES

The Construction Zone: Working for Cognitive Change in School
Denis Newman, Peg Griffin, and Michael Cole

Situated Learning: Legitimate Peripheral Participation
Jean Lave and Etienne Wenger

Street Mathematics and School Mathematics
Terezinha Nunes, David William Carraher, and Analucia Dias Schliemann

Understanding Practice: Perspectives on Activity and Context
Seth Chaiklin and Jean Lave, Editors

Distributed Cognitions: Psychological and Educational Considerations
Gavriel Salomon, Editor

The Computer as Medium
Peter Bøgh Anderson, Berit Holmqvist, and Jens F. Jensen, Editors

Sociocultural Studies of Mind
James V. Wertsch, Pablo del Rio, and Amelia Alvarez, Editors

Sociocultural Psychology: Theory and Practice of Doing and Knowing
Laura Martin, Katherine Nelson, and Ethel Tobach, Editors

Mind and Social Practice: Selected Writings of Sylvia Scribner
Ethel Tobach et al., Editors

Computation and Human Experience
Philip E. Agre

(Continued after index)

Games, Learning, and Society

Learning and Meaning in the Digital Age

Edited by

CONSTANCE STEINKUEHLER
University of Wisconsin-Madison

KURT SQUIRE
University of Wisconsin-Madison

SASHA BARAB
Arizona State University

CAMBRIDGE
UNIVERSITY PRESS

CAMBRIDGE
UNIVERSITY PRESS

32 Avenue of the Americas, New York NY 10013-2473, USA

Cambridge University Press is part of the University of Cambridge.

It furthers the University's mission by disseminating knowledge in the pursuit of education, learning and research at the highest international levels of excellence.

www.cambridge.org
Information on this title: www.cambridge.org/9780521144520

© Cambridge University Press 2012

First published 2012
Reprinted 2013

A catalog record for this publication is available from the British Library.

Library of Congress Cataloging in Publication data
Games, learning, and society : learning and meaning in the digital age / [edited by] Constance Steinkuehler, the University of Wisconsin, Madison; Kurt Squire, the University of Wisconsin, Madison; Sasha Barab, Arizona State University.
    p. cm. – (Learning in doing)
Includes bibliographical references and index.
ISBN 978-0-521-19623-9 (hardback) – ISBN 978-0-521-14452-0 (paperback)
1. Video games – Study and teaching. 2. Video games – Psychological aspects.
3. Learning, Psychology of. 4. Video games – Design. 5. Video games –
Social aspects. I. Steinkuehler, Constance, 1970– II. Squire, Kurt.
III. Barab, Sasha A.
GV1469.3.G423 2012
794.8–dc23   2012011690

ISBN 978-0-521-19623-9 Hardback
ISBN 978-0-521-14452-0 Paperback

Contents

Contributors

Sasha Barab
Arizona State University

Rebecca W. Black
University of California, Irvine

Trina Choontanom
University of California, Irvine

Sarah Chu
University of Wisconsin-Madison

Douglas B. Clark
Vanderbilt University

Bob Coulter
Litzsinger Road Ecology Center

Drew Davidson
Carnegie Mellon University

James Paul Gee
Arizona State University

Melissa Gresalfi
Indiana University

Erica Rosenfeld Halverson
University of Wisconsin-Madison

Elisabeth Hayes
Arizona State University

Soren Johnson
EA2D

Yasmin B. Kafai
University of Pennsylvania

Eric Klopfer
MIT Scheller Teacher Education Program

Richard Lemarchand
Naughty Dog

Greg LoPiccolo
Harmonix Music Systems, Inc.

Colleen Macklin
Parsons The New School for Design

Thomas M. Malaby
University of Wisconsin-Milwaukee

Mario Martinez-Garza
Vanderbilt University

Nathan McKenzie
Independent Game Designer

Bonnie Nardi
University of California, Irvine

Yoonsin Oh
University of Wisconsin-Madison

Kylie A. Peppler
Indiana University

Judy Perry
MIT Scheller Teacher Education Program

Patrick Pettyjohn
Indiana University

Stephanie M. Reich
University of California, Irvine

David Williamson Shaffer
University of Wisconsin-Madison

John Sharp
Savannah College of Art and Design–Atlanta

Josh Sheldon
MIT Scheller Teacher Education Program

David Sirlin
Independent Game Designer

Maria Solomou
Indiana University

Kurt Squire
University of Wisconsin-Madison

Constance Steinkuehler
University of Wisconsin-Madison

Series Foreword

This series for Cambridge University Press is widely known as an international forum for studies of situated learning and cognition. Innovative contributions are being made by anthropology; by cognitive, developmental, and cultural psychology; by computer science; by education; and by social theory. These contributions are providing the basis for new ways of understanding the social, historical, and contextual nature of learning, thinking, and practice that emerges from human activity. The empirical settings of these research inquiries range from the classroom to the workplace, to the high-technology office, and to learning in the streets and in other communities of practice. The situated nature of learning and remembering through activity is a central fact. It may appear obvious that human minds develop in social situations and extend their sphere of activity and communicative competencies. But cognitive theories of knowledge representation and learning alone have not provided sufficient insight into these relationships. This series was borne of the conviction that new and exciting interdisciplinary syntheses are underway as scholars and practitioners from diverse fields seek to develop theory and empirical investigations adequate for characterizing the complex relations of social and mental life – and for understanding successful learning wherever it occurs. The series invites contributions that advance our understanding of these seminal issues.

Roy Pea
Christian Heath
Lucy A. Suchman

Foreword

James Paul Gee

People of all ages spend massive amounts of time watching television. In his book *Cognitive Surplus*, Clay Shirky argues that we could change the world if we could get people to devote many of those hours to important causes. And, indeed, more and more people today are turning off the television and using digital media to produce and not just consume, to participate and not just spectate, and to innovate and not just replicate. Video games are one important medium that has siphoned cognitive energy from television. However, for nongamers, video games are often not what they think they are based on what mainstream media often makes them out to be.

Games are not like books, movies, or television. Books, movies, and television are all about their content. In these media, content is king. Games have content, but they are not about their content. They are about doing, making decisions, solving problems, and interacting. Content is there in a game to facilitate and serve acting, deciding, problem solving, and interaction. In good games, content (including story or plot) needs to be a loyal vassal to *game mechanics*, that is, all that players must do and decide in order to succeed. *War and Peace* is about war and peace; *Grand Theft Auto* is not about crime – it is about players coming up with good strategies for success in a virtual world with multiple constraints, some stemming from the story and many from the design of the virtual world and the game play in it.

People certainly can learn things from books, movies, and television. But learning is, for nearly all good games, a core game mechanic. Gamers do not just do things and make decisions. They must learn things and even master them. If they don't, they don't leave the first level of a game. Imagine a book that constantly had quizzes and tests at the end of each section (oops, that's a textbook). Few people would consider it fun (few people consider textbooks fun). But games constantly assess players. Every action is a test with feedback, and the boss at the end of a level is a "final exam" for that level. Games have found that both learning and constant assessments of that learning are a "turn-on" for people. And players pay lots of money for this turn-on. The textbook makers can only marvel in envy.

Good games work because they know that learning is a deep drive for humans, a drive that school has managed to kill for many. Games are simply spaces of learning and problem solving with a "win" condition (beating each level and the game as a whole). But to sell, they have to organize learning in engaging and highly motivating ways. They have to tap into the innate drive for learning and mastery that is inside all human beings.

As learning systems, games are not traditional pedagogy (tell the learner everything through overt instruction) or liberal pedagogy (just turn the learners loose in a rich environment). Games make it feel like the player has been turned loose in a rich environment. But the game mentors, guides, and teaches the player all the time. Games do this by designing experiences in the game world in such a way that they shape players' goals, decisions, and actions while still leaving players a good deal of freedom and responsibility for their own decisions and actions. It is a sort of magic: design as mentor and teacher.

Games honor "tacit knowledge," that is, knowledge about how to act (do things) gained from experience. But they also know that knowledge gets deeper when we can articulate it and think about it overtly. Not all tacit knowledge can be rendered overt, conscious, and articulated. But a good deal can. School tends to rarely honor tacit knowledge. It fails to realize as well that moving from tacit knowledge to explicit knowledge is a route that ensures the ability both to solve problems and store relevant facts and information. Simply teaching and assessing information and facts, as school so often does, gets paper-and-pencil tests passed but does not lead to problem solving.

Games often build into their designs lots of language, exposition, and explanation, so that players can learn some explicit articulated knowledge from game play itself. But very often games rely on interest-driven, fan-based communities associated with the game to accomplish this goal. In these communities (which I have elsewhere called *passionate affinity spaces*), gamers reflect on, critique, and analyze the game, game play, and different strategies. They even use software tools to redesign ("mod") aspects of the game or to design devices (such as damage meters) that can be used in the game by other players, tools that often require a deep understanding of the statistical model underlying a game.

School is about "belief." It is about what others have claimed and what is true or not. Although belief is important, games and game play are about "design knowledge." Design knowledge is not just about belief but also about which beliefs, facts, and tools are adequate or not for various purposes and goals.

As I have mentioned, games engage in constant assessment. In school, assessments are about "knowledge," about what facts and information and formulas one can articulate or write down. In games, assessment is about knowledge in that sense as well (and you are, in particular, in trouble in a game-based passionate affinity space if you cannot articulate your knowledge). But they also assess three others things: (1) problem solving, (2) the quality of one's choices and decisions across time in terms of their short- and long-term consequences, and (3) preparation for future learning, that is, how well the player is prepared to go to the next harder level, not just what the player has mastered in the level. Games do not want you to pass tests if you can't pass the next one and win in the end.

All in all, good games are a model of twenty-first-century learning. The same principles that games use to "hook" gamers can be used to "hook" learners on anything worthwhile, including school "content" such as science, civics, and math (which, then, must be seen as things to do and not just facts to repeat).

Many have hoped that the cognitive surplus drawn away from television to more interactive and social media will lead to transformation in the real world. It may then seem surprising that gamers use a lot of that cognitive surplus to engage in theory crafting, modding, and designing for games and other virtual environments. They study the underling statistical models in games; they use scientific thinking, and even carry out experiments, to argue about the complex interaction of variables in games; they study the economics of massive multiplayer games so that they can manipulate it; they use digital 3D tools to design all sorts of different things for games (e.g., *the Sims* and *Spore*) – such as houses, environments, creatures, clothes, cities – and virtual worlds such as *Second Life*.

Some worry that all this intellectual effort and all these skills will not "transfer" to the real world. But the reality is that games – which today, for the most part, involve real people collaborating and working and playing socially with each other – are the real world. The models gamers build and the designs they make influence others across the world and sometimes lead to new businesses selling virtual or real goods. The evidence that the cognitive surplus devoted to games transfers to other aspects of the real world is the large number of game players, modders, and designers who have moved on to other technical, artistic, and entrepreneurial enterprises. Games are, without doubt, a great source of a secondary, value-added, enhanced cognitive surplus that spills out into many aspects of the world.

However, in my view, the real contribution games studies – when they involve papers such as the ones in this volume – has to make is to show us that we swim in a new sea of possibilities. We can learn from games and gaming not just new ways to build better games but also ways to build better learning, assessment, production, participation, design, and creativity for all people, old and young, in a fast-changing, high-risk, global world. Levi-Strauss once said that people in oral cultures used myths to show that objects in nature were "good to think with" and not just to eat or use. This discovery was one of the origins of science and theory building. Games are good to think with as well and not just to play. They, too, can be the origins of new ways with learning and knowledge.

Acknowledgments

This book is the culmination of many brilliant people creating the future of new media, unpacking how they operate, and applying how they operate to try and transform education. This community (and book project) reflects the work of game developers, academics, and teachers, many of whom play all three of these roles from time to time. We are indebted to everyone in this community and particularly to James Paul Gee, Henry Jenkins, and Connie Yowell, who have paved the way for this collaboration through building this field. This particular book project, which seeks to engage the learning sciences community in these conversations (where all three of us were trained as scholars) from a situated learning perspective, is also indebted intellectually and practically to John Seely Brown, Jean Lave, Etienne Wenger, Lucy A. Suchman, John Bransford, Roy Pea, and Ann Brown.

As is always the case, our thinking in conceptualizing this work is deeply indebted to our graduate students. We are greatly indebted to Crystle Martin without whose indefatigable conceptual and practical management "up" we would never have been able to finally pull this volume together. Her work has made all of ours better in numerous ways. We would also like to acknowledge Tyler Dodge whose wonderful spirit was engaging, sincere, and deeply committed to using media for social justice. Much of the thinking in Sasha's chapter comes directly from Tyler, who has shaped all our thinking on games. Tyler will be missed by this community, but most profoundly by Sasha, who is deeply grateful for Tyler's selfless willingness to share his contributions so generously.

Section I

Games as Designed Experience

1   Introduction to Section I

Kurt Squire

This section, "Games as Designed Experience," is the result of years of conversation among game developers, educators, media theorists, and indeed most of the authors (at times all three) at venues such as the Games+Learning+Society (GLS) Conference. This section features game developers theorizing about their practice and the social changes suggested by it. Much of this work is motivated by game developers trying to understand their practice in real time. As designers, these authors are mostly outside mainstream educational research discourse. However, they all do educational activities, including teaching university courses on game design, leading workshops for game developers, or just training team members informally on the job.

Many of the essays that make up these chapters have appeared in other venues ranging from *Game Developer* magazine to academic journals on digital media and learning. As such, their primary audiences include professional game designers, educators, and media theorists. Rather than revamp the pieces for this audience, we chose to leave them relatively intact, hopefully providing a window into the language and value systems that each author brings to his or her work.

A goal of this section is to invite educators who might be unfamiliar with game-developer discourse into this world and provide a window into how some leading developers theorize their practice. Hopefully, this section also lays a foundation for educators to understand how games are constructed, how potential meanings are encoded into them, how players learn to think in games, how game cultures operate, and what the implications of this medium are for learning and society writ large.

Several essays first appeared in venues directed toward game developers, and each has become a classic within certain circles. David Sirlin's "Yomi: Spies of the Mind" certainly fits these criteria. Sirlin uses *Virtua*

Fighter 3, a 3D fighting game to illustrate the concept of *Yomi*, which is for a player to get inside another player's mind and understand his or her thinking. The discussion might get esoteric unless you are familiar with *Virtua Fighter*, but hopefully it communicates to skeptics just how complex a "mindless, button-mashing" fighting game can be. More broadly, Sirlin's work is interested in competitive games, games that are clearly skill-based (as opposed to games in which success comes from luck or simply time spent playing, which many have argued is true for too many contemporary video games – including Sirlin himself (see Sirlin, 2006). Ironically, it may be fighting games such as *Virtua Fighter* that hold the key to games for education.

Soren Johnson's series of articles on theme, mechanics, and meaning, which were first published in *Game Developer* magazine, asks a question of central importance to educators: How do games convey meaning? Johnson, who has a background in history, computer science, and historical modeling from Stanford, has worked on *Civilization* and *Spore* (among others), which are two touchstone games for educators. Johnson articulates why criticism of *Spore* as a bad evolution game were the result of focusing on theme rather than mechanics and how meaning arises at the intersection of mechanics, theme, and player experience (for a similar but different framework, see Hunicke, LeBlanc, and Zubek, 2004). Johnson also critiques the *Civilization* series from this perspective, concluding that games more firmly rooted in a particular time period may be best for encouraging historical thinking. Johnson's distinctions are crucial for educators, media theorists, and game designers who hope to better understand what meanings youth may be taking from games, why they play what they play, and what the potential of the medium is for more formal learning.

Nathan McKenzie uses another touchstone game, *SimCity*, to outline the contemporary game-development ecology in "Nurturing Lateral Leaps in Game Design," suggesting how a game-development environment that could encourage the kinds of games that educators would want might very well look like. McKenzie is a veteran game developer in both the mainstream AAA (game title) community, where he worked on such games as *Soldier of Fortune*, *Hexen*, and *Quake4*, and the independent community, where he has launched a number of ground-breaking games through his own development studio, Ice Cream Breakfast. McKenzie reflects on these experiences to show how the modern game-making environment, as a heavily industrialized, sociotechnical enterprise, is deeply shaped by the kinds of games that have been made, with software tools, techniques, and developers' skill sets co-evolving with such games. To create *new* kinds of games, we will need new tools, methodologies, and skill sets. McKenzie also calls our attention to the importance of competing *values* – something that most educators who have partnered with game developers well understand. Particular visual 3D programmers, for example, may tend to value beautifully rendered water, whereas educators may value accessible game play. Developing a robust, mature educational gaming market will require an interplay between innovative games and more derivative games that consolidates proven design innovations and brings them to broad markets. McKenzie surveys entertainment games, modding communities, student projects, and quasi-commercial spaces (such as Multi-User Dungeons [MUDs]), providing both a useful analysis of games culture and a blueprint for how educators might create a thriving business sector.

"Uncharted 2: Among Thieves – How to Become a Hero" emerged out of the *Well Played* (aka *Gaming with Drew*) series at the GLS Conference. The idea behind this series is to feature game players and game designers discussing a given game in real time in ways that "close the loop" across game players, designers, and the designed object. The resulting chapter is a collaboration between Drew Davidson (who directs Carnegie Mellon's Entertainment Technology Center in Pittsburgh and is both an academic and a former developer) and Richard Lemarchand, who is a lead game designer at Naughty Dog. The chapter is an inside look at both how the game was designed, on the one hand, and how it is experienced by skilled players, on the other. Understanding how skilled players experience games is central to Davidson's work in the *Well Played* series (see also Sirlin's *Yomi*, Chapter 6 in this volume). How can scholars "keep up" on the wide range of experiences available to gamers, particularly when participating in a forty-person *World of Warcraft* raid, a competitive *Quake* clan, or a *Civilization* modding community each can be a nearly full-time job? By engaging developers in a dialogue around the game, this chapter illustrates one crucial theme within the field: Academics must study game-development techniques so as to understand how they shape and influence the medium and therefore gamer experiences.

In "Interview with Harmonix," Sarah Chu and I interview Greg LoPiccolo, vice president of product development for Harmonix Music Systems, to better understand how Harmonix approaches game design. Its music games, which include *FreQuency*, *Karaoke Revolution*, *Guitar Hero I* and *II*, and the *Rock Band* series, are revolutionary, launching a multi-billion-dollar sector of the games industry and, in the case of *Rock Band Pro*, likely candidates for transforming music instruction as well. LoPiccolo describes how, through constant iteration and user testing, Harmonix develops games that produce particular *emotional experiences* such as the experience of making and performing music in a group.

Finally, my contribution to the volume is a study of Apolyton University, an online community within the Apolyton.net affinity space. This piece began with a conversation with Soren Johnson, lead designer of *Civ4*, who suggested that I use Apolyton as a model for how to organize an after-school gaming club. I was frankly shocked by the depth of thinking in Apolyton, and as I shared the story, James Paul Gee suggested that I study the community's structures more formally. Ethnographies of social practices (including institutions) surrounding media build on the tradition of cognitive ethnographies in the learning sciences (see Hutchins, 1995; Lave & Wenger, 1991) but seek to understand how the nature of participation in social life may be changing in a digital age (cf. Gee, Hull, & Lankshear, 1996). In truth, the broader GLS community has become a refuge of a sort away from institutional and political pressures for research that narrowly responds to the immediate needs of teachers or increases standardized test scores (Stokes, 1997; Shavelson et al., 2003).

Taken together, these chapters suggest new directions for thinking about games as an expressive medium both for how learning takes place within them and for how they might be leveraged for more formal instruction. A few key themes are especially important for educators seeking to design game-based interventions for education.

The first is that making a good game for entertainment, let alone for learning, is a nontrivial task and one that, as a field, we have yet to do particularly well. McKenzie's challenge is the appropriate one, although with games such as Douglas Clark's *Surge*, Filament Games' *Resilient Planet*, and Education Arcade's *Labyrinth* (to name a few), we now have some *new kinds of games*, to use McKenzie's terms, to generate energy in the field. Still, we are in no position as yet to answer the question posed by many educational researchers and institutions: "Is there evidence that games work?" (cf. Tobias and Fletcher, forthcoming). Aside from the fact that this question is always temporal (the effective game-based curricula may be one that doesn't exist yet), we still need more rounds of iteration and experimentation. A challenge for the field, however, is to devise ways to develop and share this knowledge. Ultimately, that elusive killer app may be something like *Guitar Hero Pro*, which comes entirely outside the educational establishment.

Johnson's chapter, "Our Cheatin' Hearts," reminds us that although we can look at games in the tradition of earlier media, there are unique affordances to games to which educators will need to respond. Games value different forms of thinking and suggest different modes of interpretation. Given educators' widespread difficulties "getting" the meaning of *Spore* (or, otherwise put, their difficulties "reading" the game), it may be a while before an education community is sufficiently literate with the medium to produce (i.e., to "write") innovative games that wed content, thinking, and game play. Sirlin and Davidson remind us that to understand games, we need to get personally good at them on some level and understand the game that is in the player's mind. My own thinking has been profoundly shaped by conversations with each of these designer-authors, although it's also worth noting that these conversations have happened *despite* academic and educational institutional structures, not because of them. These designers take personal days off of work to attend the GLS Conference and other events in order to engage in conversations with us, and academics from social sciences traditions are largely disincentivized from digging deeply into design.

Indeed, if, as McKenzie suggests, educators of the sort to be writing in this volume are akin to the AAA game publishers, then perhaps the more effective task would be to stop making games and to instead create tools and resources for communities of developers to make a lot of games, most of which will be spectacular failures. Perhaps funding agencies such as the National Science Foundation (NSF) and the Department of Education need to realize that games coming from academics may never even get the 100,000 players that one of McKenzie's beloved failures gets on Kongregate. However, if academic communities can manage to function like these independent developer communities, in which they create a lot of games, steal ideas from one another, and build on one another's successes, they could build enough novel games for a highly specialized and skilled group to create a polished instance of a game that truly could have mass appeal.

Even then, we must be sure not to focus on the game but rather to focus on the *game-playing context* as the real driver of learning. Learning through game-playing communities is frequently interest-driven, multi-generational, specialized (i.e., people learn different things), productive (i.e., you make complex artifacts), and authentic (i.e., learners often engage in activities with consequences beyond the classroom). These conditions, which are found in many alternative schools or "experimental" programs such as Montessori, have values that fly in the face of mainstream education – indeed, even in the face of so-called gold standard educational research methods. If a precondition to good learning is that a student learns something new, something unanticipated that goes beyond what the teacher knows (which is, after all, how much of learning works in the real world), then we will have to invent new research methods that are able to capture such genuine production rather than continue to haphazardly adapt methods from agriculture or medicine (as though learning were like optimizing crops).

My own hunch is that in the upcoming years, great games of this sort will get built and played and that, as devices such as iPads proliferate, students will play those games regardless of educators' intentions. As any parent of young children in the past decade is aware, there is a robust, highly profitable multi-billion-dollar home edutainment market for young children. It is not difficult to imagine parents spending similar amounts on older children – especially if designers can create ways for parents and youth to play together. It is also not difficult to imagine attending a museum exhibit on evolution with my children and then playing a multiplayer evolution game with them at home afterwards. The ultimate question, then, is equity. Who will have access to these experiences, be resourced in ways necessary to take advantage of them, and have the intellectual, social, and technical tools needed to participate in something such as Apolyton University? Current educational rhetoric from Washington nearly ensures that public schools will cater to the lowest common denominator, allowing in only those curricula that "work" as defined by antiquated and narrow measures, whereas the educated and affluent will continue to enrich their children through designed experiences such as games.

References

Gee, J. P., Hull, G., & Lankshear, C. (1996). *The new work order: Behind the language of the new capitalism*. Boulder, CO: Westview.

Hunicke, R., LeBlanc, M., & Zubek, R., (2004). MDA: A formal approach to game design and game research. *Proceedings of the Challenges in Game AI Workshop, Nineteenth National Conference on Artificial Intelligence*, San Jose, CA. Last retrieved October 1, 2010, from http://www.cs.northwestern.edu/~hunicke/MDA.pdf.

Hutchins, E. (1995). *Cognition in the wild*. Cambridge, MA: MIT Press.

Lave, J., & Wenger, E. (1991). *Situated learning: Legitimate peripheral participation*. New York: Cambridge University Press.

Shavelson, R. J., Philips, D. C., Towne, L., & Feuer, M. J. (2003). On the Science of Education Design Studies. *Educational Researcher*, 32(1), 25–8. Last retrieved October 4, 2010, from http://www.jstor.org/stable/3699932.

Sirlin, D. (2006). *World of Warcraft* teaches the wrong things. *Gamasutra*, February 22. Last retrieved October 5, 2010, from http://www.gamasutra.com/features/20060222/sirlin_01.shtml.

Stokes, D. E. (1997). *Pasteur's quadrant: Basic science and technological innovation.* Washington, DC: Brookings Institution Press.

Tobias, S., & Fletcher, J. D. (eds.) (forthcoming). *Computer games and instruction.* Charlotte, NC: Information Age Publishers.

2   Designed Cultures

Kurt Squire

As educators investigate the power of games for learning, much attention has been paid to the learning principles underlying video games (Gee, 2003/2007), their *design* features (also called *formal abstract design tools*; Church, 2005), such as the use of narrative for creating investment (Davidson, 2009), or rhythmic immersion (see Squire, 2011). An understanding of these design tools and patterns is critically important to enable understanding of learning at the human-computer level. Indeed, much of educators' interest in games lies in understanding their design so as to better understand cognition as a materially situated, digitally mediated phenomenon (see Shaffer & Clinton, 2006; Lemke, 2005), as well as how to design more compelling, effective learning materials ranging from multiuser virtual environments (MUVEs) to digital textbooks (Squire et al., 2003).

Consistent with the sociocultural approach, it is equally important for researchers and theorists to understand the socially situated nature of game play. Social structures such as families, guilds, informal gaming networks, and broader cultural notions of play further mediate game play and thus learning. For example, familial rules (such as the length of time that a child is permitted to play) make some forms of gaming practice available while prohibiting others; if a child is permitted limited gaming time, it is unlikely that he or she will have opportunities to engage in sophisticated practices such as modding. Within multiplayer games, guilds function as a remediating force, pushing particular values for how games ought to be played as instantiated through formal and informal participation structures (such as dragon kill point [DKP] systems, looting rules, and rules for membership). Such structures may be on par with the software itself when constituting the game-play experience in such contexts (Squire & Steinkuehler, 2005).

Nitsche (2009) offers a framework of five planes of gaming that is useful for unpacking these distinctions. The first plane is the game as it is encoded as software (in the box, back when games primarily came that way). The second plane is the game that unfolds on screen. These are the actions and events, often emergent, that arise from player action. Notice already that there is no "game" to speak of without the player. Game action cannot be examined on screen without taking into account the player. The third plane is the game being played in the player's mind. Will Wright discusses this plane in terms of *The Sims*. I might, for example, play a game based on my family. The people on screen aren't "my family," but in my mind, they are. The fourth plane is the action occurring in real space (the mouse clicks and so on). This is the "button mashing" plane, as well as the "dancing plane" (in *Dance, Dance, Revolution*). Studies of games with strong physical components have emphasized the expressivity that players showcase through such movements in real space in order to augment games' relatively constrained choices (see Smith & Squire, 2002).

The fifth plane, which will be discussed more extensively in this chapter, is the social plane. This plane is gaming in its social context, which might involve performative dimensions (as in *Rock Band*) or competitive play (as in *Team Fortress 2*). House *Madden* tournaments, *Starcraft* matches, *Metroid* speed runs, classic gaming tournaments, and *Golden Tee* golf tournaments are all examples of such social structures that have been formalized. Often, as in *World of Warcraft* (but also in games as diverse as *Madden* and *Civilization*), one game has multiple, overlapping, and contradictory social structures affiliated with it, as evidenced by the game's Battle Ground teams, Progression Guilds, and Social Guilds.[1] In a very real way, massively multiplayer online game (MMO) players are often playing very different games, and the game play that emerges is at the intersection of designed structures, players' goals, and broader cultural context (e.g., other media properties). Thus, understanding the cultural context of games is critical to understanding both the game experience (see Jenkins, 2006) and games' potential (and perhaps limitations) for supporting learning.

The game "experience" spans all five planes, and the intersection across them (i.e., how a game design feature might support collaboration) is in many respects the place where game play becomes interesting for learning. How do particular game features (e.g., direct competition) facilitate social interaction? As will be explored in this chapter, what impact on learning might robust game design and development tools have?

The qualities of these gaming communities are especially important for educators. First, such communities are constitutive of the game-play experience, so it's difficult to understand learning through gaming in any meaningful way without accounting for them. To claim to understand *Quake* without understanding the many clans, tournaments, and encompassing social structures that mediate play would be impossible (much as golfers could miss a lot about golf if they don't study Tiger Woods). As such, this chapter is meant to contribute to a growing body of interdisciplinary research empirically examining such communities in order to characterize gaming communities, identify the participant structures that affect learning, and theorize about the nature of learning in a networked, digitally mediated world (see also Gee & Hayes, 2010; Steinkuehler, 2006). Indeed, as youth spend more and more time affiliating with such organizations, it is critical that we understand how they operate – particularly given most parents' and educators' lack of familiarity with them (Squire, 2005b).

Second, they might serve as design inspiration for educators seeking to create game-based curricula. Much as Lave and Wenger (1991) developed the notion of legitimate peripheral participation in communities of practice by studying apprenticeships, such studies might provide new models of social arrangements that can support learning. Gee (2003/2007) used *Rise of Nations* forums to develop his notion of *affinity spaces*, a description of spaces that support interest-driven learning and that, Gee argues, are increasingly common within the digital, networked world. However, much as Lave and Wenger's notions were meant to be descriptive and not prescriptive, such a study ought to provide guidance, but not a template, for education. As educators, we have both the freedom and responsibility as designers to create systems reflective of our (and community) values.

This chapter is one such analysis, a study of Apolyton University, an online, self-organizing community of *Civilization* players (hereafter called *Civ* when referring to the general franchise or *CivI, II, III*, or *IV* when referring to a specific title). I first became aware of Apolyton while completing my dissertation. I was looking for historically accurate scenarios and soon found a treasure trove of accurate maps, historical mods, and development tools designed to support players in modding. For those unfamiliar with gaming communities, it is worth emphasizing this last point: There is a robust third-party software-development community dedicated to designing tools to support *Civ* players creating mods.

My dissertation investigated the potential for using *CivIII* in formal and informal school environments to teach world history and showed how game play could lead students to sophisticated ways of thinking about world history. However, as I concluded this research, I was left wondering how different learning might be free from the constraints of school (e.g., limited time periods, content coverage pressures). The true power of a game such as *Civ*, designed to be played over hundreds of hours, might be in players taking the game home, playing with friends, and even designing their own scenarios. How would you set up such an organization? What sorts of participant structures would guide players from being novices to becoming experts?

"Take another look at Apolyton.net," Soren Johnson, lead designer of *CivIII*, suggested. "Look into Apolyton University. It's one of the most sophisticated gaming communities I've seen."[2] When I did finally visit Apolyton University, I was *deeply* humbled.

Apolyton University

I would like to propose a new group effort.

For several reasons I want to get a lot sharper at *CivIII*. First, I just enjoy it. Second, I've really liked some of the tourney and tournament discussions, have learned a bunch, and have been waaay impressed by some of the strategies and tactics employed. Third, MP [Multiplayer] is coming and while I never participate in MP that way, I intend to this time around.

Also, although I still enjoy playing the stock game, it definitely could be more of a challenge.

So what I want is a combination boot camp and war college leveraging a varied group of players and a variety of techniques, to polish collective skills.

...

We should do experiments, like Aeson's iceberg, Arrian's UP™, Sir Ralph's effort to create WWIII, etc.... I also think it will be useful to start developing a more advanced lexicon for strategies, tactics, and exploits. We've been doing that informally, but it will make life a lot easier for new players.

—Theseus

With this post, Theseus launched Apolyton University, an online school of strategy, in which "students sharpen their *CivIII* skills and share their experiences in a series of thematic games." This was unbelievable. A group of players started their own *school* for *Civilization*? Their energy was impressive and their skill level humbling. Hundreds of players were designing custom games, holding tournaments, and even writing *courses* on advanced strategies.

Theseus's post contains many insights about how learning unfolds in this (and other) digital communities. First, note that Theseus is motivated primarily by "enjoyment." Learning is fun, and fun, for Theseus, is learning (becoming sharper), as it is in many gaming communities (see also Koster, 2004; Steinkuehler & Johnson, 2009). Theseus already has considerable expertise, but he wants "more of a challenge" to extend this expertise further.

Second, learning is deeply social. Theseus learns by observing and studying games and receiving feedback on his own games from other players. Social interaction pushes his own thinking and creates an audience for his work. This motivation is also future-oriented. Theseus wants to play in multiplayer games and recognizes that he needs to sharpen his skills in preparation. So Theseus is not learning for abstract reasons but preparing for future *action*.

Unlike most schools, which are focused purely on transmitting knowledge, Theseus's school is also focused on knowledge *production* (like universities). Theseus uses two metaphors – "boot camp" and "war college" – to describe the school. This combination suggests both enculturation into specific practices (boot camp) and the production of new knowledge (war college). Here, we see an intriguing contradiction between schools – and indeed many game-based learning approaches that seek to enculturate learners into particular viewpoints (e.g., Shaffer, 2006/2008) – and Apolyton University, which also seeks to produce new knowledge. Apolyton University is inquiry- and interest-driven, seeking to transform game-playing practices, generate new knowledge, and – as we shall see – transform the game itself.

The final paragraph in which Theseus explicitly mentions several "experiments" drives this point home. These experiments, basically design experiments in which the stock rules are changed, enable players to gain new insights into the stock rules, discover new strategies, and in some cases create entirely new games. As such, Apolyton University looks as much like a research laboratory as it does a school.

Over the next six months, Levi Giovanetto and I enrolled in Apolyton University, played its games, took its courses (see Figure 2.1 for a list), and studied its participants. The full methods are described in our article, "The Higher Education of Gaming" (Giovanetto & Squire, 2008), but one idea to emphasize here is that enrolling in dozens of courses and playing collaboratively online was both time-intensive and *deeply* personal. I thought of myself as a sophisticated *Civ* player, yet my analyses were elementary compared with those of veterans.

Theseus further set the tone for the school in the following post:

> When playing an Apolyton University game, gaining and sharing knowledge is more important than getting a high score, or even winning the game. Participants are encouraged to share their strategy after the game, and even to try several attempts.

Table 2.1. *Apolyton course listings*

Course number	Course title	Author
AU 101	Crowding and War	Theseus
AU 102	All We're Sayin' Is Give Peace a Chance	Alexman
AU 104	Banana Island	Sir Ralph
AU 201	The Quest for Ultimate Power	Nbarclay
AU 203	The Power of Communism	BRC
AU 206	Gallic Glory	Alexman
AU 210	UN Peacekeepers	Rhothaerill
AU 302	OCC (One-City Challenge)	Dominae
AU 401	They Came Down from the Mountains	Konquest02
AU 502	Celtic Power – Swords and Ploughshares	Ducki

This ethos builds on aspects of gaming culture (such as the importance of debriefing after a game) while also differentiating it from subcultures in which high score is indeed paramount. The point of *this* community was learning. Because Apolyton University was organized learning rather than credentialing (or administrative needs), many structures (such as permitting multiple attempts at a test) emerged differently than at most formal learning institutions.

Soon, courses formed (see Table 2.1 for sample courses). They ranged from "Give Peace a Chance," a course designed to teach players the diplomatic system, to the "One-City Challenge," which required players to win with only *one* city. Each course was based on a downloadable game. Periodically, players take notes and post them as "Duration Action Reports." These reports are the backbone of class discussion and, indeed, the university. At the time of this analysis, Apolyton University consisted of 19,302 posts by 74 registered members with perhaps another 100 lurkers (estimated through analyses of "reads" per post). Participants monitor the forums fairly closely; the median response time for feedback is between two and five hours.

As the number of courses increased, the university formed a curriculum committee. The curriculum committee reviews course submissions, identifies subjects lacking course coverage, researches how to best develop courses, and reviews which changes go into the "official" game mod. Based on its experiments, the university began designing an "official" game mod, which was the best, most well-balanced game. Building an official mod encouraged synthesis and oriented the school toward a common form of knowledge production.

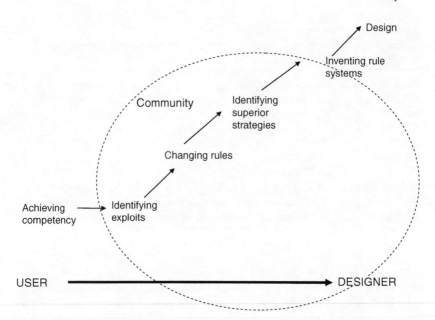

Figure 2.1. Trajectories of experience within game communities.

One might contrast this content-creation system with those in traditional schools. Rarely in school do we gather to *make* anything. When
we do (such as a school float), it's not tied to learning. Curricular decision
making is centralized, pushed more and more away from teachers (let alone
students) and toward the federal government. In Apolyton University, curricular decision making is *entirely* open – in terms of both *who* can participate and how the curriculum is determined. Students are *encouraged* to
post courses, ideas for courses, criticisms on courses, and suggestions for
additions to the "canon." If a student wants to know why a course isn't in
the canon, he or she can begin a discussion about it.

Although Apolyton University's participant structures can be contrasted
with schools' in that they are not geared toward credentialing, this is not to
suggest that *expertise* is devalued. Rather, expertise is recognized through
accomplishment in joint practices. As participants play together and are
exposed to one another's thinking, particular players become recognized as
experts. Indeed, Apolyton University members such as Theseus have earned
incredible status through their participation. Recall how Theseus's initial
post described several efforts by name (i.e., Aeson's iceberg, Arrian's UP™,
and Sir Ralph's effort to create WWIII). Participating in courses, developing strategies, and designing new courses all give players credentials.

During Action Reports: Cognitive Artifacts
That Organize Practice

During Action Reports (DARs) became the central community practice. A DAR begins with a *recap* to help the reader understand the player's goals, motivations, and thinking. Next, the player crafts *narrative*, interweaving his or her actions, goals, and interpretations of the game's underlying model. The player ends with descriptive statistics about his or her civilization, which other players use as raw data for comparisons with their own.

Discussing DARs puts participants simultaneously in the role of student, teacher, and researcher. These DARs function as *cognitive artifacts* to coordinate distributed game play. I might be playing in Madison, Wisconsin, in January of 2005, whereas another player may be playing Greece in the fall of 2007. Through DARs, we could play together.

Studying multiple games enabled *me* to see new things, such as that I built cities too far apart. The following post by Aqualung captures how I felt:

> Wow! I think I'm finally starting to learn this game! My first eight turns were pretty much the same as yours, except I went for a Warrior before the Granary to help with the happiness!

Later, Aqualung analyzed another colleague's game. He compliments the player's opening moves but notes that not investing in infrastructure (granaries and workers) will haunt him.

> Freud – Reasonable early expansion, though you are going to pay for it in the next DAR. Your city placement seems a trifle wide and your build priorities have promoted early expansion at the expense of some more important things. Granaries and Workers! You don't seem to have built any Granaries, though you have at least one underway.... this will hurt you in the longer term.

This advice is like the advice I gave students in my dissertation, but because Apolyton University players *all play the same game together*, there is a shared sense of the problem space. As a result, feedback is that much more sharp. The next passage illustrates just how specific this feedback could be.

> With a Granary, Delhi can spit out a Settler every four turns or a Worker every two.... I'd also suggest a few Warriors, which may prevent that AI

Persian Warrior from declaring war on a civ with four cities and not a single military unit! I see you've got another Settler heading out to capture the Dyes. Next town should probably be near the Flood Plains to keep growth moving along, which helps with commerce.

Playing the same game enables novices and experts to work on the *same problem*. Alan Collins and others call this commentary on thinking *cognitive apprenticeship*.[3] In cognitive apprenticeships, newcomers are apprenticing with experts, but the focus is on *learning* and *thinking* (rather than, say, making a coat, as in a tailoring apprenticeship). Through DARs, participants' game play – and thinking that goes into it – becomes visible and codified for further reflection. Cognitive apprenticeships are some of the most powerful arrangements for learning. Players gain access to experts' reflection on action and then can discuss it explicitly.

These exchanges often went on and on for pages, providing multiple rounds of feedback. The following exchange was typical. It begins with the newcomer asking for advice on military units (upgrading a knight to a cavalry). Theseus responds by helping the newcomer reframe the problem in a more nuanced way.

> *Newcomer*: (Should I upgrade knights to cavalry) 5/3/3 versus 4/3/2?
> *Theseus*: I'd upgrade in a New York minute. I would upgrade, but the question is would *I want to research the tech*. Remember you will soon be in the next age and have the better units. Especially if you are a scientific civ. Largely the AI [artificial intelligence] will not be a big problem for you at this point with the knight type unit. Of course you will have some games that make that strategy wrong; that is what is good about *Civ*, you cannot do the same thing in all cases. Anyway, I am not presenting this a sure thing, only as a food for thought, a consideration.

Theseus takes the newcomer's presentation of a single-variable problem (Is it worth spending the gold to upgrade a military unit?) and reframes it in terms of broader priorities: Should the player invest in more military technology when it soon will be made obsolete? Theseus pushes the newcomer to consider the larger intersecting game systems (i.e., future technologies, characteristics of civilizations, patterns in the artificial intelligence). He then *acknowledges* the *ambiguity* and reminds the newcomer that *Civ* is an ill-defined problem space where no one correct answer will work in all situations.

Soon, successful strategies were identified. Rapid expansion (i.e., creating a lot of cities early on at the expense of anything else) emerged as an effective opening strategy. Rapid expansion (shortened to "REXing") encompasses many smaller concepts, such as "settler pumps." Settler pumps are cities designed to "pump out" a never-ending supply of settlers (which can start new cities).[4] Tracing the development of these ideas, we see how personal experiences became articulated in DARs, were codified into a particular language (i.e., REXing, rushing, culture flipping) through discussions, and then employed to analyze games.

The DARs differ from traditional apprenticeships – and indeed many cognitive apprenticeships – in that participants are explicitly engaged in the *production* of new knowledge. Recall that Apolyton University is one part boot camp (enculturation and transmission of knowledge) and one part war college (investigating new strategies and ideas). In developing new strategies, courses, and critically, the master "Apolyton University mod" (which, recall, seeks to be a "more perfect" version of the game), players are creating *new* knowledge.

This rapid knowledge development created a specialized vocabulary that is cryptic to outsiders – similar to other domains of expertise when experts discuss a problem. See if you can make heads or tails out of this post:

> Unlike everyone else I didn't road the silks … but game/forest to the north, as my playstyle usually means researching hard and prioritising trade roads early on. I wouldn't need the silk just yet, but I wanted the income ASAP, and obviously wanted to work the game tile. Nor did I start with barracks and warriors, but with a warrior-warrior-settler, planning on a Ralph-style archer rush from four cities.

Simply parsing a post requires background knowledge of game mechanics and players' histories. Anyone who could "read" this post understands *Civ*.[5]

This exchange exemplifies the situated but also transportable nature of knowledge. Concepts come from experience, but they are also living, evolving entities that morph through use. Some concepts (such as culture flipping) are discernible to casual players, whereas others (such as the Eternal China Syndrome) are unique to how this group thinks about the game.[6] The "shared saved game" mechanic enables players to enter others' experiences. Knowledge is a tool for understanding, and formalizing knowledge eases communication. Saying "Ralph's archer rush" is simpler than recapping his entire game.

In response to this growing body of knowledge, the Apolyton community developed a "handbook." Lemmy suggested it because he thought the following post was impenetrable:

GA can also be triggered peacefully now by building GW with the same CSA as your civilization, but since only one *Civ* can build each GW, a peaceful GA can also be prevented. The peaceful GA trigger could also allow *Civ*'s with modern UU, to have an early GA, and if a GA can be declined, *Civ*'s with early CSU can have their GA late, if they can complete the GW with the right CSA.

So the community developed a compendium of terms and strategies. Before long, they nominated an official dean to accommodate the growing number of courses, students, and materials.

Never did Apolyton University create a list of "important terms and concepts" as a prerequisite for enrollment. Instead, it honors Gee's (2003/2007) "performance before mastery" principle: It's very difficult to comprehend specialized texts until you've been immersed in situations in which they are useful. First start playing. Then post your game. Then you can start reading. When you are in the middle of a game, these posts make total sense. But before you've ever played a scenario, it's not worth trying to understand. Gee notes that a problem in secondary schools is that we "give people the book before they are ever allowed to play the game." In games, you play before you read the book.

Design Thinking

So what did participants learn? After studying posts, interviewing players, and reflecting on notes of what we learned, players developed "design" understandings of the game as a system. This process begins with people (such as our newcomer) entering the community as *competent* players. This novice player knows game terms and understands their general meaning. As players identify superior strategies, the community pushes them to explore new game systems (identifying and transcending exploits). Posts such as Theseus's made connections across systems, leading to systemic thinking. In order to "enforce" this strategic thinking, the community identified and "fixed" broken rules in their "best of the best" mod (changing rules). This mod encouraged tinkering with rules while staying true enough to history (design).[7] In advanced courses, players created unique mods that illuminated relationships (designing rule systems). Thus the games *themselves* become pedagogical artifacts designed to teach one another game systems.

We interviewed players to see how this design thinking might transfer to thinking about history or current events. The following excerpt from an interview with a twenty-year-old American male suggests how *CivIII* remediates players' thinking:

> Interviewer: Do you ever draw comparisons between current events and *Civ*?
> Steve: Yes. The culture in *CivIII*. Stronger cultures make it harder to occupy other countries. We already saw the Golden Age of America – that's behind us now. There is a *CivIII* term: "Golden Age."

Steve immediately uses *Civ*'s concept of culture to think about contemporary efforts at military occupation. *Civ*'s concept of "Golden Age" is also interesting for Steve. He believes that the United States was in a golden age at some point but no longer is. He returned to current events, particularly the Iraq War (this interview was conducted in 2004).

> The situation in Iraq might flip back to the Baathe party, flip back to its original owner. But in some ways our culture is very strong. Go to Europe and see our commercial products. Capitalism – that's the American culture – that mind-set. In *CivIII* terms, the American mind-set is influencing so much of the world that basically we've won a cultural victory already. You know how the *CivIII* city screen, they still retain their identity of being Iraqi but they're a part of our culture? We want to give them an American mind-set, an American ideology. Like a cultural outpost, you're building all the cultural buildings.

The ease with which Steve applied these *Civ* concepts to the Iraq War was surprising. Steve believes that the United States is trying to "culture flip" Iraq so that Iraquis act like Americans and "join" American civilization, which for Steve is best described as capitalism.

Steve's read on U.S. foreign policy via *Civ* is a sophisticated one, one that runs counter to the official narrative provided by the Bush administration. In fact, it isn't entirely present in the game. Steve's read of the American strategy to export capitalism is a synthesis of many factors that he has created, some of which come from the game and some of which are from other experience. *Civ* (and its encompassing community) provides a set of representations (like "culture flipping") that he draws on in his interpretations. Participation in Apolyton University did not predict attitudes toward politics or global events. Steve was "for" the Iraq War but wasn't supportive of its execution.[8] Many others (particularly European participants) were critical of the war. There was no dominant view expressed in Apolyton University. In fact, discussions of politics or sensitive historical issues generally was discouraged given the diverse and global nature of the community.

Thus, playing *Civ* didn't inspire one particular read of history or politics but instead provided a language for thinking about it. Some of its ideas – such as "culture flipping" or the mix of cultural identity and participation in a civilization – are unique and quite useful. For Steve, the more he thought about it, the more he thought that technically speaking, the Americans may have *already* won a cultural victory (and indeed, under some rule sets, they would have). This would relegate Al Qaeda's operations to essentially that of a small group of "resistors" in the game's language. We wanted to know how this kind of interpretation compared with his school-based study of history.

> *Interviewer*: How does *CivIII* compare with your Western *Civ* class?
> *Steve*: I actually learned a lot more history and geography through *CivIII*. I will probably learn more through scenario design and *CivIII* than I will in this class because it's so basic to me.

Steve recently built a historical Rome scenario and was sharing it with his professor. Steve enjoyed playing through content related to his studies, and the two went hand-in-hand.

The upshot for Steve was to develop a form of *design thinking*. Steve used *Civ*'s model, it's grammar and lexicon, to think through historical questions. *Civ* gave Steve a symbol system and interconnected set of rules to use in analyzing historic scenarios. Steve's interpretations are quite flexible. *Civ* doesn't provide one "answer" or interpretation but is instead a set of possibilities for thinking through the problem.

By having such flexibility in their rule sets, games give players substantial degrees of freedom in interpretation – particularly as players become accustomed to modifying the underlying rules to meet their fancy. To a player such as Steve, *Civ* is a *game* to play, a *framework* to think with, and a *toolset* to author with. How Steve uses *Civ* in his academic work emphasizes its flexibility. Steve understands *Civ*'s underlying rules, but he must modify them substantially to model the growth or fall of Rome. He must choose starting and ending dates, include portions of the world and exclude others, and add and subtract resources. Further, he chooses technologies and military units and assigns values to different structures. *CivIII* can't be used to simulate *everything*; it could never be used to simulate the interworking of the Roman Senate. In fact, Steve could model most prevailing theories, including the Sassanid (Iranian) threat, plague, crop failures, improper growth (causing political instability), and good, old-fashioned invasions. Yet theories such as Joseph Tainter's "diminishing returns on investments in social complexity" are tough to simulate with *Civ*. So Steve is ultimately locked into *Civ*'s grammar when using it as a model to think with, but he can use that grammar quite flexibly.

Games function differently than other media in this regard (and also perhaps closer to fiction than nonfiction). Books typically tell stories or make arguments. Films typically tell a story from the point(s) of view of a character or characters. Games, in contrast, set up *frameworks* with which players think. A key component of *Civ* is that there is no "one" game. Players play *Civ multiple* times at *multiple* time scales with *multiple* rule sets. As players experience different versions, they experience differences in the feel of each model. Each scenario further expands this by emphasizing different relationships. *Civilization* involves so many different size maps, difficulty levels, and scenario rules (indeed, Apolyton University's "One-City Challenge" is now an official setting in *CivIV*) that it's hard to remember what the "real" rules of each *Civilization* installment is, let alone a particular mod. The *game* isn't so much a set of rules as much as a defined set of relationships and possible interactions. These possible interactions aren't wholly set by the designer; the player can change any number of settings from the main menu, in addition to digging under the hood to change rules as desired. As such, the designer and player write the rules "in collaboration."

Participation in Apolyton University is ultimately about design, but could Apolyton University really teach you to become a designer? Surely there's a meaningful difference between sitting in your living room arguing about the "One-City Challenge" with random strangers on the Internet and *really* designing the game, right?

It turns out, not really.

Midway through a course, Apolyton University was discussing the game's artificial intelligence (AI). Out of nowhere, the AI programmer on *CivIII*, Soren Johnson, popped in to clarify a misconception. He then "thread-jacked" the discussion by challenging students to decipher the algorithm determining barbarian uprisings. (Recall that barbarian uprisings are triggered events in which barbarians attack, which is meant to simulate such occurrences as the Mongolian horde's sacking of Asia and Europe). This was amazing stuff. *Civ*'s lead AI programmer found this little corner of the Internet, had read the discussion, and now was issuing a challenge to the students' collective intellect.

As you might imagine, the place went nuts. About seventy-five posts followed in the next week. Players ran in-game experiments. Side topics spun off – including the origin of the word *barbarians*. Some Europeans explained the historical roots of the term. Finally, Soren declared DeepO, a German Ph.D. student and former AI programmer the victor because he had most closely deciphered the pattern.[9] The school was elated. Soren's participation was tacit approval that they were onto something, and as we will find out later, this was hugely consequential for more than a few students.

Designing CivIV

The claim that "participating in Apolyton University is to become 'a designer'" soon became concrete. As we were completing the study, Apolyton University had slowly been dying. We were trying to figure out what happened. Levi rushed into my office with the following data point: A participant explained that Apolyton University was winding down because, "Well, we're done learning."

> *Interviewer*: Do you think Apolyton University will jump to *CivIV*?
> *Jacko*: Yes, certainly, but as so many veteran members of Apolyton University are on the beta test team, maybe we won't have to do much modding. I will definitely help to test the mod, although I doubt I will be able to help with the modding.

Soren Johnson, leader of that AI experiment had been promoted to lead developer on *CivIV*. One of his first actions was to recruit leaders from Apolyton University to participate in a unique "closed beta program." Johnson wanted Apolyton University and *Civ*Fanatics' War Academy players to play-test *CivIV*, just as they did with *CivIII*, but this time *before* the game came out. Over a hundred gamer testers were included in the credits on *CivIV*, so open its credits and you see many of our participants – Dominae, DeepO, and Gramphos all right there. Indeed, before it was all done, three of the most active modders actually were *hired* by Firaxis as scenario designers.

By treating players as designers, Firaxis is extending this idea of play and design and instantiating within the design process. Firaxis recognized that collectively, communities such as Apolyton University contain infinitely more game knowledge than a handful of designers working alone. This relationship between knowledge and communities suggests a formal real-ization of Pierre Levy's notion of collective intelligence. Collective intel-ligence is the idea that in modern society, knowledge is distributed among collectives rather than in individual heads. Intelligent things are produced by collectives applying their "brainpower" to problems. The production of *CivIV* embodies this thinking. How do you most efficiently play-test a game with nearly infinite possibilities? Call in the collective.

For his part, Soren Johnson felt that Apolyton University taught *him* something about game design. In an open letter to the gaming community posted in 2006, Soren explains that he started participating at Apolyton University long *before* he held a job at Firaxis.

> I moved to Maryland a few weeks later, eager to start my job. My head was full of ideas based on my experience with *Civ* and *Alpha Centauri*. I thought I knew all of the ins and outs of *Civ*. I had logged countless hours playing the game, had always wanted to make historical strategy games, and was full of enthusiasm to make my mark in gaming. If anyone was an expert on the *Civ* series, it must be me. [Johnson had previously worked at Electronic Arts and had degrees in computer science and history from Stanford.]
>
> I was dead wrong.
>
> The world of *Civ* was far, far bigger than I had ever imagined. As I began to wade through the Apolyton forums, I began to discover just how little I knew about the game itself. Certain acronyms, like ICS (Infinite City Sleaze) and OCC (One-City Challenge) were being thrown around with an assumption that everyone understood them. Massive lists of improvements and fixes were being compiled. Clearly, a culture had grown around *Civ* that I was just beginning to understand.
>
> At the start of 2000, I had never played a game of *Civ* in multi-player. I had never played a scenario. I had never opened up the editor. I knew nothing about the events system of *CivII*. I had never heard of Democracy, Diplomacy, Succession, or Story games. I was just beginning to discover the wealth of fan-sites available on the web. I had a lot to learn.
>
> From that point on, my most important source of information, my compass, so to speak, was always the online community. Game design, of course, always involves the iterative cycle of internal development and testing and refinement and more testing and so on. However, the topic of *Civ* was so broad, so all-encompassing, and so flexible that no one person could understand all the ways the game could be played or approached.
>
> As I discovered more and more paths to *Civ*, I became a better game designer. If *CivIV* succeeded in areas where *CivIII* failed, it is largely because our understanding of the *Civ* community increased so much over the intervening years. In fact, the one-hundred-person private test group for *CivIV* – critical to the game's development – was culled from our personal interaction with the many different groups and sites that existed on the net.

Apparently, I wasn't the only one humbled by Apolyton. This example illustrates how right now, a young student interested in game design has access to game communities so robust that lead game developers *themselves* consult them as compasses.

Apolyton University is unique in terms of its organization and professionalism, but it is indicative of how game communities work. Recall Apolyton University's "rival school," *Civ*Fanatics' War Academy, which is a rival school that is every bit as impressive as Apolyton University. Similar trends exist in other genres. MMO designer Raph Koster has long noted how "official" MMO designers have always been a "step behind" the player communities in "knowing" the details of their games. Quasi-professional sites are popping up around *World of Warcraft* (where, like Thotbott, they collect data from players' games, aggregate them, and publish them for gamers to use when researching).

This example suggests how the future of games-based pedagogies could be in situating games within and facilitating such participatory communities. If Apolyton University is any example, then studying the social structures surrounding games suggests to me the importance of structuring activities that springboard learners out from the game and into domains in which their design-level understandings can be applied.

Indeed, as educators, we have fewer and fewer excuses for denying students opportunities to participate in professional or quasi-professional learning communities. This move toward participatory learning can happen via any number of digital media channels; participatory learning occurs everywhere from sports to politics (see Jenkins, 2006). However, there is a deep impulse in games culture toward learning through *participation*. Game cultures value learning by diving in, mucking around, and joining people who know something about that topic (see also Beck & Wade, 2004).

If this blurring of lines between pro-am communities is indeed indicative of broader trends, then educators face serious challenges and opportunities. In most *every* field, a novice can participate in communities of practice that lead toward authentic participation in complex activities. "Professionals" and "amateurs" work side by side, enabling enculturation into communities of practice (such as game design) and producing new knowledge.

Participatory communities expand students' *professional networks* way beyond what schools can do. Apoltyon University enabled DeepO, despite living in Germany, to connect with Soren and the *Civ* team in Maryland. When Johnson left Firaxis to work at MAXIS (Will Wright's company, makers of *Sim City*, *The Sims*, and *Spore*), he further broadened Apolytonians' networks.

Designing Education for Participation

Sites such as Apolyton University put a crucial piece in place for educators seeking to design learning systems involving games. In addition to the compelling learning principles operating in games, they give us participant structures such as DARs that can be used to structure learning. Further, they suggest models for how to engage players in *design* so that they develop critical understandings of games' underlying rules. One fruitful approach may be to design games so that they become the fodder for pro-am communities, communities that feature professionals and amateurs designing solutions to problems. Such communities enable newcomers and experts to rub elbows. Participants might design *artifacts* such as *Civ* mods with experts but also design the social systems themselves (such as Apolyton University).

This way of thinking about design and learning hasn't widely penetrated schools, but it is an idea with deep roots in education, most forcibly argued in the New London Group's (1996) manifesto. The New London Group articulated the idea that design knowledge is a critical skill for the digital age and new economy. We need to understand things such as books, movies, and games as designed objects, especially how they are designed for particular audiences and purposes (and being able to design them for others). Knowing *how* to design – as a skill to applied to messages (i.e., books, images, web pages, Facebook profiles, Twitter presence, and video games) and the identities they constitute (i.e., work identity, play identity) – is core to being competent today. The New London group goes further, saying that we are responsible for designing our own *social* futures. The large companies that care for us are long gone. We all need to think as entrepreneurs, designing our identities online and offline for colleagues and employers alike.

Apolyton University suggests a model for how to teach design understanding and then springboard people into participating in even more complex activities. In effect, it offers a way to tie together the kind of learning we do through games in pursuing our own interests and the forms of apprenticeship that happen in massively multiplayer online games (see Steinkuehler & Oh, Chapter 12). What's exciting about this for educational designers is that we don't have to "turn everything into an MMO" to make good educational games.[10] There are *many* models beyond *World of Warcraft* for learning through participation.

One cannot discuss models of game-based learning through participation without revisiting the intersection between play and work. The story of Apolyton University is very much about people taking their life's love and turning it into their "job." This same thing occurs across participatory cultures, ranging from politics to sports. There is something about how these participants follow their passions that needs to be preserved, or we may lose what makes games special. There is something life-enhancing, something transformative about meaningful game play. There is a playfulness about "fixing" one of the best video games ever developed, and there's something playful about "starting an online university to make people better video game players." There's something playful in the lead programmer derailing the entire "university" by throwing down a challenge, and there's something playful about him later hiring these same people to work with him.

Apolyton University has so many nifty features, such as DARs, that it's easy to lose sight of this playful spirit (or ludic stance). This same playfulness can be found in gamers across various domains. For example, when I was a teacher, my elementary students once designed a level for *AVATAR* (an online game) based on their school and found a real joy in creating the "teacher's red pen," an epic weapon that caused enemies to quiver once they were in its presence (reported in Squire, 2011). Similarly, the students I interviewed in my dissertation found joy in adopting the logic of colonial imperialism to justify Native American expansion (Squire, 2005a). Even if we never build a decent educational game, maybe we can interject this playfulness that is central to learning in these instances back into our conversations about education. Today's discussion has become so mired in the particulars of schooling (i.e., issues of scalability, test scores, and teacher accountability) that the ethical dimensions of designing experiences for other people seem to have been hopelessly lost.

Notes

[1]   WoWiki says the following about *WoW* guilds: "Guilds are often classified into types, such as Raid Guild, Social Guild, PvP Guild, Roleplaying Guild, and leveling guild." Keep in mind that these categories are not mutually exclusive, and many overlap (e.g., some Raid Guilds like to participate in PvP Guilds, some Roleplaying Guilds raid).

[2]   This is no slight to *Civ*Fanatics, an equally sophisticated community of *Civ* players and designers.

[3]   See Collins, Brown, & Newman, 1990.

[4]   Normally, a city loses two population points every time it produces a settler. With a settler pump, the city grows quickly enough that it gains back those population points by the time it produces the settler, allowing the player to create settlers without the city collapsing owing to food shortages.

5   One of my favorite moves that he makes is to use *road* as a verb (meaning to build roads in order to obtain access to silk, a luxury resource). Also note how he references "Ralph-style" archer rushes, which is another example of a player observing one game, using those ideas in his or her own game, and reflecting on its value. It's typical of Apolyton University, and indeed of many game communities, to retain the history of the idea within the language itself, something common to games and perhaps language more generally.

6   Eternal China Syndrome is the problem the game has with modeling every civilization essentially as "eternal China," starting in 4000 BC and continuing without interruption for 6000 years. The community was dissatisfied with how *Civ* deals with this, and some attempted custom mods to rectify it, but the general problem as outlined by the developers – that it's hard to create easily understandable and workable game mechanics – still holds true.

7   How they think about this balance is really interesting – and is worth further exploration. The primacy in Apolyton University to some extent is game balance. However, some adherence to historical rules is required; you don't see people adding implausible features. There may be a belief that history *itself* is a well-balanced game, and what *Civ* players do is interpret it.

8   The more I thought about it, the more curious I was about how to model these events via *Civ*'s rules. A similar *Civ* strategy might involve an initial attack to create civil unrest and cripple the infrastructure. With sufficient cultural pressure, players might "flip" to your side (although they also could become "Persian," depending on how you model Afghanistan and Pakistan). As Steve observes, it's *really* difficult in *Civ* to "convert" a civilization with long-established cultural structures (i.e., temples, art) to another. I'd never try it, or at least not without realizing it would take several generations to take root. Regardless, I'd inundate the civilization with *cultural* rather than *economic* buildings, particularly libraries, schools, universities, and temples. Economic buildings may bring in money – to the centralized government (not necessarily to the people) in the short run, but without overwhelming troop presence, it would never last (and maybe not even *with* significant troop presence). Indeed, with such little civil support and distance from the capitol, Iraq would be a cesspool of corruption and ultimately a giant money pit.

9   It turned out that the barbarian uprisings were, in the words of Johnson, "triggered the second time a civ enters a new age (once for the middle ages, once for the industrial age, once for the modern age, …). The intention was to basically simulate the barbarian hordes that knocked out Rome and (to a lesser degree) the Mongols. This made a little more sense back when barbarians were more destructive, but having half your civ knocked out for seemingly random reasons was deemed not much fun. Instead, we flipped the concept around and gave a temporal bonus (the Golden Age) instead of a temporal penalty." This is an illuminating illustration of how designers wrestle with historical modeling (how to create barbarian uprisings) and entertainment (no one enjoys random penalties) in a manner that results in a reasonably realistic yet satisfying play experience.

10   My favorite two real-life examples are MMOs for dentistry and MMOs for street sign navigation.

References

Beck, J. C., & Wade, M. (2004). *Got game: How the gamer generation is reshaping business forever*. Boston: Harvard Business Press.

Church, D. (2005). Formal abstract design tools. In K. Salen and E. Zimmerman (eds.), *The game design reader: A rules of play anthology* (pp. 366–80). Cambridge, MA: MIT Press.

Collins, A., Brown, J. S., & Newman, S. E. (1989). Cognitive apprenticeship: Teaching the craft of reading, writing and mathematics. In L. B. Resnick (ed.), *Knowing, learning and instruction: Essays in honor of Robert Glaser* (pp. 453–94). Hillsdale, NJ: Erlbaum.

Davidson, D. (2009). From experiment gameplay to the wonderful world of Goo and How Physics Is Your Friend. In D. Davidson et al. (eds.), *Well played 1.0: Video games and value and meaning* (pp. 334–67). Pittsburg, PA: ETC Press.

Gee, J. P. (2003/2007). *What videogames have to teach us about learning and literacy*. London: Palgrave Macmillan.

Gee, J. P., & Hayes, E. (2010). "No Quitting Without Saving After Bad Events": Gaming Paradigms and Learning. *Sims International Journal of Learning and Media*, 1(3), 49–65. Available from http://dx.doi.org/10.1162/ijlm_a_00024.

Giovanetto, L., & Squire, K. D. (2008). The Higher Education of Gaming. *E-Learning*, 5(1), 2–28.

Jenkins, H. (2006). *Convergence culture: Where old and new media collide*. New York: NYU Press.

Koster, R. (2004). *Theory of fun for game design*. Scottsdale, AZ: Paraglyph.

Lave, J., & Wenger, E. (1991). *Situated learning: Legitimate peripheral participation*. Cambridge, England: Cambridge University Press.

Lemke, J. L. (2005). Theory of complex self-organizing systems. Retrieved March 7, 2005, from http://academic.brooklyn.cuny.edu/education/jlemke/theories. htm.

Nitsche, M. (2009). *Video game spaces: Image, play, and structure in 3D worlds*. Cambridge, MA: MIT Press.

Shaffer, D. W. (2006/2008). *How computer games help children learn*. London: Palgrave Macmillan.

Shaffer, D. W., & Clinton, K. A. (2006). Toolforthoughts: Reexamining thinking in the digital age. *Mind, Culture, and Activity*, 13(4), 283–300.

Smith, J., & Squire, K. D. (2002). *Sound screen: Points of convergence in recorded sound and digital gaming*. Paper presented at Media in Transition 2, Cambridge, MA.

Squire, K. (2005a). Changing the Game: What Happens When Video Games Enter the Classroom. *Innovate: Journal of Online Education*, 1(6). Available at http://www.innovateonline.info/pdf/vol1_issue6/Changing_the_Game-__What_Happens_When_Video_Games_Enter_the_Classroom_.pdf

(2005b). Toward a Theory of Games Literacy. *Telemedium*, 52(1–2), 9–15.

(2011). *Video games and learning: Teaching and participatory culture in the digital age*. New York: Teachers College Press.

Squire, K., & Steinkuehler, C. (2005). Meet the Gamers: They Research, Teach, Learn, and Collaborate. So Far, Without Libraries. *Library Journal*, 130(7), 4.

Squire, K., Jenkins, H., Holland, W., Miller, H., Tan, K. P., & Todd, K. (2003). Design Principles of Next-Generation Digital Gaming for Education. *Educational Technology*, 43(5), 17–23.

Steinkuehler, C. (2006). Massively Multiplayer Online Video Gaming as Participation in a Discourse. *Mind, Culture, and Activity*, 13(1), 38–52.

Steinkuehler, C., & Johnson, B. Z. (2009). Computational Literacy in Online Games: The Social Life of a Mod. *International Journal of Gaming and Computer-Mediated Simulations*, 1(1), 53–65.

Steinkuehler, C., & Oh, Y. (2012). Apprenticeship in Massively Multiplayer Online Games. This volume.

3   Theme Is Not Meaning: Who Decides What a Game Is About?

Soren Johnson

At first glance, the popular board game *Ticket to Ride* seems to be another link in the great chain of rail baron games, such as *Age of Steam*, *Eurorails*, and the *1830* series. During the game, the player draws unique route challenges to connect certain pairs of cities – New York to San Francisco, Miami to Chicago, and so on.

To complete them, the player must claim a series of tracks that connect adjacent cities while also trying to block opponents from finishing their own challenges. There are subgoals too, such as having the longest contiguous rail line and completing one's network first, which ends the game for everyone.

Thus most players would describe *Ticket to Ride* as a game about building the best rail service by grabbing choice routes and cutting off the competition. However, the Introduction in the rules tells a different story:

> On a blustery autumn evening five old friends met in the backroom of one of the city's oldest and most private clubs. Each had traveled a long distance – from all corners of the world – to meet on this very specific day…October 2, 1900 – twenty-eight years to the day that London eccentric Phileas Fogg accepted and then won a £20,000 bet that he could travel *Around the World in 80 Days*.

> Each succeeding year, they met to celebrate the anniversary and pay tribute to Fogg. And each year a new expedition (always more difficult) was proposed. Now at the dawn of the century it was time for a new impossible journey. The stakes: $1 million in a winner-takes-all competition. The objective: to see which of them could travel by rail to the most cities in North America – in just seven days.

Originally published in *Game Developer* magazine (February 2010). Available at http://www.gdmag.com/archive/feb10.htm.

The official story comes as a surprise to many players, even veterans of the game, because the theme simply does not match the game play. For example, how can a player "claim" a route just by riding on it? Do the trains shut down, preventing anyone else from using that line? On the other hand, claiming routes matches perfectly the fiction of ruthless rail barons trying to control the best connections.

Furthermore, routes can be claimed in any order – there is no sense that the player actually exists in the world as a traveler with real, physical limitation. Instead, claiming routes feels a lot more like buying them rather than traveling on them.

Mechanics Give Meaning

This disconnect leads to some interesting questions. Does a game's designer have the right to say what a game is about if it doesn't match what's going on inside the players' heads? And if the designer doesn't have this right, then does a game's official "story" even matter at all because it can be invalidated so easily? Isn't a game about what one actually *does* during play and how that feels to the player?

Ultimately, designers need to recognize that a game's theme does not determine its meaning. Instead, meaning emerges from a game's mechanics – the set of decisions and consequences unique to each one. What does a game ask of the player? What does it punish, and what does it reward? What strategies and styles does the game encourage? Answering these questions reveals what a game is actually about.

Furthermore, whereas people buy games for the promise of the theme ("I want to be a space marine!"), the fun comes from the mechanics themselves (actually shooting the aliens). When there is a severe dissonance between the two, players can feel cheated, as if the designers executed a bait and switch.

The reception of *Spore*, a game sold with an evolutionary theme, provides a recent example. In the October 2008 issue of *Science* magazine, John Bohannon wrote the following about how the game delivered on the theme's promise:

> I've been playing *Spore* with a team of scientists, grading the game on each of its scientific themes. When it comes to biology, and particularly evolution, *Spore* failed miserably. According to the scientists, the problem isn't just that *Spore* dumbs down the science or gets a few things wrong – it's meant to be a game, after all – but rather, it gets most of biology badly, needlessly, and often bizarrely wrong.

The source of this dissonance is that even though it was sold as such, *Spore* is not really a game about evolution. *Spore* is actually a game about creativity – the reason to play the game was to behold the wonder of other players' imaginations as they used (and misused) the editors to create objects not imagined by the game's designers – from musical instruments to fantastical creatures to dramatic scenes.

However, even though *Spore* is not about evolution, the scientists should keep looking because one of the most popular games actually *is* about evolution – *World of Warcraft* (*WoW*). The game may have a swords-and-sorcery theme, but the mechanics encourage the players to conduct their own form of natural selection when deciding how to develop their characters.

Over years of experience, veterans of *WoW* have established a number of upgrade paths (or *builds*) for each class depending on what role the player wants the character to fill. For example, the Paladin class has three main builds: Holy (for healing), Protection (for tanking), and Retribution (for damage per second). Further, underneath these main categories, sub-builds exist for player-versus-player, player-versus-enemy, and mob grinding. These paths have evolved organically over the years as players tried out different combinations depending on what the game rewarded or punished.

Seeing Past the Theme

One can look at any number of games through the lens of how the mechanics affect the user experience to find out what the game actually means. *Super Mario Bros.*, for example, is a game about timing, certainly not about plumbing. *Battlefield* games are about teamwork, not World War II or modern combat. *Peggle* is a game about chaos theory, not unicorns or rainbows.

Indeed, games with the same theme actually can be about different things. For example, human conflict with aliens certainly has been a popular theme across video game history. Nonetheless, each alien-themed game can mean something very different depending on the rule set. *Galaga* is actually about pattern matching. *X-Com* is about decision making with limited information. *Gears of War* is about using cover as a defensive weapon. *StarCraft* is about the challenges of asymmetrical combat.

Conversely, games with different themes but the same mechanics are actually about the same thing. *Civilization* and *Alpha Centauri* are set on completely different planets, but the mechanics are largely the same. *Alpha Centauri*'s mind worms, probe teams, and Secret Projects are essentially identical to *Civilization*'s barbarians, spies, and World Wonders. Players can easily see past the game's chrome to see that they are still making the same decisions with the same tradeoffs.

Genre choice also can affect the meaning of a game. Players expect a theme to deliver on certain nouns and verbs ("I am a Mage – I can cast powerful Magic!"). Unfortunately, genre conventions often put a barrier between a player and the game he or she imagined while holding a copy in the store. Once again, players buy games for the theme – if the mechanics and traditions of the genre are wildly unfamiliar to the player, at odds with the game in his or her head, he or she may feel cheated.

For example, two recent console games – *Halo Wars* and *Brutal Legend* – surprised players by being strategy games. With the former, many players expected a *Halo* game to be about reflex-based combat; with the latter, heavy-metal music is not inherently strategic. Because strategy games are often played at a considered distance, players expecting the visceral thrill promised by these games' themes were disappointed. The designers may have built fun and interesting rule sets, but the themes sold the games to the wrong fans.

Uniting Theme and Mechanics

One interesting comparison is the board games *Risk* and *Diplomacy*, which have identical themes of world conquest. Indeed, at first glance, the two games also seem quite similar mechanically. The game board is split up into territories, which the players control with generic army or (in the case of *Diplomacy*) navy tokens. These territories switch hands as battles are fought, and – in turn – the victors are able to field larger militaries from their new lands.

However, a small difference in the rules makes the two games about something very different. In *Risk*, turns occur sequentially, whereas in *Diplomacy*, they execute simultaneously. This difference makes *Risk* a game about risk, whereas *Diplomacy* becomes a game about diplomacy. In the former, players must decide how much they can achieve during their own turn and then hope the dice are not unkind. With *Diplomacy*, however, there are no dice; players can succeed only with the help of others, which can only be promised but not actually delivered during the negotiation round. Only when the secretly written orders are revealed between turns is it clear who is a true friend and who is a back-stabbing traitor.

Diplomacy, in particular, is a perfect marriage between theme and mechanics. Indeed, President John F. Kennedy considered it his favorite game. The game is about exactly what it claims to be about – the twists and turns of diplomatic negotiations. On the other hand, when a game's theme and mechanics are sharply divorced, players can react negatively to the dissonance. Such a dissonance can leave players feeling lost, perhaps even cheated. Thus designers should strive to keep the two in harmony. At the very least, they should not be fighting each other.

When they do, the game's mechanics actually can undermine the theme that the designers want to deliver. For example, *Bioshock* presents players with a true ethical choice – "harvest" Little Sisters by destroying them or "rescue" them by releasing their minds? The reward for harvesting is double Adam (the game's genetic modification currency), which tempts players to choose a morally disturbing path.

However, the game sprinkles other rewards on players who rescue Little Sisters, so the ultimate difference between the two paths is negligible from a statistical perspective. Players are told by the game's fiction that their choice matters – that they are making a sacrifice by deciding to rescue the little girls – but the game's mechanics tell them a different story. Of course, when theme and mechanics are in conflict, players know which one actually matters, which one is actually telling them what the game is about.

Similarly, many traditional role-playing games (RPGs) put the player in an odd position. By giving the player an epic goal ("Kill the evil wizard!") from the beginning, the game casts him or her in the role of the world's savior. However, the actual game play involves roaming the countryside killing most of what falls in the player's path and looting everything else. The story tells the player that he or she is a hero, but the game rewards him or her for being something else. Richard Garriot directly attacked this dissonance when he designed *Ultima IV* by making the game about achieving eight virtues instead of simply killing a Foozle at the end.

A Perfect Union

Sometimes a designer does achieve a perfect union of theme and mechanics. One example is Dan Bunten's *Seven Cities of Gold*, the classic game of exploration. Bunten lost his way one day while hiking in the Ozarks and imagined a game in which the player struggles to keep her bearings in an unfamiliar landscape. From that seed, Bunten took the next step and chose a perfect theme – the age of the conquistadors, of Columbus, Cortez, and Pizarro, who were always partially lost – that provided wonderful raw background material with which to work.

Certain categories match theme and game play particularly well, including Wii games (*Wii Sports*), music games (*Rock Band*), tycoon games (*Railroad Tycoon*), sports games (*Madden*), flight sims (*Wings*), and racing games (*Gran Turismo*). Notice that while these examples are based on real-world activities, which helps to keep the mechanics tied to the theme, a designer does not need to put verisimilitude above all else.

In fact, one could argue that *Mario Kart* is more truly about racing than *Gran Turismo* is – the former's rapid exchange of player position as shells fly around the track is perhaps closer to many players' ideal concept of racing than a stodgy simulation's more fixed positioning. Put another way, which object is more about Guernica – a photograph of the city's ruins or Picasso's masterpiece of anguish?

Further, great games can emerge when the theme simply provides an excuse to experiment with certain mechanics. *Left 4 Dead* is not really a game about zombies, after all – it's a game about teamwork. The designers created each special zombie to encourage players to work together as a team – the hunter punishes loners, the tank requires concentrated fire, the witch demands close communication, and so on. The zombie theme simply gave the designers a plausible backdrop in which they could experiment with game mechanics that encouraged teamwork over solo play.

Does *Civilization* Fail?

The *Civilization* series provides an interesting study in the challenges inherent in trying to match theme with meaning. The games are purportedly about the sweep of world history, but one does not have to play long before cracks start to show.

To begin, societal progress is constant throughout the game – the player's civilization never can fall into a dark age or split apart in a civil war. The user community has dubbed this dynamic the *Eternal China Syndrome*. The only entropy a player experiences comes from external invasion.

Indeed, the game actually provides a "Start a Revolution" button so that the player can change government, but only when convenient. (I'm sure Louis XVI would have appreciated such a system!) Indeed, all actions in the game are conducted top-down – the player is some strange combination of king, general, tycoon, and god.

The source of these conflicts with real history is the problem of *player agency*. In order to be fun, the player needs to be in control. Moreover, the consequence of each decision needs to be fair and clear so that players can make informed choices, plan ahead, and understand their mistakes. Real history, of course, is much messier and difficult to understand, let alone control.

In fact, the game's mechanics tell us less about world history than they do about what it would be like to be part of a league of ancient gods who pit their subjects against each other for fun. These immortal opponents, after all, are the only characters that can destroy the player. The people themselves have little say in how history will develop.

However, player agency is actually a good thing; indeed, it is at the very center of what makes games so powerful. Perhaps some topics are simply too broad or vague or slippery to be addressed by a game's mechanics, and – sometimes – themes can just be themes, with the player knowingly entering a fantasy space that speaks not directly to the topic but to some other need or desire.

In the case of *Civilization*, the desire is to control history, which may not teach us much about it, but it is not without value. Indeed, the game fares well when compared with other artistic disciplines. Few works of art tackle the sweep of world history, and the ones that exist (*Birth of a Nation*) are often dangerous works of ideology.

Designers who care to make games that actually speak to us about history should focus on a specific era or event, such as Bunten's *Seven Cities of Gold* or Meier's *Railroad Tycoon*. Put the player in the shoes of a flesh-and-blood person – let him or her explore the challenges and opportunities of the times, but within mortal limits.

Why Theme Matters

Although a game's theme and mechanics can tell different stories, society at large does not understand that there is a difference between the two, and if the theme is appalling to the mainstream, a good game can be tarred unfairly. For example, *Grand Theft Auto* (*GTA*) has a theme of crime and urban chaos, but the game is actually about freedom and consequence. Every crime increases the player's notoriety, which can end the game if the police send enough firepower.

Nonetheless, to the mainstream, *GTA* was simply about killing hookers and running over pedestrians – for outsiders, the game couldn't be "about" anything else. Players, however, understood that the game was giving them something different – an open world in which their decisions actually mattered. Consequence was the true killer feature.

Crackdown provides an interesting contrast in that it delivers the same open-world simulation with consequence as *GTA*, but with a theme (fighting crime as a supercop) much more palatable to the average person. *Rockstar* may have record sales to show for their work, but designers who believe that they have a responsibility to society at large should take note that the criminal theme was not inevitable.

Today, many designers strive to achieve two worthy goals – reaching a mass audience and creating great art. However, both are at risk if theme and mechanics are in dissonance. The average consumer, who is not highly literate in the standard tropes of game design, expects video games to be about whatever is on the cover. Pulling a bait and switch – or simply not thinking critically about the lessons that a game actually teaches – will only turn new players away.

As for the question of art, one must first recognize that many great works of art are abstract. Lyrics may give some meaning to a song, but a symphony generally is meant to be interpreted and enjoyed however the listener prefers. Similarly, games can stand on their own without specific themes – *Tetris* being the obvious example.

Furthermore, even a pasted-on theme can work if the designers are not promising more than the game can deliver – *San Juan* and *Race for the Galaxy* are both brilliant, yet similar card-based adaptations of *Puerto Rico*. That one is set in the Caribbean and the other in outer space is not a problem because the games are clearly not marketed as re-creations or simulations. The theme simply adds flavor.

However, great art never has theme and meaning in open conflict, in the way that many games do. *Othello* is actually about the "green-eyed monster" of jealousy and not just the life of a Moor in the sixteenth-century Venetian military, but the latter does not detract from the former. Can the same be said about *Bioshock*? About *Spore*? About *Civilization*? These games do claim to be about something – do their mechanics tell the same story? To touch people, the play itself needs to deliver on the theme's promise.

4   Our Cheatin' Hearts

Soren Johnson

The designers of *Puzzle Quest* have a frustrating burden to bear – everyone thinks they are a bunch of dirty cheaters. The game centers on a competitive version of *Bejewelled*, in which players duel with an artificial intelligence (AI) to create the most "match-three" colored patterns.

The problem comes from how the pieces on the game board are created – when, for example, a column of three green orbs is lined up and removed from play, new pieces fall in to take their place. However, sometimes, these three new pieces happen to be of all the same type, which means that a new match is made automatically, and the player scores again. The odds of such a result are low (around 2 percent for getting three of the same colors in a row), but they are still high enough that a player will see it many times with enough games played.

Of course, the AI is playing the same game, so the player will see this lucky match fall into the enemy's lap as well. At this point, human psychology takes over. Because the new pieces are hidden from view, how does the player know that the computer is not conducting some funny business and giving itself some free matches?

The human mind is notoriously bad at grasping probability, so many players are convinced that the AI is cheating. The developers have pledged over and over again that everything is fair and even, but whether they like it or not, the player experience has been affected by the simply possibility of cheating.

Trust Me

Games do not start with a player's trust – this trust needs to be earned over time. Our audience is well aware that we can make a game do whatever we

Originally published in *Game Developer* magazine (May 2009).

want under the hood, so the transparency and consistency of a game's rules contribute significantly to player immersion. The worst feeling for a player is when he or she perceives – or just suspects – that a game is breaking its own rules and treating the human unfairly.

This situation is especially challenging for designers of symmetrical games, in which the AI is trying to solve the same problems as the human is. For asymmetrical games, cheating is simply bad game design– imagine the frustration that would result from enemies in *Half-Life* warping around the map to flank the player or guards in *Thief* instantly spotting a player hiding in the shadows.

However, under symmetrical conditions, the AI often needs to cheat just to be able to compete with the player. Accordingly, designers must learn what cheats feel fair to a player and what cheats do not. As the *Puzzle Quest* team knows, games need to avoid situations in which players even suspect that the game is cheating on them.

Cheating is not the same thing as difficulty levels – by which the players are asking the game to provide extra challenges for them. Cheating is whether a game is treating the players "fairly" – rewarding them for successful play and not arbitrarily punishing them just to maintain the challenge. Unfortunately, in practice, the distinction between difficulty levels and cheating is not so clear.

Show the Mechanics

Fans of racing games are quite familiar with this gray area. A common tactic employed by AI programmers to provide an appropriate level of challenge is to "rubber-band" the cars together. In other words, the code ensures that if the AI cars fall too far behind the human cars, they will speed up. On the other hand, if the human cars fall behind, the AI slows down to allow the player to recover.

The problem is that this tactic is often obvious to players, which either dulls their sense of accomplishment when they win or raises suspicions when they lose. Ironically, games that turn rubber-banding into an explicit game mechanic often become more palatable to their players.

For example, the *Mario Kart* series has long disproportionately divvied out rewards from the mystery item boxes sprinkled around the tracks relative to the riders' current standings. While the first-place racer might receive a shell only useful for attacking other lead cars, players in the rear might get a speed bullet that automatically warps them to the middle of the pack.

These self-balancing mechanics are common to board games – think of the robber blocking the leader's tiles in *Settlers of Catan* – and they don't feel like cheating because the game is so explicit about how the system works. Thus players understand that the bonuses to the AI also will be available to them if they fall behind. With cheating, perception becomes reality, so transparency is the antidote to suspicion and distrust.

Cheating in *Civilization*

Sometime, however, hidden bonuses and cheats are still necessary to provide the right challenge for the player. The *Civilization* series provides plenty of examples of how this process can go awry and drive players crazy with poorly handled cheating.

Since the game is turn-based, the developers could not rely on a human's natural limitations within a real-time environment. Instead, *Civilization* gives out a progressive series of unit, building, and technology discounts for the AI as the levels increase (as well as penalties at the lowest levels). Because of their incremental nature, these cheats have never earned much ire from players. Their effect is too small to notice on a turn-by-turn basis, and players who pry into the details usually understand why these bonuses are necessary.

On the other hand, many other cheats have struck players as unfair. In the original version of the game, the AI could create units for free under the fog of war, a situation that clearly showed how the computer was playing by different rules than the human. Also, AI civilizations occasionally would receive free "instant" Wonders, often robbing a player of many turns of work. While an AI beating the human to a Wonder using the slow drip of steady bonuses was acceptable, granting it the Wonder instantly felt entirely different.

How a cheat will be perceived has much more to do with the inconsistencies and irrationality of human psychology than to any attempt to measure up to some objective standard of fairness. Indeed, while subtle game-play bonuses may not bother a player, other, legitimate strategies could drive players crazy, even if they know that a fellow human might pursue the exact same path as the AI.

For example, in the original *Civ*, the AI was hard wired to declare war on the human if the player was leading the game by 1900 AD. This strategy felt unfair to players – who felt that the AI was ganging up on the human – even though most of them would have followed the same strategy without a second thought in a multiplayer game.

In response, by the time of *CivIII*, we guaranteed that the AI did not consider whether an opponent was controlled by a human or a computer when conducting diplomacy. However, these changes still did not inoculate us against charges of unfairness. *CivIII* allowed open trading – such as technology for maps or resources for gold. Enterprising human players would learn when to demand full price for their technologies and when to take whatever they could get – from a weak opponent with very little wealth, for example.

We adapted the AI to follow this same tactic so that it would be able to take whatever gold it could from a backwards neighbor. To the players, however, the AI once again appeared to be ganging up against the humans. Because the AI civs were fairly liberal with trading, they all tended to be around the same technology level, which led players to believe that they were forming their own nonhuman trading cartel, spreading technologies around like candy (or, in the parlance of our forums, *tech-whoring*).

Perception Is Reality

Once again, perception is reality. The question is not whether the AI is playing "fairly," but rather, what is the game experience for the player? If questions of fairness keep creeping into the player's mind, the game needs to be changed. Thus for *CivIV* we intentionally crippled the AI's ability to trade with other AIs to ensure that a similar situation did not develop.

The computer is still a black box to players, so single events based on hidden mechanics need to be handled with great care. Sports game developers, for example, need to be very sensitive to how often a random event hurts a player, such as a fumble, steal, or ill-timed error. The dangers of perceived unfairness are simply too great.

Returning to our original example, the developers of *Puzzle Quest* actually should have considered cheating, but only in favor of the *player*. The game code could ensure that fortunate drops happen only for the human and never for the AI. The ultimate balance of the game still could be maintained by tweaking the power of the AI's equipment and spells – changes that appear "fair" because they are explained explicitly to the player. The overall experience thus would be improved by the removal of these negative outliers that serve only to stir up suspicion. When the question is one of fairness, the player is always right.

5   Playing the Odds

Soren Johnson

One of the most powerful tools a designer can use when developing games is probability, using random chance to determine the outcome of player actions or to build the environment in which play occurs. The use of luck, however, is not without its pitfalls, and designers should be aware of the tradeoffs involved – what chance can add to the experience and when it can be counterproductive.

Failing at Probability

One challenge with using randomness is that humans are notoriously poor at evaluating probability accurately. A common example is the *gambler's fallacy*, which is the belief that odds will even out over time. If the roulette wheel comes up black five times in a row, players often believe that the odds of it coming up black again are quite small, even though clearly the streak makes no difference whatsoever. Conversely, people also see streaks where none actually exist – the shooter with a "hot hand" in basketball, for example, is a myth. Studies show that, if anything, a successful shot actually predicts a subsequent miss.

Also, as designers of slot machines and massively multiplayer online games (MMOs) are quite aware, setting odds unevenly between each progressive reward level makes players think that the game is more generous than it really is. One commercial slot machine had its payout odds published by wizardofodds.com in 2008:

1:1 per 8 plays
2:1 per 600 plays

Originally published in (2009, October) *Game Developer Magazine*.

5:1 per 33 plays
20:1 per 2,320 plays
80:1 per 219 plays
150:1 per 6,241 plays

The 80:1 payoff is common enough to give players the thrill of beating the odds for a "big win" but still rare enough that the casino is at no risk of losing money. Furthermore, humans have a hard time estimating extreme odds – a 1 percent chance is anticipated too often, and 99 percent odds are considered to be as safe as 100 percent.

Leveling the Field

These difficulties in estimating odds accurately actually work in the favor of the game designer. Simple game-design systems, such as the dice-based resource-generation system in *Settlers of Catan*, can be tantalizingly difficult to master with a dash of probability.

In fact, luck makes a game more accessible because it shrinks the gap – whether in perception or in reality – between experts and novices. In a game with a strong luck element, beginners believe that no matter what, they have a chance to win. Few people would be willing to play a chess Grandmaster, but playing a backgammon expert is much more appealing – a few lucky throws can give anyone a chance.

In the words of designer Dani Bunten, "Although most players hate the idea of random events that will destroy their nice safe predictable strategies, nothing keeps a game alive like a wrench in the works. Do not allow players to decide this issue. They don't know it but we're offering them an excuse for when they lose ('It was that damn random event that did me in!') and an opportunity to 'beat the odds' when they win."

Thus luck serves as a social lubricant – the alcohol of gaming, so to speak – that increases the appeal of multiplayer gaming to audiences that would not normally be suited for cutthroat head-to-head competition.

Where Luck Fails

Nonetheless, randomness is not appropriate for all situations or even all games. The "nasty surprise" mechanic is never a good idea. If a crate provides ammo and other bonuses when opened but explodes 1 percent of the time, the player has no chance to learn the probabilities in a safe manner. If the explosion occurs early enough, the player will stop opening crates immediately. If it happens much later, the player will feel unprepared and cheated.

Also, when randomness becomes just noise, the luck simply detracts from the player's understanding of the game. If a die roll is made every time a *StarCraft* Marine shoots at a target, the rate of fire simply will appear uneven. Over time, the effect of luck on the game's outcome will be negligible, but the player will have a harder time grasping how strong a Marine's attack actually is with all the extra random noise.

Further, luck can slow down a game unnecessarily. The board games *History of the World* and *Small World* have a very similar conquest mechanic, except that the former uses dice and the latter does not (until the final attack). Making a die roll with each attack causes a *History of the World* turn to last at least three or four times as long as a turn in *Small World*. The reason is not just the logistical issues of rolling so many dice – knowing that the results of one's decisions are completely predictable allows one to plan out all the steps at once without worrying about contingencies. Often, handling contingencies is a core part of the game design, but game speed is an important factor too, so designers should be sure that the tradeoff is worthwhile.

Finally, luck is very inappropriate for calculations to determine victory. Unlucky rolls feel the fairest the longer players are given to react to them before the game's end. Thus the earlier luck plays a role, the better for the perception of game balance. Many classic card games – pinochle, bridge, and hearts – follow a standard model of an initial random distribution of cards that establishes the game's "terrain," followed by a luck-free series of tricks that determines the winners and losers.

Probability Is Content

Indeed, the idea that randomness can provide an initial challenge to be overcome plays an important role in many classic games, from simple games such as *Minesweeper* to deeper ones such as *NetHack* and *Age of Empires*. At their core, solitaire and *Diablo* are not so different – both present a randomly generated environment that the player needs to navigate intelligently for success.

An interesting recent use of randomness is *Spelunky*, which is indie developer Derek Yu's combination of the random level generation of *NetHack* with the game mechanics of 2D platformers such as *Lode Runner*. The addictiveness of the game comes from the unlimited number of new caverns to explore, but frustration can emerge from the wild difficulty of certain, unplanned combinations of monsters and tunnels.

In fact, pure randomness can be an untamed beast, creating game dynamics that throw an otherwise solid design out of balance. For example, *Civilization III* introduced the concept of strategic resources that were required to construct certain units – chariots need horses, tanks need oil, and so on. These resources were sprinkled randomly across the world, which inevitably led to large continents with only one cluster of iron controlled by a single artificial intelligence (AI) opponent. Complaints of being unable to field armies for lack of resources were common among the community.

For *Civilization IV*, the problem was solved by adding a minimum amount of space between certain important resources so that two sources of iron never could be within seven tiles of each other. The result was a still unpredictable arrangement of resources around the globe but without the clustering that could doom an unfortunate player. On the other hand, the game actively encouraged clustering for less important luxury resources – incense, gems, and spices – to promote interesting trade dynamics.

Showing the Odds

Ultimately, when considering the role of probability, designers need to ask themselves, "How is luck helping or hurting the game?" Is randomness keeping the players pleasantly off balance so that they can't solve the game trivially? Or is it making the experience frustratingly unpredictable so that players are not invested in their decisions?

One factor that helps to ensure the former is making the probability as explicit as possible. The strategy game *Armageddon Empires* based combat on a few simple die rolls and then *showed* the dice directly on-screen. Allowing the players to peer into the game's calculations increases their comfort level with the mechanics, which makes chance a tool for the player instead of a mystery.

Similarly, with *Civilization IV*, we introduced a help mode that showed the exact probability of success in combat, which drastically increased player satisfaction with the underlying mechanics. Because humans have such a hard time estimating probability accurately, helping them make a smart decision can improve the experience immensely.

Some deck-building card games, such as *Magic: The Gathering* or *Dominion*, put probability in the foreground by centering the game experience on the likelihood of drawing cards in the player's carefully constructed deck. These games are won by players who understand the proper ratio of rares to commons, knowing that each card will be drawn exactly once each time through the deck. This concept can be extended to other games of chance by providing, for example, a virtual "deck of dice" that ensures that the distribution of die rolls is exactly even.

Another interesting – and perhaps underused – idea from the distant past of gaming history is the *element-of-chance* game option from the turn-based strategy game *Lords of Conquest*. The three options available – low, medium, and high – determined whether luck was used only to break ties or to play a larger role in resolving combat. The appropriate role of chance in a game ultimately is a subjective question, and giving players the ability to adjust the knobs themselves can open up the game to a larger audience with a greater variety of tastes.

6   Nurturing Lateral Leaps in Game Design

Nathan McKenzie

SimCity

In 1984, Will Wright released his first game – a free-roaming shooting game called *Raid on Bungeling Bay*.[1] As an unsurprising game in an established genre, *Raid* was an inauspicious start to a career that later included such innovative titles as *The Sims* and *Spore*. Yet *Raid* provided the backdrop for *SimCity*, the commercially successful and educationally fruitful game that established Wright as one of the most important game designers working today

In a 2009 interview, Wright recounted the design path he took to get from *Raid on Bungeling Bay* to *SimCity*:

> *Raid on Bungeling Bay* was a super shoot 'em up where you bomb these little islands. I had to create an editor where I could scroll around and create these little worlds to bomb. I found in playing with the editor that I was having a lot more fun creating these worlds than I was blowing them up. After I finished that game, I started kind of playing with the editor, and I started to add a little bit more dynamic to it. I wanted to keep traffic moving on the roads. I wanted to see kinds of dynamic systems operating. So I started reading about city planning. At first, I didn't find the subject that interesting, but as I started developing very simple simulations of the theories I was reading, it became fascinating to me, because I had a little guinea pig city that I could sit there and experiment and play with.

In an additional interview, also taken from a Will Wright fan site,[2] Wright describes how playing with the *Raid* editing utility evolved into designing it to be a game.

> Eventually I finished the shoot-'em-up game part [of *Raid*], but for some reason I kept going back to the darn thing and making the building utilities

more and more fancy. I wanted to automate the road function. I made it so that when you added each connecting piece of island, the road parts on them would connect up automatically to form a continuous road. Then I wanted to put down buildings automatically, so I built a little menu choice for buildings. I started asking myself, why am I doing this since the game is finished? The answer was that I found that I had a lot more fun building the islands than I had destroying them. Pretty soon I realized that I was fascinated by bringing a city to life. I wanted to add more behavior to it. I wanted to add traffic, and see the world kind of come alive and be more dynamic. At first I just wanted to do a traffic simulation. But then I realized that traffic didn't make a lot of sense unless you had places where the people drove to…and that led layer upon layer to a whole city: *SimCity*.

In the world-building tool that he used to construct a "super shoot 'em up," Wright saw the potential for a whole new kind of game – one based on balancing and manipulating the complex systems of a city. Or, more to the point, he found building the *Raid* islands fun and then followed that path toward more fun. When he followed that path, he did not have a master plan of *SimCity*. Instead, he pulled on one thread of his interest in world building, unraveling the design of one game until he found himself in the middle of another, quite-different game design. Because Wright functioned as programmer, artist, tool builder, *and* game designer on *Raid on Bungeling Bay*, his independence allowed him to shift gears into a new game design.

The story of *SimCity*'s genesis is partially striking because it's rare in game development for the road map of such new kinds of games to be so clearly documented. Even more striking, perhaps, is what *SimCity* portends: Not only was it a bold example of a new kind of game, but it also pointed in new directions that games could take generally. It showed how games could build on patterns in the world at large, including topics in which educators traditionally have been interested.

This chapter argues that there are deep patterns to be gleaned from the story of *SimCity*'s creation that are valuable to game designers, artists, and educators. These lessons are not, in general, the kinds that can be drawn from more recent, larger-budget games that dominate game industry sales and which dominate the tools and organizational process of the current game industry.

In particular, there is an important distinction between creating *new* kinds of games rather than high-quality, market-facing instances of *existing* kinds of games – that the former acts essentially as a vital but unpredictable input for the latter, that changes and evolution in game-creation techniques are driven almost entirely by creating higher-quality instances of existing kinds of games and hence provide poor resources for those lacking strong working models of new kinds of games, and that there are alternate models and communities to pay attention to that provide better road maps and processes for creating new kinds of games with some degree of success.

Instances of Games versus Kinds of Games

The core argument in this chapter hinges on the idea that there is a chasm between *kinds of games* and *instances of games* and that game-development processes look radically different for each. Hence we will elaborate on this distinction. Kinds of games are similar to genre but also not really the same. *Genre* is an encompassing term that suggests established patterns of market categorization. Indeed, many of the games discussed here are categorized as within the *indie* category at the moment. For example, is *Katamari Damcy* a game genre? Assigning games with unique game-play patterns each their own genre category leads to endless numbers of genres and therefore is not useful. Rather, we want to talk about something closer to, perhaps, recipes for games or broad blueprints.

So let's begin with a cooking metaphor – that exasperating cliché of game design discussions that can't be put to rest because it's simply too apt. Imagine for a moment that you run a restaurant in which you prepare, among other things, lasagna. At some point you grow bored of your menu and decide that you need to differentiate your food, so you change your lasagna to get people talking about it. You might use chicken or lamb as the meat, or you might change other ingredients to accommodate the new taste and texture. You might try out different cheeses and spices or change the proportions of ingredients to aim for different flavors and textures. You even might try getting higher-quality ingredients to really get some expressive flavors in your lasagna.

This process, for a paying audience, potentially could result in quite a number of new lasagna variations. You're getting constant feedback as you try out your recipes on a vocal and finicky audience. This is hill-climbing with feedback. It is evolution. It's astonishingly effective in all sorts of design contexts, especially when employed by hundred or thousands of cooks.

It is also not a process that could ever, in a million years, invent stir-fry out of lasagna.

Why is this? Well, there are not likely many intermediate points between lasagna and stir-fry that people would pay for or eat willingly. The kinds of recipes are dissimilar enough that some of this, some of that generally is going to be much, much worse than where you started from rather than better. If every meal you cooked had to be better than the last – because that's what your paying audience demands, after all – you can't move far enough to find strikingly new islands of successful meal types. This is a great process for refining working-recipe templates but not so effective for creating entirely new meal types. In other domains, this has been referred to as the *valley of death problem* (see National Materials Advisory Board, 2004). Educational reformers (particularly with technology) face similar problems (see Papert, 1980).

Most commercial game development takes place in an environment very much like the lasagna variation example just mentioned; the rough ingredients and proportions are inherited, and it is possible to rely on hill-climbing, making slight changes to the formula and then adjusting the system until it returns to some sort of appealing equilibrium. Rinse and repeat.

There's nothing wrong with this process. If you're a serious gamer, there's a good chance that many of your favorite games were the end result of this process. The recipe for a first-person shooter is a fine one: Create several weapons that bob in your view as you run, tweak some artificial intelligence (AI) agents (chatty, wise-cracking buddies are greatly outnumbered by ugly, vicious cannon-fodder enemies, of course) who will populate your largely linear roller-coaster ride with a fun variety of visually interesting locals. Figure out how to handle cover, inventory systems, and drivable vehicles, and viola! Cheese, meat, noodles, sauce. Experimentation happens in solid, sure-footed ways. The introduction of the recharging shield mechanic in *Halo* is a perfect example of what innovation looks like in this recipe; recharging shields let players perform reconnaissance with the less precise console controllers without relying on excessive saving and reloading. This simple game-play change was quickly absorbed back into the genre by most shooters that followed. Working on *Soldier of Fortune* and *Quake 4*, we at Raven Software monitored what game mechanics were used in recent successful shooters and exploited them in our designs.

There are upsides and downsides to this approach. It is, in general, more consistent and predictable for development, an issue that matters quite a lot to investors. It means, too, for developers that they inherit a game design that is already known to be fun, so as long as care is taken not to fundamentally break the game design, the game should remain so. Players can come into the game with a great deal of genre knowledge, which means that games can be complex without being inaccessible, at least to a certain sort of player. Further, marketing games (and marketing budgets have gotten terrifyingly large for many games) is much easier when they have a family resemblance to other successful games. Nevertheless, all these choices made in the service of creating predictably fun games for a wide swath of players make the space for genuine player surprise smaller and smaller.

There is no hard and fast either-or distinction between games that are pure evolutions versus games that spring forth from nothing. There is a family resemblance among *Virtua Fighter*, *Dead or Alive*, *Tekken*, *Soul Caliber*, and the lion's share of 3D fighting games. There is also a distinct family resemblance among *Street Fighter*, *Guilty Gear*, *Samurai Shodown*, and other 2D fighting games. *Virtua Fighter* clearly took many of its cues from the success of *Street Fighter 2*, and yet it's also enough of its own system that subsequent successful 3D fighting games clearly draw from *it* and *not Street Fighter 2*.

There are degrees to which a new game can represent a new kind of game, a new combination of parts that seem to work successfully together. Perhaps it wouldn't be too far off to compare it to lasagna and spaghetti; they're not the same recipe, but they belong in the same branch of a family tree. Experiments with one can inform and inspire experiments with the other.

Compared with all of this, it's not entirely obvious where *Super Mario Kart*, *Facade*, *Metroid*, *Warcraft 1*, *Grand Theft Auto*, *Katamari Damacy*, or *Street Fighter 1* come from. While each of them draws from other games and genres (often from radically disparate sources), they are all working systems without obvious road maps leading to their particular blends of mechanics and game-play structures. As I worked on *Soldier of Fortune*, its antecedents were on the whole obvious – and the game was in no sense impaired by that fact. Where *Wolfenstein 3D* came from, on the other hand, is a little more difficult to trace despite its massive impact on the first-person shooter genre.

The point is not to lionize these games. Some of them are not very fun. For quite a few of them, their evolved sequels are vastly better games. However, it's just as essential to point out that each of them served as a baseline for those later games. *Street Fighter 2* is a much more fun and important game than *Street Fighter 1*, but it's nearly baffling to go back and look at the first game and recognize how much of what was good in the sequel was already present in the original. The framework is nearly there; the proportions and components just weren't quite right yet.

SimCity fits comfortably into this model. Without question, if you were interested in playing *SimCity* right now, it would be a strange choice to track down the C64 original. It might very well be, from a current perspective, a bad game. And yet, as an exemplar of a kind of game, as an arrow pointing in a fruitful direction that game design could go, it has been extremely important.

Before turning to the evolution of game-development practices, a few more distinctions among kinds of games and specific instances of games need to be articulated. In general, *kinds* of games are the bedrock for subsequent game designs. Once there is an established kind of game, specific instances that pull together different components emerge. *Metroid: Zero Mission* for the Game Boy Advance might be a much better game than the original 1986 NES *Metroid*, but *Zero Mission* certainly couldn't exist with the original. Most of the game design was already present. *Grand Theft Auto 1* is a prerequisite for *Grand Theft Auto 3* to exist. *EverQuest, Ultima Online*, and *Dark Age of Camelot* all contributed to *World of Warcraft*.

Markets are not predictable tools for encouraging the creation of new kinds of games. It may be serendipity that *Metroid, Street Fighter 1, SimCity*, and *Grand Theft Auto* found enough of an audience to keep their creators afloat long enough to evolve these games into the more fleshed out, polished games that they became. If comparable games were created and shipped today exploring an interesting new game design but hamstrung by uneven execution, it is likely that most of them would fail miserably in the marketplace because games must sell 100,000s of copies to break even.

The key is that game buyers do not preferentially seek out and reward new kinds of games. They reward extremely well-executed instances of games. This is not to say that game players are not sometimes grabbed by new kinds of games; of course, far from it. But the massive prevalence of sequels and solid genre entries in the market point toward buyers' default behaviors.

This combination of facts – the role of kinds of games as input for making high-quality instances of games and the market's preference for well-executed instances of games – is essential for understanding why blindly copying techniques and processes from the game industry can be a recipe for difficulty, especially for educational game makers. What educational game developers need is a robust ecology for developing new kinds of games and then mechanisms for improving them to create very well polished instances of quality games.

The Evolution of Game-Making Processes in Action

The rapid evolution of production processes in the commercial game industry has been staggering to watch, and it is little wonder that people in adjacent fields are anxious to reap the fruits of that evolution. With few lulls, commercial games have enjoyed dramatically increasing success since the early 1980s.

To map out some of those changes and draw attention to their consequences, let's return to *Raid on Bungeling Bay*. Will Wright made and was able to sell this Commodore 64 game at a very specific moment in time with very specific market competition. His follow-up game was *SimCity*, which bore little resemblance to the original game. But what would it look like if *Raid on Bungeling Bay*'s sequels were to follow the trajectory of commercial game design since the 1980s? The following description is hypothetical, based in common games industry practices as documented by Wright himself in his 2005 Game Developer's Conference keynote address on innovation.

Let's start by picturing a hypothetical *Raid on Bungeling Bay 2*, released in the late 1980s or early 1990s. By this time, teams for game design were bigger; it was nearly impossible for one person to do the bulk of the work for a commercial game. Four to six developers might be involved at this point. Communication still would be relatively easy, though, and nearly everyone would have at least a vague idea about what everyone else on the team was doing. In terms of the design process, easy-to-understand tool chains for developers, as well as processes for getting content into the game in a routinized and predictable fashion, would begin to be a priority. As the development process became more routinized at this time, there was greater separation between duties for team members on a game. *Programmer* and *artist* began to differentiate. Increased graphics capabilities meant that Will Wright's clumsy "programmer artwork," while serviceable on the Commodore 64 in 1984, would not have competed successfully in this market. *Raid on Bungeling Bay 2* almost certainly would have full-time artists working on it to have any chance of selling. Design of game worlds still was largely handled by programmers; however, the procedural design that Wright used to generate worlds for *Raid* in 1984 likely would have been replaced with hand-crafted levels.

Fast forward a few more years to *Raid on Bungeling Bay 3*, hypothetically released in the late 1990s, and the construction of the islands themselves would be handed off to people who were neither particularly artistic nor overwhelmingly technical and who conceived of themselves as *level designers*. The island surfaces would be handled by dedicated artists. Programmatic tools for level creation – which had been the seeds of *SimCity* – would be met by stiff resistance by both the level designers and the artists, each of whom would be appalled at the loss of control. New programmers would show up who had only a passing interest in game design qua game design. Instead, some would be handling the rather prestigious and technical task of finding novel and quick ways of doing terrain and water rendering, and others would try to make level editing tools considerably more full-featured. The publisher of the game might begin wondering if perhaps a professional writer needed to provide a narrative arc. Much would come down not to individual components but to successfully coordinating communication among the level designers, the technology programmers, the writer, the tools programmers, and the level artists. There's a reasonably good chance that for the game to be successful, it would need to copy another general game template to ensure that everyone on the team knew in which direction to pull. Counting technical and game programmers, level designers, writers, and artists, twenty-five to forty people might be involved in the game at this point.

Let's imagine that *Raid on Bungeling Bay 4* was released in the mid-2000s. Suddenly, the chance of the game existing at all approaches nil – or at least not with that clunky name. Maybe the game would be called *RAID 4*. Or more likely, publishers would have tracked down a preexisting license from some other form of media to give consumers positive brand awareness. Off-site experts from the holder of the brand would be required to vet nearly every major decision made by the game makers to ensure that the brand's integrity was preserved. The game itself would be built on one of several very powerful, very complicated, full-featured game engines, complete with optimized rendering, physics, and networking code, and integrated with a robust level editor that allowed level designers to edit levels in real time to see changes immediately. This engine might come preequipped with code from other shipped games. While the engine will promise that it can serve as an infinitely reconfigurable game-making tool, the designers will slowly discover that subtle choices in its design make it much better at making games just like the one it shipped with originally. The job for programmers will be less about creating new kinds of technology and more about tweaking the enormously complicated game engine and tool chain. Attempting to cut costs, the publisher might outsource music, sound, cinematics, and some kinds of art and animation to external shops around the globe, all puttering along in different time zones. Hollywood talent will provide performances for the obligatory story about why players are raiding islands. Marketing departments at the large publishing company also will want to vet as much of the game as possible to make sure that they can sell it to target demographics. Multiple demos and greenlight meetings will reshape development progresses to allow the publisher and other stakeholders a chance to pull the plug or change teams around if they are not pleased with how the enormously expensive project is progressing.

Teams in the mid-2000s radically exploded in the size and range of their expertise. The team of the mid-2000s dwarfs poor Will Wright in its ability to do the isolated tasks that Wright did when making *Raid on Bungeling Bay*. The technology programmers are experts at optimizing speed and performance. The artists are highly trained and highly paid professionals who can make things look just right. And the infrastructure for making games likewise is radically better; the game engines, the painting programs, the programming languages, the compilers, and the debuggers are all astronomically better than what Will Wright had access to.

The Battle Against Complexity and the Control of Information in Making Bigger and Better Instances of Games

For anyone on the outside looking in, it's easy to view these changes in the game industry's production processes as unabashed progress. Games look more beautiful, sound better, and are better written. Programming languages are more robust and full-featured. More and more specialists are honing their crafts, bigger teams are capable of pulling together ever more impressive projects, and more capital is being turned into larger and larger projects that find bigger audiences. More middleware means more competition and more options for developers. It's easy to view this all as a kind of progress, and it certainly is greater organization, but examined more closely, some deep and vexing tradeoffs appear. Anyone who wants to inherit the successes of the game industry needs to understand why it has followed the arc that it has and to make sure that their goals thus are aligned.

It is tempting to describe contemporary game development as the rise of specialization. Will Wright was a lone developer donning all hats; there was no freedom to develop hyperfocused skills, such as the real-time procedural grass animation used frequently in racing games. Game development, as evolved by the industry, has created people with amazing abilities. If you are a smaller group trying to mimic current big-budget game-development techniques, the array of talent on display in a modern successful team can feel intimidating, as though it is an insurmountable difference between what their teams can achieve and what yours can.

Nevertheless, while it is highly tempting to conclude that "games have gotten more impressive because they have had the resources to bring in, and develop, so many specialists," this is, I argue, a side story to the much, much more important central story: *Game development has evolved as it is because game developers have chosen particular approaches to taming the rise of complexity and information flow and change in projects.* Specialization is the result of that process, but that process is the true driver and has much farther-reaching consequences on game production.

To continue, a lone developer such as Will Wright on *Raid on Bungeling Bay* operates in what we might call a prerationalized state (captured brilliantly in Boyer's 2010 "More Rock Less Talk"). All production is implicit and ad hoc; there is no documentation to plan or communicate other than whatever notes Wright might make for himself. The collection of Wright's skills and knowledge is entirely arbitrary and unrepeatable. The Will Wright of 1985 knows what he knows, and he will make games that reflect that knowledge. His art production might rely heavily on programming. His level designing might rely heavily on his reading of urban planning literature. Radical new designs can emerge midway through a project based on information gleaned from the production process itself, and the design can veer to incorporate that. If he were to be hit by a bus, his unfinished projects essentially would have to be thrown away; there would be no real way for someone else to fill in his shoes. The knowledge generated by his successes doesn't really contribute to anyone else's, except at the macro level of the complete and full integrated games that eventually are made public.

There is no consistent way for an outside party to invest in making tools for Will Wright and what he is doing at this point (not even *PhotoShop* is used). There is no way to build professional organizations except in the loosest of senses of communities of game developers. There is no way for universities to craft programs to train students to help Will Wright do whatever it is that he is doing or to repeat his successes.

In the lone-developer scenario, every kind of knowledge and every kind of skill potentially can inform, in entirely unpredictable ways, every other skill. The lone developer can change anything in the project at any time, and those changes can be inspired by information gleaned from any other part of the project. The flow of information during development is unconstrained, perhaps even seemingly stochastic.

As the teams grow slightly larger, and as different developers evidence different skill sets and expertise, this lack of constraints grows into a larger and larger problem. At first, when team sizes are small and the production quality expected from games is still rather low, it can be managed. The number of people who need to be informed of any particular change or new interaction in development is still fairly small. Although people begin to adopt fuzzy titles, communication from anyone to anyone else is still fairly quick because they may occupy the same office (or proverbial garage).

But the ability for everyone to change anything arbitrarily and for job descriptions to be amorphous and communication pathways between makers to be completely unpredictable becomes crippling as teams get larger. Communication becomes a much larger burden, as does staffing, morale, consensus, vision, scheduling, and all the difficulties that large organizations of all stripes have always wrestled with.

The rise of specialization largely has been a reaction to these problems. While it is true that the rise of character animation means that game development has access to much higher-quality animation, it may be more important that game development has developed information interfaces to black-box character animation from the rest of game development. The rise of specialist character animators means that character animation can occur in isolation from the rest of game development – at least for many kinds of games. Character animation can happen in rough parallel without frequent communication or collaboration with other stakeholders. Employees can be hired who know almost nothing about other disciplines involved in game making, but they still can be successful character animators. Character animation can be scaled up safely; new animators can be brought on board, and as long as they respect the information interface between character animation and the rest of the project, they can be integrated (and replaced) safely. Special tools can be built to support the tasks of character animation, and other firms can outsource character animation duties. Universities can collaborate with industry and identify the skills needs to be a character animator, books can be written, professional organization can develop, and character animators can develop their own value systems.

The most important aspects of the rise of the modular boundary of character animation are the guarantees about what a character animator *doesn't* need to know to be successful, the guarantees character animators have about what infrastructure within a game that they count on as remaining relatively firm as they work, and the guarantees about what other aspects of a project any particular character animator cannot change during development. Such modularity is at the root of many complex phenomena, as Edwin Hutchins (1995) documented in his study of ship navigation.

This process largely is repeated for all the other disciplines that have emerged for game development, including various types of technology programmers, special-effects artists, texture and skin artists, writers, musicians, game balancers, level architects, scripters, and the other vast assortment of job descriptions in the credits of a modern game, and this is only growing in scope.

One not entirely obvious result of this process is the value for middleware game engines, not just as technology solutions but also as sociotechnical infrastructures that organize work (see Hutchins, 1995; Barab, Kling, & Gray, 2004). Game engines aren't valuable simple because of the features their code supports, or their optimization for specific desirable hardware, or their tools and examples. Buying a well-supported game engine is also buying a workflow. Middleware manages expectations about the flow of information, team structure, job descriptions, and ultimately, modular boundaries between kinds of expertise. A game engine represents not just features but ways of working. A good game engine gives you job descriptions and soft guarantees about what character animators won't be required to know while still being productive.

As enormously successful as this sociotechnical infrastructure has been at managing complexity to reliably produce games, there are a number of deep tensions and problems embedded in this transition. Anyone who mimics the game industry without understanding those tensions is likely to suffer their consequences.

The modular boundaries for disciplines are historical rules of thumb, created and constrained temporally. As an example, for many games, character animators can work in rough isolation from other disciplines, especially on art assets such as idle animations, friendly nonplayer character (NPC) animations, ambient animations that add personality to characters, and noninteractive and cinematic animations. Action-adventure games such as *Shadows of the Colossus* that privilege beautiful, lengthy animations over responsive controls have been critiqued for poor game play. Even within an entirely modular production process, animators are forced to deal with hardware limitations and tool paths, but in general, these are tasks that can be handled in isolation or at least within the confines of an art department.

So can we safely say, a priori, what sorts of things animators cannot know and still be successful? Well, unfortunately, not really. In some severe cases, as in fighting games such as *Street Fighter 2*, the majority of the game design and game balance *is* located in the timings of the animation system and the interconnected web of damage, timings, and priorities between animation sequences (see Sirlin, Chapter 9 of this volume). Game design and animation are essentially the same thing in this genre. This coupling is true to a lesser degree in many other genres; in such games as *Prince of Persia: The Sands of Time*, the relationship between player control and player animation is, again, central to game design (see Davidson, 2008). It can't be isolated out.

This process pops up again and again. Music composition is frequently one of the most modular of all disciplines in game making, which allows for easy outsourcing and the use of licensed scores. Many, many studios rely on the fact that they can hire out for music cheaply and consistently to keep their staffs leaner. Thus, what can musicians be excused from knowing while still being successful, and what can game teams be excused from knowing about music while still making good games? Well, in most cases, really quite a lot. And yet games such as *Guitar Hero* require a deep, deep connection between music as an expertise and game design, level design, and user-interface design (see LoPiccolo, Chapter 8 of this volume).

Or another example. In general, wall, floor, and character skin textures are the tasks that tend to be easiest to make modular, to farm out to teams of artists, and to scale up. And yet even this can have sharp edges. For example, while working on *Quake 4*, we noticed that players were having a much harder time telling if they were shooting monsters successfully than in *Doom 3* (a similar title using the same technology). After reviewing the combat mechanics, it became clear that the major issue was an art one: The monsters in *Doom 3* often were fleshy, smooth, and off-white in color, which meant that, when shot, their surfaces would be bloodied and visibly hurt. The art direction on *Quake 4*, hoping to differentiate itself from *Doom 3*, included dark monsters with lots of high-frequency metallic surfaces. This is a pretty reasonable art decision aesthetically, and if *Quake 4* had been a movie or a turned-based role-playing game (RPG), it probably would have been an uncontroversial decision. However, in a fast-paced first-person shooter, it meant that players had a lot less feedback and information about their primary task, which was shooting foes. *Monster texture art was game design.* So what can we safely say, a priori, that texture artists cannot know and still be successful at their jobs?

The answer is, we can't. We can't make any good global claims about which modular boundaries and disciplines will function well in game design in general. Animators for *Final Fantasy* don't have to know anything at all about game design (barring avoiding extravagances such as thirty-second-long animations in the middle of battles, a rule they have violated at times). Animators for *Ico*, *Shadow of the Colossus*, *Prince of Persia*, and *Street Fighter 2* are deeply embedded in game design.

But there is one rule of thumb on which we can rely, and it brings us back full circle to the beginning of this chapter. It is, ultimately, the source of the great success of modularity of information in game making. That rule is this: When making high-quality instances of games that are following existing recipes, the flow of information and the requirements of knowledge and information for various disciplines largely will be similar to previous instances of those same kinds of games.

We cannot say, in general, what an animator can safely not know to function as a good animator. If, however, we are making *Halo 3*, we can get a pretty good guess about the knowledge requirements for an animator by looking at the process that produced *Halo 2*.

We cannot say what sorts of music knowledge a game designer needs to have access to in the general case (surely none in most cases but quite a lot in a few others), and we cannot say what sorts of music knowledge a game designer needs to invent *Guitar Hero* when we don't know that *Guitar Hero* could exist, but we have a pretty good method for identifying the job boundaries for *Guitar Hero 2*. We can just look at the production process of *Guitar Hero 1*. Perhaps not surprisingly, Harmonix, inventor of *Guitar Hero*, is a company full of musicians.

The changes that have happened in the game industry have been driven largely by creating the sociotechnical network to manage this complexity. If you are looking to huge-budget game-crafting iterations of existing game styles using tools specially made for those tasks, you are not looking at a process that is trivially copyable. Rather, you are looking at the end results of a specific kind of evolutionary process, most steps of which are inherently distributed and not contained within any one team or any one project.

The industry, in short, has evolved to make high-quality instances of particular kinds of games, with those kinds of games an extrinsic, preexisting resource for the process. It is a machine for doing just that. If you are in a similar situation – working with game systems or kinds of games that are already fertile and somewhat successful and needing to scale up the quality of components – current game industry practices make quite a lot of sense to replicate.

Embracing Complexity and Making New Kinds of Games

These questions of knowledge, communication, and the managing of complexity and its inherit risks are the central story of the history of game development, and this is where the difference between making new high-quality instances of games and new kinds of games becomes thorny. Making new kinds of games is not, ultimately, a task that benefits from the industrializing processes and industrializing value systems that have so radically improved the production quality of big-budget games.

The difficulty hinges on this question: What didn't Will Wright need to know to create *SimCity* from his *Raid on Bungeling Bay* tools? After the fact, we can easily make a giant list of all the varieties of human knowledge and expertise that one safely could be ignorant of (such as character animation) and still have the requisite knowledge to build *SimCity*, and we'd still be wrong because we don't have access to the fruitful and generative intermediate false steps Wright took. *SimCity* evolved (what if he did try advisors with facial animations, as in later installments of *Civilization*, but found that they hindered the experience?). After the fact, we can point out lots of things not involved in that system. Unfortunately, though, even such a list wouldn't really be helpful in for supporting designers in building *other* kinds of games. The list essentially would be singular and useless, highly specific to creating *SimCity*.

This is the central tension: The game industry has rationalized itself by stabilizing interactions among components of game development along more and more predictable lines. The more that interactions within games can happen only along prescribed paths, the more that tools and processes can be evolved, jobs can be decoupled, institutions can be formed, and specialist practices and value systems can be evolved.

And yet, large-scale innovation in game design, especially the creation of new kinds of games, almost always involves radical and unexpected interactions between the various components of game development. The further apart the components are, the more radical is the innovation. *Guitar Hero* couples music with controller input and new kinds of visual representations. *Facade* connects animation with AI and natural-language parsing. *SimCity* connects level building with world simulation. *Metroid* splices level design with power-ups, player control, and weapon behaviors. *Street Fighter 1* embeds game balance in an enormous database of animation timings and positions.

It's a peculiar dilemma. Large game-development teams often house astonishing amounts of talent in aggregate, but the process of modularity itself prevents any one person from having the right kinds of disparate knowledge to pull together unexpected systems and interactions. Worse still, too, the value systems that experts develop, which, as always, are directed toward the crafting of extremely high-quality instances of particular games (such as well-crafted procedurally animated grass), often devalues innovations *across* systems. If the creators of *Facade* had had some typical game industry writers on staff, there's reasonably good odds that they would have pushed back on *Facade*'s game design choices. If *Portal* had been created from scratch inside of *Valve*, rather than being a project based on an external game, there's a reasonably good chance that the AI programmers and character animators on staff might have tried to pull the game design in other directions that highlighted their particular kinds of expertise (or let them work on the project at all).

If the story of Will Wright creating *SimCity* doesn't seem to lend itself to the changes that have evolved in the broader commercial game industry, is all hope lost? Is the creation of new kinds of games essentially a random event, vital to the creation of large-scale games but ultimately something that can't be encouraged or fostered?

It turns out that the history of the evolution of game-development practices just recounted, while broadly accurate for big-budget, high-prestige game development, is in a very important sense incomplete. If this description captures the broad central currents of game development, there have been very consistent eddies and pockets of turbulence in game design that are complementary to this process but spiraling back in other directions.

It is in taking notice of these spaces and drawing out some recurring patterns from them that we can see alternate models for helping spur the creation of successful kinds of games rather than just high-quality instances of games. One such space has been the various mod communities that have sprung up around first-person shooters such as *Quake*, *Unreal*, and *Half-Life* and other games that provide software development kits (SDKs) to their end users. These games have had very large grass roots communities of game development spring up, with users variously creating tools, documentation, asset repositories, maps, and especially new kinds of games from these original big-budget games.

Mod communities have been the source of a lot of game-development experimentation. Operating largely in a noncommercial context, game mods often reuse most of the game code and art assets from the games on which they are built. At their most successful, they often create, and only create, new kinds of interactions and play structures on top of a largely final base of the games on which they are built. The teams that create them tend to be quite small, the experimentation often takes place in a highly public iterative way, with feedback from players helping to inspire new game changes; development cycles are fairly short; and no money is required for players to enjoy the fruits of someone else's experimentation. The line between audience and peer group is relatively fuzzy, and game makers can find audiences that are receptive to new kinds of game play without needing lavish stories, new art styles, or other extremely expensive production value components. New game types such as *Counterstrike, Team Fortress*, and *Defense of the Ancients* all have been the products of this kind of development.

Another surprisingly fruitful set of communities has turned out to be student projects and experimentation. Although the rise of students having officially sanctioned contexts to create games and find audiences is recent, giving the very recent recognition that game creation may be a legitimate area for academic study, it has already proven to be a space where new kinds of games can be created. *Narbacular Drop, Tag: The Power of Paint*, and *flOw* are all fascinating game design projects stemming from student game creation spaces.

Rising at roughly the same time as these student communities and often interacting with them has been a robust independent game-creation scene. Consisting of small teams and low budgets and relying on distribution networks such as Steam, XboxLive arcade, and especially just installers downloaded from websites on the Internet, the recent explosion of truly independent games has brought with it a multitude of game designs that are striking in their originality. Games such as *Minecraft, Dwarf Fortress*, and *Facade* once again are pushing the boundaries of the kinds of games that are being made and expanding the space of the possible in game development.

One especially important facet of the independent game-making scene has been the rise of browser-based Flash games. Despite providing relatively paltry technical capabilities and requiring games to have small downloads, the Flash game-making scene has seen an absolute explosion of independent games being made and as such has been the birthing grounds of many new kinds of games.

Although recent years have been particularly good for building communities where kinds of games can find an audience, it would be mistaken to think that this is a new phenomenon. Many of the patterns and properties of these spaces were already present in the early years of the multiuser dungeon (MUD) development community (which evolved into MMOs) and in the titles created for early cheap PCs, such as the Commodore 64 and the Apple 2. These are not new ways of working.

There are a number of extremely important patterns and similarities that show up in these spaces. One is that the rate of failure tends to be radically higher than in more established spaces. The majority of indie games, Flash games, mods, and student games that are released are flatly terrible, and they're often terrible in ways that would never make it through the filter of the big-budget game-making process. And that, of course, only applies to the designs that see the light of day; these are spaces rife with unfinished projects.

On the other hand, they're also extremely cheap. Many of the games made in the spaces are pulled together with essentially no funding at all. One consequence of this is that development teams are often forced to find art styles, game designs, and methodologies that allow them to work effectively without budgets. In some cases, this means building on top of existing infrastructures, as in the mod communities. In other cases, it means relying on extremely stylized art styles, as in the Flash space, or even text, as with MUDs. In all cases, it makes the drastically higher failure rate endurable.

With such bare bones teams, the game-building styles also force all developers to wear an extraordinary number of hats, meaning that while the teams tend to lack the sheer depth of specialist talent big teams have, the chances of any individual having enough exposure to disparate kinds of knowledge and being able to discover new kinds of unexpected interactions actually are greatly increased.

This lack of specialist identities has a number of deeper consequences. No real permission is required from outside specialized experts for work to be performed and with it no real attendant communication bottlenecks or frictions. There's no real intermediate vetting, which means, of course, that many things that shouldn't be made are, but this also means that premature or incorrect vetting doesn't happen either. Specialist expert value systems are brought to bear after the title has been finished and made public, not before.

The communities that grow up around many of the spaces also radically change evaluation. Rather than looking toward market acceptance as the final arbiter of success, with its aggressive bias toward rich instances of existing kinds of games, and rather than turning toward specialist experts with their decontextualized and modular value systems, game makers in these communities often turn toward each other for their most important feedback and support. Mod makers, MUD makers, indie developers, and students often serve both as makers and audiences for works in progress or for games that are testing the boundaries of new kinds of interactivity, and their dual role can make them uniquely appreciative of games that have uneven production values, are too short, or otherwise are hamstrung relative to the broader market and yet evidence striking new ideas that are still worth trying and praising.

Several of these factors – the huge amount of shallow experimentation, the presence of local control, the nonmonetization of so much work occurring in these spaces, and the importance of peer-community feedback – have another highly beneficial consequence. Whereas prototyping in large firms, when it happens at all, tends never to see the light of day except in instances where it leads to new big-budget games, many of these games in essence are evolved in public regardless of their ultimate commercial viability. In this sense, the knowledge generated by these game-development processes, regardless of whether the kinds of games created are ultimately viable, and regardless of whether the games in question are ever turned into high-quality instances of games, acts as a kind of public good; these communities are generating information that is accessible to everyone, everywhere, about game design. This form of design research is one that educators may seek to emulate.

If the evolution of the game-development process in big-budget spaces represents a certain attempt at taming complexity and managing the flow of knowledge and information in projects, what can we say about these alternative spaces? These niche spaces represent an entirely different evolutionary path with values and practices that embrace rather than tame certain kinds of complexity and unexpected large-scale interactions. Where big-budget games rely on repeatability and consistent, replaceable modular job roles and communication paths, the makers of indie games, Flash games, student games, and mods generally work in ad hoc fashions that, at their best, aggressively leverage the highly particular knowledge, skills, and interests of their specific game makers. In this sense, they do not stray so very far from Will Wright's starting point back in the mid-1980s.

But there are very specific traits here that help to raise the chances of general success and sustainability. Clearly, minimizing costs through clever asset use (be it the reuse of mods, or the art styles of Flash, or aggressive reliance on procedural content-creation techniques that would be inappropriate for larger teams) is one trait. Another is cultivating audiences that can appreciate the core kind-of-game innovation happening in these spaces; players or peer developers who are excited to try out new kinds of systems or interactions can be quite forgiving of production quality if expectations are calibrated properly.

The most important trait, however, is an even more aggressive relationship with controlling information, knowledge, and change than big-budget games. If large-scale games have wrestled to control the flow of knowledge, information, and change in games by creating modular boundaries and hierarchical structures for making change more predictable, these smaller-scale teams essentially get rid of multidirection communication or change entirely. In one sense, Will Wright worked alone on his transition from

Raid on Bungeling Bay into *SimCity*. In another sense, Will Wright worked closely with every urban planner who wrote a book that he read, every user-interface designer whose game he played and was inspired by, and every other developer with whom he shared production knowledge. He simply didn't give any of them permission to make any changes or impose their value systems on his work.

Would *SimCity* have been a better game if Will Wright had brought in official urban planners at the prototyping/evolution stage? What about better artists or user-interface designers? The reality, of course, is no; the friction and coordination costs introduced almost certainly would have meant that *SimCity* simply never would have existed, and even if such experts had been brought on board, it's not obvious that they would have understood what it was that deeply worked, on a systemic level, about *SimCity*. Comparable constraints would hold for most successful small and indie games, and educational developers wrestle with similar issues all the time as they seek to juggle subject-matter experts, game design, and production realities (see Squire, 2008).

The successes of these smaller spaces at generating many great new kinds of games, despite the overwhelming sea of cheap failures that come with them, seems to imply that kinds of games are best developed in extremely inexpensive, very loosely coupled spaces with small, ad hoc, arbitrarily skilled teams with high amounts of local control and peer communities that appreciate what valuable experimentation looks like. And recognizing the value in publicly capturing those successes and failures, and nurturing them even when markets won't, is paramount for anyone who eventually will need successful kinds of games as inputs to their ultimate high-quality instances of games.

Educational Games

This discussion of game-development processes oddly was inspired through many conversations with educational developers and watching various educational game projects come and go (including those I have worked on in various capacities). Needless to say, a lot of hard work is taking place in educational game development right now. A lot of effort is going into making bigger, better, more technically impressive games. Developers and educators are slowly amassing some of the modular specialist skills and technology that make commercial game development so technically demanding.

This effort is all to the good. Nevertheless, it is striking that where the canon of great entertainment games, after a few short decades, is astonishingly rich and deep, the stable of truly great educational games – the titles that would be clear, obvious, and uncontroversial exemplars of everything that is amazing and possible in the educational space – is still surprisingly thin. There are commendable efforts, to be sure. But some process that is happening automatically in entertainment game development is not quite clicking on the educational side.

Often, it is suggested by developers that if they just had the tools, capital, and talent of large-scale, big-budget teams, obviously, educational games would be just as successful. *SimCity* didn't have those tools, capital, and talent. What it had was highly personal ad hoc talent, hundreds of comparable but terrible also-ran attempts being made by other concurrent developers at the same time, and a kind of total local freedom to truly swing for the fences without premature outside interference.

In the last several years, the indie, Flash, and student game spaces have produced many, many games, with none of the tools, capital, and talent of big-budget teams, that have sewn the seeds for all sorts of fantastic new genres and kinds of games. But what they have had are robust communities, local control, small, particular teams, freedom to fail in astonishingly embarrassingly spectacular ways, strong traditions of publicly capturing successes and, far more often, failures, and ultimately, numbers. Educators need to facilitate this type of ecology today if we hope to see great games emerge.

There is no question that a many heavyweight processes are necessary before any learning game ultimately is used by students on a large scale. Many of the same quality-control and bureaucratic impulses that have been evolved by the commercial game industry for creating high-quality instances of games likewise are necessary for making student-facing games for schools, museums, or even homes. A *SimCity* built to be rolled out for students needs the involvement of urban planners and user-interface specialists and amazing artists and dozens of other specialists besides. Again, though, we need the seeds of compelling new kinds of games before we apply such highly specialized processes to particular game instances.

Learning game makers everywhere would be in much more robust positions to make high-quality instances of games if they had even a fraction of the entertainment game industry's giant pool of research that comprises successful recipes for kinds of games. There is no precise formula for creating and collecting these recipes, but there are things that can be done at the institutional level to nurture the processes that make these experiments, such as Will Wright's efforts with *SimCity*, happen and happen in ways in which their results are captured publicly and can inspire and inform other new kinds of work.

Research and development of educational games has to be respected as its own special kind of task, with its own special methods for evaluation and success, separate from the task of making games for student- or learner-facing audiences for educational games ultimately to thrive.

Valve

If people outside the game industry are interested in copying powerful ideas, techniques, and technologies from successful game makers, perhaps no company can serve as a better model than Valve Corporation, the studio responsible for *Half-Life 1* and *2, Counterstrike, Team Fortress 2, Left 4 Dead,* and *Portal*.

Valve has all the traits and technologies that educational game makers of all stripes wish they had access to. The company has large budgets, cutting-edge technologies, and large stables of enormously talented developers from an assortment of disciplines. The company is staffed and funded to make great instances of games.

This can't be the whole picture, though. Plenty of other studios are staffed with just as much illustrious talent, have at least as powerful middleware, and have even more funding. Few other studios can boast of such a great record of getting award-winning games to market, particularly such a diverse range of games.

So what makes Valve special? I'm not here to claim that any one feature can account for Valve's success at being not only monetarily successful but also innovative on a large scale. Nevertheless, a close look at the history of several of the company's titles is illuminating.

Team Fortress, the first death-match game to really explore class-based team death match with classes that complement each other in deep, interesting, asymmetrical ways largely was fleshed out as a free mod for *Quake 1* in the *Quake* community in 1996 by Robin Walker, John Cook, and Ian Caughley. Valve barely existed at the time of *Team Fortress*'s noncommercial creation, but the company wasted no time in snatching up the creators, going on to release *Team Fortress Classic* and, later, *Team Fortress 2*.

Valve further benefited from the shooter mod community with the massive popularity of *Counterstrike*, another free mod, this one for *Half-Life*, by Minh Le and Jess Cliffe, first released in 1999. *Counterstrike* tossed out most of the rules of first-person shooter multiplayer competition and replaced them with a tense, addictive round-based format that has been highly influential. Once again, Valve brought these developers on board and leveraged their internal talent to make more polished and extensive versions of *Counterstrike*.

Another highly interesting free game was released in 2005. The senior project of students attending DigiPen, *Narbacular Drop* was a peculiar first-person puzzle game in which the player had no weapons but only two portals that could be fired at walls and floors, which then could be teleported through to solve puzzles. The game went on receive some attention from various contests and festivals. The team that built *Narbacular Drop* then was hired by Valve, and in 2007, Valve released *Portal*, a critically acclaimed genre-breaking puzzle game that in many ways fulfills the promise and potential of *Narbacular Drop* and then some.

At the time of this chapter's writing, Valve has released press material for *Portal*'s sequel. Although it is not yet finished, it is known that the company incorporates new game-play mechanics from another DigiPen student project, *Tag: The Power of Paint*, and yet again, Valve looks like it's crafting another genre-defying game on top of new game designs that have already been shown to hang together successfully.

So what exactly is Valve doing here?

Following the massive success of *Half-Life* in 1998 (which was itself a very innovative title), Valve was sitting on a working, interesting formula and one of the most important brands in gaming. Were it any normal studio, it would have released six or seven sequels by now, none straying too far from the proven formula, and all of them with escalating technology and production values.

But this hasn't been the road Valve has taken. For all intents and purposes, it looks like Valve has outsourced the process of kind-of-game innovation itself to giant, decentralized spaces where failure and production are both extremely cheap and where Valve can harvest the fruits of that chaotic process and turn those recipes for games into successful high-production-value games in a somewhat more predictable fashion after the fact – and all with essentially no investment or directing on its part. But this works only because someone at Valve knows how to look at unfinished, rough, incomplete games and recognize what counts as potential.

The fascinating thing here is how low risk and cheap this is for Valve. For every *Counterstrike*, there are literally thousands of terrible or derivative mods out there. For every *Narbacular Drop*, there are hundreds of incomplete and incomprehensible student projects with terrible writing and distracting artwork. On average, student games, mods, and other small indie projects are much, much worse than games from established studios and vastly more prone to embarrassing failure. And yet, because that failure is so cheap, and because the freedom of those developers is so great, the odds of developers stumbling on legitimately new kinds of games turns out to be much higher. Valve seems to recognize this and to use it as an amazing resource.

Conclusion

This chapter hopefully suggests a few observations relative to the space of educational game production. One is that educational game makers would do well to firmly recognize and emphasize that the creation of kinds of games as a type of production and research is a necessary and vital task with entirely different characteristics and needs from making high-quality learning-facing instances of games. Too often governments, academics, and industry want games to be both new kinds of games and highly polished instances of a canonical game type. Because the game industry uses massive marketing departments to foreground their amazing instances of games, it's easy to overlook the essential role that low-budget, grass roots, decentralized, public game experimentation plays in seeding the ground for bigger games. But this resource is a critical input to those games.

Another is to recognize that market popularity and end-user reactions have not been the guiding force in nurturing and furthering kind-of-game experimentation. The communities that spring up around independent game development, MUDs, student projects, mods, and so on have been essential in giving makers of new kinds of games useful, receptive audiences and in amassing, collectively, huge amounts of distributed communal knowledge about who is trying what and what sorts of interesting experiments are in the process of being tried or that should serve as starting points for the works of other creators. What counts as fruitful or valuable kind-of-game experimentation has a frustrating *je ne sais quoi* kind of quality to it, and yet these communities of peer experts are absolutely capable of recognizing what sorts of things are worth checking out, discussing them, and championing them. In this sense, these communities function with interesting parallels to idealized academic communities: Idea production is decentralized and relatively cheap, rates of failure are quite high, public capture of as much information as possible, for successes and failures, is critical, and peer experts are able to identify powerful and fruitful ideas even if housed in rocky production values.

Based on these observations, anyone interested in nurturing success-ful educational kind-of-game development would do well to invest in, and help to build, communities and social spaces where kinds of games are explored and iterated, particularly from a grass roots and decentral-ized perspective, with aggressive public sharing and peer experts as the primary audience. For reasons that are not entirely clear, these kinds of communities have sprung up again and again for entertainment games. The Flash game-making community, for instance, is (incidentally) doing massive amounts of cheap, decentralized public game design research right now, following very much in the mold of mods and MUDs before them. How to nurture communities from the top down that participants invest in properly is, of course, always a sensitive and tricky issue, and yet the role of id Software and Valve Corporation in nurturing mod communities or the major portals such as Newgrounds.com in helping expand the Flash gaming scene provide perhaps useful models in central bodies playing a productive role. The specifics of how to build and fund such communities are, of course, devilish questions – particularly questions about control, permission, content, values, and outside vetting – but I'm convinced that focusing on this part of the equation and striving to build the communities that create these kinds of experiments and capture the kinds of knowledge they generate rather than just any one instance of a game is the critical place to invest and explore.

Notes

[1]   This discussion of Will Wright draws from will-wright.com, an excellent fan-developed resource on Wright's work.
[2]   See http://www.will-wright.com/willshistory2.php.

References

Barab, S. A., Kling, R., & Gray, J. H. (2004). *Designing for virtual communities in the service of learning.* Cambridge, England: Cambridge University Press.

Boyer, B. (2010). More Rock Less Talk: A Manifesto by Indie Game Dev Superbrothers. *Boing Boing*, March, 24, 2010. Last retrieved October 1, 2010, from http://boingboing.net/2010/03/24/less-talk-more-rock.html.

Davidson, D. (2008). Well Played: Interpreting Prince of Persia: Sands of Time. *Games and Culture*, 3(3–4), 356–86.

Hutchins, E. (1995). *Cognition in the wild.* Cambridge, MA: MIT Press.

LoPiccolo, G., Squire, K., & Chu, S. (2012). Interview with Harmonix – Transcript June 22, 2010. Chapter 8 in this volume.

National Materials Advisory Board (NMAB). (2004). *Accelerating technology transition: Bridging the valley of death for materials and processes in defense systems.*

7 *Uncharted 2: Among Thieves* – **How to Become a Hero**

Drew Davidson and Richard Lemarchand

With this chapter, we're going to unpack how the design of a game (*Uncharted 2: Among Thieves*) can offer players the chance to explore and learn all the possibilities within the playing experience. In other words, a good game can teach you how to play it through the very act of playing it. And players can develop a literacy of games as they learn through the playing of a variety of games.

In *Well Played 1.0*, a book I edited, contributors performed in-depth close readings of video games to parse out the various meanings to be found in the experience of playing a game and how it can be well played.

To clarify, we used the term *well played* in two senses. On the one hand, well played is to games as well read is to books. Thus a person who reads books a lot is "well read" and a person who plays games a lot is "well played." On the other hand, well played as in well done. Thus a hand of poker can be "well played" by a person, and a game can be "well played" by the development team.

With this in mind, Richard Lemarchand (lead game designer at Naughty Dog and Co-Lead Game Designer of *Uncharted 2: Among Thieves*) and I are going to explore the making and playing of the game. We're going to analyze sequences in the game in detail in order to illustrate and interpret how the various components of a game can come together to create a fulfilling playing experience unique to this medium. With this chapter, I wrote a complete first pass, unpacking my game-playing experience (which included some discussions with Richard). Richard then added in his thoughts and responses to my analysis, to which I, in turn, replied. Therefore, the bulk of this chapter is from my perspective, but we've called out specific comments from Richard and my replies. Throughout, we've tried to capture the range of dialogue we've had around and about the game.

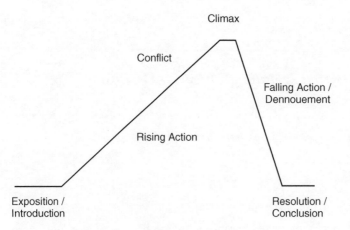

Figure 7.1. A classic literary plot diagram.

From a game-play experience perspective, we're going to walk through how game design and narrative development unfold. To help track this process, we'll refer to two diagrams. The first diagram used (Figure 7.1) is a classic literary plot diagram (Davidson, 2005).

Using this diagram, we can follow the story of *Uncharted 2* as it develops across key moments in the game. Next, we'll use a diagram illustrating the stages of interactivity (Figure 7.2).

This interactive diagram was developed in a previous paper (Davidson, 2005) and outlines the interactive experience of playing a game. Briefly, the experience is posited to have three stages: *involvement*, being initially introduced into the game; *immersion*, becoming engaged with the game play and the game world; and *investment*, feeling compelled to complete the game successfully. The interactive diagram illustrates these three stages. The x axis shows the relationship of the time spent playing the game, from start to completion. The y axis shows both the level of interactive engagement (starting from the top left moving to the bottom right), from shallow to deep, and the percentage of game experienced (starting from the bottom left moving to the top right), from none to all.

Comparing the results from both the preceding diagrams helps to illustrate the relationship between a game's story and its game play and how they can fit together to create a satisfying and engaging interactive experience. Of course, this approach wouldn't necessarily be the most apt for analyzing all the different genres and types of games, but we think that it works well for *Uncharted 2*.

One method that isn't explored directly is the procedural, computational nature of how this experience is created. Michael Mateas (2005) and

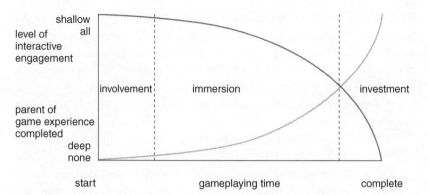

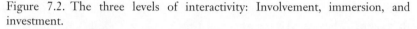

Figure 7.2. The three levels of interactivity: Involvement, immersion, and investment.

Ian Bogost (2007) have written on the importance of procedural literacy, but for the purposes of this interpretation, the focus is kept more on a gaming literacy and an exploration of the game play and narrative. Also, James Paul Gee (2007) has written on thirty-six learning principles associated with games that illustrate how a game teaches us to play. And in performing this interpretation, Bogost's (2007) ideas on *unit operations* as an analytical methodology in which the parts of an experience are viewed as various units that procedurally interrelate together to create the experience as a whole are not explicated in detail but are combined with Gee's ideas of learning principles to inspire an exploration of how the game play and story can be seen as learning units of meaning that interrelate in a variety of ways and lead us to a literacy and mastery through the playing experience (Davidson, 2008b).

Needless to say, this article is full of spoilers on *Uncharted 2* (and some for the first *Uncharted*), so consider this your fair warning. While it's not necessary, we encourage you to play the game before you read on. A goal of this chapter is to help develop and define a literacy of games as well as a sense of their value as an experience. Video games are a complex medium that merits careful interpretation and insightful analysis. By looking closely at a specific video game and the experience of playing it, we hope to show clearly how a game can be well played.

Introduction to *Uncharted 2*

Uncharted 2: Among Thieves is the sequel to the hit game *Uncharted: Drake's Fortune*. Released in the fall of 2009 for the Sony Playstation 3

(PS3), it garnered critical acclaim (with a 96 MetaCritic score) and many game-of-the-year awards (in addition, it often came close to sweeping many award shows across all categories). Within the world of the game, it develops on the experiences of the first *Uncharted* as we join in on the new adventures of Nathan Drake, the player character from both games. For the scope of this chapter, we won't delve too deeply into details about the first game, just enough to help explain any events and characters that span both games.

Before we dive into the game in detail, let's start with a more high-level overview. Naughty Dog was known initially for its *Crash Bandicoot* and *Jak & Daxter* series of games and is a subsidiary development studio of Sony Computer Entertainment. As a Sony subsidiary, all its titles are exclusive releases on Sony platforms (currently the PlayStation 3). In 2007, the company branched out with a new title, *Uncharted: Drake's Fortune*. The game was a third-person action-adventure game that drew favorable comparisons to the *Tomb Raider* video game franchise in terms of game play and game world and *Raiders of the Lost Ark* in terms of story and cinematic presentation, and it was the sleeper hit of 2007. It should be noted that Richard was the lead game designer on both the *Uncharted* games (sharing lead design with Neil Druckmann on the second).

In *Uncharted: Drake's Fortune*, players play as Nathan (Nate) Drake, a contemporary fortune hunter, and they join in an adventure to find the lost treasure of Sir Francis Drake (see Figure 7.3). This adventure leads to a forgotten island in the Pacific, and Nate and his companions discover clues, secrets, maps, and more that help them unravel the mystery and find the treasure. Game play consisted of plenty of combat (hand to hand and gunplay) as well as a lot of exploratory platforming as they work their way through the exotic environments.

Uncharted 2: Among Thieves picks up after the events of the first game. Drake is tempted back into his next adventure with a new group of mercenary companions. Characters from the previous game come to play a role in this adventure as well. Unlike the first game, which takes place primarily on one island, this adventure takes Drake to exotic locales all over the world on the search for the legendary Himalayan valley of Shambhala.

Richard Lemarchand: When Drew invited me to add some remarks to a chapter he was writing about *Uncharted 2: Among Thieves*, I was immediately interested in having the opportunity to look at the game through a different lens – that of an academic review. Of course, since *Uncharted 2* was released, my friends at work and I have been studying the reviews that both critics and fans have written, looking for insight into where we had been successful with the game and where there was room for improvement.

Figure 7.3. Screenshot from the game *Uncharted: Drake's Fortune*.

I have become increasingly interested in games criticism in past years as my understanding of how film and literary criticism works has expanded, and I now see that a robust professional and academic critical context is an important adjunct to the creative culture that produces games and that advancement in a form is rarely possible without it. I thought that *Well Played 1.0*, the book that Drew edited and partly authored, offered fresh and interesting takes on the games that it looked at, and I was curious as to what we would uncover if we looked at our game in a new way.

My personal experience of *Uncharted 2* had been intense and rewarding. The game took twenty-two months to conceive and create, and I was involved in the process from before the beginning, and we began to discuss ideas for a sequel during the closing stages of the first game in the *Uncharted* series, *Uncharted: Drake's Fortune*.

We had always imagined *Uncharted* as a series of games, and our contemporary reinvention of pulp adventure tropes gave us lots of potentially rich subject matter. Our decision to push both cinematic game play and character-driven storytelling beyond anything seen in video games before provided many challenges but also the singularly most rewarding and satisfying game-development experience of my career. I'm excited to have an opportunity to share a glimpse behind the scenes of the process in the course of Drew's narrative.

Full Disclosure: Drew Davidson

In case it's not apparent, I should share that Richard and I are friends, and that fact helped to spur the idea for writing this chapter together. In the past, I've approached the analysis of a game mostly from my perspective as a player, although I recently did an analysis of *World of Goo*, and knowing Kyle Gabler (game designer) enabled me to participate in the beta testing of the game as well as ask a lot of questions. And last year at Games + Learning + Society 5.0, I did a live play and analysis of the latest *Prince of Persia* with James Paul Gee and François Emery, the lead level designer on the game. François and I were introduced by a mutual colleague, and we prepared through e-mail, but we first met the morning of the presentation. The session went very well, with a lot of shared details coming out during the play-through in front of the crowd. In fact, it led to an invitation to do a similar presentation for the Games + Learning + Society 6.0 Keynote. I thought of asking Richard about doing the keynote together because I was excited about playing *Uncharted 2*, which, in turn, has led to our writing this chapter.

At the time of this writing, I've played *Uncharted* only about one-quarter to one-third of the way through twice now. I started playing it during the winter holidays of 2007 and was enjoying it, but it ran into the start of spring semester classes, and I had to put it aside and just didn't get a chance to pick it back up at the time. When *Uncharted 2* came out in 2009, I had the idea that I should go back and revisit the first game before I jumped into the second, but on discussing this with Richard, he encouraged me to play *Uncharted 2* first to enjoy all the new content and game-play improvements the company was able to put into the second game.

Taking Richard's advice, I played through *Uncharted 2* one complete time and also played some specific sections several times (I have yet to take advantage of the multiplayer game play). I then thought about starting the first game over again for the sake of being thorough, but I got only a little further along in the game before I got too frustrated with the game-play controls of the first game compared with the improved controls of the second game (more on this below). During my play-throughs, I visited GameFAQs from time to time to double-check to make sure that I didn't miss anything major (although both games are fairly linear in their experience, so this wasn't too much of an issue). Finally, I should note that *Uncharted 2* is one of the rare games that my wife enjoyed watching me play from start to finish, as long as I was playing on the "Easy" setting (more on this below as well).

Narrative and Game-Play Analysis

I'm going to start doing a close analysis of the game. It's such a large experience that I'm not going to cover everything that happens in great detail, but I do want to highlight key points and sequences in the game that contributed to the overall experience of playing.

Uncharted 2 starts with a bang that sets the tone for the pacing of the story and game play and how the two are blended into the game through the use of what Naughty Dog calls *in-game cut-scenes* (IGCs). IGCs are intricate moments that combine real-time interactivity (or briefly nonin-teractive but real-time-rendered moments) with techniques from the language of cinema. In a lot of games there are *quick-time events* (QTEs) that are extended interactive cut-scenes in which a player has to press a button at key moments in order to advance through the cut-scene event success-fully. Naughty Dog came up with IGCs as a term to help emphasize how the IGCs in *Uncharted 2* are more seamlessly interactive and integrated into the game play than a normal QTE.

In the first moments of *Uncharted 2*, we find ourselves as Drake coming to consciousness, wounded and bleeding, alone in a train car hanging pre-cariously from a mountain in a roaring blizzard. You then gain control over Drake as you try to climb out of the train to safety. Throughout this initial sequence are several IGCs that introduce players to a highly polished cine-matic perspective meshed with integrated interactive game-play moments. Thus you have very short periods where you actually don't have control of Drake, but you watch sudden events happen and then immediately gain control again. In this instance, the action comes to a climax with the train jerking and sliding off the cliff while you race to get out before it does. You start getting a good sense of how the platforming game play works as you jump, swing, and climb. Climbing out of the train gives you a good intro-duction to all the platforming mechanics. You work your way up and out, climbing the interior and exterior as stuff falls on you, handholds break, and you finally make a leaping run onto solid ground as the train goes crashing away below you.

Drake then loses consciousness, and this leads to a more traditional and extended flashback cut-scene that you get to watch. In this scene, Drake is at a beach bar and is met by an old acquaintance, Harry Flynn, along with a femme fatale, Chloe Frazer. They have a job (presumably the reason Drake is currently unconscious on a snowy mountainside), and they want to rope Drake into joining them. This job has something to do with some lost treasure related to Marco Polo and his travels, and Drake is uniquely qualified because he is the only person to have pulled off this particular heist. Drake resists at first, but slowly gets tempted into helping out, the scene ends with them toasting to the adventure, and Drake saying, "What could possibly go wrong?"

Richard Lemarchand: I was glad to see your remark, that the job that Chloe and Flynn are offering in Drake is presumably the reason that he's now passed out in the snow in the Himalayas, because that is exactly the kind of thing we wanted the player to think during the cut-scene.

By showing Drake in a dangerous situation and an inhospitable environment at the very start of the game, our normally empathetic, curious audience starts to ask how Drake came to be in such a situation – even if they've never seen him before. By making our flashback cut-scene start to tell the story of a chain of events that might lead to Drake's disastrous circumstances, we naturally grab and hold our audience's attention, right from the very beginning of the game.

This definitely worked on me as a player because I was instantly drawn into the action (and what the heck has happened?). What could go wrong indeed. You wake up in control of Drake again, back on the icy cliffs in the middle of a blizzard. And now you get your first sense of the combat game play. Like the climb out of the train, this section of game play briefly introduces you to the combat mechanics as you get a sense of how to use various weapons that are strewn all around in the wreckage of the rest of the train, along with some soldiers who appear to be after Drake. As you work your way through the wreckage from carriage to carriage, there are also explosions that rock you around, and Drake loses consciousness again.

This cues up another cut-scene that you get to watch. This one shows Drake and Chloe together. There are hints that Flynn is actually onto something real, and there seems to be a love triangle brewing, as well as some trust issues among the three of them. The scene ends with Drake regaining consciousness on the icy mountainside.

Richard Lemarchand: In fact, as Drake regains consciousness, we seized the opportunity to add an interactive moment. When control returns to the player after the cut-scene, Drake appears to be still unconscious. He is lying prone in a smashed train car, with one arm slightly swinging and his eyes closed. Only when the player touches the analog stick will he start to stir and then stand up.

It's one of those chances for us to give the player one of those "Oh, cool, I'm back in control" moments. It might be a little fourth-wall-breaking, but players generally remark positively on that moment of revelation as at least novel, and I think that we probably can leverage this type of experience toward both game-play and storytelling ends in the future.

Interestingly, I didn't pick up on this initially, but I did notice it after the fact. For me, I was eager to get Drake back up and on his feet and start actively playing the game. And so you stumble back out into the blizzard, and you come upon a unique-looking dagger – one that shows up spinning every time a scene loads in the game. Therefore, this dagger must be important (and in some way the reason behind all the catastrophe on this mountainside). As Drake cradles the dagger, the scene fades out, and then a new scene fades in as you're told that it is four months earlier in Istanbul.

> **Richard Lemarchand:** One more comment about your not noticing that interactive moment when Drake regains consciousness: We've found that it's often the case with this kind of interactive finesse – many players will never notice it. Some game developers will use "hardly anyone will notice that" as a reason not to put something in a game, and of course, you have to draw the line somewhere. But when an opportunity such as this one takes relatively little effort to put into the game and doesn't require the creation of new assets, I always jump at the chance to make our game even a little richer. Players also love the feeling that they've discovered a secret.
>
> I'd also like to grab this opportunity to mention that *Uncharted 2*, like all of Naughty Dog's games since *Crash Bandicoot*, streams data from the disc so that players only have to experience load times at the start of a play session and never during the flow of the game's action and story. This is very important for us – maintaining the pacing we've carefully constructed – and is so critical to our creation of a cinematic experience that players get caught up in.

And this definitely helps to create a more seamless experience. So you leave Drake on the mountainside, and back in time you find him in Istanbul with Harry and Chloe, ready to run the heist they were discussing in the first extended cut-scene. Before I get into the details of this first heist, I want to take the time to comment on the cinematic storytelling that has been used to introduce you to the game world. On a high level, in terms of the plot diagram, we're still getting some great introductory exposition, but also with hints of things having all gone awry (that's a huge mess on the mountainside). And I'd like to note that the game story is broken up into titled chapters (so far, everything discussed has been in Chapter 1, "A Rock and a Hard Place"). To help with orientation, I'll refer to these chapters as we move through the analysis of the game (and there are twenty-six chapters in all). Considering the interactive diagram, we're still firmly in the involvement stage, we've had some initial practice with the platforming and combat, and we've been shown how the IGCs work as well.

But this doesn't quite do justice to the highly polished craft in which all of this is blended seamlessly together into an amazingly engaging and gripping experience. The IGCs are used to great effect, and you're able to watch and play your way into this game world. Naughty Dog has crafted the video game equivalent of a thrilling action-adventure movie. Pushing this comparison deeper, Naughty Dog has used the narrative conventions of these types of movies to help shape the story beats as they play out across the game (which I believe helps to make it such a watchable experience). *Story beats* are the smallest units of a story, like an exchange between characters in a scene, that advance the narrative, and this initial sequence really does drop you right into the action. You then have some flashbacks to help break up the tense action but also to start filling in some back story on how it all started and how wrong things went awry. Simultaneously, you're gaining a sense of how the game-play mechanics work as you play through the scenes, establishing how you, as Drake, are able to survive the straits laid out before you. The game pulls you into the story by requiring you to play through it successfully (as the hero in a movie would do as well).

And now you're back in Istanbul four months prior, at the start of it all. From here, the high-rolling, globe-trotting adventure kicks into gear. You're here to steal an artifact from a museum that should provide you with a clue to the ultimate treasure you're seeking. Chloe is the driver for the escape after the heist, and Harry and Drake go through the sewers to enter the museum from below. This is the beginning of Chapter 2, "Breaking and Entering," as you make your way through the museum to the artifact. There are some interesting dynamics to this chapter that again blend game play and storytelling well. For instance, Drake makes it clear that he doesn't want guns involved so as not to risk accidentally killing the innocent museum guards. This gives you some sense of Drake's character and motivations while also setting up a level that is more about sneaking around than shooting it out. Harry has brought two tranquilizer guns, though, so you can shoot some, but your focus is more about traversing through the museum while remaining undetected.

That said, there is a contradictory moment in this level where it appears that Drake actually kills a guard. He is hanging from a ledge high up on the roof of the museum, and a guard walks by, and the game prompts you to hit a certain button, which causes Drake to grab the guard and toss him off the roof to his apparent death. I've seen online that this moment disturbed players in terms of their sense of who Drake is and what he would and wouldn't do (Wardrip-Fruin, 2010).

Richard Lemarchand: We were, of course, very focused on preserving the idea that Drake didn't want to take any innocent life during his time in the museum. When the level's layout offered us the opportunity to showcase our "pull an enemy off a roof" stealth mechanic (one of a number of new "action-stealth" moves that we'd added to *Uncharted 2*), we couldn't resist seizing it, but we still didn't want Drake to appear inconsistent.

So we made sure that there was water below the roof for the guard to fall into, and we even went so far as to create an animation that showed the guard swimming to safety, having survived the fall, and clambering onto a nearby rock to recover.

However, we now realize, based on what we've read on the Internet, that many players don't notice that the guard survives the fall, and they think that Drake has suddenly stopped caring about whether the guards get hurt. It's just one of those times where we have to realize that what we added doesn't "sell" or "read" – it's not completely, transparently obvious to nearly every player – and we just have to chalk this one up to experience and try not to make the same mistake next time!

To be honest, this moment didn't register strongly with me at the time I played through it, but I can see how players may not have "read" Drake's intentions. Moving on, Drake and Harry continue through the museum. Before we get to the treasure, I want to unpack how this buddy system works on two levels as well. In terms of story, you get to listen to the two characters banter back and forth while they're together, so it helps to establish their relationship for the player. In terms of Drake and Harry, you get the sense that while they don't fully trust one another, they do have a camaraderie in which they joke with each other. The dialogue pulls you into the characters in terms of content but also in terms of delivery. The voice acting behind the characters is excellent, and it's obvious that Naughty Dog took great care in making sure that the characters come across in the voices. Granted, often their dialogue is reminiscent of Hollywood blockbuster action movies, but this is the genre they're emulating, so it fits fairly well to the adventure in which you find yourself as Drake. And on a gameplay level, the buddy system is used to help keep you on the right track. Throughout the game, you're almost always with a companion (here it's Harry), and this buddy often is able to serve informally as a guide to lead the way so that you don't spend too much time getting lost, and the buddy also to give hints when you're trying to solve environmental puzzles that always seem to require two people (such as boosting Harry up to grab a ladder that he can then drop down to you). Once again, Naughty Dog is working with a high level of integration throughout the experience.

Drake and Flynn get to the treasure (and ancient oil lamp) that has a resin that burns blue and enables them to read a scrap of paper from the lamp that tells of a tsunami that left Marco Polo shipwrecked in Borneo and the first hints that Polo may have found Shambhala (Shangri-La) with the help of a cursed Cintamani stone (that actually still may be on a prominent mountain in Borneo).

So now they know roughly where in the world they need to go next on this adventure. But here the subtitle of the game ("Among Thieves") really comes to the fore as Harry double-crosses Drake, leaving him stuck in the museum while also setting off all the alarms. So now you have to try to find some other way to escape, and you can manage to get out of the museum through the sewers, but when you exit, you find yourself surrounded by armed guards.

> **Richard Lemarchand:** The characters that accompany Drake through the game are crucially important for creating an emotional reality for the player, and we think that it's this emotional reality that makes our game engaging. We use the characters that Drake interacts with to show different sides of his (often conflicted) character, and we work hard at every stage of the process – from their character designs, to our scriptwriting and performance capture processes, to the implementation of the characters in game play – to make sure that the people in our game are believable and nuanced in their characterization. We try to use techniques that are both narrative and interactive to set up and pay off situations that deepen and enrich the world of the game.

And I found that the character interactions definitely helped to flesh out the world and where you thought Drake stood within it. Three months later, you find that Drake is (still) in jail. Victor Sullivan (Sully) shows up to spring Drake. Sully is Drake's friend from the first game. Their friendship was called into question throughout that earlier adventure, but it all turned out to be a misunderstanding, and Sully is one of the few people Drake trusts.

> **Richard Lemarchand:** We think that Drake probably mostly trusts Sullivan, but I don't think he trusts him completely. The world that Drake and Sully exist in rarely allows for certainty about anything, and we try to use that to our advantage whenever possible to heighten the mystery, wonder, and romance of our game's world.

This is definitely taken advantage of because the reunion is complicated by the fact that Chloe is with Sully. As they dance around regaining some trust, it is revealed that Harry and his client (Lazarevic) have found Marco Polo's lost boats in Borneo but have yet to find the Cintamani stone.

So Sully, Chloe, and Drake team up to try to go to Borneo to sneak the stone right out from under Flynn and Lazarevic.

So off to the jungles of "Borneo" (Chapter 3), and in this part of the adventure you partner up with Sully. As you work your way into the jungle toward the camp, the stakes are raised because now you get into more deadly firefights with Lazarevic's men. This is where you really get familiar with the combat game-play mechanics, with multiple encounters and a variety of weapons from which to use. At the same time, you're also becoming more adept at traversing through the territory in which you find yourself. Chloe is acting as a double agent, getting in close to help create a diversion and enable Drake and Sully an opportunity to get access to all of Lazarevic's notes, journals, and plans (in Chapter 4, "The Dig"). This helps them to realize that Lazarevic is off track in looking for the treasure. So they have a chance to find it as soon as they shoot their way out of the camp.

Stepping back for a second, this is where the story really aligns with action-adventure movie blockbusters from the past, particularly *Raiders of the Lost Ark*. You definitely can see the similarities quite clearly, but it also helps you to fall into the role of Drake. The familiar story beats give you a direction for how you should act if Drake is indeed the hero of this adventure. This, in turn, aligns with your game goals as you play your way through the experience.

Back in the game, Drake, Sully, and Chloe manage to find the resting place of the ancient survivors deeper in the jungle. They don't find the Cintamani stone, though; instead, they find the unique dagger (a Phurba) from the earlier scene on the mountain, which appears to be some sort of key to Shambhala, which they now figure out is in Nepal. Then Chloe fulfills her double-agent role twice. First, it appears that she turns Drake and Sully over to Flynn, but then it becomes clear that it was to help save them and gives them a chance to escape. And as they flee, we get a scene straight from *Butch Cassidy and the Sundance Kid* as Drake and Sully leap from a cliff into a raging river below and float away free and clear.

Richard Lemarchand: We hope that we don't draw on any preexisting narrative too much, and we are always walking a fine line between appealing to adventure stories from the past, whether it's the more recent past of 1980s action movies or the distant past of Robert Louis Stephenson, and approaching everything with a fresh eye that invigorates the characters and prevents them from feeling like clichés or types. It's always a compliment to be compared with films as beloved as *Raiders of the Lost Ark* or *Butch Cassidy and the Sundance Kid*, though!

From my perspective as a player, the familiarity of the story conventions helped to draw me into my (or Drake's) role within the adventure. Speaking of which, now it's off to Nepal to try and find Chloe and the Cintamani stone. At this point, we're solidly into some rising action on the plot diagram, with the major conflict coming into better focus (although I'm still not sure who I can trust). And we're getting solidly immersed in the interactive experience. The last adventure gave you a lot practice in game play (both combat and platforming), and at this point, I've noticed that I'm much better at both. I'm more accurate with my gunplay and more strategic about taking cover. And I've learned to adjust the camera view to search around my environment to help find my way around when I need to jump and climb.

The experiences in Nepal last for several game chapters as we start with Chapter 5, "Urban Warfare," and it lives up to its title right away. As Drake is driving through the war-torn streets, it's apparent that the city is overrun with fighting. And we get to see a classic Naughty Dog gameplay sequence in which the perspective shifts and you have to run toward the screen. This is something Naughty Dog has done across many of the different games it has created. It adds a unique control moment because everything is reversed, which adds an intensity to the game play because you have to adjust to the backward perspective and controls on the fly. In this case, Drake ends up running down an alley with a large military truck barreling after him. You have to run forward while shooting backward in order to cause the truck to crash as you flee from the wreckage in the alley. The switch of perspective makes it a challenging game-play experience that adds to the cinematic action of watching as a truck comes bearing down on you. It's another great sequence that makes you feel like a hero when you survive (although, truth be told, it took me several tries before I did).

There are some other interesting game-play twists that happen in Nepal. Right after the alley sequence, you're on your own for a bit before you find Chloe. So, for almost the first time in the game, you're not buddied up with someone. This increases your immersion because you have to find your way on your own. Once you meet up with Chloe, the two of you work your way through the war-torn city, traversing alleys and up and down buildings. There is a nice mix of platforming and combat because many of the buildings have been bombed or damaged, and there are soldiers and guerillas all around.

There's also an interesting story moment on the roof of a hotel that happens to have a pool. You're up there to scout for the right temple in this city full of temples, but you can have Drake jump into the pool, where he goofs around and jokes about playing the Marco Polo game. This shows a great level or attention to detail by the developers. Unlike many of the more sandbox emergent games (such as the *Grand Theft Auto* franchise), where players have an open world to wander around in, *Uncharted 2* is linear in progression, so you're always moving forward through the experience. But little moments such as the pool scene open up the game world and make it feel fully fleshed out, and you're just moving through it on your adventure.

> **Richard Lemarchand:** It's always very satisfying when players call out this moment as enjoyable because it was a particular labor of love for a number of us, including the actors who partly improvised the dialog and the game designer who carefully added the dialog to the game and made his implementation interactive – there are different dialogue flows depending on whether the player keeps Drake in the pool for a while or makes him climb out quickly. We even went so far as to rejig our trophy scheme at the eleventh hour, adding two bronze trophies, one for when Drake first jumps into the pool and yells "Marco" and another one for the player who keeps Drake in the pool long enough for him to coerce Chloe into saying "Polo"!

I've enjoyed how trophy schemes have developed to help track a variety of player achievements across a game; this provides players with another level of motivation to fully explore a game. And I really like how there are trophies for these little narrative moments. It encourages me, as a player, to explore the world some more, which resonates well with the theme of the game overall. And so, shortly after the pool, Lazarevic finds out that Drake is in the city and sends out attack helicopters to deal with him. This leads to an amazingly cinematic game-play sequence. Drake and Chloe are trapped high up in a building with soldiers chasing from floor to floor when a helicopter joins in the fight and starts shooting missiles at the building. As a player, it was a confusing experience for me. I was in an office room using a desk as cover as soldiers entered the room, when the perspective started shifting and all the furniture and people started tumbling across the room as the building tilted. I wasn't sure what was going on, but noticed I was sliding toward a window and could see that we were crashing toward the building next door. It all felt crazy, but I made a run for it with Chloe, and we jumped through the window, landing in the adjacent building. And then it jumps to a quick IGC as Drake and Chloe turn back and watch the other building collapse completely. This is definitely an intense moment that made me feel like a hero. I was psyched to have survived (and actually managed to do it on my first try) and was impressed by how the designers created the game-play sequence to line up with the story beats and enable me to perform like an action-adventure hero.

> **Richard Lemarchand:** This sequence was very important for us – it was among the first of our major cinematic set pieces that we polished, and it showed off a system that represented an important technical leap forward for us: our Dynamic Object Traversal System. This system let Drake, and all his enemies and allies, use all their moves on any arbitrary moving object in the world, and without it, we couldn't have realized either this collapsing hotel or other emblematic sequences such as the train level. A system like this is pretty much the Holy Grail for character-action-game designers because it lets us do things that we'd only been able to dream about previously, and it was incredibly difficult to implement, causing our programmers to change or touch almost every core system in the game. We felt that the sequence was very successful, and it inspired us to push ourselves ever further with our set pieces. It certainly seems to make an impact on players, and it was planned to punctuate the peak of action that this part of the game reaches.

What's important to consider is how seamless the playing experience was. It makes me realize that the technical challenges going into the Dynamic Object Traversal System paid off because I didn't even notice them (which meant that I felt like I was able to play the set piece – and feel like a hero – even in the chaos of a collapsing building). Staying with this concept of being a hero, shortly after escaping the collapsing building, Drake and Chloe run into Elena Fisher and a cameraman (Jeff). Elena is a gutsy reporter from the first *Uncharted*, and through those earlier adventures, Elena and Drake developed complicated feelings for one another. Chloe argues to leave them on their own, and Elena and Jeff seem a bit wary of joining Drake and Chloe. Based on previous experience, Elena assumes that Drake is up to something (and most likely it's no good). Drake insists that they could use their help, so he talks everyone into sticking together. What I liked about having this short-story experience shortly after feeling like such a hero jumping from a collapsing building is that it underlined for me that being a hero isn't just about those feats of derring-do; it's also about doing the right thing. And you see Drake stepping more into the role as a hero in this moment.

So you now have a party of four, deep in a city surrounded by enemies out to get you. As you make your way through the violence around you, Elena reveals that Lazarevic is a psychopathic war criminal, and she's here to expose his war crimes to the world (so now you know who you're up against). The group works its way to the right temple, and then there is some amazing environment puzzle solving within in the temple that requires a lot of platforming by Drake as he uses his trusty notebook and works to unlock the clues found within and beneath the temple (Chapters 8 and 9). Once you negotiate the puzzle platforming successfully and use the Phurba as a key, you're shown the location of Shambhala deep in the Himalayas.

Of course, Lazarevic's men find you, and you have to fight your way out. In the ensuing firefight, Jeff gets wounded pretty badly, and Drake has to help carry him away. This adds a game-play wrinkle as well because Jeff really slows you down, so you have to work at a much slower pace. Again, this is combined with a story element as Chloe argues to leave Jeff, but Drake insists on carrying him. And once again, it looks like Chloe turns on you, as Flynn shows up, and we finally get to meet Lazarevic. Although it looks like Lazarevic suspects Chloe and has her taken away to the train. He then kills Jeff and threatens Elena in order to get Drake to share what he's discovered. Once he has the information, Lazarevic leaves and asks Flynn to kill them. Elena and Drake manage to get away and head to the train yard to rescue Chloe from Lazarevic.

Richard Lemarchand: I'm not sure that I agree with your characterization of Drake at the meeting with Elena and Jeff as heroic, at least not at the start, but this scene certainly is a pivotal one for him. We use this moment to reset the rhythm of the action, and we do it somewhat at Drake's expense (and perhaps partly to his credit).

For a start, Elena openly challenges Drake about the nature of his quest, saying, "So let me get this straight: You're competing with a psychopathic war criminal for a mythological gemstone?" In a single sentence we say everything we need to say about the breakdown of any romantic relationship that may have formed between Drake and Elena at the end of the first *Uncharted* game, and we characterize Drake, rather negatively, as both a criminal and a dreamer. We've grounded our story in the context of the real world (or at least *a* real world), and we've moved both Drake and Elena's characters forward a step in their relationship.

Second, this is the first time that Elena, a woman for whom Drake may have had deep feelings, meets Chloe, Drake's sexy sort-of current lover. Amy Hennig, our creative director and head writer, says that this scene was one of the most difficult to write in the whole game, and commentators have paid us the compliment of remarking that many games – indeed, many films – would have played this scene badly, perhaps showing Drake as swaggering or cocky as his conquests past and present cross paths and leaving all the characters stuck playing out banal stereotypes that do nothing to honor them.

But instead Drake seems awkward and embarrassed – it betrays a kind of vulnerability that I think is appealing and also indicates that he's not just a regular Joe in terms of his sloppy fighting style and frequent clumsiness: He can be conflicted and self-conscious, just like the rest of us. The women are confident and funny in counterpoint to Drake and even seem to rather like each other, even in the midst of a difficult situation.

So I think that the scene works tremendously well not just to tamp down the pace of the game after such an intense crescendo of action (and before a relatively sedate sequence of exploration and puzzle solving in the temple complex) but also to shed some new light on the characters and the relationships between them, as well as to bond the player to Nathan Drake as a likable guy with some serious flaws.

I would agree, that within this scene Drake isn't necessarily heroic. But for me, having him being awkward also read as a moment where he was having to assess what he's doing and why he's going it, and that got me thinking that in order for Drake to become a hero, he has to figure out how to do the right thing. We're now at Chapter 12, and looking at the plot diagram, we're well into the conflict of rising action, so this mirrors the conflict Drake is displaying in this scene as well. I'm feeling empathy with the characters and want Drake to help thwart Lazarevic and save the day. In terms of interactivity, I'm solidly immersed in the game play. I'm at the point where I don't even have to think about what buttons to push. For the most part, I'm able to maneuver Drake as I need to, and now the designers do a nice job throwing another wrinkle into the mix.

With Elena's help and a lot of improvising with many different vehicles, you're able to get onto the train for a thrilling extended action sequence in Chapter 13. In addition, if you recall, the game began on a wrecked train on a snowy mountainside, so even though you're down in the valley, this very well might be that train because Lazarevic knows that Shambhala is up in the mountains. Now Drake has to work his way through, under, over, and around the train as he makes his way forward toward Lazarevic, Flynn, and Chloe. The train is a limited spatial environment so you have to be careful (and you can fall or get knocked off). And this train is loaded for war: There are soldiers, weapons, tanks, and helicopters. This is one of the longest combat sequences, although because you're goal is to get to the front of the train, there is a lot of platforming as well. And the combat is mixed up as well because you have to take on soldiers in train carriages, on top of the train, and on the sides of the train, and you can have helicopters flying beside the train. In addition, the environment the train is moving through comes into play. You have to watch out for and avoid signs near the side of the train as well as signals above the train. And then the next thing you know, you're in a long tunnel, and you come out in the mountains (Uh-oh!).

Drake finally finds Chloe, who asks him to leave. As they argue, Drake gets shot by Flynn. Then Chloe starts arguing with Flynn, and Drake is able to run to another carriage followed by some soldiers. Wounded and trapped, Drake takes aim and shoots some propane tanks, setting off some huge explosions, causing a massive train wreck.

We're now back at the same sequence that started the game. Recall that the game up to this point essentially has been an extended flashback from the start of the game. And once again, we have to climb Drake back out of the train. And then you have to fight your way through the exploding wreckage and surviving soldiers trying to kill you. You manage to get out and away, but now you are basically wounded and lost in a blizzard on a mountain. Drake collapses in the snow, and someone walks up to him as he loses consciousness (again).

> **Richard Lemarchand:** It's good to read your remarks here. It was easy for even us on the team to forget that nearly the first half of our game takes place in flashback (when viewed in a certain context, at least).
>
> Nonlinear temporal flow is a hallmark of some of my favorite films, from *Rashomon* to *Lola Rennt* to *Memento*. Indeed, discontinuity of space and time, bridged by the edit, is a character of nearly all film.
>
> I think that partly because of pragmatic issues to do with camera control in third-person character-action video games and partly because we perceive a relationship between digital games and digital simulations, both developers and players are somewhat overfocused on maintaining temporal and spatial continuity in narrative video games.
>
> Few games have taken advantage of the opportunities offered by thinking about time and space as the plastic, collapsible continua that they are in cinema. When we remember that games are different from simulations, new creative possibilities open up, and I'm happy that the talented team members that came up with the temporal sequencing of our game did so.

As a player, the nonlinear way the story is revealed created a more complex set of expectations in terms of how I was experiencing the set pieces across time and places. In the back of mind, I always had this feeling that I was heading for a catastrophe on the side of the mountain, so I was paying attention to the choices and consequences of Drake's actions. Moving forward, Drake comes to in a small hut with a small girl looking at him and the man who rescued him. The man speaks to Drake in Tibetan, which Drake doesn't understand, but he notices that his wounds have healed. We're now in Chapter 16, and it feels like we're both literally and metaphorically getting close to reaching the climactic moment in the story. And I'm starting to feel invested in the game-play experience. I want to find Shambhala and keep Lazarevic from ruining it.

The Tibetan man beckons Drake to follow him out of the hut. This starts a short sequence that has a similar effect to the earlier game of Marco Polo in the pool. As Drake exits the hut, he finds himself in a Tibetan village, and he can follow after the Tibetan rescuer or walk around and play soccer with some kids and pet a yak. Again, what's nice about these little moments is that you don't have to do any of them, but if you do, you can feel more of the world in which you find yourself. Also, in talking with Richard, he related how they designed these particular moments so that players couldn't go around and punch the villagers. Instead, those familiar button presses lead to Drake offering handshakes or waves of hello because Drake doesn't speak Tibetan.

> **Richard Lemarchand:** Indeed, the idea for those hand-shaking interactions emerged directly from play testing. I was in charge of the "Peaceful Village" level, and I noticed that about half our play testers ran straight up to the villagers and threw a punch at them when they arrived in the village for the first time. By talking to them afterwards, I worked out that they weren't really trying to hurt the villagers – they wanted to test the bounds of our system by attempting an interaction with the world.
>
> Experimentation of this kind is a fundamental aspect of the way that players relate to video games – they make hypotheses about the game and then test them out, and by doing so, they learn the rules of the game and how to succeed. Video game players are a lot like scientists investigating the world in this regard.
>
> We'd initially set up the villagers so that if Drake threw a punch at them, nothing happened. Games that reward experimentation on the part of the player with reactions that are interesting or entertaining generally are considered better than those which don't, so we decided to make the extra effort to add a set of animations to show Drake and the villagers shaking hands or waving to each other, should the player try to throw a punch at a villager. I'm still very grateful to the animators and programmers who expended elbow grease on this.
>
> It's a moving experience whenever I hear that a player was delighted with finding himself or herself shaking an old man's hand or patting a yak on the nose. It feels like the realization of a playful dialog between the player and me, the designer.

And building on the earlier scene with the pool, players have been encouraged to explore, so it's like they'll encounter these unique interactions, which again enhances and expands the feeling of the world in the game. Back in the village, the Tibetan rescuer leads you into a house, and lo and behold, there's Elena (who speaks Tibetan to boot!). She followed the tracks from the train wreck and found Drake. Elena introduces Drake to Karl Schafer, an older man who went on an earlier expedition to find Shambhala. Schafer introduces Tenzin (the man who rescued Drake) and shares some advice and warnings learned from his experiences, and he lets Drake know that the Phurba is the key to Shambhala, so Lazarevic is going to be coming for it. He also relates how the Cintamani stone will give Lazarevic great power to rule the world. During this conversation, Drake wavers about doing anything more; he feels as though it's all been a big mess and actually says that he's through playing the hero. Elena argues that they should try to stop Lazarevic, and Schafer offers to show Drake proof by having Tenzin take Drake into the mountains to the remains of Schafer's earlier expedition.

Richard Lemarchand: In terms of Joseph Campbell's monomyth (1949) as reconfigured by Chris Vogler in his screenwriting book, *The Writer's Journey*, this is a moment where Drake makes his final and most emphatic refusal of the call to adventure. It's a low point for Drake's character and an important point for us because it helps us show that Drake isn't a straightforwardly crusading altruist. He doesn't want to get killed in the service of some abstract, even ridiculous-seeming quest. His world is a serious, dangerous place – just like ours – and he's a sensible guy – someone just like us. Having Drake pass through this moment – where he simply can't accept that he's a hero – grounds his character is reality and helps us to relate to him.

This underscored for me how Drake really struggled with doing the right thing (which is more important than "playing the hero"). So Drake now buddies up with Tenzin and heads off into the mountains for Chapters 17 and 18. You make your way into a mountain cave system, where you start finding some of the dead men from Schafer's expedition. There is a lot of platforming game play here with Tenzin as you make your way through the icy cave system. You also start getting hints that there is some sort of monster in the caves with you, and then you are attacked by a ferocious yeti. Together with Tenzin, you are able to fend off the beast and continue deeper into the caves. Soon you come upon a huge underground area with large statues. This leads to another intense sequence of puzzle platforming as you work your way through the environment with Tenzin. They then discover more dead men and find out they were Nazis after the "Tree of Life" and immortality. And it's apparent that Schafer killed the Nazis to prevent them from succeeding in the quest.

This discovery significantly raises the stakes of our current adventure, and it is followed by an attack by a bunch of the yetis. So Tenzin and Drake have to fight them off and escape by activating an ancient elevator that gets them above ground, away from the monsters. From their perch in the mountains, they can see that Tenzin's village is being attacked.

So they rush down into the village and into Chapters 19 and 20. They find Elena, who confirms that Lazarevic has found them. Tenzin is worried about his daughter, and Elena tells them that she is hiding with Schafer, before telling Drake that this terrible destruction that has been brought down on the Village is all their fault – people are dying because of Drake and Elena. Drake and Tenzin head out to find Schafer and Tenzin's daughter, only to run into a tank, which then pursues them through the village. This leads to an out-of-control action sequence as you and Tenzin play cat and mouse with the tank. One moment stands out in particular for me, and it reminds me of the scene in the *Bourne Ultimatum* in which Bourne is chasing an assassin through the medina in Tangiers. Except in this game scene, I'm running with Tenzin, trying to keep some houses between us and the tank. And there's this intense moment when the tank actually crashes through the walls of the house that we're running through.

In this moment, a quick (all of a couple of seconds) IGC happens to show Drake getting bowled over by crashing tank, but the camera angle during the IGC is such that I'm instinctively trying to guide Drake out of the room, so when I do regain play control, I'm already heading in the right direction. This is some very clever design because it makes me feel as if I'm playing through the short IGC while also using the IGC to up the intensity of the moment. I've talked to some friends who wondered if they actually were in control at all or not, but for me, it all lined up. This was yet another moment when I felt heroic in performing some crazy feat of action.

Drake is able to take care of the tank finally, and Tenzin find his daughter, but Lazarevic's men have taken Schafer away with them in a convoy of trucks. Drake and Elena manage to hijack the last truck and take off in pursuit and into Chapter 21. This leads to a game-play sequence somewhat like the train but ramped up a level because you now have combat while also jumping from truck to truck across crazy terrain.

Richard Lemarchand: This long sequence, leading from the peaceful village, to the ice caves, to the frozen temple, and then back to the now-besieged village is a pivotal section of the game. As you've identified, there's a lot going on there in terms of cinematic game play – sequences where complex set pieces play out almost entirely in game play, with the player directly in control of Drake nearly all the time.

We switch things up a few times, using moments of constrained game play in a narrative way – such as the climax of the first encounter with the yeti – and we pull out every single trick in our bag to guide and sometimes push the player from A to B to C, using "characters" like the tank or the transformed village to effect moment-to-moment emotional change in the player. We even sucker-punch the player a second time, having already brought Drake low by his near-refusal to continue with the quest, by having Elena blame him for the awful transformation of the formerly idyllic community.

But Tenzin occupies the heart of this sequence, of course. Drake and Tenzin do not share a common language, and this gives us an opportunity not only for a few gags but also for the player to become bonded to this unusual, dynamic character almost entirely through their collaborative game-play actions. As Tenzin sets up ropes for Drake to swing on, boosts him up to otherwise inaccessible ledges, and catches him as he is about to fall to his death, we hope that a connection is slowly growing between Tenzin and the player (or Drake, by proxy) in a way that the player barely notices.

When Tenzin's village comes under attack – and his small daughter's safety is in doubt – we hope that the groundwork we've carefully laid gets activated and that the experience of fighting through the war-torn village is charged beyond what one might expect from even the most epic, awesome battle scene in another video game.

Interestingly, I really wasn't thinking about Tenzin specifically during this (he was just another buddy as I was playing), but I really felt the responsibility of causing the attack on the village and putting everyone's lives, especially Tenzin's daughter's, at risk.

Richard Lemarchand: I should be clear in saying that the effect we were trying to have wasn't one that the player would or should notice, and it is interesting that you weren't really thinking about Tenzin during this sequence. Either we did our job really well, or what we did with Tenzin didn't make much difference! I do think that this sequence would have had far less – or perhaps just different – emotional impact if you'd played through the ice cave with Chloe or Elena.

I would agree that playing through with Tenzin gave it a better context in which to have that emotional impact. Again, I felt like I needed to step up and do the right thing. Back in the game, Drake and Elena end up getting forced off the pass and over a cliff. The soldiers assume that they've died, but Drake and Elena (of course) survive, climb up, and follow the convoy on foot to a monastery. Spying from afar, they see that Lazarevic has Schafer. So now in Chapter 22 they sneak into the monastery to rescue Schafer and stop Lazarevic. This requires a lot of combat and platforming, as Drake and Elena work their way through the monastery, fighting off soldiers as they go. They get to Schafer in Chapter 23, but they're too late. Schafer has been shot and left for dead, and Lazarevic has the Phurba and is off to find Shambhala. Schafer tells them that the monastery hides the entrance to Shambhala, and as he dies, he implores Drake and Elena to stop Lazarevic.

This further underscores how high the stakes are in this adventure. So Drake and Elena decide that they've got to find a way to save the day. As they try to pull together some sort of plan, they notice that the yetis are loose in the monastery as well, adding to the challenges ahead of them. They split up so that Drake can get the Phurba and Elena can find the secret entrance. Drake manages to find Chloe with the Phurba (with Lazarevic and Flynn nearby). Using the Phurba and his notes, Drake is able to solve a tricky environmental puzzle to find the secret entrance, which is cleverly hidden in plain sight.

They manage to sneak into the entrance and into Chapter 24. Of course, Lazarevic manages to trap them in the entryway. Lazarevic threatens to kill Chloe and Elena if Drake doesn't help him. Under this coercion, Drake solves the puzzle that opens the entrance and leads to some puzzle platforming with Flynn and some combat with some yetis as well. Lazarevic enters and kills the yetis just as they're about to kill Drake and Flynn, and in looking at the corpses, they discover that they're actually men, guardians of Shambhala (granted, really strong men who are extremely hard to kill). They now finally enter Shambhala, which is a large ancient city overrun with greenery, and they're immediately attacked by more guardians.

> **Richard Lemarchand:** Chapter 24 gave us an opportunity to do something we hadn't ever done before: a sequence of play where Drake is accompanied by someone with whom he is in an antagonistic relationship. Drake and Flynn still need to cooperate to complete the sequence, but we had a lot of fun with the banter between them as they travel through the area, and we hope it is another technique that to helps raise the emotional stakes as we race toward the game's climax. We also took the opportunity to add in another bit of finesse interactivity, as anyone who decides to take a swing to Flynn's irritating grin will discover.

It does add a tension having to work with Flynn in this scenario (although I didn't take a swing). And in the confusion, Drake, Elena, and Chloe escape into Shambhala and into Chapter 25. Here, you have combat with both soldiers and guardians as you try to beat Lazarevic to the Cintamani stone. Drake is not adamant about setting things right (and saving the world). He's become a hero, and it's up to you to succeed and save the day. As they make their way through the ruins of the city, they notice more of the blue resin on trees, and when it's shot, it explodes. This becomes a way to clear a path as well as a weapon to use against others. They work their way to a temple and solve some puzzle platforming, which leads them to the Cintamani stone, which is embedded in the Tree of Life. Drake starts worrying that something is not right. He then figures out that the stone isn't a gem but is made of resin that can be eaten to gain immortality (or at least you're pretty near invincible).

They then spot Lazarevic by the tree, but before they can go, Flynn shows up, mortally wounded and holding a grenade with the pin pulled. He sets off the grenade, killing himself, leaving Drake and Chloe woozy, but severely wounding Elena. Chloe ends up carrying Elena while Drake goes to stop Lazarevic and into the final chapter of the game.

At this point in the plot diagram, we are firmly in the climax of the story, we're out to stop the villain or die trying. This gives you a clear sense of where you are in the interactive diagram, deeply involved and committed to successfully finishing this experience.

Drake moves toward the Tree of Life and sees Lazarevic drinking from the pool of sap. Drake shoots at Lazarevic, but the bullets don't seem to have any effect now, and Lazarevic now comes after Drake. In game-play terms, we're in the final battle, the climax of the story. You then have to figure out how to kill Lazarevic (*Hint:* Use the exploding blue tree sap), and once you've managed to catch him in enough explosions, he weakens and falls.

Drake approaches Lazarevic, and Lazarevic calls him out on how similar they are (look at how many people Drake has killed, just today even). In the end, though, Drake doesn't kill Lazarevic in cold blood – the guardians do. In this moment, Drake makes the right choice and acts as a hero. And now, of course, the whole city starts collapsing. So Drake finds Chloe and Elena, and they manage to narrowly escape. You have a great scene where the perspective shifts again, and you're running toward the screen on a bridge while everything collapses around you. This is another effective use of the perspective because you really get to see the chaos all around you as you try to stay just ahead of it at all and to escape (to be honest, it took me a couple of tries) as we fade to black with Drake holding Elena, hoping she'll survive.

And now we're in the denouement, the active game play is over (we won!). As we return to the village and see Drake standing over a grave, at first it's not clear if this is Elena's grave, but it turns out that she did survive. Chloe says her goodbye (they joke about playing the hero), and she encourages Drake to tell Elena about his feelings for her, and Sully shows up to help with the recovery. The scene, and the game, comes to an end with Drake and Elena joking about how much he cares about her as the boy (might actually) gets the girl.

Meaning and Mastery

With this, we've completed the narrative experience of *Uncharted 2*. There is the multiplayer game play (which I have yet to experience), but I want to discuss how the game-play controls were improved in this game compared with the first *Uncharted*. As I mentioned at the start of this chapter, I actually played a bit of the first game initially, then played through all the second game, and then I tried to go back to finish the first. But Naughty Dog didn't rest on its laurels between the two games. The game-play controls have been refined and improved (in terms of responsiveness and accuracy in both combat and platforming). Thus, after playing all the way through the second game, it was hard to go back to the first game with the older controls. Interestingly, in talking with Richard about this, he noted that the development of the multiplayer portion of the second game played a big part in how they improved the controls.

> **Richard Lemarchand:** When we first announced that *Uncharted 2* would have a multiplayer component, some Internet-posting fans of the first *Uncharted* were concerned that the single-player game of *Uncharted 2* would suffer as a result of the fact that our attention would be divided between two different parts of the game. As Drew says, it turned out that multiplayer actually *helped* our single-player game.
>
> In order to make the online multiplayer game as on-the-button responsive as a great multiplayer game needs to be, we had to tighten up our player mechanics and make them even snappier than they'd been in *Uncharted: Drake's Fortune*, and this fed back directly into a better feel for single-player, which used the same executable (i.e., the same game code).

And this made for a more playable game from my perspective because I felt that I had better control of Drake's actions throughout the game. At this point, I want to take a step back to discuss how the meaning of the game came through a mastering of the game-play mechanics across the experience of the story. In a well-designed game, the experience is kept pleasurably frustrating: It's not too easy, nor is it too hard. Ideally, you get increasing challenges followed by a reward and possibly increased abilities that make it a little less challenging for a bit, but it soon ramps up again.

Crawford (1984) refers to this as a smooth learning curve in which a player is enabled to advance successfully through the game. Costikyan (2001) notes that "play is how we learn" and move from one stage to the next in a game. Csikszentmihalyi's (1991) notion of flow, in which a person achieves an optimal experience with a high degree of focus and enjoyment, is an apt method for discussing this process as well. And Gee (2004) notes that well-designed games teach us how to play them through rhythmic, repeating structures that enable a player to master how to play the game. In terms of unit operations, the units are being juxtaposed well so that meaning and mastery build as you play. I believe that this creates an aesthetic experience unique to games.

In *Uncharted 2*, the developers do a nice job of striking this balance on three levels. First of all, the game has a fairly even mix of the two major types of game play (combat and platforming) so that you are continually doing one or the other (and often both) throughout the game. Second, there is a good flow to the increasing level of difficulty across the game. It builds on your successes with more daunting challenges. And finally, it blends the narrative and game play quite seamlessly. The clever use of IGCs throughout the game helps to create the feeling of being an integral part of an amazing action adventure. Combined together, the overall effect is one in which you start out as a bit of a bumbling ne'er-do-well, and as you play through this experience, you become a hero who saves the day.

Richard Lemarchand: Thanks very much for the kind words, Drew, and for the favorable comparisons with the academic work around this subject. We worked hard to create a structure for our game where the peaks and valleys of its respective narrative and game-play rhythms would be well aligned, creating synergistic effects for our audience of players.

We tried to create patterns of rhythm that would be irregular enough to avoid the repetitive feelings from which some games suffer. We feel like we did pretty well in this regard, with the exception of a sequence of game play in the monastery that doesn't have quite enough story beats to support the ongoing gunplay action and where the pace of the game starts to flag a little.

We also worked hard to introduce the game's mechanics in a way that would allow the player to learn about them without ever feeling like he or she were being taught something. Our usual technique was to couch the "tutorial" in terms of an action sequence, the opening train wreck "climbing lesson" being a good example. This fed into a ramp of action where we offered successively more complex challenges, building on the player's previous experiences and the skills the player had acquired from them.

We do our best to plan these things in advance, but there's also a good deal of iteration and trial and error involved. We try to constantly put ourselves in the mind-set of someone who has never seen the game, and we do a lot of play testing with people who haven't played before to help us find and fix problems.

In truth, we use a lot of gut instinct, too. As well as the conscious approach we try and take to these issues, there's also a little bit of something intangible and unpredictable involved. So, for me, when everything comes together – as it did for *Uncharted 2: Among Thieves* – it makes the creative process all the more satisfying.

Now that you mention the monastery, that actually still sticks out in my mind as the longest gunfight (and I recall my wife mentioning it as well). This leads us into some ideas on what good game design can do to create an engaging experience.

Ludic Narrans

A good game can and should teach players what they need to know and do in order to succeed. Ideally, the very act of playing the game should enable players to master the game-playing units of the gaming situation so that they can master the rising challenges and complete the experience successfully. If a game gets too hard, too easy, or too confusing, or if it is just too long and seems never-ending, players may not finish. For these reasons and more, players can reach a point where they drop off the curve and lose their sense of engagement, becoming bored, frustrated, and tired of playing the game. However, if a game enables players to stay on course and continues to hold their attention, players will advance to a point where their immersion develops into an investment in which they truly want to complete the game experience successfully. And when there is a lack of balance in the interactivity, the story actually can help to keep the player engaged in order to move from involvement through immersion to investment and successfully completion of the game (Davidson, 2008a).

Richard Lemarchand: We've noticed from the online data that we gather that about half our players complete the single-player narrative part of

Uncharted 2. This figure is quite high for contemporary video games, which famously have poor completion ratios. We'd like to drive this number higher, though, in the future.

This gets me thinking about the various reasons people play games (because completion rates are normally low) and how some games are designed in such a way as to help make this happen. *Uncharted 2* is an example of how a game can combine game play and story together in a resonant manner. As I mentioned at the start of this chapter, my wife actually enjoyed watching me play through the whole game because she engaged with the story experience, but only if I was playing on the "Easy" difficulty level (the levels are very easy, easy, normal, hard, and crushing). I usually play games on normal, but I sometimes switch to easy depending on how a game fits my skill level, as well as the amount of time I have to devote to playing the game. Similarly, I sometimes will use GameFAQs when I get stuck for a while (again, this depends on the amount of time I have to play the game). What was interesting about *Uncharted 2* is that I started on normal and was doing fine, but the fire fights took me long enough (owing to the number of enemies or the times I would die) that my wife would lose interest in watching because she lost the thread of the narrative and didn't have fun watching the seemingly endless fire fight. But if I set it on "Easy," this enabled me to advance through fire fights more readily and kept the story beats coming at a pace that was enjoyable for her to watch.

In talking with other colleagues and Richard, it seems that a lot people enjoy watching people play this game. I think this says a lot about how well it does blend the two together and how games are becoming an even more performance medium, akin to theater or sports. *Rock Band* and games on the Nintendo Wii are other examples of games that are fun to watch. It seems as if designers are becoming more cognizant of creating games that enable performance experiences that are fun to play and to view.

I think that it has been useful to consider this game (and games in general) from a variety of perspectives. In so doing, we can, as Marie-Laure Ryan (2001) notes, observe features that remain invisible from other perspectives. Engaging this medium of video games, we tell our stories of the game as we relate the varied and visceral experiences of the games we play. Noah Falstein (2004) discusses the "natural funativity" of games – how they are activities that help us live in the world. Stories are how we stitch together a continuity of our experiences. They are our "mystories" – our stories that enable us to understand the world (Ulmer, 1989). Narratives are how we convey the perspective of our experiences (Meadows, 2002).

Thus we are both *Homo ludens* and *Homo narrans*, or as Greg Costikyan (2001) states, "Play is how we learn; stories are how we integrate what we've learned, and how we teach others the things we've learned ourselves through play."

Now, in following the idea that humans begin life in a prelinguistic consciousness as babies, it seems that we start solely as *Homo ludens*. We literally learn everything through play as we interact with the world. And then we learn language, and a new phase of consciousness begins, one that dominates, shapes, and constrains our worldview for the rest of our lives (Huizinga, 1950). We are now *Homo narrans*; we discursively talk about what we play, what we learn, and what we feel, believe, think, etc. (Schank, 1995). But being *Homo narrans* does not erase our foundational *Homo ludens* character; we are always already *Homo ludens* – it's just that now we talk about it.

I believe that games are an interesting medium because there are definite paralinguistic activities involved, and meaning is conveyed through gesture, space, color, sound, and activity and agency. And all these can combine into engaging aesthetic experiences. I think one of the reasons that these experiences are so compelling is that they enable us to tap more directly into our prelinguistic *Homo ludens* consciousness as we play them. Of course, we then step back and talk about it, which engages our discursive *Homo narrans* consciousness. Hence, *ludic narrans*, "playful stories" (Davidson, 2008a). I bring this up because I believe that *Uncharted 2* is good example of a playful story.

Playing Well

On reflection, I think that the dual approach of analyzing both the narrative plot and the interactive levels enabled me to show the moments in this game in which units of both elements were working together to truly engage me in the experience. It also was a useful method for exploring moments throughout the experience that didn't work as well as they could have. Overall, the story development and rhythmic game play help players to understand the gaming situation – the "combination of ends, means, rules, equipment, and manipulative action" required to play through the game (Eskelinen, 2001). That said, I kept my analysis with both diagrams at a general high-level progression of the plot and the stages of interactivity. I think that this was useful, but I also believe that it could be interesting to get even more granular with both diagrams and really dig into units that show the details of the diversity of peaks and valleys of interest curve in the development of the plot as well as the moments of engagement, disengagement, and reengagement that occur during the progressive stages of interactivity. I think both macro and micro perspectives would be worthwhile to pursue in analyzing and interpreting interactive experiences.

> **Richard Lemarchand:** As we create and play test our games we gather metric data about how long our play testers take to travel between the game's automatic save points and the numbers of attempts – how many times each player dies and restarts – in each of these intervals. We look at the maximum, minimum, and median values for these data, and doing so helps us to discover potential problems with the game – places where some aspect of the game is making it arbitrarily or needlessly too difficult (or, more rarely, too easy).
>
> These data also can be viewed as a kind of intensity chart for the game, with peaking median attempt counts denoting places where the game reaches a crescendo of challenge. It's a crude method of visualizing the data, but it does help us to ensure that the plans we've laid, in terms of the rhythms of play we've attempted to present to the player, are bearing the right kind of fruit.
>
> As new technologies appear that gather biometric data such as pulse rate, galvanic skin response, and even electroencephalographic (EEG) activity to interrogate the player's biological state and attempt to make inferences about their emotional state from that data, we will have even more opportunities to confirm that the experience we've crafted is having the effect on players that we intended.
>
> However, planning and designing an experience such as that of *Uncharted 2* probably will remain a craft that relies partly on our experience as designers and players, partly on our skill as craftspeople and storytellers, and partly on what our gut instinct tells us for the foreseeable future.

This helps to summarize what we've been exploring in this chapter – how the meaning of playing a game is designed and experienced. A game can be well played in two senses (Davidson, 2008b). First is well played as in well done, so a game can be looked at in terms of how well it was created. Second is well played as in well read, so through the experience of playing games you can develop a literacy of games. Lev Manovich (2001) notes that when engaging new media (or playing a game), we oscillate "between illusionary segments and interactive segments" that force us to "switch between different mental sets," demanding from us a "cognitive multitasking" that requires "intellectual problem solving, systematic experimentation, and the quick learning of new tasks." Together, an aesthetics is formed out of the game design and the experience of playing through it. Thus, when the units of story are intertwined effectively with the units of game play, the rising action of the plot can parallel the rising challenges of the game play and enable us to have a compellingly engaging experience. Overall, *Uncharted 2* does an elegant job of combining its narrative and game play to provide a fulfilling interactive experience. It is a game well played.

References

Bogost, I. (2007). *Unit operations: An approach to videogame criticism.* Cambridge MA: MIT Press.

Campbell, J. (1949). *The hero with a thousand faces.* Princeton, NJ: Princeton University Press.

Costikyan, G. (2001). *Where stories end and games begin.* Available at http://www. costik.com/gamnstry.html.

Crawford, C. (1984). *The art of computer game design.* New York: McGraw-Hill.

Csikszentmihalyi, M. (1991). *Flow: The psychology of optimal experience.* New York: HarperCollins.

Davidson, D. (2005). Plotting the Story and Interactivity of the *Prince of Persia: The Sands of Time.* Delivered at the Media in Transition 4, MIT, Cambridge, MA.

(2008a). *Stories in between: Narratives and mediums @ play.* Pittsburgh, PA: ETC Press.

(2008b). Well Played: Interpreting *Prince of Persia: Sands of Time. Games and Culture*, 3(3–4), 356–86.

Eskelinen, M. (2001). The gaming situation. *Game Studies*, 1(1). Available at: http:// www.gamestudies.org/0101/eskelinen/.

Falstein, N. (2004). *Natural funativity.* Available at: http://www.gamasutra.com/ features/20041110/ falstein_01.shtml GameLab *Institute of Play.* http://insti-tuteofplay.org/. *Games and Storytelling.* http://www.gamesandstorytelling.net/. Game Studies. http://www.gamestudies.org/.

Gee, J. P. (2004). *Learning by design: Games as learning machines.* Paper presented at the Game Developers Conference, San Jose CA. Available at: http://labweb. education.wisc.edu/room130/PDFs/GeeGameDevConf.doc.

(2007). *What video games have to teach us about learning and literacy*, revised and updated edition. New York: Palgrave Macmillan.

Huizinga, J. (1950). *Homo ludens.* Boston: Beacon Press.

Manovich, L. (2001). *The language of new media.* Cambridge, MA: MIT Press.

Mateas, M. (2005). Procedural Literacy: Educating the New Media Practitioner. *On the Horizon*, 13(2), 101–11.

Meadows, M. (2002). *Pause & effect: The art of interactive narrative.* New York: New Riders.

Ryan, M.-L. (2001). *Narrative as virtual reality.* Baltimore: Johns Hopkins University Press.

Schank, Roger (1995). *Tell me a story*. Chicago: Northwestern University Press.
Ulmer, G. (1989). *Teletheory*. New York: Routledge.
Wardrip-Fruin, N. (2010). *Uncharted 2's sloppy fiction*. Available at: http://kotaku.
    com/5437484/uncharted-2s-sloppy-fiction.

8   Interview with Harmonix

Greg LoPiccolo, with Kurt Squire and Sarah Chu, Interviewers

The following interview between Kurt Squire and Greg LoPiccolo of Harmonix Games (on June 22, 2010) tries to get at how Harmonix thinks about designing games to elicit particularly musical experiences. Harmonix, developers of FreQuency, Amplitude, Karaoke Revolution, Guitar Hero I and II, and now the Rock Band series, is known for its pioneering work in rhythm action games, taking them from a niche genre to broad mainstream success. Sarah Chu, who transcribed and cleaned up the transcripts, contributed interview questions as well.

Kurt Squire: Can you talk a little bit about the game design philosophy at Harmonix and a little about how you think about game design?

Greg LoPiccolo: Well, the company charter from day one was to use technology to provide nonmusicians with the tremendous experience of creating music. Most of the people here are musicians or frustrated musicians or some version of that. There's a strong consensus here that if you have proficiency in an instrument, performing music is one of the great joys in life. It is enormously fun and rewarding, but this experience is denied to most people because the learning curve is so steep. It really requires multiple years of focus, dedication, and time to get good enough on a traditional instrument to really express yourself. So, broadly conceived, the ambition here has always been to try to use technology to bring more people into that experience. Harmonix was not originally games-specific. It wasn't until maybe about four or five years ago that we realized that games are an appropriate platform to bring this vision to life.

Kurt Squire: If I recall correctly, once folks at Harmonix saw the rhythm-action genre emerging with such games as *Parappa the Rappa*, people started thinking, "We could take this genre and push it even further."

Greg LoPiccolo: That's right. There were games coming out of Japan in the 1999–2000 time frame, none of which were very big here. But we would buy them as imports, and we soon realized that games are the mass-market platform that is developing cultural momentum, which has only accelerated since. So we started thinking that this would be a good medium to work in. We started making music games, and the first several that we made, I think, were creatively successful – we're proud of them – but they certainly weren't commercially successful.

Kurt Squire: Actually, I was a big fan of *FreQuency*, played it a lot, and loved it to death. I know there were a lot of others like me, but we were fairly big music nerds already. In your subsequent games, it seemed like a lot went into how to make them accessible, tune them properly, and really ramp up the experience for novices. What did you learn from those games?

Greg LoPiccolo: We learned a few things. We learned that you couldn't just present an abstract concept; people really needed to associate the experience with some kind of musical concept that they already held. For us, it found its first expression in *Karaoke Revolution*, which was definitely an evolutionary step for us because it came with a mic. You sing into the mic, and you know what you're supposed to do: You're a singer. So we built game play around that. The idea really found its purest expression in the first version of *Guitar Hero* that we worked on and then subsequently *Rock Band*. For *Guitar Hero*, the insight was that you need to create the illusion of a musical experience. We got feedback saying, "Oh, this thing is really dumb, who wants to hold a plastic guitar?" But once we put in star power and rock poses and built it well, we were able to create an illusion that you were playing guitar, and that was powerful enough to propel people toward that experience. We then just expanded across multiple instruments for *Rock Band*. And the other significant contribution of *Rock Band* was that we were able to capture some of the feeling of an ensemble, the interplay between among band members and the idea that you were collaborating in a group, fusing together a bigger sound.

Kurt Squire: Yeah, I want to talk a little bit about that. It often was a profound experience when you got in the flow. I guess in some ways it's like performing music when you're sight reading because you're taking in information and performing it back. But it seemed like *Rock Band*, by going the extra step of having it really be collaborative – when it clicked – it created an even deeper experience. Does that resonate with your experience? Did you feel that happening early in the game design, or did you really have to work to get that?

Greg LoPiccolo: It was very much a high-concept goal, where many of us were either in bands or had been in bands, and we were proud of *Guitar Hero*, but it seemed like it provided just a small slice of the experience that we had in bands where you're feeding off the energy of other people. You know, there's something about four or five people working together to perform rock music; it's just very emotionally powerful. And so we wanted to capture that feeling. There were basically two parallel development efforts: One was to develop game play for the other instruments because there are some similarities, but there are a lot of differences that we had to painstakingly work out for drums and for vocals. We had some experience with vocal game play, so we had some basis to work from, but we had to develop the game play for those instruments. The other, more challenging thread was to try to figure out some game mechanics to fuse people into a unit, to make them aware of each other. In the first version, we figured out drum game play, and we figured out vocal gameplay. We stitched it all together, and we had four single-player games running in parallel, but everyone was just staring at the screen. Nobody cared about everybody else. Then there was a long iterative process of figuring how to get people to relate to each other, so there are a bunch of ancillary mechanics that attempt to do that.

Kurt Squire: Describe what kinds of insights you may have gained from that? Like things that either worked or how you went about thinking that? Because that's the kind of thing that a lot of folks in education I think would be really interested in trying to understand a little bit better. It can be simple, like how a mechanic seemed to work.

Greg LoPiccolo: So one thing that we already knew but was reinforced for us was that perceptually if you're sight reading one of these games, your attention is very much focused on the spot you need to be looking at, and you don't have a lot of brain space available for complicated interactions with other things. So, basically, if you want to intrude on that little bubble, you have to do it in a very *big* way because you need a big hit to pull people's attention off of their little zone of focus. I think the most successful specific thing that we did was this idea that if someone fails out, that he or she can be saved by other band members, so if you earn enough overdrive power, you can deploy overdrive to save somebody who's failed out. This fulfilled multiple functions: It gave people a specific, concrete interaction with each other, like somebody would die and then somebody else would save them, and they form that bond where you have somebody saving somebody else, which was emotionally really powerful. It also added this whole strategic angle, and added a lot of cliffhanger moments where if there was a weak person in the band, they would bank their overdrive and not use it, so they'd have it to save the weak player. Or occasionally, you get in a situation where somebody fails out and has banked enough overdrive phrases to be able to save – you have to beat two, I think, to have a big enough reservoir to save – so people are waiting for the next overdrive phrase and hoping they nail it so that they'll keep the band in the game. And that all actually worked out pretty well.

Then there were a few smaller mechanics such as unison phrases where if everybody hits the phrase at the same time, you get a big graphic in the middle of the screen, and you get extra points. There was a mechanic whereby if multiple people deploy overdrive at the same time, it doubles up the score multiplier, so experienced players very quickly figure out, "Oh, okay, if we coordinate our actions, if everyone gathers and deploys overdrive together, we can get an eight times multiplier and crank our score up significantly." Then there are just a few other goofy, fun things such as the big rock endings that were an attempt to emulate an aspect of live performance, where everybody can just thrash away for a couple of bars at the end, but then they have to hit the final note. So it was this nice juxtaposition of anarchy and then a little bit of precision – when everybody hits it, then you get this kind of communal positive payoff.

Kurt Squire: Can you talk about anything that *didn't* work that one might have assumed would work?

Greg LoPiccolo: You know, there's a whole list of things. There were *all sorts* of variants on band energy. What we ended up with is that everybody has their own little pointer on the health meter, so everyone's tracking it separately, but in the same space on screen so that you can easily see where others are. I think we tried a lot of different ways of tracking the ensemble's health. We had more sophisticated, complicated designs that seemed mechanically more clever and engaging, and generally, we would discover that they were too complicated for people to grasp in real time. We evolved toward a design in which for new players there's a bunch of stuff they don't really understand, but it's okay. They understand health, they understand being rescued, and that's about all. Then there's a level above that where experienced players start to strategically coordinate a little bit. But generally we moved away from things that were more complicated and more sophisticated because they were not really graspable.

Kurt Squire: There is a lot of talk about games being part of moving us toward a culture of production and away from consumption. Can you talk about ways that you've thought about games encouraging players as producers or stories you've heard from players? Does that resonate with you at all? Is that something you people think about? Games seem like a very interesting middle ground in the sense that you're playing a game, playing other people's songs, but you are learning to do things, which then in some weird way you're playing the song, and it seems like an interesting middle space in between those kind of poles, if you will.

Greg LoPiccolo: There are a lot of ways for us to approach our metagoal of engaging people with music. I think we're very far from complete. The area we've explored so far is in some ways the easiest to accomplish. We've been fortunate enough to be successful commercially, which has allowed us to devote our development resources to new iterations. So for *Rock Band 3*, for instance, we've tried to move – you know, one of the cultural criticisms that has come our way has been that we've got all these players grinding away developing these impressive skills, but they're completely abstract – it's mimicry. You're just developing proficiency in pretending to play music. And I guess our initial defense has been, "Well, that's all we've really intended, that it's an entertainment experience; our ambitions do not rise beyond that."

   But point in fact, they do. I think the next set of evolutionary steps we've taken with *Rock Band 3* is a set of features called *Rock Band Pro* that gives players a pretty big shove toward proficiency on real instruments – for keyboards, drums, guitar, and bass. We have new peripherals and a new visual language that really matches the actual interface of actual instruments. So one evolutionary thread is just that – to try to push people in the direction of actually developing proficiency with actual instruments so that they can make the evolution to making music, so that they're not just imitating music through game play, they actually can move over to actual music play. The other evolutionary thread we're very interested in but hasn't seen any market expression yet is the idea of allowing people actually to create music within the game environment, and that is a very difficult thing to accomplish, but it's something that we remain fascinated by and hope to tackle one day.

Kurt Squire: I confess that I love the remix mode in *FreQuency*; I thought it was hilarious. Have you thought about doing something like that?

Greg LoPiccolo: Yeah, that's as close as we got to making music in game play. A couple things we learned: There's a zillion low- to mid-end sequencer-style music applications all over the place. And we've enjoyed working on sequencing, and we refined it somewhat for *Amplitude*. There are aspects of that we're really proud of – the fact that you can write a song collaboratively online, that you can play with somebody else online and get the song you made to their console – and this is on the PlayStation 2.

That was all fairly advanced for its time, but in a world that has things like *GarageBand*, there's really no reason to jam another midi sequencer into a music game. It's not the appropriate interface. If you want to use a digital workstation or sequencer, you should pop open your Mac or PC and use one of the many incredibly advanced, evolved programs of various competencies that already exist for that, but there's no reason to try to shove that into one of our games.

So that evolutionary direction is not particularly interesting to us because it assumes that you already know how to write music. Whereas for us the interesting design challenge would be to take people who don't know how to write music – you know, in the same way that nonmusicians figure out how to feel like they're performing with *Rock Band* – to basically take that same leap and try to warp people into a creative mind-set and give them the right kind of tools, but in a context that they're comfortable with. Because if you try to bolt some kind of remix mode or sequencer onto a music game, five percent of the audience enjoys it, and nobody else cares about it.

Kurt Squire: The same five percent may be just likely to use an actual one is what I hear you saying.

Greg LoPiccolo: Yeah, and are the actual ones better products, because the companies who make applications such as Cubase or Logic have spent the last two decades refining them.

Kurt Squire: Yep, yep. So there are two main things I want to follow up on. I just went to a session in which Alan Kay was decrying the guitar play in *Guitar Hero* and by extension, I guess, *Rock Band*, saying, "It is nothing like the guitar, etc.," which is fair enough because, as you said, you never pretended that it was. But it still seems to miss the point because there are some skills one develops that have some musicality, and it seems as if there is the potential for someone to say, "I like doing this and have been doing it a lot, so maybe I should pick up the guitar or drums." In fact, there are tips in the game that say, "Maybe you should pick up the drums or the guitar." Could you talk a little bit about that sort of progression, if it's something you thought about in terms of designing, with either *Guitar Hero* or *Rock Band*? Either stories you've heard about folks doing that, either picking up an instrument and so on.

Greg LoPiccolo: Well, we have a lot of anecdotal evidence to the effect that it has happened, that there are a lot of guitar and drum teachers in this country now that are seeing steady business because people started with *Guitar Hero* or *Rock Band* and then developed a taste for the real thing. I think it's fair to say – I mean, I don't really want to belabor the point, we never claimed our games are akin to actual music making – but I do think that we deserve a fair amount of credit for cluing people, particularly kids, into some of the fundamentals; here are the roles in the band, here's what a bass guitar part is like, and this is what a rhythm guitar part is like. We've got lots of feedback from people who now have just developed an appreciation for these fundamentals, which seems like a small thing, but if you don't even know what a rhythm guitar is, it's a big thing.

Kurt Squire: What's interesting is that when I play with nonmusicians, the ability to listen, to hear that it's a snare and that's a kick, it's things like that they tend to pick up.

Greg LoPiccolo: Yeah. It's not complicated. It's learning by doing. It's the simplest kind of teaching tool where there's no musical theory. And I think the most powerful manifestation of that we've seen, which is really the thing that drove us to develop *Rock Band Pro*, is watching people at the drums, where we put a lot of work into as good an emulation as we could. There, what we found was people who put the time in and got proficient at it, learned the basics of drums. If you can play *Rock Band* drums at hard and you sit down in front of a real kit, you can basically play drums. There are a lot of nuances and theory, and maybe your technique is terrible, but we've gotten a lot of feedback from drum teachers who had this flood of kids come in whose technique was awful – they couldn't hold the sticks right because no one was there to tell them to do it – but their independent limb coordination was phenomenal, and they know like thirty, forty drum parts. And that I think is significant.

It's found its most powerful expression in the *Rock Band Pro* guitar stuff. I don't know if you've seen it, but it's phenomenal. If you get a controller and you spend six months, you can play guitar. We are just enormously proud of it. It breaks it down into simple concepts, it flattens the learning curve out, and it gives you rewards at each stage, which really is just the culmination of everything we've learned about how to present this kind of material to people. I think it's going to have a seismic impact. We're all very excited. We showed it to Fender, who is collaborating with us – they're actually making a Strat specially wired up with fret sensors embedded in the fret board – and they were just blown away.

Kurt Squire: One of my best friends, Adrian Martin, has been a guitar teacher for thirty years, so we go back and forth about aspects of this, so it would be hilarious to actually do a piece for some magazine where you sit down and actually side by side talk about them.

Greg LoPiccolo: We actually had the assistant chair of guitar studies at Berklee come to consult with us – he was sort of our conscience through our development. So it's not meant to replace conventional instruction by any means; it's very light on theory; but in terms of developing people's muscle memory to form chord shapes and pick and fret and so forth, it's awesome.

Kurt Squire: I want to talk to you about art direction and how you think about the relationship between that and game play. Any time I'm talking to educators, I try to tell them that it's not eye candy, that it actually is a part of the experience. Is there anything you want to say about just how you people think about that?

Greg LoPiccolo: Well, I guess there are two main threads. One would be just the mechanics of it – if you're trying to build a visual language where people can understand what's going on and they have to parse all the data that's moving very quickly – that's very pragmatically driven, where there's certainly an art style to it, but all the iteration and refinement goes into just trying to figure out how to be legible.

And then the polar opposite of that is the characters and venues and all the rock ambience that we've tried to build up, where there we had a lot of freedom to fashion the world that we wanted. We had this desire to construct a virtual alternate idealized rock world, like any fantasy experience really, but our conception of what the idealized rock world would be, in terms of the clothes and the characters and the stage moves – which, again, sees its most advanced expression in *Rock Band 3*, where there are vignettes. Once you make your character, you can actually see them go to their first rooftop party or go to Tokyo or set out on a tour in the van for the first time – all these seminal moments are expressed cinematically.

So I think, really, the overall ambition of the art direction has been to try to build this beautiful, kind of timeless environment. One of the things we were careful about is that there are no cell phones – it's not explicitly of any era – but it's really rooted in the mid-1970s, kind of like the era of flamboyant arena rock, such as Bowie and Queen and Stones of that era, that vibe. It's been fun to coalesce around that to try to get that to breathe. And frankly, I can't tell how well it works; I can't tell if anybody is picking up on that or not. We like it. So that's something I think we somewhat made for ourselves.

9   *Yomi*: Spies of the Mind

David Sirlin

> *What enables the wise sovereign and the good general to strike and conquer, and achieve things beyond the reach of ordinary men, is foreknowledge. This foreknowledge cannot be elicited from spirits; it cannot be obtained inductively from experience, nor by any deductive calculation....the dispositions of the enemy are ascertainable through spies and spies alone.*
>
> —Sun Tzu, *The Art of War*

Sun Tzu held spies in the highest regard, saying that they should be rewarded more liberally than any other relation in war because the foreknowledge they can provide is more valuable than any other commodity. When one knows where the enemy will strike, one doesn't need to spread one's forces thin protecting a dozen possible targets. When one knows when the enemy is unprepared, one can strike and be assured of victory. When one knows the habits of the enemy general, those habits can be turned against him. The use of spies to gain foreknowledge is like being able to see into the future.

> *I see only one move ahead, but it is always the correct one.*
> —Jose Raoul Capablanca, Third World Chess Champion

Yomi

In competitive games, there is little more valuable than knowing the mind of the opponent, which the Japanese call *yomi*. All the complicated decisions in game theory go away if you know exactly what the opponent will do next. Sun Tzu says that reading minds is for the spirit world, and on

Reprinted with permission from Sirlin, D. (2006). *Playing to win: Becoming the champion.* Lulu.com that I cannot comment, but I have witnessed firsthand the ability of some players to "achieve things beyond the reach of ordinary men" through eerily powerful *yomi*. Perhaps these players are simply adept at "studying the details of the enemy," but it seems to go far beyond that in some. There is one player whom I would even say has a supernatural ability to spy on the minds of others, knowing which moves they will next make – if it weren't such an absurd thing to say. But believe me, those who have witnessed Japan's fighting-game player Daigo Umehara do speak of these things in hushed tones, fancying that they may be true.

As a side note, I would even argue that the "strategic depth" of a game should be defined almost entirely on its ability to support and reward *yomi*. For a silly example, consider tic-tac-toe. There are only nine opening moves, and only three of them are functionally different. Even if through some witchcraft you know the move your opponent will make next, it doesn't really matter. The game is so constrained that the opponent is forced to make certain moves, so both the novice player and the master of divination basically will be on the same footing. There is no room to develop "tendencies" or a certain "personality" or style of play in tic-tac-toe. There is only a simple algorithm at work and no room for *yomi* at all.

Yomi Layers

Any decent competitive game needs to allow you to counter the opponent if you know what he or she will do. What happens, though, when your enemy knows that you know what he or she will do? The opponent needs a way to counter you. He or she is said to be on another level than you or another "*yomi* layer." You knew what the opponent would do (*yomi*), but he or she knew that you knew (*yomi* layer 2). What happens when you know that the opponent knows that you know what he or she will do (*yomi* layer 3)? You'll need a way to counter his or her counter. And what happens when the opponent knows that you know…

I'll nip this in the bud: There need only be support up to *yomi* layer 3 because *yomi* layer 4 loops back around to layer 0. Let's say that I have a move (we'll call it *m*) that's really, really good. I want to do it all the time. (Here's where the inequality of risk/reward comes in. If all my moves are equally good, this whole thing falls apart.) The level 0 case here is discovering how good that move is and doing it all the time. Then you will catch on and know that I'm likely to do that move a lot (*yomi* layer 1), so you'll need a counter move (we'll call it *c1*). You've stopped me from doing *m*. You've shut me down. I need a way to stop you from doing $c1$. I need a counter to your counter, or $c2$.

Now you don't know what to expect from me anymore. I might do m or I might do $c2$. Interestingly, I probably want to do m, but I just do $c2$ to scare you into not doing $c1$ anymore. Then I can sneak in more m.

You don't have adequate choices yet. I can alternate between m and $c2$, but all you have is $c1$. You need a counter to $c2$, which we'll call $c3$. Now we each have two moves.

> Me: m, $c2$
> You: $c1$, $c3$.

Now I need a counter to $c3$. The tendency for game designers might be to create a $c4$ move, but it's not necessary. The move m can serve as my $c4$. Basically, if you expect me to do my counter to your counter (rather than my original good move m), then I don't need a counter for that; I can just do go ahead and do the original move – if the game is designed that way. Basically, supporting moves up to *yomi* layer 3 is the minimum set of counters needed to have a complete set of options, assuming that *yomi* layer 4 wraps around back to layer 0.

This is surely sounding much more confusing than it is, so let's look at an actual example from *Virtua Fighter 3* (which almost certainly will confuse you even more).

Example of *Yomi* Layer 3 from *Virtua Fighter 3*

Let's say that Akira knocks down Pai. As Pai gets up, she can either do a rising attack (these attacks have the absolute highest priority in the game), or she can do nothing. A high rising attack will stop any attack that Akira does as she gets up, but if Akira expects this, he can block and retaliate with a guaranteed throw. Pai does the rising kick and Akira predicts this and blocks. Now the guessing game begins.

Akira would like to do his most damaging throw (that's his m) and be done with it. Even though the throw is guaranteed here, all throws can be escaped for zero damage if the defender expects the throw and enters the throw reverse command. The throw is guaranteed to "start," but Pai may reverse it. In fact, Pai is well aware that a throw is guaranteed here (it's common knowledge), and it's only obvious that Akira will do his most damaging throw. After all, this situation has happened a hundred times before against a hundred Akiras, and they all do the same thing. It's really conditioning, not strategy, that tells Pai that she needs to do a throw escape here (that's her $c1$). In fact, it will become her natural, unthinking reaction after a while.

Akira is tired of having his throw escaped again and again. He decides to be tricky by doing one of his very slow, powerful moves such as a double palm, a reverse body check, a two-fisted strike, or a shoulder ram (we'll just lump all those into $c2$). Why does a big, slow move work in this situation? First of all, if Pai does her throw escape and there is no throw to escape, the escape becomes a throw attempt. If her opponent is out of range or otherwise unthrowable for some reason, her throw attempt becomes a throw whiff. She grabs the air and is vulnerable for a moment. One important rule in *Virtua Fighter* is that you cannot throw an opponent during the startup phase or the hitting phase of a move. Thus, if Akira does a big, powerful move, he is totally unthrowable until after the hitting phase of the move is over and he enters recovery (retracting his arm or leg).

Back to our story. Akira is tired of getting his throw escaped all day, so he does the standard counter to any throw: a big, powerful move. This $c2$ move does a decent amount of damage, by the way. The next time this whole situation arises, Pai doesn't know what to do. Her instincts tell her to reverse the throw, but if she does, she is vulnerable to Akira's slow, powerful move. Rather than go for the standard reverse, Pai does her $c3$ move: She simply blocks. By blocking, she'll take no damage from Akira's powerful move, and depending on exactly which move it was, she'll probably be able to retaliate.

So what does Akira do if he expects this? In fact, he needs no $c4$ move because his original throw (m) is the natural counter to a blocking opponent. A throw is a special kind of move that grabs an enemy and does damage regardless of whether they are blocking. It's designed specifically to be used against an opponent in block who is afraid of an attack.

In summary,

Akira has throw and powerful, slow move.

Pai has throw escape and block.

As I tried to show, it's actually pretty reasonable to expect players to be thinking on *yomi* layer 3, 4, or even higher. This is so because conditioning makes doing the throw escape an unthinking, natural reaction. But against a clever opponent, you'll have to think twice about doing a standard throw escape or blocking. The Akira player will do the occasional powerful, slow move just to put the enemy off balance and abandon his or her instinct to escape the throw. Then Akira can go back to his original goal: Land the throw.

Another very interesting property is *beginner's luck*. Notice that a beginner Akira in this situation will go for the throw because that works on other beginners who haven't learned to throw escape. The beginner Akira will never land the throw on an intermediate player, though, because the intermediate player knows to always throw escape. But strangely, the beginner sometimes will land the throw on an expert because the expert is aware of the whole guessing game and may block rather than use throw escape. Of course, the expert soon will learn that the beginner is, in fact, a beginner, and then he or she will be able to *yomi* almost every move.

Just as a final note on *Virtua Fighter* to further demonstrate the complexity of its guessing games, I actually greatly simplified the preceding example. I left out, for example, that Pai could attack with a fast move rather than block. And Akira has another *c2* move besides a slow, powerful move. He also can do what's called a *kick-guard cancel*, or *kg*. This means that he can press kick, which will make him unthrowable until his kick reaches recovery phase. If Pai tries to throw, she'll whiff. But then Akira can cancel the kick before it even gets to the hitting phase. Now he's free to act and take advantage of Pai's whiffed throw vulnerability. Now Akira has a guaranteed throw, putting him back in the exact same situation in which he began. The catch is that if Akira does kg-cancel and then goes for the throw he originally wanted to do, Pai probably will not have time to react with a throw escape. It's just too fast. She'd have to be on the next *yomi* layer. She'd have to expect Akira to throw, enter a throw escape, see the kg-cancel, and then immediately enter her next guess (probably an attack or throw escape). Any hesitation and she'd be thrown.

The point I'm making here is that despite *Virtua Fighter*'s absurd complexity, players really are able to think on the levels I'm hinting at. While having a mental mastery of the structure and payoffs of these guessing games is important, the master of *yomi* can cut to the chase by guessing correctly in a particular situation rather than merely following a theoretically good rule of thumb for similar situations.

Section II

Games as Emergent Culture

10   Introduction to Section II

Constance Steinkuehler

In Section I we heard from game design luminaries on themes core to both industry practice (how designers think about the titles they create) and their role in learning (which we argue for throughout this book). Games, however, are more than *designed artifacts*, hewn from the creative labors of a designated team of experienced and thoughtful designers. They are, in fact, *emergent cultures* – social groups or organizations that share common knowledge, practices, and dispositions that emerge around a given game title. The attributes and tendencies of these cultures are not merely under the dictates of the creators of games themselves; more often than not, in fact, they surprise, if not confound, those original authorial intentions. Examples abound. *Lineage II* players forgo the core activity of the game, guild versus guild castle sieges, in order to ban together in cross-guild alliances to wage collective war on so-called Chinese adena farmers that they believe to be a "cancer" on their game (Steinkuehler, 2006a). *LambdaMOO* members establish their own forms of self-governance after an "evil clown" uses a code-based voodoo doll to rape another player's character (Dibbell, 1993). *CivIII* players mobilize online to support their own learning, establishing online universities complete with deans, faculty, students, and curricula, all based on a collective desire to hone their gaming expertise (Squire et al., 2005). An enterprising PlayStation Network (PSN) user creates a fully functioning calculator within the game *Little Big Planet* (Pereira, 2008). If game play cannot be accounted for solely by the way that the games themselves are designed to be played but, in fact, proves contingent on player practices and norms, then what about the forms of learning we argue throughout this volume that are associated with game play itself? In other words, what role do emergent game cultures play in learning?

In this section we explore the nature and function of game communities as naturally occurring, self-sustaining (often at least in part online) learning communities, ones that rival (if not oblique) communities overtly intended to teach, architected out of federal grant dollars, and built on widely accepted sociocultural and cognitive theories of mind in psychology and education (Steinkuehler 2006b). Chapters in this section review their affordances for fostering deep and meaningful learning (Gee & Hayes, Chapter 11; Steinkuehler & Oh, Chapter 12), the specific forms of production and labor such communities engage in (Choontanom & Nardi, Chapter 13; Halverson Chapter 16), and the ways in which particular game design choices sustain or thwart them (Black & Reich, Chapter 14; Malaby, Chapter 15). Together they offer more than a mere plausibility argument: They are collectively emblematic of a field that now has taken root and continues to grow in breadth and depth to include theoretical, empirical, and critical scholarship.

Chapter 11 takes a broad view of emergent gaming cultures, emphasizing the structural features of such game-based learning communities and their contrast with the structural features of school. Using *The Sims* as a generative example, Gee and Hayes detail the social practices or *metagame* that takes place around the game title to create what they refer to as a "nurturing affinity space." Gee and Hayes call such practices *soft modding* to emphasize their co-constructive role in the game as it is actually played and experienced. They then detail fourteen specific features that an affinity space needs in order to be considered "nurturing" – features that include, for example, (number 1) the primacy of a common endeavor, (number 5) open access to production and not just consumption, (number 7) knowledge distribution, and (number 11) multiple routes to or forms of status. Gee and Hayes use of terms here is strategic, leveraging existing veneration of more technical forms of modding practice (such as changing the code base of the game rules) within game (and game studies) communities toward new and more subtle ends of cultural and social forms of rule modification. Thus the chapter both provides a foundation for the section in its articulation of general principles of productive gaming culture – productive in terms specific to learning – and, at the same time, does significant political work. Their choice of terms, whether intentional or inadvertent, bestows the same high status accorded the *technical* to the *social*, the same authority accorded to *design* to *codesign* (or *redesign*; New London Group, 1996), and the same recognition given historically to *male forms of production* to *a wider range of intellectual creation and property*. It is perhaps this more subtle point, then, that reverberates most with this section's main goal: to demonstrate that game cultures and communities and not just game titles play a vital, constitutive role in the production of objects, knowledge, worldviews, and identities and that this production is both the means and the ends of the learning that games foster in the first place.

Chapter 12 complements Chapter 11 by drilling down to detail one of the specific mechanisms for learning within gaming communities (or most any community for that matter): *apprenticeship*. Steinkuehler and Oh give a detailed analysis of three spontaneous episodes of apprenticeship from three separate massively multiplayer online game titles. Using Gee's (1996, 1999) "Discourse analysis," they unpack the ways in which expert players mentor novice players through engagement in joint activity with a mutually understood goal. Comparison across the three cases highlights common structural features to the social interaction that foster learning, but perhaps the most interesting and dramatic point to their analysis is the fact that what learners are apprenticed into is not simply the *practices* of the dominant game culture but their *perspectives* as well: Masters show learners the ropes not merely in terms of strategies and tactics for how to play well but also and as crucially in terms of adopting the "right" set of values and attitudes toward the game, its content, its goals, world, and other players. Thus the "soft modding" that Gee and Hayes describe in Chapter 11 – the modification of game-play rules through cultural means rather than code – is both more ubiquitous than we might imagine, resulting from even the most seemingly mundane social interactions (as detailed in Chapter 12), and perhaps more potent. Based on Steinkuehler and Oh's analysis, its effect is not just the modification of game play but indeed the incremental alteration of values, dispositions, and identities.

Chapter 13, by Choontanom and Nardi, examines the actual content of what such gaming cultures produce intellectually. In it they detail the theorycrafting practices of *World of Warcraft* players – gamers' collective out-of-game analysis (on game-related forums and blogs) of in-game mechanics using the basic tools of spreadsheets, "napkin math," argumentation, logic, and scientific inquiry. While the authors are careful not to justify pleasure and play based on some external functional, utilitarian value, their rich ethnographic account of how players systematically work through explanations and understandings of in-game phenomena functions as a kind of "existence proof" of sorts of the intellectual value of online game play. Again, as in previous chapters, we see that the "game" players are actually engaged in is not driven by the designed technology alone. In the case of theorycrafting, it is driven by the community's need not just for tools and strategies for problem solving within the game but also for shared strategies for interpretation and community understanding of somewhat subtle concepts such as validity and reliability.

With Chapter 14, by Black and Reich, we shift gears toward a discussion of what design features enable or thwart the development of game culture and community. Here, the authors examine *Webkinz World*, a browser-based shared virtual environment designed to enable young children to socialize and play with their virtual counterparts to material plush toy animals. The central question they pursue is, "How do the multimodal resources both within and beyond the virtual space contribute (or fail to contribute) to a *Webkinz* culture or community?" Their findings suggest that in-game design choices made in the name of safety (e.g., heavy mediation of all interactions through nested drop-down menus, some of which require an understanding of language beyond the grasp of most children, if not young adults) actually inhibit genuine, productive sociability. Systems intended for the social well-being of the children whose virtual animals inhabit *Webkinz World* actually impede important prosocial behaviors and inadvertently emphasize consumerism (i.e., shopping for clothes, toys, and other items for one's pet) over actions with any (virtually) real import. The result is an ironic reminder of the old adage that, sometimes, "if you close the door, it just goes on out the window." In the case of *Webkinz World*, social interaction moves entirely outside the company-designed virtual space to that dense, unregulated, and user-generated network of fan sites, fan blogs, and discussion forums that surround the title, far beyond the watchful eye of designers (and perhaps parents). In the context of this section's theme, one take-home message is clear: Players have a strong drive to engage socially. When the technology thwarts those intentions, users do not appease themselves with shopping and decorating houses. Instead, they go find alternative avenues to connect.

Chapter 15 continues this discussion of how game design can function in ways orthogonal to sociability – and therefore, by extension, to many important forms of learning. In it, Malaby explores the basic *asocial* conceptualization of the human underlying the architecture of *Second Life* and the ways that imagining has very little room within it for the emergence of culture in its most generic sense. As in Black and Reich's account of *Webkinz World* (Chapter 14), sociability among players emerges *despite design* rather than because of it. In the case of *Linden Lab*, however, the situation is more insidious. Here, it is the design team's "technoliberal sensibility" and not merely paternalism or greed that leads them toward the creation of a virtual world in the image of humans as master of systems, solitary problem solvers, and virtuosos of code. In contrasting response, their users then reconstruct *Second Life* in their own, contradicting image of humankind, one that is socially organized, self-governing, collaborative, and competitive in turns – but always acting within in a context as social as it is technical. The result is a forestalling of the former will toward creation by a community with ulterior intentions and a frustration of the latter will toward co-creation by an underlying architecture of code that enables and rewards some creative acts but not others. With this discussion, we return to the core issues raised in Chapter 11 by Gee and Hayes: There is push and pull between game design and the gaming communities that inhabit them, transforming the "game" proper into what I have elsewhere called the "mangle of play" (Steinkuehler, 2006c), borrowing from Pickering (1995) – "an evolving field of human and material agencies reciprocally engaged in a play of resistance and accommodation where the former seeks to capture the latter" (p. 23).

The final chapter, by Halverson, provides a useful bridge toward the third and final section entitled, "Games as Twenty-First-Century Curriculum," remaining squarely centered on issues of culture that is participatory in nature (of which gaming culture is only one subset) yet shifting our focus toward their purposeful design. Rather than empirically documenting and analyzing existing participatory cultures and their role in informal, every-day, so-called casual or incidental learning, Halverson explores the concept of "participatory media spaces" as the design of participatory cultures for intentional learning. Drawing from two years of research on youth media arts organizations, as well as previous research on on- and off-line games, Halverson details three basic design principles for fostering productive youth experiences in the creation of digital stories: cycles of production, the affordances of digital tools, and embedded assessment addressing both product and process. These three principles lie at the core of what it means for youth to participate in the creation of digital artifacts in ways that are not only individually and culturally meaningful but also transformative in terms of *learning* explicitly. As such, this chapter rounds out our collective discussion of games as emergent culture and segues seamlessly into thoughtful discussion of what it might mean to cultivate curricula based on games.

References

Dibbell, J. (1993, December 23). A Rape in Cyberspace, or How an Evil Clown, a Haitian Trickster Spirit, Two Wizards, and a Cast of Dozens Turned a Database into a Society. *Village Voice*.

Gee, J. P. (1996). *Social linguistics and literacies: Ideology in discourses*, 2nd ed. London: Taylor & Francis.

(1999). *An introduction to discourse analysis: Theory and method.* New York: Routledge.

New London Group (1996). A Pedagogy of Multiliteracies: Designing Social Futures. *Harvard Educational Review*, 66(1), 60–92.

Pereira, C. (2008, October 7). Working Calculator Constructed in *Little Big Planet:* Adding and Subtracting Has Never Been This Mind Blowing. *1up. com*, October 7. Available at http://www.1up.com/news/working-calculator-constructed-big-planet.

Pickering, A. (1995). *The mangle of practice: Time, agency, & science*. Chicago: The University of Chicago Press.

Squire, K., Giovanetto, L., Devane, B., & Durga, S. (2005). From Users to Designers: Building a Self-Organizing Game-Based Learning Environment. *TechTrends*, 49(5), 34–42.

Steinkuehler, C. (2006a). The Mangle of Play. *Games & Culture*, 1(3), 1–14.
   (2006b). Why Game (Culture) Studies Now? *Games and Culture*, 1(1), 97–102.
   (2006c). The Mangle of Play. *Games and Culture*, 1(3), 199–213.

11 Nurturing Affinity Spaces and Game-Based Learning

James Paul Gee and Elisabeth Hayes

In this chapter we will argue that to understand how gaming supports learning, as well as to design games for educational purposes, educators and scholars must think beyond elements of the game software to the social practices, or *metagame*, that take place within and around games. Based on studies of fan sites associated with the popular computer game *The Sims*, we identify features of what we call *nurturing affinity spaces* that are particularly supportive of learning and contrast these features with how schools are typically organized. How such spaces are developed and sustained remains a central question for future research on games and learning, and we conclude by identifying key areas for further investigation.

Games and Learning

Those of us who have made the claim that games are good for learning have meant, of course, that well-designed games are good for learning, not poorly designed ones. While an empirical enterprise is under way to test whether and how games are good for learning, too often these studies do not first ensure that they are assessing games that are well designed.

The question of what makes a good game is, of course, different from the question of what makes a game good for learning. However, we have argued in earlier work that the very design of good games incorporates good learning features (e.g., Gee, 2003, 2007). Good learning features are, in fact, a key aspect of good game design because games are fundamentally problem-solving spaces that are meant to engage players. Games designed around problems people could not learn to solve and did not enjoy solving simply would not sell.

Obviously, different types of players like different types of games. However, fundamentally, all good games have good game mechanics (the actions players take to solve problems) and engender in players a desire to persist past failure, thereby engaging in a good deal of practice and time on task. Good games also engage players in reflection on strategy because to win such games, players must figure out the rules of the game and how they can be used to the players' advantage (Gee, 2004; Hayes & King, 2009).

Even the term *game* in the claims that good games are good for learning needs explication. Commercial designers and designers of nonentertainment games for learning have realized that both engagement with a game and learning are enhanced by building social engagement inside a game and outside it, in communities organized around an interest in the game (Salen & Zimmerman, 2003). Thus *World of WarCraft* players socialize within the game, and they come together in fan sites to discuss, critique, analyze, and mod the game. Learning potentially stems from both the game play (i.e., the play structured by the game as software) and the social practices going on in and around the game, as well as from the interaction between the two.

The term *metagame* has been used increasingly to describe "'the game beyond the game,' or the aspects of game play that derive not from the rules of the game, but from interplay with the surrounding context" (Salen & Zimmerman, 2003, p. 481; see also Garfield, 2000). We will use the term *game* to describe just the software that sets up game play, that is, what comes "in the box" or, increasingly, is downloaded from the game distributor's website. We will call the social practices that happen inside and/or outside the game, the *metagame*. We will call the combination of the two – game and metagame – the *big G Game*, with a capital G (see Gee, 1990, for a similar distinction between *discourse* and *Discourse*). We argue that the claim "good games are good for learning" should be rephrased as "good Games are good for learning." Like many others today – game designers as well as game scholars – we see game design as Game design (in addition to Salen & Zimmerman, 2003, see, for example, Gee & Hayes, 2009; Gresalfi et al., 2009; Matos, 2010; Morgenstern, 2007).

There is an aspect of modern game design, well exemplified now in the commercial industry, that is, in our view, an important "value added" for learning in and through games, especially in regard to twenty-first-century skills. This is the way in which many games today stress the role of players as designers. Many games allow players to modify (mod) them by using design software that comes with the game. Players can make small or big changes; they can design new levels and even whole new games. Further, many games today involve players as designers in the very way the game is played; that is, game design is a game mechanic in the game. This is true, for example, of *Spore*, where players constantly alternate between playing and designing (Morgenstern, 2007). *Spore* also has a robust fan community devoted to design for the game. *The Sims* operates similarly, as does *Little Big Planet* and *GameStar Mechanic* (a game made for teaching game design; see Games, 2008; Salen, 2007).

Designing, thinking like a designer, reflecting on the interaction between design and human interaction (as in a game), and thinking of complex relations in systems (as in the rule set of a game and the way it interacts with players and they interact with it) are all twenty-first-century skills (Zimmerman, 2007). In a sense, however, all games treat players as designers, as an inherent property of good games, in that players must figure out the game rules and interactions so that they can use those rules and interactions to their advantage to win the game. Players are, in this way, codesigners of the game, recruiting the rules (as well as taking advantage of flaws or bugs in the rules) in certain ways to customize their own play and thus their own game.

However, games that stress the involvement of players as designers in the first sense, by making game design a core game mechanic, facilitating modding, and encouraging robust design communities to develop around the game, are, we believe, particularly good for fostering skills with technology, design, systems thinking, and sociotechnical engineering (i.e., thinking about and creating good interactions between people and technology). We believe there is true "value added" with such games for learning in the twenty-first century. We will call such games *big G Games* with a plus: *Games+*. We can claim that "Games+ are particularly good for learning."

In earlier work we have spelled out a number of learning principles that we believe good games incorporate as part and parcel of their design (Gee, 2003). It would be useful also to identify a set of guiding principles for games that support players as designers, as well as to ascertain the relationship between these two sets of principles. However, in this chapter we wish to focus on aspects of Game (metagame) design concerned with social engagement and, more specifically, principles for good learning found in good metagame design. Of course, we will argue that a principle of good metagame design is involving players as designers. That is, most positive social engagement in and around games involves, in part, players acting and thinking like designers.

Affinity Spaces

When we think about fan communities associated with games, the concept of *community of practice* (Lave & Wenger, 1991; Wenger, 1998) is one that comes readily to mind. However, this term has been applied to so many different types of communities, some of which are not very "communal," that it has lost its conceptual clarity (Barton & Tusting, 2005). Furthermore, the concept of community of practice was based originally on studies of face-to-face groups that do not bear much resemblance to the geographically distributed, technologically mediated, and fluidly populated social groupings that comprise online game fan communities. In earlier work (Gee, 2004; Gee & Hayes, 2010), we used the terms *affinity groups* and *affinity spaces* to characterize these forms of social organization. We have used – and will use here – the term *space* instead of *group* because often in the modern world a group is defined by a space in which people associate rather than some readily identifiable criterion such as registering with a political party or completing professional training. On a fan site devoted, say, to *Age of Mythology*, who "belongs" and who does not? What does *belonging* really mean?

Most fan sites are completely open; anyone can find them and access their content. Some sites require visitors to become "members," which typically merely involves creating a username and profile. Accordingly, one of easiest and best ways to answer the question of "who belongs" is simply to say that whoever enters the space (the fan site) is in the group and belongs. This sets up a sense of group membership that ranges from short-term lurkers to wholesale aficionados and everything in between. This continuum is often one of the attractive features of affinity spaces, although, of course, the space can be organized to reshape this continuum in various ways. Within a space, various other sorts of (sub)group membership criteria or norms can be set up.

The concept of affinity space stresses that the organization of the space (the site and what it links to, including real-world spaces and events in some cases) is as important as the organization of the people. Indeed, the interaction between the two is crucial as well. Using the term *group* overstresses the people at the expense of the structure of the space and the way the space and people interact.

Affinity spaces do not have to be virtual, although the Internet lends itself extremely well to the creation of such spaces. A high school newsroom can be an affinity space. This space (e.g., the newsroom) is organized to structure social interactions of various sorts. There are varying degrees of participation; even a visitor who has come only once to the newsroom is "in" the affinity space and part of what defines the space, just as much as the news reporters and editors who are there frequently.

In earlier work we have outlined features that we consider to be definitive of an affinity space (Gee, 2004; Gee & Hayes, 2010). However, these features, which we will discuss below, are not absolute. In most cases, an affinity space can reflect the "ideal" or prototype to a greater or lesser extent. Furthermore, some affinity spaces may be missing some features. Affinity spaces are a "fuzzy concept" in the logical sense that they are defined by fuzzy boundaries and not necessary and sufficient conditions (Rosch, 1975, 1983). In practice, affinity spaces that are high on all the features we discuss below are hard to achieve and take work to sustain.

Not all affinity spaces are alike, of course. They may share common features but realize those features in different ways. Furthermore, affinity spaces can differ from each other on features that may not be part of the definition of an affinity space, such as the appearance of the space or the types of content available. We will discuss some of the more salient differences among affinity spaces below.

Our discussion of affinity spaces is based on research we described in a recent book (Gee & Hayes, 2010). The book focused on girls and women as gamers and in particular as game content creators. In this research, we investigated various affinity spaces associated with *The Sims*, the best-selling PC game series in history.

There are many different types of affinity spaces (and other kinds of communities) on the Internet and out in the real world (Barton & Tusting, 2005; Hellekson & Busse, 2006; Rheingold, 2000; Shirky, 2008; Wenger, 1998; Wenger, McDermott, & Snyder, 2002). Some are inclusive, supportive, and nurturing, whereas others are not. Affinity spaces and other sorts of communities can give people a sense of belonging, but they also can give people a sense of "us" (the insiders) against "them" (the outsiders). People can be cooperative within these spaces and communities, but they also can compete fiercely for status. They can communicate politely and in a friendly fashion, or they can engage in hostile and insulting interaction (which is so widespread that a distinctive term, *flaming*, is now used to describe it).

The Sims affinity spaces we studied in our book are organized around a passion for building and designing for *The Sims*. They are affinity spaces of a distinctive type. They function in certain ways that we believe are good for learning and human growth. Since not all affinity spaces function this way, we will call these *nurturing affinity spaces*. We will soon list a variety of features that characterize affinity spaces in a general sense and discuss more specific instantiations of these features that comprise nurturing affinity spaces. Later we will discuss how a nurturing affinity space can weaken or even cease to be nurturing by losing one or more of the features that define such a space.

We want to argue that human learning becomes deep, and often life-changing, when it is connected to a nurturing affinity space. The following list is the set of features associated with *The Sims* nurturing affinity spaces we have studied. This is an "ideal" list; many real spaces and communities tend more or less toward these features, thus coming closer or not to being an "ideal" nurturing affinity space. It is difficult for human creations to remain close to any ideal, and spaces or other sorts of communities that are close to any ideal can change over time for the worse. However, during the time we studied them, these *Sims* affinity spaces came close to this ideal. An important question for further research is how nurturing affinity spaces are initiated, by whom, and how they are sustained over time.

As we list the features of a nurturing affinity space, it will become apparent how different school is from a nurturing affinity space. If human learning and growth flourish in a nurturing affinity space, then it is of some concern that schools have so few features of such a space. To make this point, we will discuss how schools compare with each feature listed below. We will, to make the contrast clear, talk about "traditional" schools or school as we traditionally conceive of it. Of course, in this age of school reform, there are many people trying to break the mold of traditional schooling; nonetheless, this traditional model still prevails.

Features of Affinity Spaces

Here we describe fifteen features of an affinity space and the ways in which nurturing affinity spaces implements them:

1. *A common endeavor for which at least many people in the space have a passion – not race, class, gender, or disability – is primary.* In an affinity space, people relate to each other primarily in terms of common interests, endeavors, goals, or practices – defined around their shared passion – and not primarily in terms of race, gender, age, disability, or social class. These latter variables are backgrounded, although they can be used (or not) strategically by individuals if and when they choose to use them for their own purposes. This feature is particularly enabled and enhanced in virtual affinity spaces (Internet sites) because people can enter these spaces with an identity and name of their own choosing. They can make up any name they like and give any information (fictional or not) about

themselves they wish. This identity need not, and usually does not, foreground the person's race, gender, age, disability, or social class.

There is an interesting paradox here: What people have a passionate affinity for in an affinity space is not first and foremost, at least initially, the other people in the space but rather the passionate endeavor or interest around which the space is organized. The passion that fuels an affinity space can, however, lead to quite different ways of behaving, depending on how the other features (see below) of the affinity space are implemented. While people eventually may come to value their fellow members as one of the primary reasons for being in the affinity space, the shared passion is foregrounded as the reason for being there.

This shared passion can lead to good behavior if everyone sees that spreading this passion, and thus ensuring the survival and flourishing of the passion and the affinity space, requires accommodating new members and encouraging committed members. This is how nurturing affinity spaces implement this feature. Other affinity spaces may restrict full participation in the space only to people who have already proven themselves by passing various "tests" (e.g., newcomers may be flamed when they unknowingly break a norm or fail to already know what they "should" know).

School: Children in school rarely share a common passionate endeavor. In fact, children often have quite different views from each other and from the teacher as to why they are doing what they are doing in school (Willingham, 2009). Too often factors such as race, gender, social class, or disability play a prominent role in school without the student's ability to choose how to define and use his or her own identity. Finally, school is usually not about trying to spread a passion to as many people as possible.

2. ***Affinity spaces are not segregated by age.*** They involve people of all different ages. Teenage girls and older women, and everyone else in between, interact on *The Sims* sites we studied. There is no assumption that younger people cannot know more than older people or that they do not have things to teach older people. Older people can be beginners; indeed, anyone can begin at any time. Older and younger people judge others by their passion, desire to learn, and growing skills and not by their age.

In nurturing affinity spaces, the older and more advanced members set a standard of cordial, respectful, and professional behavior that the young readily follow. Such respectful behavior norms do not, of course, apply in all affinity spaces. A significant proportion of adult participants seems to be one necessary condition. These norms also appear to be connected to an attitude that expertise is like a candle flame – sharing it never diminishes it or the person who has it. In some other affinity spaces, experts will share their knowledge as mentors to only a restricted number of people who already show commitment and talent (which is also true of many a graduate advisor in Ph.D. programs).

School: School is, by and large, segregated by age with a low proportion of adults to young people. Knowledge is assumed to be associated with age, and students are measured in terms of standards for their age group, not, for example, in terms of the opportunities they've had to learn.

3. *Newbies, masters, and everyone else share a common space.* Affinity spaces do not segregate newcomers ("newbies") from masters. The whole continuum of people from the new to the experienced, from the unskilled to the highly skilled, from the slightly interested to the addicted, and everything in between, is accommodated in the same space. Different people can pursue different goals within the space based on their own choices, purposes, and identities. They can mingle with others as they wish, learning from them when and where they choose (even "lurking," or viewing but not contributing, on advanced forums where they may be too unskilled to do anything but listen in on the experts). While passion defines a nurturing affinity space, not everyone in the space needs to be passionate or fully committed. They must, however, respect the passion that organizes the space; the space will offer them the opportunity, should they wish to take it, to become passionate.

Nurturing affinity spaces make entry for newcomers easy. They do not haze or test them, although they do demand norms of respectful behavior and willingness to be a proactive learner. Some other affinity spaces, on the other hand, are rather like frat houses, treating newcomers like new pledges and seeing to it that they "pay their dues."

School: School segregates newcomers from more expert students through tracking and grade levels. As a result, students are rarely exposed to the discussions and practices of more advanced learners; they have little sense of the possible learning trajectories available to them. Indeed, learning trajectories are, for the most part, determined for the learners by others rather than by their own choices or passions.

4. *Everyone can, if they wish, produce and not just consume.* People who frequent a *Sims* affinity space often go there to consume, that is, to get content other fans have created, and that is fine. But the space is organized to allow and encourage anyone to learn to build and design. Tools, tutorials, and mentorship are widely offered. In some game-related affinity spaces, fans create new maps, new scenarios for single-player and multiplayer games, adjust or redesign the technical aspects of a game, create new artwork, and design tutorials for other players. In an affinity space, people are encouraged (but not forced) to produce and not just to consume – to participate and not just to be a spectator.

Most affinity spaces set high standards for the quality of production. There is rarely "social promotion" or lowered expectations. Indeed, as in other groups of experts (Bereiter & Scardamalia, 1993), the standards for production typically rise continuously as individuals innovate, create new tools, and otherwise push the collective bar for achievement. Nurturing affinity spaces enforce high standards through respectful and encouraging mentoring based on the assumption that no matter how expert one is, there are always new things to learn and people who know more than you do. Everyone is always a potential "newbie," continually learning and being mentored, no matter how often they may mentor others.

School: School stresses consuming what the teacher and textbook say and what other people have done and thought. When students produce (e.g., a writing assignment), they do what they are told because they are told to, not because they have chosen it. Furthermore, student productions rarely become a lasting feature of school; that is, students do not see and learn from prior student work, nor do they use that work as a starting point for their own innovations and achievement. They have no sense that their own work might be used and appreciated by others.

5. *Content is transformed by interaction.* The content available in an affinity space (e.g., all the *Sims* houses, rooms, furniture, clothes, challenges, and tutorials) is transformed continuously through people's social interactions. This content is not fixed. People comment on and negotiate over content and, indeed, over standards, norms, and values. Most of what can be found in an affinity space is a product of not just the designer (and certainly not just the company, e.g., the makers of *The Sims*) but of ongoing social interaction in

the group. This is particularly evident in forum discussions around, for example, tutorials, in which people add information, ask questions, and otherwise contribute a whole set of new information. Content producers in an affinity space, especially in a nurturing affinity space, also are sensitive to the views, values, and interactions of other members of the group.

School: School content is fixed by teachers, curricula, and textbooks, and the students' interactions with each other and with teachers rarely changes anything in any serious way (with the proviso that some teachers, of course, try to adapt material to different sorts of learners, although often without these learners having much say in the matter).

6. ***The development of both specialist and broad, general knowledge is encouraged, and specialist knowledge is pooled.*** Affinity spaces encourage and enable people to gain and spread both specialist knowledge and broad, general knowledge. People can readily develop and display specialized knowledge in one or more areas, for example, learning how to make meshes in *The Sims* or how to tweak a game's artificial intelligence (AI). At the same time, the space is designed in ways that enable people to gain broader, less-specialized knowledge about many aspects of the passion they share with a great many others in the space. Thus, for example, a *Sims* player may learn that Milkshape is a 3D modeling tool that can be used to mod *Sims* content, although not learn how to use the tool. This fosters the development of people who share knowledge and common ground but who each have something special to offer. It also means that experts are never cut off from the wider community (Surowiecki, 2004).

In a nurturing affinity space, it is important that each person with specialist knowledge sees that knowledge as partial and in need of supplementation by other people's different specialist knowledge for accomplishing larger goals and sustaining the affinity space. Knowledge pooling is enhanced by the fact that everyone in the group shares a good deal of knowledge about *The Sims* and design.

School: In school, most children rarely become experts or specialists in anything. Further, the children in a classroom or school rarely share a lot of general knowledge about something about which they all deeply care, which lays the foundation for each child's development of different forms of specialist knowledge that they can use to achieve common goals.

7. ***Both individual knowledge and distributed knowledge are encouraged.*** An affinity space encourages and enables people to gain both individual knowledge (stored in their heads) and the ability to use and contribute to distributed knowledge (Brown, Collins, & Dugid, 1989; Hutchins, 1995). Distributed knowledge is the collective knowledge accessible through, in this case, the affinity space and includes knowledge possessed by people, stored in material on the site (or links to other sites), or in mediating devices such as various tools, artifacts, and technologies to which people can connect or "network" their own individual knowledge. Such distributed knowledge allows people to know and do more than they could on their own. For example, a player who wants to create a new kitchen table for *The Sims* might ask questions on a forum, read tutorials, download modding tools, and analyze tables created by other players. Once the player has created a new table, he or she may upload it to the site along with instructions for other players. Thus these spaces encourage and enable people to interact with others and with various mediating devices in such a way that their partial knowledge and skills become part of a bigger and smarter network of people, information, and mediating devices and tools.

Nurturing affinity spaces tend to foster a view of expertise as rooted more in the space itself or the community that exists in the space and not in individuals' heads. "Experts" know that their expertise is always partial and limited, and they draw on the knowledge stored in the community when they need to supplement their individual knowledge or learn new things. The public display of individual expertise is less important than contributing to the collective knowledge of the space. In less nurturing spaces, individuals place more of a premium on establishing their expertise in relation to other people in the space and may vie to lay claim to the possession of unique knowledge or skills. As we will discuss below, even nurturing affinity spaces provide opportunities for the recognition of individual achievements and skill, but more in the service of encouraging individual growth and contributions to the collective good.

School: In school, the development of individual knowledge is valued, and the use of distributed knowledge is given short shrift. We still debate whether students should use tools such as calculators in math class. There are few sophisticated knowledge-building tools and technologies present in most schools; even access to computers, for example, is limited, and software is often outdated. Students rarely are encouraged to draw on each other's knowledge to supplement their own in academic tasks; in school that is often called *cheating*. The evaluation of students and schools is predicated on individual achievement, typically measured by assessments of students' recall of facts and application of skills in isolation from other people, resources, or tools.

8. ***The use of dispersed knowledge is facilitated.*** An affinity space encourages and enables people to use dispersed knowledge: knowledge that is not actually on the site itself but can be found at other sites or in other spaces. For example, in some *Sims* affinity spaces, there are many software tools available on site made by the designers of *The Sims*, but there are links to all sorts of other groups, software, and sites that have tools to facilitate building and designing for *The Sims*. In an affinity space devoted to the game *Age of Mythology*, as another example, people are linked to sites where they can learn about mythology in general, including mythological facts and systems that go well beyond *Age of Mythology* as a game. When a space provides access to dispersed knowledge, it recognizes the value of local and particular knowledge available in other places and created by other groups and the necessary limitations of its own knowledge base and resources.

The concepts of distributed knowledge and dispersed knowledge sometimes are used interchangeably, but they have different origins and implications. Distributed knowledge, as described earlier, refers more to an aggregate of knowledge possessed by individuals associated with a community or within a space and available for problem solving. The concept of dispersed knowledge originated as way of describing economic systems in which the knowledge of the relevant facts (e.g., on supply and demand for particular products) is dispersed among many people and localities (Hayek, 1945). In this case, it is assumed that it's not possible or even desirable to accrue all relevant knowledge in one place; dispersed knowledge is assumed to be necessarily specialized and context-specific. Thus, for example, a *Sims* affinity space devoted to fan fiction might link to individual authors' websites, where fans can find more detailed information about these authors and their work.

Of course, affinity spaces differ in their connections with other spaces, based on what "counts" as worthwhile knowledge and expertise in the eyes of those responsible for the space. While we don't have systematic data on the types of linkages associated with different sites, we speculate that nurturing affinity spaces tend to be more inclusive. For example, The *Sims Resource*, a site we consider to be nurturing, has a section in its forums specifically devoted to posting links to other sites, many of them personal sites created by individuals. A site we considered to be less nurturing and that fostered a sense of elitism among participants did not seem to have any section with links to other spaces or resources perhaps because of the attitude that all "important" knowledge could be found in the space itself.

School: In school, too often valid knowledge is to be found primarily in the classroom and restricted to general facts and principles found in textbooks or other "sanctioned" material. Specific, localized, and contextualized knowledge typically is considered inferior [despite efforts of educators to acknowledge the "funds of knowledge" brought by students to the classroom (Moll et al., 1992)]. The potential of the Internet to connect learners with other sources is viewed more as a threat to "safety" than as a means of accessing important, decentralized knowledge systems, and many links are banned or heavily policed.

9. ***Tacit knowledge is used and honored; explicit knowledge is encouraged.*** An affinity space encourages, enables, and honors tacit knowledge: knowledge members have built up in practice but may not be able to explicate fully in words (Polanyi, 1967). For example, designers of *Sims* content typically learn primarily through trial and error, not by memorizing tutorials and manuals. While tutorials (explicit or codified knowledge) are found in abundance in these spaces, designers rely on personal contact, through forums, and messaging to pass on their own craft knowledge and tricks of the trade. Indeed, some spaces foster the expectation that tutorial authors also will be available to answer questions as other designers try to use their guides. As we've observed, even the most well-written tutorial cannot capture every potential application of a process, and at times, players will share object files in order to troubleshoot without spending more time trying to articulate the problem. At the same time, the affinity spaces offer ample incentives for people to learn to articulate their tacit knowledge in words (e.g., when they contribute to a forum thread or engage in group discussion about a shared problem).

Since affinity spaces are often centered on a shared passion for producing things, not just consuming them, they all tend to honor tacit and craft knowledge (even producing fan fiction, for example, requires more than an explicit knowledge of grammar or techniques of fiction). Nurturing affinity spaces, however, tend to be tolerant of a wider range in people's abilities to articulate knowledge in specialist technical language. They create better conditions for people to learn and develop professional-like varieties of language (Hayes & Lee, forthcoming).

School: In school, unlike in many workplaces, tacit knowledge counts for little or nothing (at least in the more "academic" – and valued – subject areas). Indeed, students often learn to articulate knowledge (say it or write it down) that they cannot apply in practice to solve problems.

10. ***There are many different forms and routes to participation.*** People can participate in an affinity space in many different ways and at many different levels. People can participate peripherally in some respects and centrally in others; patterns can change from day to day or across larger stretches of time. Sometimes people lead and mentor, and other times they follow and get mentored. In nurturing spaces, this variation is wider than in less nurturing spaces.

School: In school, by and large, everyone is expected to participate in the same way and do all the same things. Students (and teachers) are expected to show up at the same times and do the same things at regular intervals. A student can't choose, for example, to spend weeks just "observing" what happens in school or to devote a day to tutoring younger students. Appropriate forms of participation tend to be narrowly defined.

11. ***There are many different routes to status.*** An affinity space allows people to achieve status, if they want it (and they may not), in many different ways. Different people can be good at different things or gain repute in a number of different ways. For example, in the *Sims* affinity spaces we've studied, some people are recognized for their skills as content creators, others for their tutorials, and still others for their roles in creating and managing the spaces themselves. Again, in nurturing spaces there is likely to be more variation and more routes to status, as well as more acceptance of people who do not want high status (and the corresponding commitment), than in less nurturing spaces.

School: In school, there certainly are different routes to status (e.g., being a good student, a good athlete, class president, and other such things). Unfortunately, in the "official" reward system of school, too often the only route to status is being a "good student," which means being good at being a student, not necessarily being good at solving problems or innovating.

12. ***Leadership is porous, and leaders are resources.*** Affinity spaces do not have "bosses." They do have various sorts of leaders, although the boundary between leader and follower is often porous because members often become leaders and leaders often participate as members. Leaders in an affinity space, when they are leading, are designers, mentors, resourcers, and enablers of other people's participation and learning. They do not and cannot order people around or create rigid, unchanging, and impregnable hierarchies. Obviously, there are degrees of flexibility in leadership, and while nurturing spaces foster respect for experts and those with more advanced skills, they tend toward less hierarchy and a view of leadership as "teaching," with an emphasis on mentoring and providing resources, not necessarily instructing, although this can happen as well.

School: In school, teachers are leaders and bosses and often are expected to see their role as telling rather than resourcing learners' learning and creativity. Even when students are given leadership roles, the ultimate authority always resides with the teachers or school administration.

13. ***Roles are reciprocal.*** In an affinity space, people sometimes lead, sometimes follow, sometimes mentor, sometimes get mentored, sometimes teach, sometimes learn, sometimes ask questions, sometimes answer them, sometimes encourage, and sometimes get encouraged. In nurturing spaces, even the highest experts view themselves as always having more to learn as members of a common endeavor, and they are not in it only for themselves. They want others to become experts, too. There is, as some of our interviewees reported, a desire to "give back" to others in the space.

School: In school, roles are not reciprocal. Teachers teach, mentor, and lead, whereas students "learn," get mentored, and follow. Despite the occasional assertion that teachers are learners, rarely is it assumed that teachers will learn anything directly from their students, nor do students expect to teach their "teachers" or anyone else, for that matter.

14. ***A view of learning that is individually proactive but does not exclude help is encouraged.*** Affinity spaces tend to encourage a

view of learning where the individual is proactive, self-propelled, and engaged with trial and error and where failure is seen as a path to success. This view of learning does not exclude asking for help, but help from the community is never seen as replacing a person's responsibility for his or her own learning. Nurturing affinity spaces tend to promote a view of requests for help (when other resources have been exhausted) as a means for enhancing the knowledge base of the space as a whole as participants engage in collective problem solving. There is considerable tolerance for newcomers who may not yet be able to locate information readily and thus ask redundant questions. In less nurturing spaces, such requests can be treated as evidence of stupidity, or at least inexperience, and there is little tolerance for newcomers who have difficulty locating existing information on their own.

School: Ironically, in school, students are expected to be dependent on teachers and textbooks for information, yet getting help from other students often counts as "cheating." Few students learn to adopt a proactive, self-directed, and trial-and-error approach to learning. Indeed, since learning objectives and methods are determined by the teachers and curricula, there is little opportunity for students to be self-directed, except perhaps in how they master predetermined content.

15. *People get encouragement from an audience and feedback from peers, although everyone plays both roles at different times.* The norm of a nurturing affinity space is to be supportive and to offer encouragement when someone produces something. This support and encouragement come from one's "audience," from the people who use or respond to one's production. Indeed, having an audience, let alone a supportive one, is encouraging to most producers. Many *Sims* affinity spaces provide mechanisms for this feedback, such as guest books where people can post messages to content creators.

At the same time, producers get feedback and help (usually also offered in a supportive way) from other creators whom they consider either their peers or people whom they aspire to be like some day. Who counts as a peer changes as one changes and learns new things. Everyone in an affinity space may be audience for some people and potential peers for others – again, more so in a nurturing affinity space than in less nurturing ones. In some less nurturing spaces, most of the visitors are considered "audience," and few are allowed to contribute content or are considered capable of providing meaningful feedback.

School: In school, children rarely have an audience that really cares about their work other than the teacher. Feedback comes, by and large, from the teacher, who is not a peer (not simply in the sense of age but also in the sense of expertise) or someone most students aspire to be like, in terms of their own passions. Furthermore, students rarely have the opportunity to be an audience for other students or to provide meaningful feedback to each other.

The preceding list is based on the online *Sims* affinity spaces we have studied. Other affinity spaces have these features as well. It is possible to implement these features in face-to-face groups, but it is likely to be more difficult owing to institutional constraints, preexisting status differentials, and even geographic boundaries that prevent people with common interests from coming together.

The preceding features are not easy to achieve, in either nurturing or less nurturing versions, and they can deteriorate over time. Affinity spaces with positive learning and growth features present in nurturing affinity spaces are miracles of human interaction. We need to know a great deal more about how they are initiated and sustained. We also need to study how such spaces can be designed to support learning in areas we care about as educators and citizens, locally, nationally, and globally.

Content, Knowledge, and Choice

The contrast between affinity spaces and traditional schooling may seem unfair. People choose to be in an affinity space, whereas schools are expected to force (or "motivate") students to do things they may not want to do. In an affinity space, many people share a passion. Schools (supposedly) cannot be about passions because everyone has to do, learn, and know the same things, namely, "what every educated person ought to know" (Hirsch, 1987). Too often this leads to everyone knowing next to nothing or at least nothing very deeply.

Here is the sad fact: Humans do not learn anything deeply by force. Humans do not learn anything in depth without passion and persistence. That is why, for most people, what they learn in school is short-lived unless they practice it in work or other settings after school. It is also why so many people, children and adults, learn more important things in their lives out of school than in it.

Think, for example, about learning geometry. Forcing people to learn geometry all in the same way because they are "supposed" to know geometry is not effective. Few people learn it well enough to remember and use it unless their jobs (or other life experiences) give them opportunities to practice with it outside school. They take geometry (or chemistry or algebra) as school subjects to progress to the next level of schooling. The subject serves as a gateway. Some people master it at school because they choose to and have a passion for it, if only for a high grade and getting into a good college.

Now consider how geometry learning happens when someone wants to design things in the virtual world *Second Life*. The building tools in *Second Life* are software tools for designing 3D environments. Mastery of these tools requires a big learning curve, a learning curve that people take on by choice, driven by their passion for being designers in *Second Life*. These tools require the application of a good deal of geometry to fit all the angles and shapes together perfectly. In fact, the tools build in some nice representations of geometric information, such as vectors.

In our book we discuss a woman who is a skilled and widely respected designer in *Second Life*. She failed to learn geometry well in school but now feels quite confident in her geometric knowledge. This woman did not master geometry because someone told her she "had to" or "should." She learned it because she wanted to design in *Second Life*, and knowledge of geometry is required to do that. Further, she had the support of the people and resources in *Second Life* affinity spaces devoted to design. Geometry became a tool for something she wanted to do.

The things we teach in school, subjects labeled "algebra," "physics," "civics," and so forth, are all tools (Gee, 2007). For example, "physics" is a set of tools for doing physics, that is, for solving problems that involve forces such as motion, friction, and energy. These tools are also used in other enterprises, for example, in building roller coasters in *RollerCoaster Tycoon* or in designing rockets in real life, much like geometry is used in designing for *Second Life*. "Civics" is a set of tools for understanding and participating in government and society. These tools, too, can be used in other enterprises, for example, in designing virtual worlds with their own economies and governing structures. Humans learn things such as facts, information, and principles ("content") well and deeply only when they are learned as tools for doing something meaningful and important to them (diSessa, 2000; Gee, 2004; Shaffer, 2007).

This brings us to "knowledge," or what school is supposed to be "about." Lots of the features of an affinity space as listed earlier use the word *knowledge*. Indeed, affinity spaces are, in a sense, knowledge communities. Such spaces build, transmit, sustain, and transform knowledge. But this knowledge is always in the service of something beyond itself. This does not mean that such knowledge has to be practical in the sense of serving the needs of society as a whole, but it has to be in the service of doing, that is, in the service of solving problems.

In an affinity space, people do not judge what other people know by asking them to list what they know and to write down the facts, information, and principles they know (i.e., what they have stored in their heads). They judge what other people know based on what they can do and how they can put their knowledge to work in solving problems for themselves and in helping others to solve problems.

The philosopher Wittgenstein (1953/2001, p. 52) once said that we know whether someone knows something if they know "how to go on" in a course of action. If someone is doing something, they have to act. Then they have to ask themselves, did my action work, and did it bring me closer to my goal or not? If the answer is "no," then they have to choose how to "go on," or how to proceed on a trajectory of actions that will, eventually, lead to success. All the knowledge in the world will do you no good in geometry, civics, or designing for *The Sims* if you do not know how to assess the success of your actions and how to go on in a successful trajectory to accomplish your goals (sometimes one way to go on is to change your goals). This is the main thing affinity spaces teach.

The learning scientist Dan Schwartz at Stanford University has said that looking at the choices people make in a course of action devoted to solving problems in a certain area is a much better assessment both of what they know and of how well prepared they are for future learning in the same area (personal communication; see also Schwartz, Sears, & Chang, 2007). He suggests that we should teach and assess choices, not knowledge, as content. For example, in solving a problem in science or mathematics or designing a building in *Second Life*, what are good choices to make when something has not worked? Should one try multiple solutions even if one solution already works? Is it more helpful to write down representations on a piece of paper as one goes along or leave everything in one's mind? Imagine the transformation in schools if learning in school became about how to make good choices in science, mathematics, art, and civic participation.

Affinity spaces are organized to help people make better choices. They are organized to share information so that new and better choices can be discovered. They are organized as well to share information about choices that work and ways to learn how to make better and better choices. These choices are not just about designing things. They are also about how to socially interact in the affinity space and outside it as well, including in "real life," so that goals are accomplished and people grow, no matter what their age. When this focus on discovering and making good choices lessens, affinity spaces deteriorate. They may become sites devoted more to socialization or popularity, and fights arise over status, belonging, and how to behave.

The Pareto Principle

The ways in which participation and production work in an affinity space are quite different from school. Schools operate by the bell curve. In a bell curve, the great majority of people are in the middle range of achievement, with a few much better than the rest and a few much worse. Game-related affinity spaces and other interest-driven spaces such as *Flicker* (a photo-sharing site), for example, tend to operate by the principle called the *80/20 principle* or the *Pareto principle* (Shirky, 2008). Eighty percent of the people in an affinity space produce 20 percent of the content (designs, pictures, mods, or whatever the activity of the group is), and 20 percent of the people produce 80 percent of the content.

This 80/20 organization means that such groups can recruit everyone's contributions while allowing the most dedicated to produce a great deal more. If we believe that young people today learn a great deal in such interest-driven groups, then it is important that there are many of them and that everyone can find ones in which they can be in the 20 percent of high contributors, if they wish, while making contributions in others where they are in the 80 percent.

Many people think that the bell curves we find in school, where nearly everyone is clumped in the middle at average, are just a reflection of people's "nature," that is, their genetics, like a normal distribution of height. Most of us, we think, are average performers, and only a few are really good or really poor. In reality, though, as Gould (1981) long ago pointed out, the standardized testing industry assumes bell curves and designs tests to get them. The design and scoring method of such tests are normative, just as is grading "on a curve." There always must be some students who have lower scores than all others and some who have higher scores, even if the actual difference in their performance is quite small. In addition to how tests are designed, the way that schools design instruction contributes to an artificial view of people's abilities to learn.

When people are organized to learn something like algebra, with little choice, passion, or lucid understanding of why they learning what they are learning, the result is a bell curve. Most people cooperate and learn something, if not much. A few resist and learn nothing, and a few find their own deep reasons for learning algebra. It is not that some people simply are not "gifted" at something like mathematics. What people learn outside school shows that nearly anyone can learn such things if they need and want to do it. Consider the woman we discussed previously, who hated geometry in school and now uses geometry regularly, with confidence, because she has a passion for building in *Second Life*, and such building requires geometry.

Not everyone has a passion for the same things. People join different groups that support their learning and resource them. In some cases, this is enough. In other cases, they get hooked on the community and the passion the community supports and join the top 20 percent.

In our book we look at women participating in two sites that constitute nurturing affinity spaces: *The Sims Resource* (TSR) and Mod *The Sims 2* (MTS2). These sites offer a good deal of support and encouragement for people with quite diverse skills and backgrounds. Not all sites devoted to *The Sims* operate like these sites.

An interesting contrast to these two sites is a site called More Awesome Than You (MATY). This is a site whose participants pride themselves on being at the "cutting edge" of *Sims* hacks and mods. The participants are, for the most part, quite technically adept. The norms of behavior for the site favor dealing harshly with anyone with whom one disagrees and especially with newcomers ("newbies") or people who are not highly skilled.

MATY is not, using the phrase of one post, "a standard buddy-buddy forum" (Rohina, 2009, reply 25). The post goes on to say that "you don't come here to be loved or fawned upon or greeted with open arms, you come here for information and downloads to make your game More Awesome .... If you don't want chunks bitten off you, don't play with tigers." Another post includes the admission that MATY regulars "tend to give new arrivals a particularly hard time." The post says that this "affords us a great deal of entertainment." It is also a way, the post says, to separate the "wheat from the chaff" and keep only newcomers who are tough and skilled (Rohina, 2009, reply 94).

MATY members are no fans of sites such as TSR. In fact, MATY contains one thread that is a vicious rant against the TSR site owner, whom the thread accuses of "brown-nosing" Maxis in order to get prerelease access to *The Sims 3* and trying to co-opt *Sims 3* modding tools (Merlin, 2009). To MATY members, TSR probably would be a "standard buddy-buddy forum," and in the words of another post (which tells people who do not like MATY that they can go elsewhere), "There will be other places where you can have a group sing-a-long of 'Kumbaya' and pretend to care about each other's days, your Special Sisters, your 'creative' abuse of the English language, your made-up attention-seeking disorders and diseases, and your emotional ups and downs" (Rohina, 2009, reply 43).

MATY has many features we associate with an affinity space. It is clearly a site of very high-level knowledge production – its mods are among the best available. Indeed, MATY had out an extensive mod of *The Sims 3*, a mod that corrected many errors in the code and made many improvements to the game, within two weeks of its release. However, its failure to accommodate a wide diversity of skills and backgrounds and its treatment of newcomers make it by our definition not a nurturing affinity space or, at least, only a partial one.

Designers such as a woman whose virtual name is "Tabby Lou" – a woman respected widely on TSR – are not respected on a site such as MATY. In fact, the site contains several criticisms of Tabby Lou. MATY participants look at themselves as hard-core technical experts. Tabby Lou and many of the other women we studied do not view themselves as such hard-core experts. They appear, rather, to view themselves as advanced learners. Furthermore, they see their expertise as part of the community, something that adds to the community but is also always supplemented by the community. Finally, women such as Tabby Lou do not see their technical and design expertise as separate from the social relations they have contracted in the community and the emotional intelligence they seek to combine with their technical expertise.

How people behave in these communities is not, in fact, a fixed property of them as individuals. It is certainly not due just to the presence of women or men. There are women on MATY and men on TSR. In fact, we have tracked the same individuals engaged with both sites. On MATY they behave harshly, and on TSR they behave cordially. How these communities behave is ultimately a matter of the culture a group grows and attempts to sustain.

We do not have a label for "experts" such as Tabby Lou, although we are much more familiar with the sort of hard-edge, high-tech expertise of many MATY participants. However, we now live in a world where individual expertise, especially expertise that overvalues what it knows and undervalues what it does not know, is dangerous, as was the case with Alan Greenspan's inability to predict the current global economic meltdown (Andrews, 2008).

Problems are too complex today to trust individual experts. They tend to trust their knowledge too much and pay too little attention to what they do not know and to what others, perhaps those quite unlike them, do know. We need to grow not expert individuals but knowledge communities (or spaces or whatever term we ultimately settle on to describe them). Some undoubtedly will be like MATY, which for all its harshness does network people together for knowledge building. But some will be like the affinity spaces we have discussed – sites of shared learning with people devoted to spreading passion and knowledge and not restricting it to hard-core experts. True innovation is as likely, or even more likely, to grow in a space that allows and encourages diversity of skills and backgrounds than one that is more narrowly defined, no matter how high its status.

How these affinity spaces are developed and sustained remains an important question not only for game studies but also for the learning sciences as a whole. In the sites we observed, considerable effort was devoted by site managers as well as members to sustaining the site's focus, content, and positive social interactions. In addition, we do not know the extent to which the focus of these spaces – in this case, a computer game or, in particular, *The Sims* – contributed to their features, including the extent to which they were more or less nurturing. Maxis, the company that created *The Sims*, has made noteworthy attempts to foster a sense of community and participation among *Sims* fans, for example. Maxis also has allowed and even encouraged fans to engage in a wide range of content-creation and modding practices, thus providing opportunities for diverse forms of participation and expertise. Despite *The Sims'* reputation as a "dollhouse" for little girls, the game is quite complex, with many affordances for learning technical and design skills. Indeed, before the release of *The Sims 3*, many fans expressed concerns that the tools incorporated in this new version of the game would render their expertise obsolete and even lead to the demise of some *Sims* fan sites (so far this has not been the case).

Lastly, we need to understand how affinity spaces are tied to other aspects of the metagame (Game or Game+) that play a significant role in learning associated with games and how these spaces might lead people to other spaces and types of knowledge that are not specific to games. For example, we found that some girls and women who learned technical skills through *Sims* content creation went on to take formal courses in graphic design or explored affinity spaces devoted to architecture. While such individual learning experiences cannot be designed per se, it is clear that affinity spaces have much to teach us about fostering people's passion and commitment to learning.

References

Andrews, E. L. (2008, October 23). Greenspan Concedes Error on Regulation. *New York Times*. Retrieved from http://www.nytimes.com/2008/10/24/business/economy/24panel.html.

Barton, D., & Tusting, K., eds. (2005). *Beyond communities of practice: Language, power, and social context*. Cambridge, England: Cambridge University Press.

Bereiter, C., & Scardamalia, M. (1993). *Surpassing ourselves: An inquiry into the nature and implications of expertise*. Chicago: Open Court.

Brown, A. L., Collins, A., & Dugid, P. (1989). Situated Cognition and the Culture of Learning. *Educational Researcher*, 18(1), 32–42.

diSessa, A. A. (2000). *Changing minds: Computers, learning, and literacy*. Cambridge, MA: MIT Press.

Games, I. A. (2008). Three Dialogs: A Framework for the Analysis and Assessment of Twenty-First-Century Literacy Practices, and Its Use in the Context of Game Design within *Gamestar Mechanic*. *E-Learning*, 5(4), 396–417.

Garfield, R. (2000). Metagames. In J. Dietz (ed.), *Horsemen of the Apocalypse: Essays on roleplaying* (pp. 16–22). Sigel, IL: Jolly Rogers Games.

Gee, J. P. (1990). *Sociolinguistics and literacies: Ideologies in discourses*. London: Taylor & Francis.

(2003). *What video games have to teach us about learning and literacy*. New York: Palgrave/Macmillan.

(2004). *Situated language and learning: A critique of traditional schooling*. London: Routledge.

(2007). *Good video games and good learning: Collected essays on video games, learning, and literacy*. New York: Peter Lang.

Gee, J. P. & Hayes, E. (2009). No quitting without saving after bad events: Gaming paradigms and learning in *The Sims*. *Int J Learn Media*, 1(3), 49–65.

(2010). *Women as gamers: The Sims and 21st century learning*. New York: Palgrave.

Gould, S. J. (1981). *The mismeasure of man*. New York: W.W. Norton.

Gresalfi, M., Barab, S., Siyahhan, S., & Christensen, T. (2009). Virtual Worlds, Conceptual Understanding, and Me: Designing for Consequential Engagement. *On the Horizon*, 17(1), 21–34.

Hayek, F. (1945). The Use of Knowledge in Society. *American Economic Review*, 35, 519–30.

Hayes, E. R., & King, E. M. (2009). Not Just a Dollhouse: What *The Sims2* Can Teach Us About Women's IT Learning. *On The Horizon*, 17(1), 60–9.

Hayes, E. R., & Lee, Y. N. (forthcoming). Specialist Language Acquisition and Trajectories of IT Learning in a *Sims* Fan Site. In S. C. Duncan & E. R. Hayes (eds.), *Videogames, affinity spaces, and new media literacies*. New York: Peter Lang.

Hellekson, K., & Busse, K. (eds.) (2006). *Fan fiction and fan communities in the age of the internet*. Jefferson, NC: McFarland.

Hirsch, E. D. (1987). *Cultural literacy: What every American needs to know*. Boston: Houghton Mifflin.

Hutchins, E. (1995). *Cognition in the wild*. Cambridge, MA: MIT Press.

Lave, J., & Wenger, E. (1991). *Situated learning: Legitimate peripheral participation*. Cambridge, England: University of Cambridge Press.

Matos, X. (2010, March 3). Designing the Meta-Game. *GamePro*. Retrieved from: http://www.gamepro.com/article/features/214260/designing-the-meta-game/.

Merlin (2009, May 28). TSR Has Already a Workshop for CC.... *More Awesome Than You*. Message posted to: http://www.moreawesomethanyou.com/smf/index.php/topic,15059.msg433718.html#msg433718.

Moll, L. C., Amanti, C., Neff, D., & González, N. (1992). Funds of Knowledge for Teaching: Using a Qualitative Approach to Connect Homes and Classrooms. *Theory into Practice*, 31(2), 132–41.

Morgenstern, S. (2007, Feb. 8). The Wright Stuff. *Popular Science*. Retrieved from: http://www.popsci.com/entertainment-gaming/article/2007–02/wright-stuff.

Polanyi, M. (1967). *The tacit dimension*. New York: Anchor Books.

Rheingold, H. (2000). *The virtual community: Homesteading on the electronic frontier*, revised edition. Cambridge, MA: MIT Press.

Rohina (2009, May 29). Important Notice from the GRAMMAR POLICE. Plz read. This Means You. *More Awesome Than You!* Message posted to: http://www.moreawesomethanyou.com/smf/index.php?topic=15068.0.

Rosch, E. (1975). Cognitive Representation of Semantic Categories. *Journal of Experimental Psychology*, 104, 573–605.

    (1983). Prototype Classification and Logical Classification: The Two Systems. In E. Scholnick (ed.), *New trends in cognitive representation: Challenges to Piaget's theory* (pp. 73–86). Hillsdale, NJ: Lawrence Erlbaum Associates.

Salen, K. (2007). Gaming Literacies: A Game Design Study in Action. *Journal of Educational Multimedia and Hypermedia*, 16(3), 301–22.

Salen, K., & Zimmerman, E. (2003). *Rules of play: Game design fundamentals*. Cambridge, MA: MIT Press.

Schwartz, D. L., Sears, D., & Chang, J. (2007). Reconsidering Prior Knowledge. In M. Lovett and P. Shah (eds.), *Thinking with data* (pp. 319–44). Mahwah, NJ: Erlbaum.

Shaffer, D. W. (2007). *How computer games help children learn*. New York: Palgrave Macmillan.

Shirky, C. (2008). *Here comes everybody: The power of organizing without organizations*. New York: Penguin.

Surowiecki, J. (2004). *The wisdom of crowds*. New York: Doubleday.

Wenger, E. (1998). *Communities of practice: Learning, meaning, and identity*. Cambridge, England: Cambridge University Press.

Wenger, E., McDermott, R., & Snyder, W. M. (2002). *Cultivating communities of practice: A guide to managing knowledge*. Boston: Harvard Business School Press.

Willingham, D. T. (2009). *Why don't students like school? A cognitive scientist answers questions about how the mind works and what it means for the classroom*. New York: Jossey-Bass.

Wittgenstein, L. (1953/2001). *Philosophical investigations*, 3rd ed. Oxford, England: Blackwell Publishing.

Zimmerman, E. (2007). Gaming Literacy: Game Design as a Model for Literacy in the 21st Century. *Harvard Interactive Media Review*, 1(1), 30–5.

12 Apprenticeship in Massively Multiplayer Online Games

Constance Steinkuehler and Yoonsin Oh

Imagine an entire 3D world online, complete with forests, cities, and seas. Now imagine it populated with others from across the globe who gather in virtual inns and taverns gossiping about the most popular guild or comparing notes on the best hunting spots. Imagine yourself in a heated battle for the local castle, live opponents from all over collaborating or competing with you. Imagine a place where you can be the brave hero, the kingdom rogue, or the village sage, developing a reputation for yourself that is known from Peoria to Peking. Now imagine that you could come home from school or work, drop your book bag on the ground, log in, and enter that world any day, anytime, anywhere. Welcome to the world of massively multiplayer online gaming.

Massively multiplayer online games (MMOs) are highly graphic 2D or 3D video games played online, allowing individuals, through their self-created digital characters, or *avatars*, to interact not only with the gaming software (the designed environment of the game and the computer-controlled characters within it) but also with other players' avatars. These virtual worlds are persistent social and material worlds loosely structured by open-ended (fantasy) narratives where players are largely free to do as they please – slay ogres, siege castles, barter goods in town, or shake the fruit out of trees. They are notorious for their peculiar combination of designed "escapist fantasy" yet emergent "social realism" (Kolbert, 2001): In a setting of wizards and elves, princes and knights, people save for homes, create basket indices of the trading market, build relationships of status and solidarity, and worry about crime.

An earlier version of this chapter was published in the *Proceedings of the Sixth International Conference of the Learning Sciences* [Steinkuehler, C. (2004)]. Learning in Massively Multiplayer Online Games. In Y. B. Kafai, W. A. Sandoval, N. Enyedy, A. S. Nixon, & F. Herrera (eds.), *Proceedings of the Sixth International Conference of the Learning Sciences* (pp. 521–28). Mahwah, NJ: Erlbaum.

Such games are ripe for analysis of the forms of sociocultural learning that attend them given their dual status as both "designed simulation" and "emergent culture." On the one hand, they are thoroughly designed worlds whose rules reflect designers' intentions (and certainly not players'). On the other, they are worlds whose culture and climate very much depend on how they are taken up by those who play and inhabit them. In previous work (Steinkuehler, 2006), I have called this the *mangle of play* – a mangle of design-ers' intentions (represented by rules) and player's intentions (represented by emergent shared practices of the in-game community) and the broader eco-nomic, legal, and cultural reality in which this interplay take place.

In fact, part of their status as technologies for learning is contingent on this very mangle. Online games function as naturally occurring online learning environments not merely in the sense that they are – based on eco-nomic pressures to reach a large audience (Gee, 2003) – technologies that are designed to be learned but also and equally they are communities of practice (Lave & Wenger, 1991) that must, in some way, educate newcomers into their shared ways of being in the world. Like most communities, MMO commu-nities use a variety of means to accomplish this – among others, tutorials, manuals, modeling, practice and feedback, and of course, apprenticeship.

This chapter presents a detailed analysis of the forms of apprentice-ship that arise spontaneously in the play spaces of MMOs and how those forms of mentoring attune learners to both the community's practices and perspectives or worldviews. Using Discourse analysis (Gee, 1996, 1999) as a way to unpack the complexities and tacit dynamics of language in social interaction and building on a corpus of cases of apprenticeship collected across five commercial game titles (*Lineage I*, *Lineage II*, *Star Wars Galaxies*, *World of Warcraft*, and *RuneScape*), this chapter presents a detailed analysis of three selected cases of apprenticeship across three distinct virtual worlds. Through close comparative analysis of these cases, we highlight common structural features to such interactions that foster learning and the tacit and overt ways that community values are expressed therein. We conclude with a discussion of how discursive analyses such as these can inform our theoret-ical understanding of sociocultural forms of learning and how the dynamics of virtual apprenticeship identified through such methods shape our under-standing of virtual communities and what it means to be a member.

Cognition as (Inter)Action

There is a growing body of work that posits that cognition is (inter)action in the social and material world. This body of theory and research includes work in activity theory (e.g., Engestrom, Miettinen, & Punamaki, 1999), d/ Discourse theory (Gee, 1996, 1999), distributed cognition (e.g., Hutchins, 1995), ecological psychology (e.g., Gibson, 1986), ethnomethodology (e.g., Garfinkel, 1967), mediated action (e.g., Wertsch, 1998), situated learning (e.g., Lave, 1988; Lave & Wenger, 1991), sociocultural theory (e.g., Vygotsky, 1978), and situativity theory (e.g., Greeno, & Moore, 1993). Despite differences among them as to the specific terms of their approach, these perspectives share a focus on interactive systems of activity of which the individual is only one part. Cognition, from this underlying paradigm, cannot be accounted for adequately by computational models of structures and processes "in the head"; rather, one must look to the intact activity systems in which the individual participates – systems that necessarily include social relationships, physical and temporal contexts, symbolic and material resources (such as artifacts and tools), and historical change. Within such systems, cognition is "a complex social phenomenon...distributed – stretched over, not divided among – mind, body, activity and culturally organized settings (which include other actors)" (Lave, 1988, p. 1). Of interest, then, are the interactional structures of such social and material systems, not structures in the individual mind per se.

From this view, it is through participation in a community of practice that an individual comes to understand the world (and themselves) from the perspective of that community. Here, semantic interpretation is taken as part of what people do in the lived-in world; it arises through interaction with social and material resources in the context of a community with its own participant structures, values, and goals (Greeno & Moore, 1993). For example, an individual becomes attuned to a particular object's constraints and affordances through the regular pattern of interaction that individual has with the object, but this regular pattern of interaction is shaped by the individual's membership in a particular community for whom the object has meaning, usefulness, and relevance for a given task with a given (individual or collective) goal. Such activities have direct import for the identity of the individual. Who one is determines and is reflexively determined by one's participations in various communities (Gee, 1999; Greeno, 1997). As Packer and Goicoechea (2000) write,

> A community of practice transforms nature into culture; it posits circumscribed practices for its members, possible ways of being human, possible ways to grasp the world – apprehended first with the body, then with tools and symbols – through participation in social practices in relationship with other people. Knowing is this grasping that is at the same time a way of participating and relating [p. 234].

Changes in knowing become changes in being: Through participation in a given Discourse community (Gee, 1999), an individual does more than merely acquire and reorganize symbolic knowledge about the world; he or she is transformed ontologically by it.

Learning, from this perspective, is progress along "trajectories of participation" (Greeno, 1997) and growth of identity within a given community of practice (Gee, 1999). Thus, accounts of how an individual interacts with his or her material and social contexts and how these interactions change over time replace accounts of individual knowledge construction occurring "in the head." It is the gradual transformation of an individual from "legitimate peripheral participant" (Lave & Wenger, 1991) to central member of a community through apprenticeship and increased participation in values community practices. At the aggregate level of the community, this learning process takes the form of an emergent reorganization of the patterns of member participation coupled with a growth of shared knowledge through changing practices and artifacts. At the individual level, however, it is ontological in nature, "a process of coming to be, of forging identities in activity in the world" (Lave, 1988).

Apprenticeship

With this view of cognition assumed, apprenticeship becomes a crucial mechanism for learning, linking individual knowledge, behaviors, and dispositions to socioculturally shared understandings, practices, and values. In apprenticeship, a master (teacher) and an apprentice (learner) jointly participate in a valued and routine community practice with a mutually understood and shared goal (Tharp & Gallimore, 1991; Lave & Wenger, 1991). That the activity is a normative one is important because participation in such practices constitutes a form of enculturationinto the predominant preoccupations of the group. Through joint activity in those practices, the master engages the learner in the unfolding activity to an extent that matches his or her current ability and models competent performance of the given community practice for the apprentice, who learns in part through observation and mimicry (Lave & Wenger, 1991). Joint activity, despite disparate ability levels between teacher and student, is made possible through scaffolding: The master adjusts the complexity of the task and the degree to which the learner is given responsibility for and control over the undertaking, thereby keeping the work within what Vygotsky (1978) calls the learner's "zone of proximal development," which is "the distance between the actual developmental level as determined by independent problem solving and the level of potential development as determined through problem solving under adult guidance or in collaboration with more capable peers" (p. 86).

In most productive apprenticing exchanges, the learner is given repeated opportunities to practice component skills (Wenger, 1999) and to receive situated feedback from the master in the exchange, often focusing the learner's attention on aspects of the context that are crucial to its success – for example, pointing out the bias of the fabric in order to make the appropriate cut. New information is provided to the learner not in advance of the activity, as a prerequisite to participation, but within the actual context of use – what Gee (2007) and others call *just-in-time information*. The focus of instructive interactions throughout the endeavor typically is sequenced so that simpler, more rudimentary subtasks are highlighted before more complex ones; however, the activity remains intact throughout the exchange (Collins, Brown, & Holum, 1991; Tharp & Gallimore, 1991) in contrast to more decontextualized "skill and drill" approaches (which break the target activity down through task analysis and then drill students on each separate subtask).

Research Methods

The research question driving this investigation is, "What is the nature of apprenticeship in the virtual spaces of MMOs?" MMOs are voluntary play spaces in which individuals with ostensibly no experience or training in education somehow must accomplish the task of teaching and being taught by presumed peers. (1) How do two equals in a voluntary play space negotiate role relationships in such a way that, temporarily, one can play expert and the other novice without any institutional sanctioning of those roles? (2) What pedagogical strategies are used by players to enculturate one another into their cultural practices? And finally, (3) what are the dispositions or "cultural models" at play in such interactions, and how are they communicated? In order to answer these questions, we collected ethnographic data across several MMO titles and analyzed the data using Discourse analysis methods based on Gee's (1996) work.

Context of the Research

For the past seven years (and counting), we have collected ethnographic data across selected globally popular MMO titles as a way to better understand the culture of such worlds, including the features of such spaces that

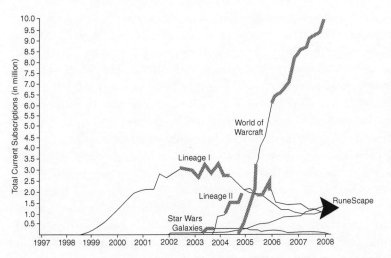

Figure 12.1. Population trends in the top-selling MMOs (Woodcock, 2010) versus the context of our data collection (depicted by the heavy line).

remain relatively stable versus those which vary from title to title (or server to server, in some cases). As Figure 12.1 shows, our data collection has followed the general migration patterns of the overall global virtual population (with the exception of *RuneScape*, which we are currently studying given its success in capturing an exclusively younger audience compared with other MMOs). At this time, the entire data corpus includes participant observation and multimodal field notes from roughly 90 months of data collection across five different titles (two from Korea, two from North America, and one from Europe).

The three cases of apprenticeship analyzed herein were chosen from three distinct MMOs. The first case comes from the Korean game *Lineage*, the second case comes from its sequel, *Lineage II*, and the third case comes from the American game *World of Warcraft*. All three titles have stable populations that inhabit them, although, like any popular media, titles fall in and out of fashion with broader audiences (again, see Figure 12.1). *Lineage I* and *II* are set during medieval times, featuring elves, knights, mages (magicians), and prince/sses, in which guilds or "blood pledges" vie for control of various castles within the virtual kingdom. *World of Warcraft* is set in the Tolkienesque fantasy world of the *Warcraft* series of real-time strategy games, featuring two factions of fantasy characters (e.g., orcs and undead on the "horde" side, humans and elves on the "alliance" side) who are in uneasy alliance against a scourge that threatens to destroy the world. Players weave their way through the complex game narrative by completing in-game quests and developing their character to level 80, after which time the game-play emphasis shifts more toward group "raids" against in-game "boss" monsters. All three game titles features "player-versus-player" content as well as "player versus environment" content, but *Lineage I* and *II* core mechanics center more on the former, whereas *World of Warcraft* core mechanics center more on the latter. All three also require collaborative play as the game advances. In *Lineage I* and *II*, advanced group play arises in the form of player-versus-player world events, which are "castle sieges" that can involve hundreds of individual players at a time. In *World of Warcraft*, advanced group play occurs primarily in the form of "instanced" group content delivered to groups of five to forty players at a given time. Both game titles feature multiple forms of social organization and networking, ranging from the short-term "pickup group" to the more enduring "guild" organizations, resulting in a complex social space of affiliations and disaffiliations constructed largely out of shared (or disparate) social and material practices – ways of behaving, communicating, interacting, and valuing that are "forms of life" (albeit virtual) through which individuals enact not just their character class, be it elf or orc, but the "kinds of people" (Hacking, 1986) they construe themselves to be and that others can recognize.

Data Collection: Cognitive Ethnography

Given the socially and materially situated perspective on cognition taken here, the proper unit of study is not the individual "head" per se but rather the intact interactional structures of social and material activity. As such, the proper method of research is cognitive ethnography (Hutchins, 1995): a "thick description" (Geertz, 1973) of the socially and materially distributed cognitive practices that constitute the given Discourse. As with most ethnographies, the researcher participates overtly in the daily life of the game (to date, in this line of inquiry, for roughly ninety months total), observing what goes on within the virtual world, taking digital video recordings and field notes, listening to what is said, asking questions, and generally "collecting whatever data are available to throw light on the issues that are the focus of the research" (Hammersley & Atkinson, 1986, p. 1). Because meaning is "not in anyone's head, but embedded in the history and social practices of the group" (Gee, 1999, p. 105), understanding what and where learning occurs and what it means for the identity of members of the Discourse is possible only through such groundwork. In addition to routine observation and field notes, informants of varying ages, ethnicities, socioeconomic positions, and levels of expertise/social status within the community are recruited and interviewed repeatedly in unstructured (e.g., informal conversation within the game), semistructured (e.g., telephone interviews about particular topics of interest), and structured (e.g., long-interview-technique; McCracken, 1988) formats. Finally, community documents (such as player-authored user manuals, fan sites, and fan fiction) and transcripts from game-related discussion boards and chat rooms are also collected in order to capture game play not only within the virtual game space itself (between login and logoff) but also beyond.

The game-play transcripts analyzed here are taken directly from the in-game chat channel of each respective title and consist of naturally occurring social interaction that was initiated by another player and not the researcher. Talk is verbatim save changes for ease of reading, such as expansions of truncated words, typographic corrections, and supplementation of dietic references with appropriate referents (in brackets). In addition, three types of changes were made to the text before inclusion for publication. Additional contextual information was added (in italics) to illuminate what actions were taken by the interlocutors and when sequentially within the exchange. Nontopical conversational turns of no immediate relevance (e.g., trade channel exchanges that appear in the ambient chat) were removed for the sake of brevity. And finally, pseudonyms replace avatar names for all participants except the researchers themselves in order to maintain (virtual) anonymity.

Analytical Method

This research draws on Gee's Discourse theory and method of analysis (1999) as a tool for understanding the situated meanings individuals construct (not just the information they process), the definitive role of communities in that meaning, and the inherently ideological nature of both. Coming out of the New Literacy Studies (e.g., Gumperz, 1982; Halliday, 1978; Kress, 1985; Street, 1984), Discourse theory provides a structured means for teasing out how particular social and material practices mark membership in the MMO gaming community and how participation in those practices shapes and is shaped by participants' identities within (and at times beyond) the game. We are keenly interested in socially distributed cognition and its role of peer interactions in learning; thus a theory of language more nuanced than the typical transmission or container model (cf. Vera & Simon, 1993) is crucial if we are to develop any viable account of the situated meanings people construct and the definitive role of communities in that meaning-making process.

Ethnographic data collected through this project are analyzed using d/ Discourse analysis methods (Fairclough 1995; Gee, 1999; Gumperz 1982; Halliday, 1978): "the analysis of language as it is used to enact activities, perspectives, and identities" (Gee, 1999, pp. 4–5). Such analyses focus on the configurations of linguistic cues used in spoken or written utterances that invite certain interpretations and not others. Such linguistic cues include, for example, word choice, foregrounding/backgrounding syntactic and prosodic markers, cohesion devices, discourse organization, contextualization signals, and thematic organization. Using Gee's (1999) theory, configurations of such devices are analyzed in terms how the language of the particular utterance is being used to construe reality in terms of

1. Semiotics. What symbol systems are privileged, how they construe the relevant context (the world), and on what epistemological basis?
2. The material world. What objects, places, times, and people are relevant and in what way?
3. Sociocultural reality. Who is who, and what are their relationships with one another? This includes the implied identity of the speaker/ writer and who the audience is construed to be, all in terms of affect, status, solidarity, and (shared or disparate) values and knowledge.
4. Activities. What specific social activities are the speaker and her interlocutors engaged in?
5. Politics. What social goods are at stake, and how are they and "ought" they to be distributed?
6. Coherence. What past and future interactions are relevant to the current communication?

Particular configurations of linguistic cues prompt specific situated meanings of these six aspects of "reality," meanings that evoke and exploit specific cultural models. These cultural models are indelibly linked to particular Discourses, which, in turn, allow speakers and hearers to display and recognize the "kind of people" each is purported to be.

Through microanalysis of how group members' utterances construe the world in particular ways and not others, we are able to infer the cultural models and concomitant Discourse(s) as play. With such analyses comes explication of the full range of social and material practices with which they are inextricably linked because the meaning of those practices is established with and through language in use. Through such Discourse analysis–based ethnographic work, then, we capture the sense human beings make of the social and material world and their (inter)action with it – in other words, we finally get at the phenomena of cognition itself in all its unbounded, situated, distributed, social, and ideological messiness.

Analysis One: Learning How to Hunt Mithril

The first example of apprenticeship is taken from transcribed digital videodata collected during the summer of 2002. In this exchange, a rather "newbie" female elf named JellyBean (level 10, played by the researcher) and a more experienced female elf named Myrondonia (level 25) jointly engage in the routine elven activity of hunting for mithril. Prior to this exchange, JellyBean ran into difficulties hunting in an area called the Elven Forest. While making her escape, she cried for help. In response, a female elf named Myrondonia inquired by whispered message to see if she could assist. Realizing that JellyBean was an experienced player, Myrondonia offers to take her hunting for mithril, a requisite raw material for many elven goods. Mithril is a rare drop from monsters in all areas except one: the Elven Dungeons. Two kinds of monsters inhabit the dungeons: undead zombies, which frequently drop mithril, and orcs, which rarely drop anything of any value. Orcs are "herd monsters": Should you hit a single one of them, they rest will gang up on you and bludgeon you to death. Figure 12.2 provides a full account of how Myrondonia apprenticed JellyBean into the elven social practice of gathering mithril. In what follows, we give a line-by-line account of what transpired.

The scene opens with Myrondonia (expert) and JellyBean (novice) in the Elven Dungeon hunting zombies. From the very beginning of the episode, Myrondonia engages JellyBean in joint participation in the target practice. She does not lecture JellyBean on the rules of the game before they enter the dungeon or quiz her before they begin in order to ensure that she understands the activity but instead dives them both immediately into the task.

As the two discuss the number of orcs in the area, JellyBean states, "I'm scared I will click on one [an orc] just walking" (line 1). By suggesting less than complete mastery over basic navigation strategy, JellyBean immediately positions herself as the learner in their collaboration, thereby positioning Myrondonia as the expert. This relative positioning tacitly sanctions, if not invites, the subsequent pedagogical exchange.

Rather than immediately shifting into overt mentoring, however, Myrondonia first prefigures her action by stating that she knows "a secret" (line 2), which elicits from JellyBean an inquiry as to what that secret is

joint
participation

JellyBean and Myrondonia are walking through the Elven Dungeons, in search of zombies to kill for their associated mithril drops. The two are discussing the glut of dangerous orcs in the area.

1	JellyBean:	I'm scared I will click on one just walking	**learner identity display**
2	Myrondonia:	I know a secret	**pre-sequence**
3	JellyBean:	what?	**sequencing instruction**
4	Myrondonia:	hold your mouse key down	1) safe navigation

I try out this navigation strategy, clicking down when the cursor is over empty ground, causing my avatar JellyBean to move to the screen location just clicked.

scaffolding

5   Myrondonia: wait [meaning, don't release the mouse key yet]

I do as instructed, causing JellyBean to move fluidly across screen.

6	JellyBean:	wow	
7	Myrondonia:	there you go	*(procedural dexterity)*
8	JellyBean:	that's so cool!	

practice

feedback

A zombie rounds the corner into the room. JellyBean shoots and kills it. It falls to the ground.

9	Myrondonia:	another rule	
10	JellyBean:	ok	
11	Myrondonia:	quickly use your mouse cursor over the dead bodies	2) efficient resource collection
12	Myrondonia:	make sure they didn't drop	

(efficiency)

I run my cursor over the zombie corpse as instructed and find a piece of mithril on the ground.   **practice**

orients
learner
to goal

13	JellyBean:	oh wow	
14	JellyBean:	I never knew that	*(virtual material good: mithril)*
15	Myrondonia:	sometimes it's sneaky	
16	Myrondonia:	you don't want to lose a mithril	

focuses
attention

A zombie walks into the room and attacks Myrondonia. Meanwhile, JellyBean is walking over to pick up the mithril on the ground from their last kill.

17	Myrondonia:	no	
18	Myrondonia:	take this one [the zombie hitting her]	**feedback**
19	Myrondonia:	try to look for zombies & hit them	

JellyBean does as instructed. The two continue the hunt, moving into a corridor. Another zombie approaches; JellyBean kills it and grabs the mithril on the ground.   **practice**

20   Myrondonia: good   **feedback**

The two continue their way to the end of the corridor. An unknown elf named IrisArker passes by.

21	Myrondonia:	another rule	
22	JellyBean:	yes?	
23	IrisArker:	^_^ [smiley face gesture while walking by]	
24	Myrondonia:	If you see someone go one way, go the other	
25	Myrondonia:	hi [to IrisArker]	
26	Myrondonia:	we are all here for mithril	*(meritocracy)*

routine
practice

Figure 12.2. Transcript of *Lineage I* apprenticeship with pedagogical moves in bold (and underlying values in parenthetical italics).

(line 3). Together, these two lines (2–3) are a presequence (Levinson, 1983) to the subsequent pedagogical exchange, acting both as an overture for the subsequent speech act (i.e., apprenticeship) and as a bid for permission from JellyBean to proceed. As an overture, the presequence is an ostensive gesture (Csibra & Gergely, 2006):

> …the teacher has to manifest not only her knowledge to be transmitted to the learner but also the fact that she is manifesting her knowledge, i.e., that she is teaching…. In other words, the teacher has to explicitly mark

her behaviour as being a pedagogical manifestation, and has to make sure that the intended recipient has received her signals…. We call this aspect of pedagogy, after Sperber & Wilson (1986), ostension [Csibra & Gergely, 2006, p. 6].

Ostensive gestures are crucial to everyday forms of teaching outside of formal classrooms. For example, Senju and Csibra (2008) found that infants will follow the actions of adults only if they are preceded by such gestures (also see Frith & Frith, 2010). Here, the presequence, "I know a secret" (line 2), followed by JellyBean's inquiry "What?" (line 3), serves this function, signaling that the subsequent exchange is intended to teach.

Myrondonia then describes a more sophisticated way to navigate that does not carry the same risk of clicking on dangerous orcs on screen: holding the mouse key down rather than clicking each specific spot along the path one hopes to take (line 4). Notice, here, that information is not orated prior to actually engaging in joint work but rather is given "just in time" (when it can be put to use immediately) and in the context of the goal-driven activity for which it is actually useful.

JellyBean attempts the new strategy. Myrondonia interrupts her action, directing her to "wait" (line 5) to release the button as she moves her mouse. JellyBean then completes the motion, successfully navigating her avatar fluidly across the screen, expressing surprise ("Wow," line 6) at the effectiveness of this new practice. Myrondonia then states "There you go" (line 7), signaling that the task has been completed successfully. Together, Myrondonia's three turns of talk (lines 4, 5, and 7) function to scaffold (Vygotsky, 1978) JellyBean's performance, providing explicit guidance during the learner's performance to support her successful completion of the task. Myrondonia's direction during the action (line 5) props up JellyBean's actions in such a way that she is able to pull off the task off without knowing herself precisely how that action should take shape. When JellyBean sees the resulting motion of her avatar on screen and realizes that she has succeeded in the task, she remarks "That's so cool!" (line 8), acknowledging the new strategy as novel. Thus, if Myrondonia's attention to the minutiae of navigation signals that procedural dexterity is something of value, then JellyBean's utterance (lines 8) indicates that she "gets" the values currently in play. Note, too, how this exchange functions as one of several cycles of practice and feedback: JellyBean completes a task; Myrondonia immediately evaluates.

The pair continues through the Elven Dungeon. A zombie rounds the corner into the room where the two are standing, and JellyBean shoots and kills it, leaving its zombie corpse on the ground. Myrondonia then gives "another rule" (line 9), telling JellyBean to "quickly use [her] mouse cursor over the dead bodies" (line 11) in order to make sure that they don't drop loot (line 12). Thus, if Myrondonia's first pedagogical "rule" targets prerequisite skills necessary for engaging in some activity (i.e., safe navigation in 3D space), then her second "rule" shifts focus toward more advanced strategies (i.e., efficient resource collection) that require that such necessary prerequisites are already in place. In so doing, Myrondonia sequences her instruction, ensuring that the basics are mastered before attention is shifted more toward matters of polish and finesse. Note, too, the premium placed on efficiency. In directing JellyBean to be doubly sure that she does not inadvertently overlook a mithril that may be obscured by a zombie's corpse, Myrondonia communicates that efficiency is to be valued in this practice.

JellyBean checks the zombie corpse as instructed, finding a hidden mithril on the ground. She expresses surprise ("Oh wow," line 13) and again positions herself as the less experienced member of the interaction ("I never [knew] that," line 14), to which Myrondonia responds, "Sometimes it's sneaky. You don't want to lose a mithril" (lines 15–16). In this exchange, Myrondonia's explanation works to explicitly orient the learner toward the immediate goal of the current practice (i.e., mithril) while at the same time reaffirming the value presumably placed on this virtual material good. While JellyBean navigates her avatar over to pick up the mithril, another zombie enters the dungeon room and attacks Myrondonia. Myrondonia corrects JellyBean's current action stating, "No, take this one" (lines 17–18). In this way, Myrondonia (re)focuses JellyBean's attention to the aspect of the activity most crucial to success – here, staying alive in place of gathering loot – by directing her to "try to look for zombies and hit them" (line 19). Note how this refocusing of attention also functions as additional feedback on JellyBean's practice: When JellyBean chooses the wrong goal as her focus, Myrondonia redirects her, and the activity proceeds. As their activity continues, JellyBean is given additional practice not just in hunting and looting but in prioritizing these subgoals in the right ways. The elven pair continue their hunt, slaying zombies and picking up mithril in their downtime, and Myrondonia's situated feedback continues ("Good," line 20), making note of JellyBean's progress.

Master and apprentice continue their way to the end of the corridor, when an unknown elf named IrisArker appears. "Another rule," Myrondonia states (line 21) as the stranger moves toward them. JellyBean inquires, "Yes?" (line 22), signaling her to continue. The stranger emotes a friendly face to the pair ("^_^," line 23) and walks by, heading into an adjacent dungeon room. "If you see someone go one way, go the other," Myrondonia whispers to JellyBean (line 24) and then shouts out a public greeting to IrisArker in response ("Hi," line 25). "We are all here for mithril" (line 26). This final line of talk communicates to JellyBean two important things: first, that their current practice is a routine one that presumably "all" elves engage in, and second, that one should ensure that all elves in the dungeon have generally equal access to gather materials (i.e., meritocracy). In this way, and by the end of their exchange, two distinct but related things are taught: One is the social practice. The other is the kind of person/elf Myrondonia wants JellyBean to be.

Analysis Two: Learning How to Group Heal

The second episode of apprenticeship is taken from transcribed digital videodata collected during the summer of 2004 from *Lineage II*. In this exchange, Adeleide, an experienced player yet beginner elf healer (researcher) and four experienced players are out in an area of *Lineage II* called the Abandoned Camp, a middle- to low-level hunting area that resides between the first and second major cities that players encounter. The group of players is out hunting packs of aggressive monsters called Ol Mahums in the area despite a somewhat significant difference in experience level between the healer (level 17) and her fellow group members (who range between levels 25 and 35). In fact, this level difference is part of the reason they are there: to help Adeleide level her avatar up and gain more hands-on experience in playing a new and dramatically different character type. While they are out hunting, a more advanced elven healer named Zena approaches the group and strikes up a casual conversation. Zena's superior expertise in the game is conspicuous: She is out hunting solo in an area intended primarily for groups, and she wears a very rare (at that time) and expensive item of equipment – a pair of cat glasses. The analysis in Figure 12.3 provides a full account of Adeleide's apprenticeship into elven healer culture in *Lineage II*.

The scene opens just after Zena has joined the hunting party, with group members overtly negotiating their functional roles for the upcoming activity. Zena asks the group whether they want her to "heal or fight" (line 1) – an unusual question given that, in *Lineage II*, most "spellsingers" (line 5) are dedicated "damage dealers," meaning that they typically specialize solely in doing high-damage spells against monsters and not in healing other group members. The fact that Zena is able to do either is a testament to her level

joint participation

Adeleide and four companions are out hunting in a popular area of moderate difficulty. Zena, a higher level elf who is out hunting the area solo, is invited to join the group.

1	Zena:	u want i heal or fight?
2	Adeleide:	dae's [the tank's] call. fight i think
3	Adeleide:	im just new to healer here. so learning hard way :/ **learner identity display**
4	Adeleide:	what about u?
5	Zena:	spellsinger [character class]
6	Adeleide:	v nice

The group sets out with Adeleide as healer and Zena fighting monsters with the other group members.

                                                     practice

7	Zena:	can i give you an advice ade?	**pre-sequence**
8	Adeleide:	yes please do!
9	Zena:	when the tank start to loose hp start your heal immediately **feedback**
10	Adeleide:	oooh ok so cast early
11	Zena:	and he will never die
12	Adeleide:	lemme *practice* some – its v [very] good advice

(tank's safety) — lines 9–11

scaffolding

Adeleide tries out Zena's strategy, casting heals earlier. The tank's HP bar is relatively stable but not 100% full.

                                                     practice

| 13 | Zena: | there life normally always be perfect   **feedback** |

Adeleide continues healing, this time casting more often so as to maintain a perfect HP bar on the tank. She struggles to keep up, however, and soon her mana runs out. Zena takes over as healer.

14	Adeleide:	low mana
15	Zena:	i heal a bit
16	Zena:	i ll try to teach a lil
17	Adeleide:	yes i can use all the help i can get! so please do advise if ur willing

modeling

18	Zena:	look life of dae [the tank] never behind 50%	*(tank's safety)*
19	Adeleide:	yes ur right!
20	Zena:	just keep safe the tank that your job ←----------- **routine**
21	Zena:	others after **focuses attention** **practice**
22	Zena:	the most important is the tank

After modeling successful healing, Zena gives the role of healer back to Adeleide, who begins a second time.

sequencing instruction

1) heal tank

                                                     practice

23	Zena:	so ade u need to keep tank life perfect
24	Zena:	because	*(tank's safety*
25	Zena:	if tank die all die too	*is group's safety)*
26	Zena:	because only tank can asume big dmg **feedback**
27	Adeleide:	kk so always keep tanks health bar at full capacity
28	Adeleide:	cast heal when his HP starts to drop at all

2) over-healing

                                                   practice

29	Zena:	yes you can heal too much not a problem	*(group safety over*
30	Zena:	better too much than not	*conserving resources)*
31	Adeleide:	kk that makes sense **feedback**

3) heal others

                                           practice

32	Zena:	and heal others when u have time	**orients**
33	Adeleide:	*nod*	**learner to goal**
34	Zena:	normally tank will have aggro on him
35	Zena:	so no one but him need heal **feedback**

Figure 12.3. Transcript of *Lineage I* apprenticeship with pedagogical moves in bold (and underlying values in parenthetical italics).

of strategic expertise. Adeleide first defers to the tank – the person in the group who stands at the front of combat and therefore purposely takes the most damage from incoming monsters ("Dae's [the tank's] call," line 2) to decide what functional role Zena should fill but then tentatively suggests that Zena "fight" (line 2) because she herself is functioning as healer, albeit at only a rudimentary level "[I'm] just new to healer here. So learning hard way :/ [sad face]" (line 3).

Again, then, at the very opening sequence of the interaction, we see two important patterns repeated: First, the entire exchange begins (and later ends) with participation in joint activity and not simply informational exchanges (such as manuals or quizzes). Second, the learner clearly positions herself as the learner and therefore her interlocutor (here, Zena) as the relative expert. As in the first episode, this relative positioning tacitly sanctions, if not invites, the subsequent pedagogical exchange. Her intimation that she is, in fact, struggling (i.e. "learning the hard way," line 3) echoes this invitation, creating a context in which Zena's expertise might be seen as salvation and not imposition.

The group sets out to hunt collaboratively, with Zena dealing damage and Adeleide trying to heal. After a few rounds of monster groups that allow Zena to observe Adeleide's work, Zena asks permission to apprentice Adeleide, stating "can I give you an advice, Ade?" (line 7). Adeleide accepts her offer with enthusiasm ("Yes, please do!" line 8). Together, lines 7 and 8 function as a presequence (Levinson, 1983), as seen in the first analysis, with Zena's query for permission functioning as the ostensive gesture (Csibra & Gergely, 2006) that signals that the subsequent exchange will be intentionally pedagogical.

Zena begins by advising Adeleide that "when the tank start to loose hp ["hit points" or "health points," which represent the relative health of the given target], start your heal immediately" (line 9). Here we see the focal point around which several concentric circles of value will be communicated throughout their interaction. Within the group, the tank is the focal point of interest, and Zena orients Adeleide to watch the tank's HP bar as the measure by which to determine whether and when she ought to heal. Adeleide restates her directive, paraphrasing it in more literal terms ("Oh, so cast early," line 10), and Zena responds, providing the rationale that, in so doing, "He [the tank] will never die" (line 11). Adeleide signals that she understands and accepts the directive, stating, "Lemme practice some – its v[ery] good advice" (line 12). If Zena's talk places explicit value on the role of tank, then Adeleide's demonstrates that she "gets" the values currently in play (much like JellyBean in the first analysis) and commits to this exclusive focus of attention. Note, too, how line 12 ("Lemme practice some – its v[ery] good advice") forecasts the subsequent cycle of practice and feedback that ensues, which will be the first of several.

The group hunt continues. Although Adeleide manages to keep the tank's HP bar relatively stable through her heals, she does not keep it perfectly full at 100 percent. As the tank's HP slowly decreases, Zena interjects, stating that "[their] life normally always be perfect" (line 13). Zena's turn provides "just in time" information that scaffolds Adeleide's performance by reminding her of the criteria for when and how to heal before the consequences of not doing so take effect. Adeleide picks up the pace, and the tank's HP bar not only stabilizes but remains perfectly filled to capacity as well.

Adeleide continues practicing, but soon her mana (the resource used to cast heals) runs out ("low mana," line 14). Zena offers to take over as the group's healer while Adeleide regenerates ("I heal a bit," line 15), taking advantage of the moment as a teaching opportunity ("I'll try to teach a lil," line 16). Adeleide accepts and again encourages such tutelage, positioning herself as the learner and Zena as benevolent master ("Yes, I can use all the help I can get! So please do advise if ur willing," line 17).

Next, in lines 18–22, Zena cognitively models successful performance of the role of healer for Adeleide, verbalizing each significant move she makes as the group's healer and explaining those moves in a way that emphasizes the primary value placed on the role of tank within the group. As the group encounters the next group of "Ol Mahums" and the tank's HP bar begins to drop, Zena immediately casts a healing spell and calls Adeleide's attention to the timing of her cast, restating the criterion for success ("Look life of dae [the tank] never behind 50 percent," line 18). Adeleide acknowledges ("Yes, ur right!" line 19), and Zena continues, now giving the rationale for this near-exclusive focus on the tank's safety above all else: "Just keep safe the tank that your job / others after / the most important is the tank" (lines 20–22).

Zena's explanation does important work on two important levels. First, it focuses the learner's attention on the care and supervision of the tank's HP bar (and not, say, the damage dealer's HP bar or the tank's mana point [MP] bar or any other variable shown in the context of the current group interface). Second, in referring to it as the healer's "job," it makes it clear that this practice is a routine one for healers, not only expected but also entirely condoned. This final detail is important one. It is by no means obvious that a designated healer ought to ignore the health status (i.e., HP bar) of all group members save the tank. By signaling that this exclusive focus is her duty, Zena denies the alternative possible interpretation of such action as discriminatory and therefore unfair.

Having modeled group healing and with Adeleide's mana resources replenished, Zena then hands control of the activity back to the learner, setting the context up again for practice and situated feedback. Here, across the next three rounds of practice and feedback, we see Zena sequencing her instruction like Myrondonia in the first analysis, ensuring that the basic skills are mastered before attention is shifted toward understanding more complex game strategies and mechanics – from (1) focusing on the tank to (2) understanding overheals to (2) healing other group members.

First, Zena begins with a more complete explanation of this emphasis on the tank. The group moves out, attacking another cluster of monsters. As Adeleide begins to cast healing spells on the tank, Zena guides her from the side, stating "So Ade you need to keep tank life perfect / because / if tank die all die too / because only tank can assume big dmg [damage]" (lines 23–26). Zena's justification communicates a second concentric circle of value whose point of origin is the tank. The tank's safety synecdochically functions as a stand-in for the group as a whole. By keeping the one safe, Adeleide keeps them all safe by proxy.

Second, Zena addresses the issue of overhealing. In response to Zena's prior explanation (lines 23–26), Adeleide again displays her understanding for inspection by restating Zena's advice in more literal terms – here, tying the directive more explicitly to the symbols in the interface and the exact timing necessary to accomplish what Zena describes ("KK so always keep tank's health bar at full capacity / cast heal when his HP starts to drop at all," lines 27–28). Adeleide's restatement goes uncorrected, and Zena continues, now taking up an important (albeit somewhat more complicated) implication of this particular healing strategy – overhealing. Overhealing is a waste of mana resources that arises when a healing spell is cast that is bigger than what is immediately needed (e.g., if a target is down 100 HP, and the healer casts a spell that increases HP by 150, often because there is no weaker healing spell available). In lines 29–30, Zena states that overhealing is acceptable ("Yes, you can heal too much not a problem / better too much than not" (lines 29–30). In this way, Zena signals that the group's safety (represented by the tank) is in practice more important than conserving one's own (mana) resources. Again, Adeleide signals uptake of the value at play ("KK [okay, okay], that makes sense," line 31).

Third and finally, Zena addresses the issue of when to heal other group members. With the tank standing in for the group's safety, Zena advises, one should heal other group members essentially as an afterthought "when you have time" (line 32). Adeleide again signals agreement, emoting a nod (line 33), and Zena explains: "Normally tank will have aggro on him / so no one but him need heal" (lines 34–35). Zena's final line reemphasizes the goal of the activity from the healer's functional point of view: to be an HP battery for the tank. And with this final explanation in place, the single-minded near obsession with the tank's safety becomes intelligible. Group composition is such that the tank should be the only member taking damage and therefore the only member in need of heals. In this way, and by the end of the interaction, again, we see two distinct but related things taught:

one the one hand, social practice of healing and, on the other, the values underlying them.

Analysis Three: Learning How to Hunt Solo

The last episode of apprenticeship is taken from transcribed digital video-data collected at the beginning of 2006 from *World of Warcraft*. In this exchange, Jezabelle, an experienced player as a healer yet a beginning "damage-dealing" shadow priest (researcher) is out hunting alone in the area called Magram Village, which is designed for players from level 33 to 34. Although Jezabelle is a level 33 priest, an appropriate level for killing monsters in the area, she is struggling owing to her recent change in her spec from a healer to a damage dealer. While she is hunting alone, a more experienced shadow priest named Synner walks by and sees Jezabelle's struggle. He casts a heal on her to help. Synner is a level 36 priest wearing a very rare and expensive item of equipment, namely, the Robes of the Archmage, which shows his high status (at that time). Figure 12.4 provides a complete account of how Synner apprenticed Jezabelle into the practices of damage-dealing shadow priests in *World of Warcraft*.

The scene opens right after Jezabelle receives help from Synner; Jezabelle displays appreciation by stating "Ur [You are] so kind!" (line 1). Synner continues helping her through periodic heals, asking whether she is "shadow specced [a damage class] or holy [a healing class]?" (line 3). Since *World of Warcraft* allows players to look at other players' information like specs, Synner simply could have looked at her character in the interface. Instead, he continues a conversation with the less-than-necessary question as a way to make character specialization a new topic in its own right. Jezabelle responds that she is a "shadow" (line 4) priest and elaborates by stating that she has "just recently changed" (line 5) and is therefore a "sorta newb [newbie, novice]" (line 5).

Thus we again find the same two important opening patterns repeated early in the apprenticeship episode: First, it begins with participation in joint activity. Second, the learner positions herself as such, thereby making Synner the relative expert. Instead of providing advice to the novice right away, however, Synner asks for her permission to give some "quick pointers" (line 6) on practices that are presumably routine for shadow priests. Jezabelle shows an interest in the learning opportunity (line 7), and Synner explicitly offers advice in the form of an *ostensive gesture* (Csibra & Gergely, 2006). As in the preceding two analyses, these two turns of conversation (lines 6–7) function as a presequence (Levinson, 1983) for pedagogical exchange.

joint
participation

Jezabelle is out hunting solo. Synner, a priest walking by, sees her struggling and casts a heal on her.

1	Jezabelle:	ur so kind!
2	Synner:	i got you keep attackin
3	Synner:	are you shadow specced [damage class] or holy [healing class]?
4	Jezabelle:	shadow [damage class]
5	Jezabelle:	just recently changed to that though so... sorta newb **learner identity display**
6	Synner:	hehe ok i can give you some <u>quick pointers for us shadow priests</u> if you want ◄──**pre-**
7	Jezabelle:	yes plz! **routine practice** **sequence**

modeling   *Synner "groups" Jezabelle, walks toward a second monster group, and stops. Jezabelle follows.*

| 8 | └ Synner: | first thing get at <u>max range</u> for your mind blast   *(personal safety)* |

Synner begins casting damage spells on the monsters, talking through each of his actions as he goes.

9	└ Synner:	mindblast them, pain, mindflay, then shield *(mana efficiency)*
10	└ Synner:	another mindblast or mindflay and then wand them to death
11	└ Synner:	if the fight is going to be tough drop pain and plague on them
12	└ Synner:	as soon as your shield breaks, hit renew *(personal safety)*
13	Jezabelle:	mindblasty, pain, flay then shield myself
14	Synner:	that works on most mobs
15	Synner:	bingo
16	Synner:	lets go <u>practice</u> *(skill development)*

sequencing instruction

1) standard   *Synner & Jezabelle attack and defeat one monster group then a second using Synner's strategy.*

2) variant 17	Synner:	up here is a caster [monster that casts spells]
18	Synner:	slightly different strat [strategy] on these
19	Jezabelle:	those r hard
20	Synner:	shield, mana burn until they are out and then pain, mindblast and wand

3) variant   *Jezabelle does as told and the monster dies. They move on to a group containing two casters.*
Jezabelle tries to cast "silence" but fails. Both casters attack her at once. Synner watches.   **practice** ⟶

21	Synner:	LOL **feedback** ◄───────────────────────────────
22	Jezabelle:	dang, wrong cast
23	Synner:	shield
24	└ Synner:	now flay
25	└ Synner:	flay him so he can't run and get more mobs ¦ **focuses**
		¦ **attention** *(crowd control)*

scaffolding   *Jezabelle casts "flay" as told and one caster dies.* **practice** ─────────────

| 26 | └ Synner: | ok, shield manaburn till she's empty pain and wand **feedback** ◄─ |

Jezabelle casts "shield" then "manaburn."

| 27 | Synner: | pain |

Jezabelle casts "pain." The second caster runs away toward another monster group on the horizon.

28	Jezabelle:	then wand more?
routine 29	Synner:	flay
practice 30	► Synner:	flay isnt always necc. but <u>a good habit</u> ¦ *(solo skill development*
31	Jezabelle:	kk [okay] ¦ *for future collaboration)*
32	Synner:	especially in instances

Figure 12.4. Transcript of *World of Warcraft* apprenticeship with pedagogical moves in bold (and underlying values in parenthetical italics).

Synner begins the tutelage by telling Jezabelle to stay as far away from the monsters as possible (" maximum range" for a spell called "mind blast," line 8) when casting. His first concern, therefore, is personal safety, an obvious focal point of interest during solo hunting for a priest wearing flimsy cloth. Synner uses *cognitive modeling* by telling and demonstrating a sequence of spells to cast on monsters as one rotation (line 9–12). His strategy is to deal a big burst of damage first with "mind blast," which slows the incoming monster and to then use a "damage over time" spell called "pain." The final move in the spell rotation is to "shield" oneself to prevent taking any damage should the incoming monster actually reach your character, thereby ensuring your own safety. Line 12 reiterates this overt concern for personal safety as Synner recommends her to recast the "shield" spell the moment it wears off.

Synner's recommendation to use "(devouring) plague" over "pain" (line 11) indicates a value placed on *mana efficiency*: While "pain" uses 22 percent of the caster's base mana to cast it on monster over eighteen seconds, "(devouring) plague" uses 25 percent of base mana to cast over twenty-four seconds but also simultaneously heals the caster for 15 percent of the damage inflicted on the targeted monster. Jezabelle restates his first sequence (line 13), signaling both attention to and understanding of the directions given. Synner then states, "Let's go practice" (line 16), forecasting a subsequent cycle of practice and feedback similar to the cycle seen in the second analysis (*Lineage II*) but, in this case, expert- and not learner-initiated.

In this way, Synner *sequences his instruction* – much like Myrondonia in the first analysis and Zena in the second analysis – across the two rounds of practice and feedback (lines 17–26). Jezabelle practices the Synner's strategy on monsters with him. Synner teaches her the second strategy that works on a new variant type of monster, a caster who can cast magic (lines 17–20). Again, his strategy of using shield first ensures her safety (line 20). Then he directs her to drain monster's mana using "mana burn" (line 20) so that it is unable to cast additional spells (because mana is the resource required for spell casting). "Pain and mind blast" (line 20) deal substantial damage. When she is out of mana, Jezabelle is told to use a "wand" (line 20) to finish the monster. Throughout, the strategy places personal safety first, efficient use of resources (mana) second, and damage dealing an important third.

Jezabelle continues to practice the new strategy given her by Synner until she runs into a problem, having failed to cast a "silence" spell, which stops the target monster from casting briefly, and two casters attack her at once, overwhelming her current ability. Synner watches her mistake (line 22) and quickly steps in to guide her action back on track, telling her to cast a "shield" (line 23) and then "flay" (line 24). He verbally (through typed talk) guides her through the new spell sequence again, again emphasizing safety first ("shield," line 23). Then, he states, "Flay him so he can't run and get more mobs" (line 25). Synner's explanation does important work on *focusing the learner's attention* on stopping monsters from running way and coming back with more dangerous monsters, which would quickly overwhelm them both – a skill called "crowd control" within the *World of Warcraft* community. Jezabelle continues her practice by doing as he has been told, and Synner gives her feedback as a reminder of the second strategy (line 26). After Jezabelle finishes her first two spells in the right sequence, Synner reminds her that the third spell is "pain" (line 27).

The second caster runs away to bring another monster group, and Jezabelle requests clarification about whether she still should use a wand to finish off the monster as she had learned earlier (line 28). Synner directs her to use "flay" (line 29) as a new practice associated with this specific situation. Finally, he concludes the apprenticeship by telling her that using flay is "a good habit"(line 30), "especially in instances" (line 32), suggesting that one reason for getting spell rotations perfected during solo hunting is important is for use in future collaborations in which such routine practices will be expected from any competent shadow priest.

Findings

Apprenticeship as Social Interaction

Table 12.1 outlines the characteristics of apprenticeship that are common across the cases analyzed. Three features of the social interaction that mark these episodes as moments of apprenticeship are worth further exploration. First, each episode begins with the less experienced player positioning herself as the learner in the exchange, thereby positioning her interlocutor as the relative expert in the context of the practice or activity. Second, such displays are quickly followed with a presequence of some form in which the designated master in the exchange makes an overture to the self-designated learner for the subsequent speech act (i.e., apprenticeship) either implicitly (first analysis) or explicit (second and third analyses). In each case, the presequence functions as an ostensive gesture that marks the master's next set of moves as a "pedagogical manifestation" (Csibra & Gergely, 2006, p. 6). Hank (Lave & Wenger, 1991) and others argue that because legitimate peripheral participation is simply one type or a subset of social interaction, then any interaction has the potential for learning. Our data suggest, however, that, in actual practice, interactions intended to teach are marked by ostension such that the learner is able to recognize the subsequent interaction as intended to teach and orient toward the master's actions and talk as such. Third and finally, in each exchange, the master overtly and covertly signals that the practice being taught is a routine and valued practice for the larger community – in the words of Myrondonia, one that "we all" do (Figure 12.2, line 26).

Together these features can be seen as characteristic of the fact that apprenticeship is a way of engaging socially, not a structure through which

Table 12.1. *Common characteristics across the three cases analyzed*

	Analysis 1: *Lineage I*	Analysis 2: *Lineage II*	Analysis 3: *World of Warcraft*
Features of the social interaction			
Learner identity display	X	X	X
Presequence (ostensive gesture)	X	X	X
Activity as routine practice	X	X	X
Features of Apprenticeship			
Joint participation	X	X	X
Scaffolding	X	X	X
Practice and feedback	X	X	X
Modeling		X	X
Sequencing instruction	X	X	X
Orientation of learner to activity's goal	X	X	
Focusing attention	X	X	X

learning somehow happens (Lave & Wenger, 1991). As such, there is work necessary at the outset of such exchanges to establish the roles of the participants (master versus apprentice), the purpose of the exchange (intentionally pedagogical), and the nature of the topic under focus (a culturally central practice). Because online game spaces such as the virtual worlds examined here are interest-driven and voluntary, roles such as "teacher" and "learner" are situated and temporary, to be negotiated, enacted, and displayed rather than designated institutionally (as in classrooms). Players must be a learner and be a teacher and have those identities recognized and sanctioned temporarily before they can engage in joint (inter)action intended to enculturate. In this way, the fact of learning as a social accomplishment and not an institutional one becomes highly salient.

Apprenticeship into Practices

In terms of the mechanisms for learning embedded in the MMO apprenticeship practices examined herein, several patterns emerge consistently. In each case, newcomers learn the game through joint participation in genuine game play with more knowledgeable/skilled others. You not only "have to play to learn" (Turkle, 1995, p. 70), but you also have to play with others if you ever hope to develop genuine expertise. During collaboration, the focus is on the activity, with information (e.g., manuals, guidebooks, and websites) playing only a secondary and supporting role (unlike most classrooms).

From the very outset of game play, the individual engages in the virtual social and material world as a complex, ill-structured, dynamic, and evolving system, not some watered-down version of it. Scaffolding is what enables this immediate engagement. By controlling the level of responsibility for the activity that the learner is burdened with and providing support for his or her actions during their execution, the master makes accessible community practices that otherwise would be beyond the scope of what the learner ordinarily could accomplish successfully (Vygotsky, 1978).

There is early overlearning – extended practice coupled with immediate feedback from both the game system (e.g., error-produced death) and other participants (e.g., "Dude, that rocked") – and one's progress and accomplishments clearly are represented in some way, if only by a displayed increased level of experience and its concomitant increase in social status. Here, failure functions as feedback. What you do risk by failing is minimal and easily recovered (cf. the high-stakes testing practices implemented by the Bush administration under the No Child Left Behind Act), particularly in the early stages of game play, and performing at the outer edge of one's current competency, which seems to sustain engagement (cf. notion of flow, Csikszentmihalyi, 1993; zone of proximal development, Vygotsky, 1978) and to constantly pull one forward into more complex and demanding tasks, is highly valued and socially promoted (challenging yourself earns you bragging rights as "hardcore" regardless of level).

In each case, the master's own actions function as a model of the practice itself (Lave & Wenger, 1991), and in two cases, he or she overtly cognitively models (Brown, Collins, & Duguid, 1989) successful performance. In the second analysis (*Lineage II*), such modeling arose in response to the learner's inability to follow previous, more general instructions successfully. In the third analysis (*World of Warcraft*), modeling was used prior to general instructions. In both, the master's modeling provides an example for the learner of what the practice ought to look like and running commentary on what features of its performance should be attended to.

Instruction is sequenced to guide learners from simple tasks (e.g., safe navigation) to variants or more complicated tasks (e.g., efficient resource collection). And in two of the three cases examined, at some point in the interaction the master overtly orients the learner to the activity's goal, making explicit the "why" behind the "what." And in each episode examined, the master overtly directs the learner's attention to the aspects of the practice that are most crucial to its success – through talk, sculpting, and shaping aspects of the phenomenal environment into cultural objects and practices that represent their own expert worldview. Thus, through such seemingly mundane moves in the social interaction that focus and shape the learner's attention, the master comes to draw the apprentice into not only the professional practices of the master but what Goodwin (1994) calls her professional vision as well – her "socially organized ways of seeing and understanding events that are answerable to the distinctive interests of [their] particular social group" (Goodwin, 1994, p. 606).

Apprenticeship into Values

Thus apprenticeship is indeed enculturation in its richest sense: The master inculcates the learner not only with a set of practices but also with a particular set of values or dispositions that hang together as an underlying "cultural model" of the Discourse, one that allows speakers and hearers to display and recognize one another as members – as "people like us." The specific values at play in each case are highlighted in italics in Figures 12.2, 12.3, and 12.4.

In the first analysis, procedural dexterity and efficient collection of virtual material goods (i.e., mithril) are prized not in and of themselves but as components of a much broader cultural value: efficiency. In fact, the *Lineage* community so values efficiency that players have been known to use stop watches to calculate subtle differences in rates of leveling across different virtual areas in the game in order to best maximize their productivity. The notion of meritocracy also plays a vital role in the exchange. What should an elf do if he or she runs into another elf during a mithril hunt? The first elf should go a different way. Why? Because the elves in that particular area safely can all be presumed to be there for the same thing: mithril. By avoiding the same areas, one can display oneself as "people like us" (like Myrondonia), the courteous kind that shares hunting territories (and, yes, the kind that help mentor newcomers in elven cultural practices as well).

In the second analysis, the role of tank in the group is the focus of attention but only synecdochically as a stand-in for the group as a whole. Because of *Lineage II* combat mechanics, the tank's safety functions to ensure the group's safety in such a way that near-exclusive focus on one player over all others (including oneself and one's own resources) is, in practice, the highest form of benevolence. Good healers, Zena demonstrates, are indefatigable in their continued assurance of the group's safety through near-obsessive concentration on the single simple variable of "tank HP."

Finally, in the third analysis, the predominant value at play is the solo development of skills for future collaboration. Personal safety, resource efficiency (i.e., mana), and strategies for crowd control all are emphasized as the requisite "good habits" (Synner, line 30) for future instances (Synner, line 32). Again, there is an emphasis on collaborative prowess, but here, in contrast to the *Lineage II* context, it is future-imagined groups (in instances), not present configurations. Here, the game design, which first foregrounds copious amounts of individual quest "grinding" and only later evolves into more consistent collaborative and large-group "end-game" play, is reflected in the cultural practices and values that develop and are passed down subsequently.

Table 12.2 shows Gee's (1996) six building tasks of language and the situated meanings at play in each of the episodes analyzed. Across all three analyses, we see an overt emphasis on the game as a space for social collaboration, on the functional roles one plays in the context of small group work (e.g., healers, tanks), and an overt cultivation of individual expertise in the service of those collaborative endeavors, immediate or imagined. In each game examined, different character classes functionally complement one another, creating an environment in which group success and individual success are reciprocal. On the one hand, an individual player cannot progress through advanced game content successfully without some form of collaborative problem solving. On the other hand, groups cannot do their joint work successfully without at least most of the functional roles represented – and filled by individuals who know how to perform those roles with expertise. The resulting space is one in which the emergent culture of learning that characterizes the technology as designed is not merely the happy by-product of a particularly benevolent assortment of individual gamers but rather an absolute necessity to successful advanced play. Because I cannot get through advanced game content without the help of others who can do their jobs well, apprenticeship becomes, in a way, simply a more collective form of "leveling up."

Conclusions

Video gaming (let alone MMO gaming) is a somewhat nascent topic in educational research, yet the broader topic of online virtual communities has a long history. A quick perusal of educational journals and conference proceedings over the past several years indicates a widespread interest in online communities and virtual worlds within the field of educational research. Indeed, online technologies provide new opportunities

Table 12.2. *The six building tasks of language (Gee, 1999) and the meanings at play in each case*

	Analysis 1: *Lineage I*	Analysis 2: *Lineage II*	Analysis 3: *World of Warcraft*
Semiotics	Cursor movement and interaction with monsters, in-game icons	Digital representations of characteristics of group members	Monster group configurations mapped to hot-key sequences (spell rotations)
Material world	Orcs versus zombies, mithril, Elven Dungeon, others players	Hit points, mana points	Monster locations and movement
Sociocultural reality	Character class, master versus learner, unknown others who have equal right to resources	Character class, master versus learner, functional group roles	Character class, master versus learner, imagined future collaborators
Activities	Hunting a resource for solo crafting	Healing in a group	Solo hunting
Politics	All have an equal right to hunt mithril for their own crafting	Resources (MP, HP) go to tank first, group function is to enable his work	Cultural capital in the form of spell rotations to be leveraged in future group work
Coherence	Present dyad works in the service of future solo work	Present group works in the service of future group work	Present solo works in the service of future group work

for "anytime/anywhere" social interaction, and the number of innovative curricular designs that incorporate online collaborative environments has been increasing steadily since such technology first emerged. Innovative initiatives such as the Games+Learning+Society Group at University of Wisconsin–Madison (Squire, 2007), the Games-to-Teach Project at MIT (Jenkins, Squire, & Tan 2003; Squire, 2003), and Indiana University's Quest Atlantis (Barab et al., 2005) are already investigating how we might leverage gaming technologies toward educational ends.

Yet, as Lave and Wenger (1991) argue, understanding the shape of learning in naturally occurring contexts and not just formal ones (e.g., classrooms) is crucial if we are to forward educational theory and practice beyond the contexts we ourselves contrive. Before designing virtual learning environments that might capitalize on MMOs' capacity for "retribalizing" (McLuhan, "Playboy Interview," 1969) people across time and place, we ought to investigate more naturally occurring, self-sustaining, indigenous virtual cultures so that our theory might be a more accurate reflection of them and our practice a better reflection on them in the days to come. The analyses presented here illustrate the kinds of learning built into MMO game play not as designed object (a simulated world) but rather as a social practice. Discourses such as those constituting MMOs are not mastered through overt instruction but rather through apprenticeship (Gee, 1999; Lave & Wenger, 1991; Tharp & Gallimore, 1998). Gamers who have already mastered the social and material practices requisite to game-play enculturate, through scaffolded and supported interactions, newer gamers who lack such knowledge and skill. And it is precisely these forms of knowledge and practice that, we argue, most shape the intellectual impact of a technology regardless of how invisible they remain in our own conversations about educational technology design.

Serious commendations are due to the educational technology designers who are leveraging gaming technologies toward educational ends. By far, video games are one of the most important entertainment media in the lives of the millennial generation (i.e., those who have grown up on the PlayStation rather than Atari 2600). However, two caveats are needed. First, we need to better understand what contemporary informal online learning environments do well and do miserably if we want to leverage those features which are productive and eschew those which are not. Designing in the dark is neither efficient nor advantageous. We know that kids are thoroughly engaged by MMOs, and some of us are fairly convinced that what they do there is far from cognitively trivial. However, without the kind of basic ethnographic work conducted here, it will remain difficult to tease out what practices, understandings, and identities MMOs recruit from those who play and whether or not they are portable, plausible, or productive. Second, this research suggests that the mechanisms for learning entailed in game play in virtual cultures/worlds are contingent on the game not only as a designed object but also as a social practice. The moral of this story is a long-familiar one for learning science researchers: Designing learning environments is not merely a matter of getting the curricular material right but is crucially also a matter of getting the situated, emergent community structures and practices right. In this case, unless we are designing appropriate social structures to accompany such technological systems (a feat that may very well not always be possible, given their situated and emergent nature), we cannot easily leverage the learning mechanisms within MMOs for play in creating MMOs for instruction.

Still, an understanding of the cultural/cognitive structures at play in online worlds one day may improve our understanding of those which emerge in life beyond them. Discursive analyses such as those presented herein can and should inform our theoretical understanding of sociocultural forms of learning by foregrounding their perspectival, ideological, and value-laden aspects as (hopefully) demonstrated here. If learning is an evolving form of membership (Lave & Wenger, 1991), then teaching ultimately is a political act. Is it easy, in our studies of learning from a learning sciences perspective, to forget that education is always ideological (Apple, 2004). Analyses that unpack how social interaction functions to calibrate one another toward one cultural model over another – to foster "intersubjectivities" (Tomasello, 1999) that are more or less representative of some folks' subjectivity than others – can enable us to better understand this fundamental cognitive link between self and society, between the machinations of "culture" and the mundanities of everyday life. MMOs are powerful spaces to examine this interaction between the macro and the micro because, in virtual worlds, the shared d/Discourses and joint practices that connect them are rendered visible, portable, and therefore up for interrogation.

References

Apple, M. (2004). *Ideology and curriculum*, 25th ann. 3rd ed. New York: Routledge.

Barab, S., Thomas, M., Dodge, T., Carteaux, R., & Tuzun, H. (2005). Making Learning Fun: *Quest Atlantis*, a Game Without Guns. *Educational Technology Research & Development*, 53(1), 86–107.

Brown, J. S., Collins, A., & Duguid, P. (1989). Situated Cognition and the Culture of Meaning. *Educational Researcher*, 18(1), 32–42.

Collins, A., Brown, J. S., & Holum, A. (1991). Cognitive Apprenticeship: Making Thinking Visible. *American Educator*, 6(11), 38–46.

Csibra, G., & Gergely, G. (2006). Social Learning and Social Cognition: The Case for Pedagogy. In Y. Munakata & M. H. Johnson (eds.), *Processes of change in brain and cognitive development: Attention and performance*, vol. 21 (pp. 249–74). Oxford, England: Oxford University Press.

Csikszentmihalyi, M. (1993). *Flow: The psychology of optimal experience*. New York: Harper Perennial.

Engestrom, Y., Miettinen, R., & Punamaki, R.-L. (1999). *Perspectives on activity theory*. Cambridge, England: Cambridge University Press.

Fairclough N. (1995). *Critical discourse analysis*. London: Longman.

Frith, U., & Frith, C. (2010). The Social Brain: Allowing Humans to Boldly Go Where No Other Species Has Been. *Philosophical Transactions of the Royal Society*, 365, 165–175.

Garfinkel, H. (1967). *Studies in ethnomethodology*. Englewood Cliffs, NJ: Prentice-Hall.

Gee, J. P. (1996). *Social linguistics and literacies: Ideology in discourses*, 2nd ed. London: Taylor & Francis.

(1999). *An introduction to discourse analysis: Theory and method*. New York: Routledge.

(2003/2007). *What videogames have to teach us about learning and literacy*. New York: Palgrave Macmillan.

Geertz, C. (1973). *The interpretation of cultures*. New York: Basic Books.

Gibson, J. J. (1986). *The ecological approach to visual perception*. Hillsdale, NJ: Erlbaum. (Original work published 1979.)

Goodwin, C (1994). Professional Vision. *American Anthropologist*, 96(3), 606–33.

Greeno, J. G. (1997). On Claims That Answer the Wrong Questions. *Educational Researcher*, 26(1), 5–17.

Greeno, J. G., & Moore, J. L. (1993). Situativity and Symbols: Response to Vera and Simon. *Cognitive Science*, 17, 49–59.

Gumperz, J. J. (ed.) (1982). *Language and social identity*. Cambridge, England: Cambridge University Press.

Hacking, I. (1986). Making Up People. In T. C. Heller, M. Sosna, & D. E. Wellbery (eds.), *Reconstructing individualism*, (pp. 222–36). Stanford, CA: Stanford University Press.

Halliday, M. A. K. (1978). *Language as a social semiotic*. London: Edward Arnold.

Hammersley, M., & Atkinson, P. (1986). *Ethnography: Principles in practice*, vol. 2. London: Routledge.

Hutchins, E. (1995). *Cognition in the wild*. Cambridge MA: MIT Press.

Jenkins, H., Squire, K., & Tan, P. (2003). You Can't Bring That Game to School! Designing Supercharged! In B. Laurel (ed.), *Design research: Methods and perspectives* (pp. 244–252). Cambridge, MA: MIT Press.

Kolbert, E. (2001). Pimps and Dragons. *The New Yorker*, May 28, 2001.

Kress, G. (1985). *Linguistic processes in sociocultural practice*. Oxford, England: Oxford University Press.

Lave, J. (1988). *Cognition in practice*. Cambridge, England: Cambridge University Press.

Lave, J., & Wenger, E. (1991). *Situated learning: Legitimate peripheral participation.* Cambridge, England: Cambridge University Press.

Levinson, S. C. (1983). *Pragmatics.* Cambridge, England: Cambridge University Press.

McCracken, G. D. (1988). *The long interview: Qualitative research methods,* series 13. Newbury Park, CA: Sage.

McLuhan, Marshall, Playboy Interview (1969, March). *Playboy Magazine.*

Packer, M. J., & Goicoechea, J. (2000). Sociocultural and Constructivist Theories of Learning: Ontology, Not Just Epistemology. *Educational Psychologist,* 35(4), 227–41.

Senju, A. & Csibra, G. (2008). Gaze following in human infants depends on communicative signals. *Current Biology,* 18, 668–71.

Sperber, D. & D. Wilson (1986) *Relevance: Communication and Cognition.* Oxford: Blackwell.

Squire, K. D. (2003). Video Games in Education. *International Journal of Intelligent Simulations and Gaming,* 2(1), 49–62.

(2007). Games, Learning, and Society: Building a Field. *Educational Technology,* 4(5), 51–4.

Steinkuehler, C. A. (2004). Learning in Massively Multiplayer Online Games. In Y. B. Kafai, W. A. Sandoval, N. Enyedy, A. S. Nixon, & F. Herrera (eds.), *Proceedings of the Sixth International Conference of the Learning Sciences* (pp. 521–8). Mahwah, NJ: Erlbaum.

(2006). The Mangle of Play. *Games & Culture,* 1(3), 1–14.

Street, B. (1984). *Literacy in theory and practice.* Cambridge, England: Cambridge University Press.

Tharp, R. G. & Gallimore, R. (1991). The Instructional Conversation: Teaching and Learning in Social Activity. Research Report #2, National Center for Research on Diversity and Second Language Learning. Santa Cruz, CA: University of California.

(1998). *Rousing minds to life.* Cambridge, England: Cambridge University Press.

Tomasello, M. (1999). *The cultural origins of human cognition.* Cambridge MA: Harvard University Press.

Turkle, S. (1995). *Life on the screen: Identity in the age of the Internet.* New York: Touchstone.

Vera, A. H., & Simon, H. A. (1993). Situated Action: A Symbolic Interpretation. *Cognitive Science,* 17, 7–48.

Vygotsky L. S. (1978). *Mind in society.* Cambridge MA: Harvard University Press.

Wenger, E. (1999). *Communities of practice: Learning, meaning, and identity.* New York: Cambridge University Press.

Wertsch, J. V. (1998). *Mind as action.* New York: Oxford University Press.

Woodcock, B. S. (2010). *An analysis of MMOG subscription growth 23.0.* Retrieved March 15, 2010 from http://www.mmogchart.com.

13 Theorycrafting: The Art and Science of Using Numbers to Interpret the World

Trina Choontanom and Bonnie Nardi

Encountering the Big Bad Wolf

A *World of Warcraft* player sits at her desk, mouse rapidly moving back and forth as the camera angle on the monitor changes to give her a better view of her surroundings and teammates. Her other hand is steadily tapping away at the keyboard, selecting teammates and in most cases giving them a much-needed heal or protection bubble. One of her other teammates, in another room across the country, is watching numbers fly by, making sure that she is applying the correct rotation of skills as well as watching her position – is she still behind the boss, or did the tank just shift him? Does she need to reapply that damage over time because the timer ran out, or can she use a finishing skill to rebuff her attack-speed increase? The boss encounter runs for roughly only five minutes, and the team is successful. While distributing the loot, one of the raid leaders posts the results of the boss fight in the form of a damage meter and a healing meter (Figure 13.1).

In this scenario, *World of Warcraft* players are "raiding"; that is, they are engaged in a tightly coordinated activity of between ten and forty people in which they collaborate to slay fantasy monsters. In their desire to play as effectively as possible – to defeat the monsters and to perform well in front of their peers – raiders engage *theorycraft*, that is, analysis of game mechanics. Game mechanics specify the rules that produce game outcomes. Paul (2009) describes theorycrafting as a metagame, a "game outside the game." Games such as *World of Warcraft* are complex, and players cannot discover everything they want to know simply by playing. Some players, then, undertake mathematical and logical analyses to interrogate the game more deeply. They share their analyses with other players on forums and blogs.

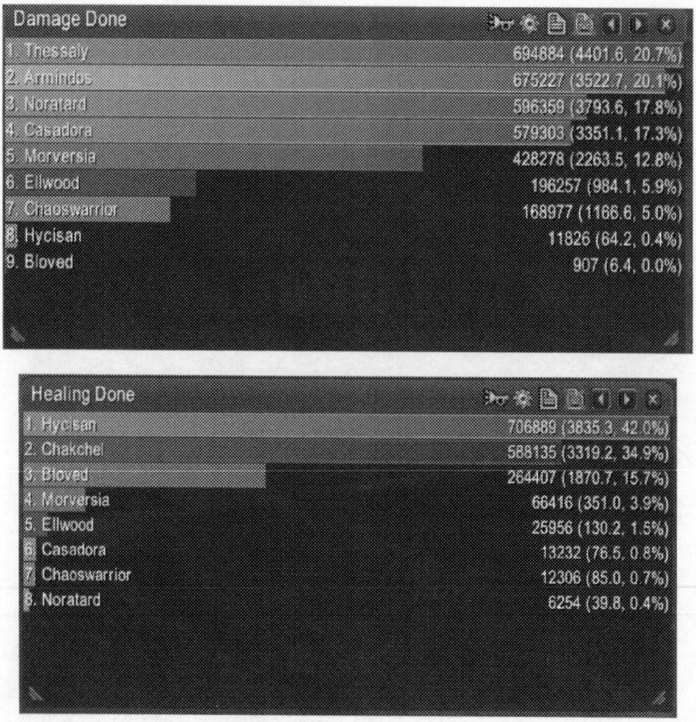

Damage Done	
1. Thessaly	694884 (4401.6, 20.7%)
2. Armindos	675227 (3522.7, 20.1%)
3. Noratard	596359 (3793.6, 17.8%)
4. Casadora	579303 (3351.1, 17.3%)
5. Morversia	428278 (2263.5, 12.8%)
6. Ellwood	196257 (984.1, 5.9%)
7. Chaoswarrior	168977 (1166.6, 5.0%)
8. Hycisan	11826 (64.2, 0.4%)
9. Bloved	907 (6.4, 0.0%)

Healing Done	
1. Hycisan	706889 (3835.3, 42.0%)
2. Chakchel	588135 (3319.2, 34.9%)
3. Bloved	264407 (1870.7, 15.7%)
4. Morversia	66416 (351.0, 3.9%)
5. Ellwood	25956 (130.2, 1.5%)
6. Casadora	13232 (76.5, 0.8%)
7. Chaoswarrior	12306 (85.0, 0.7%)
8. Noratard	6254 (39.8, 0.4%)

Figure 13.1. Damage and healing meters.

Paul (2009) reported typical player definitions of theorycraft:

> ...to hyperanalyze, mathematically, game mechanics and abilities to gain a deeper understanding and to ultimately maximize effectiveness. using math to guide your choices, instead of simply playing from your gut.

Our definition of theorycraft is the art and science of investigating game mechanics that cannot be discovered through ordinary play. With experimentation and logic, players analyze, discuss, argue about, interpret, and theorize game mechanics.

In this chapter we examine theorycrafting in *World of Warcraft*. The aim of the chapter is to explain theorycrafting as a complex social and cognitive activity derived from video games and to suggest that theorycrafting may produce or hone skills useful in educational settings and the workplace. While we do not think it necessary to justify leisure activities by claiming that they have functions beyond leisure, we cannot help but be struck by the correspondence of theorycrafting activity to authentic educational and workplace activities. We want to expose and explore potential connections.

The term *theorycraft* appears to have originated with *Starcraft*, a real-time strategy game. *Starcraft* players engaged in theoretical discussions about optimal methods of play (Paul, 2009). But players still debate the term's origins. The term *craft* is attributed to either *Starcraft* or the game *Warcraft* (of which *World of Warcraft* is a derivative). It is possible that theorycrafting activities existed even before *Starcraft* but have not been documented. Use of the term has since expanded to other games and genres, such as *Dragon Age: Origins*, a single-player role-playing game.

The allure of theorycrafting lies in digging into complex game mechanics. Theorycrafting is a rich, compelling intellectual activity involving hypothesis generation, testing, numerical analysis, logical argumentation, rhetoric, and writing. It is collaborative; theorycrafters work together to gather and analyze data and post their results in public forums to inform theorycrafters and ordinary gamers of their findings – and sometimes to engage in heated debates. Theorycrafting involves analysis of class mechanics, deploying mathematical formulas to calculate theoretical maximums, such as the maximum amount of healing or damage possible under certain conditions. Owing to the constant and changing nature of the game through software updates and expansions, theorycrafters also anticipate upcoming changes, try out projected changes on test servers, and report on their expectations of official releases. Theorycrafting analyses occur outside the game in forums and blogs, permitting players time to write, read, and reflect on posts that are often lengthy, detailed, and deeply reflective.

Theorycrafting can be interesting only if game mechanics produce enough complexity to stimulate theorizing and analysis. The complexity of games such as *World of Warcraft* (or *WoW*, as it is known) issues partly from the game's design, which organizes players to take on different, complementary roles through character types with varying abilities. It is necessary to take a moment to discuss these variable character types that we refer to throughout this chapter as we investigate theorycrafting. We will discuss these character types in the context of raiding activity, but they are relevant to other game activities as well.

WoW character types are healing, damage, and tanking. Each type is divided into "classes." Healers restore raid members as they take damage from monsters. Damage classes attack the monster. Tanks control the monsters and take as much of the damage as they can, being protected by heavy armor. Each player chooses a character class and controls the character, which accumulates equipment (armor and weapons) that adds to its

Damage Done	🔧 ⚙ 📄 📄 ◀ ▶ ✕
1. Thuringwethl	12674 (238.1, 33.5%)
2. Fluithuin	9527 (342.7, 25.2%)
3. Gothmog	8537 (261.7, 22.6%)
4. Carcaroth	5479 (170.4, 14.5%)
5. Gorthaur	1623 (117.8, 4.3%)

Figure 13.2. Thuringwethl, a rogue, and Fluithuin, a mage, are the primary damage dealers in this encounter. Gothmog, a tank, also contributes considerable damage. Carcaroth, a hunter, is undergeared and is underperforming. Gorthaur, a priest, contributes little damage because he is a healer.

powers. *Stats* are quantified attributes associated with equipment. Players are always aiming to upgrade their equipment with more powerful stats. New equipment is won as players advance in the game.

The premier theorycrafting website is elitistjerks.com. Elitist Jerks (named after the guild that started the forum) covers theorycrafting for all classes. Other forums are devoted to specific functions in the game, such as the Plusheal.com forum for healers. Blogs by individual players, such as One Rogue's Journey, also provide theorycrafting analyses.

Theorycrafters employ *mods*, that is, player-written software modifications that customize the game (Taylor, 2008; Wine, 2008; Kow & Nardi, 2009; Paul, 2009; Nardi, 2010). Mods are written by players, posted on websites, and made available for free download. Damage and healing meters, such as the in-game mod recount or the out-of-game, Java-based tool Wow Web Stats, are popular mods that can be used to indicate how well a player is doing. These mods process data from the game that are made accessible by Blizzard Entertainment, producer of the game.

The primary data used by the damage and healing meters are quantities resulting from spells cast or weapons wielded. The term *meters* is used loosely; a mod such as Recount measures both damage and healing – each reported in its own window. A *damage meter* thus is the window showing damage, and a *healing meter* is a window showing healing. Figure 13.2 shows Recount's calculation of damage done by each player in a party of five players:

In the following discussion we analyze posts from theorycrafting forums and blogs. All quotations are from posts made in 2009. The site is identified for each post, and each can be found in its entirety through a Google search. We then discuss how theorycrafting is potentially a way to gain or sharpen skills useful in the classroom and workplace.

Theorycrafting for Rogues

A rogue's sole purpose is to deal damage. Damage is measured by a unit called *damage-per-second* (DPS). Having a common unit of measure allows comparison among all the different damage classes to better evaluate performance. Damage is also measured as an absolute quantity, *damage done*, as in Figure 13.2, which shows the actual damage done in a five-person encounter.

Players engage in theorycrafting to assess their current level of play and determine the next steps for improvement in terms of gaining new equipment. They use tools such as spreadsheets and game modifications to estimate and measure DPS (see Paul, 2009). Owing to the changing nature of the game, these tools require constant attention, modification, and updates.

Players have formed online communities to collaborate in theorycrafting, including checking and posting to the community any inconsistencies or inaccuracies found in player-created tools such as Recount, as well as spreadsheets that model game mechanics. It is important to players that these tools be accurate. General discussion about spreadsheets, their uses and validity, is also found on the forums. Some of these discussions are very theoretical, analyzing what spreadsheets can and cannot do and how they articulate with *WoW* game mechanics.

Rogues have a subcommunity on the Elitist Jerks forum, where discussion is centered on the rogue class and how to maximize DPS for rogues. Players also may keep blogs to discuss their personal tactics and observations. Zaltu, a rogue, writes One Rogue's Journey. He discusses formulas that he uses for performing calculations by hand as well as his use of spreadsheets.

Spreadsheet Metagame

Conventional spreadsheet programs such as Microsoft Excel are used to analyze rogue DPS. Instead of collaborating on defeating a computer-controlled opponent, as players do in-game, theorycrafters collaborate to discover the mathematical formulas underlying game mechanics. Spreadsheets apply these formulas to calculate theoretical values. These theoretical values are ballpark estimates, or benchmarks, that players can compare with actual values found in-game.

What, specifically, do rogues do with spreadsheets? Rogues are most interested in maximizing DPS. DPS is determined by values associated with game components, including armor, weapons, and gear bonuses. The question before the rogue is, "Which combination will yield the

5		Current	
6	Helm:	Hood of Lethal Intent	▾
7	Enchant	Arcanum of Torment	
8	Meta Gem	Relentless Earthsiege Diamond	
9	Gems	Deadly Ametrine (10 Agi/10 Crit)	
10	Gems		
11	Gems		
12	Necklace	Charge of the Demon Lord (Heroic)	

5		Current	
6	Helm:	Hood of Lethal Intent	▾
7	Enchant	VanCleef's Helmet of Triumph (Heroic)	▲
8	Meta Gem	Bloodfang Hood	
9	Gems	Hood of Lethal Intent	
9	Gems	VanCleef's Helmet of Triumph	
10	Gems	VanCleef's Helmet of Conquest	
11	Gems	Conqueror's Terrorblade Helmet	
12	Necklace	Mimiron's Flight Goggles	
		Bloodfang Mask	▾

Figure 13.3. A section of a rogue spreadsheet that allows players to select their input for a headpiece.

highest DPS?" Spreadsheets calculate "theoretical" DPS, which players can compare with "actual" DPS, that is, DPS observed during game play. Actual DPS is reported in player-created tools such as Recount (shown in Figure 13.1). Theoretical DPS, calculated in theorycrafting analyses, establishes a benchmark. Players compare their actual DPS with their theoretical DPS to determine if they are performing well. Individual players compare themselves with one another, easily done by consulting tools such as Recount with their clear graphics. Players also analyze group performance. Is the general level of DPS produced by the group what is expected? Is it enough for the level of challenge of the encounter they are attempting?

Spreadsheets require user input. Input is often presented as short lists of options in the form of armor, weapons, and bonuses. Each item has its stats associated with it, that is, numerical quantities that determine the power of a class. In the case of rogues, *agility* and *attack power* are the most desirable stats. A sample set of options for a headpiece (an item of armor) is presented in Figure 13.3. The left half displays "Hood of Lethal Intent" selected with the indicated bonuses (gems) associated with the headpiece. The right half displays the set of options from which players can choose.

Figure 13.4 displays the set of alternative options in more detail, including the type of gear (helm). The "Base Score" column is in relation to other types of gear (e.g., chestpiece, legpiece) and provides a numerical comparison among options within the set; an item with a higher score tends to be more desirable.

A first-time use of a spreadsheet will require a player to match the options with what the player's character has equipped. From this point, the player knows how much theoretical damage he or she is capable of dealing. as shown in Figure 13.5.

The player can determine upgrades, that is, pieces of gear that will increase his or her DPS. When faced with multiple sets of choices, players can determine the most optimal combination through use of the spreadsheet.

Name	Type	Rank	Equipped	Base Score
VanCleef's Helmet of Triumph (Heroic)	Helm	Helm 1	0	1042.434
Bloodfang Hood	Helm	Helm 2	0	968.3842
Hood of Lethal Intent	Helm	Helm 11	1	906.4137
VanCleef's Helmet of Triumph	Helm	Helm 3	0	940.1124
VanCleef's Helmet of Conquest	Helm	Helm 5	0	850.1788
Conqueror's Terrorblade Helmet	Helm	Helm 6	0	832.9348
Mimiron's Flight Goggles	Helm	Helm 7	0	827.6415
Bloodfang Mask	Helm	Helm 4	0	876.9221
Guise of the Midgard Serpent	Helm	Helm 9	0	804.7361
Garona's Guise	Helm	Helm 8	0	815.9734
Valorous Terrorblade Helmet	Helm	Helm 10	0	787.41

Figure 13.4. A section of a rogue spreadsheet that provides additional attributes to each headpiece.

Estimated DPS: 8657.5
Offhand Poison: Deadly
Cycle: Eviscerate Only

Figure 13.5. A section of a rogue spreadsheet that displays estimated DPS given a specific set of values.

Player comments indicate the importance of these theorycrafting tools. On the Elitist Jerks forum, a rogue named Perini observed, "When in doubt, use a spreadsheet" (Perini 2009). Zaltu also advocates use of spreadsheets, remarking, "Often times a spreadsheet is your best answer to these and many other DPS questions" (Zaltu 2009), even though he also posts about the use of hand calculations.

Players' dependence on spreadsheets means that the spreadsheets must be as accurate as possible. Players report inaccuracies to the forums. For example, on the Elitist Jerks rogue forum, a poster named Byrt observed

> If I change nothing to the default spreadsheet available, except change the GoSS [Glyph of Sinister Strike] for GoSnD [Glyph of Slice and Dice] I get #VALUE errors [Byrt, 2009].

Without worrying about the details of this example, the error generated by Byrt's change raised a concern about the spreadsheet. His result when attempting to change a bonus (the glyph) indicated that something in the spreadsheet went wrong. Byrt brought this issue to the community seeking an answer:

Another poster named Wytryszek built upon this issue, asking

> *"If the spreadsheet calculations are wrong, how are we going to know how good the glyph really is?"* [Wytryszek, 2009].

As Wytryszek brings up in his question, if the calculations are wrong, he cannot evaluate the worth of a bonus successfully. Bryt's example illustrates that spreadsheets are not perfect. The close interactions players have with them provide experience – and healthy skepticism – about the use of quantitative tools. Although players may not fully understand all the calculations for which the spreadsheet is responsible, they go online to post their concerns, encouraging community collaboration and discussion.

Reliance on spreadsheets sometimes may cause players to forget about certain game mechanics they should be aware of. One such mechanic is a *cap* on a particular stat. After the player accumulates enough of a stat by equipping items, adding to the stat does not improve play. Players must keep in mind basic game mechanics – the big picture – along with what the spreadsheet indicates.

For example, Fae was trying out different headpieces in the spreadsheet. After switching a headpiece on the spreadsheet, he is returned a result that he does not expect. He generates a hypothesis about the discrepancy: If the conditions for an existing armor bonus are broken, a decrease in DPS will be observed. He tests his initial hypothesis by switching another piece of gear. The result of the second test invalidates his hypothesis. He does not understand the results. He posts his results and observations to the theorycrafting community:

> When I try to switch my headpiece for T9.25 (iLvl 245) I see ~100 dps decrease. Thats right, because of breaking T8 4-set bonus I guess. But when I try the same with gloves/chestpiece/legpiece my dps actually increases by ~40. I do not understand why there is such a difference in behaviour [Fae, 2009].

Fae observed different behavior when using the spreadsheet to switch a headpiece versus a handpiece. His original hypothesis is that when he switches a headpiece, he is breaking the requirements for a bonus, causing the decrease in DPS. However, in a subsequent test, when he switches a handpiece, which also breaks the requirements for the same bonus and is seen as an equivalent upgrade as the headpiece, he observes an increase in DPS. He tests a chestpiece and legpiece as well with the same result, invalidating his original hypothesis. Another poster replies with this explanation:

> You are over expertise cap already. Switching your helm is giving you an even bigger boost in expertise, something that is clearly wasted in your current

gear. That is why you are seeing the disparities between swapping…pieces [Nonmagical, 2009].

In this example, Fae had already attained the maximum expertise cap value, resulting in diminishing returns because the new headpiece adds more expertise than what he needs.

This example illustrates the need to learn how to use spreadsheets and understand what spreadsheets can and cannot do and what they model and do not model. Spreadsheets can calculate DPS, but they are not a complete model of game mechanics. Spreadsheets do not tell the reason for a DPS increase or decrease. This is left to the users to determine based on wider knowledge of game mechanics.

Napkin Math

Players use a set of basic formulas to determine different aspects of their DPS. These formulas have been developed by the collaborative effort of theorycrafters. The formulas are known and used by theorycrafters to perform paper calculations or what they call "napkin math." An important formula for rogues is the relationship between three stats: agility (agi), attack power (AP), and critical strike rating (crit).

In the following example, Zaltu sets up a word problem. He wants to determine whether or not to meet the requirements for an extra bonus on a chestpiece he obtained, as shown in Figure 13.6.

Gems add bonuses when added to armor with *sockets* that allow the gems to be affixed. (Players cannot boost their stats by adding as many gems as they want to.) Armor pieces with sockets have an additional bonus that can be activated if a specific color combination of gems matches the requirements (Figure 13.6). The requirements for the chestpiece are one blue gem (+10 agility, +10 critical strike rating) and one yellow gem (+10 agility, +15 stamina, although the stamina bonus is ignored because it does not contribute to DPS). If a player follows the requirements, he or she gets an additional bonus of +12 attack power. Zaltu's other option is to ignore the extra bonus and instead use two red gems (+20 agility each for a total of +40 agility). Which would be more advantageous?

To quantify this word problem, Zaltu presents the following comparison on his blog:

+20 agi versus +10 crit rating and +12 AP

The problem with this initial comparison is that the units are not the same, that is, agility versus critical rating + AP. So Zaltu uses a unit

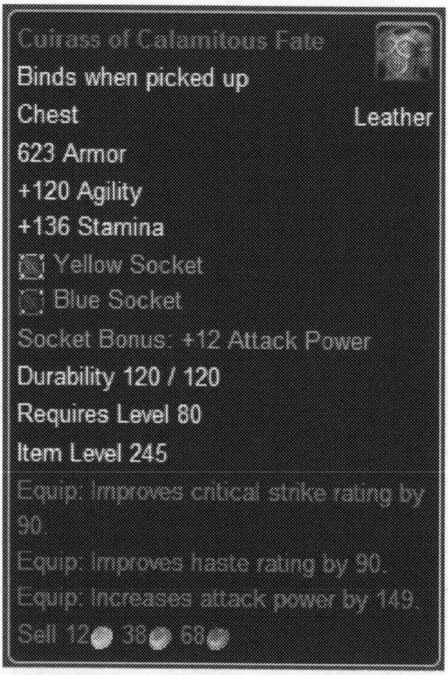

Cuirass of Calamitous Fate
Binds when picked up
Chest   Leather
623 Armor
+120 Agility
+136 Stamina
▢ Yellow Socket
▢ Blue Socket
Socket Bonus: +12 Attack Power
Durability 120 / 120
Requires Level 80
Item Level 245
Equip: Improves critical strike rating by 90.
Equip: Improves haste rating by 90.
Equip: Increases attack power by 149.
Sell 12● 38● 68●

Figure 13.6. A chestpiece with an extra bonus if the color-matching requirements are met. World of Warcraft © 2004 Blizzard Entertainment, Inc. All rights reserved. World of Warcraft, Warcraft and Blizzard Entertainment are trademarks or registered trademarks of Blizzard Entertainment, Inc., in the United States and/or other countries.

conversion to make the comparison easier. He describes his conversion as follows:

83.33 Agi ≈ 1% Crit Chance
45.91 Crit Rating ≈ 1% Crit Chance

Therefore,

20 Agi ≈ 0.24% Crit Chance
10 crit rating ≈ 0.21% Crit Chance

The quick and dirty math:

$83.33x = 1$
$x = 1/83.33$ $x = 0.012$

$20x = y$
$20(0.012) = y$ $y = 0.24$

Zaltu uses a combination of ratios and basic algebra to convert agility into critical strike rating.

Another aspect of agility is the one-to-one ratio with attack power, which Zaltu did not cover in the conversion. The concluding statement of his work is

With that known, the abstract question of which is better

+20 Agi versus +10 Crit Rating and +12 AP

is actually which is better

+20 AP and 0.24% Crit Chance versus +12 AP and 0.21% Crit change

The latter comparison makes it much easier to see the differences. It is now known, by unit conversion, that it is better to use two red gems (+40 agility) and ignore the additional bonus.

This calculation was done without a spreadsheet, just using a couple of basic formulas. Zaltu (2009) notes that spreadsheets are a player's best answer to solving this and other gear-related problems. However, just as students are taught basic arithmetic and are drilled repeatedly before being allowed to use a calculator for more advanced arithmetic, it may be desirable for players to learn how they can perform these calculations on their own to better understand how a spreadsheet works and to confront the underlying logic of unit conversions and problem formulation before worrying about the mechanics of spreadsheets.

Zaltu set up a word problem that is very similar to what students may encounter in the classroom. Students are taught to extract the relevant pieces of information from a word problem, which Zaltu does when he presents his initial comparison. Students are then expected to formulate the pieces of information to come up with the answer. Zaltu demonstrates this process by performing unit conversions and shows his work so that others can duplicate the process.

Theorycrafting for Priests

Priests are healers. Their purpose is to restore the health of other players when they are being attacked by monsters. Measuring healing is less straightforward than measuring damage. Theorycrafting priests use logic as well as numbers to define and assess their healing. While priests employ mods such as Recount to measure healing, a healer's worth ultimately depends on whether players live or die. Priests are motivated to produce high numbers on the meters, but no matter how high their numbers, if the raid "wipes" (i.e., everyone dies), it doesn't matter. Many priests argue for a simple nominal metric for healing: dead or alive.

A poster on the official *World of Warcraft* healing forum stated:

> Healer meters say nothing if you just look at who's on top. As long as everyone's alive ;-)

A priest on the Elitist Jerks site posted:

> If people aren't dying, then your healers are doing fine.

On the Plusheal.com forum, a poster wrote:

> The only effective means of measuring healing is to check weather the group is still alive.

Despite this solid logic, meters are a part of the game that players have embraced, and priests must deal with them (see Taylor, 2008; Wine, 2008; Nardi, 2010). Nearly all raiders watch meters, and raid leaders evaluate performance based on meters. But interpretation of the numbers produced by meters is complex. Priests must understand how to read the meters to improve their own performance. And they must explain the meaning of the meters to raid leaders and other raid members, who, if they play a different class, may not understand how to interpret healing numbers.

In the following discussion, we examine strategies priests have devised for interpreting meters, their understandings of the mechanics of the meters themselves, and ways priests educate nonpriests about how to interpret the numbers meters generate. We believe that the sophisticated understandings of tool mechanics and numeric interpretation priests develop have potential pedagogical value for teaching science. Measurement is a critical aspect of scientific practice, and the connection between reality and what is measured is subtle, just as it is in priestly theorycrafting. The need to communicate with a community about these subtleties – to identify, articulate, and explain them – may be one good way to practice science in the context of secondary education.

Strategies of Interpretation

Priests explain how to interpret healing meters through discussion of class mechanics, raid composition, raid encounter mechanics, and situational variation in raid encounters. A poster on Elitist Jerks stated:

> Most of your "rank" on meters depends on your...[assignment]. If you're tank-healing, you'll be bottom of the meter, just because there is not enough damage to heal, and because single-target heals have...less hps [heals per second] than group heals. If you're raid-healing, you should be in the upper part of meters.

The poster observed that to interpret the position of a particular priest on a meter, it is necessary to understand the nature of the healing assignment. If the priest is "tank healing," this means that he or she is assigned to a single player for whom he or she is responsible, that is, the tank. If the tank dies, the raid wipes; this assignment is critical to the success of the raid. The tank must be watched and healed proactively because he can take "spike damage," that is, a large instant burst of damage.

Those raid healing, on the other hand, can heal multiple players at once (using a variety of spells). No individual player is as crucial as the tank, so losing a few rogues or mages or other damage classes does not necessarily mean the end of the encounter. But because the raid-healing priest is healing multiple players at once, his or her numbers on the meters generally will be higher. As the poster said, "If you're raid-healing, you should be in the upper part of the meters."

Priests, then, come to appreciate that their particular situation, that is, their healing assignment, in part explains their position on the meters. For tank healers, the need to save a tank on the brink of death is crucial to the success of an encounter. But a heroic, death-defying act on the part of a priest is not reflected on the meters, which only show the gross amount of healing.

The Elitist Jerks poster continues to explain the situational nature of healing and how a particular situation affects healing meter numbers:

> Finally, there is often also an implicit assignment between raid-healers. I know that in my raid, one of the raid-healers focuses more on keeping low people alive, and uses less groups heals. I tend to use more group heals to top-up people, and let him heal the low-HP target that needs immediate

healing. As a consequence, I'm usually higher on meters (but I wouldn't say that I'm a better healer).

The priest acknowledges that his or her higher position on the meters is not because he or she is a "better healer" but because of the way he ort she works with his or her teammate. This is a smart strategy for raid success: One healer saves those about to die, and the other "tops people up," that is, prevents their health from getting too low (to the extent possible with unpredictable raid damage).

The poster then invokes the dead-or-alive metric:

> It's really difficult to quantify a "good" healer. The simplest metric is: "Does their assignment die?" Other than that, because healing is *so* situational, it is difficult to really say what you should be looking for. A healer that is able to consistently save the tanks and other [raid members] in potentially bad situations and save wipes is a good healer but may not top the meters.

The poster succinctly summarizes the need to interpret healing numbers by referring to the situation in which they were produced and to think beyond the simple ranking presented in the meter, which is misleading given the realities of healing.

On the Plusheal.com forum, a priest explains that he evaluates healing performance based on the fitness of the particular spells the priest is situationally using as well as whether his targets are alive:

> Meters arent that useful; if people arent dying, then everything is okay. I look at meters to verify that everyone is carrying their weight, that's about it; it's always nice to try to aim for the top, but it doesn't necessarily mean that you are doing the best. You can judge if they know what they are doing by looking at their spell usage (which changes based on the fight).

Another poster on Plusheal.com discusses the creator's strategy for evaluation. Like the previous poster, the creator also takes into account the appropriateness of the particular spells a priest is using. His advice is addressed to a question posted by another priest wondering about how to evaluate healers:

> As far as evaluation, that becomes tricky…. I'd suggest running combat logs for your raids and uploading them to something like worldoflogs.com. Finding fights where you can evaluate your healers' numbers can be tricky; there are a lot of variables you have to look at to get a good understanding

of what is happening. In a short, simple answer, what I generally will do is upload our combat logs, look at our healers' spell usage in comparison with other guilds (same class obviously), look at their uptimes and usage of various abilities (e.g., Inspiration uptime on the tank), etc.

You can find most top raiding guilds on worldoflogs if you figure out what server they are on, compare their numbers to yours while taking into account fight length, people standing in the fire, etc.

This strategy requires in-depth comparative analysis and demands an impressive amount of effort. The poster explains the complexities of the analysis, indicating the multivariate nature of the analytical materials and suggests ways to carry out a fine-grained comparison between an ordinary raiding guild and a top guild. The creator helpfully provides specific resources – much as we might expect in a scientific community. He identifies specific metrics. Details aside, the discussion of "Inspiration uptime" and so on indicates that the priest engages game mechanics at a deep level, providing a valuable means of helping other priests improve their performance through theorycrafting.

Validity and Reliability

Steinkuehler and Chmiel (2006) observed that players customizing their *World of Warcraft* characters may engage in activities somewhat like those of scientists, for example, activities such as model-based reasoning and understanding theory and evidence. Students learning to be scientists or just learning about science must develop clear understandings of reliability and validity. Is a measurement measuring what it is supposed to? Are measurements reliable across time and tools?

Healing meters present a classic problem in validity, as we saw in the preceding discussion. Changes to the game and to mod software create issues of reliability. Through theorycrafting analyses, players become sophisticated about how the tools they use entail problems of validity and reliability.

A poster on Elitist Jerks wrote:

I believe in the past there has been some discussion about how reliable "absorbtion tracking" logs/addons are, but I have been unable to find it. Is world of logs showing appropriate values for absorbs done, or is there something behind it that makes it not really reliable?

Because of changes to the game as it is periodically updated, meters may produce unreliable numbers if they are not updated properly. The "absorption tracking" the poster refers to is a particularly tricky quantity to estimate because the data from the game that the meters use are difficult to assess, but it is a quantity essential for understanding how well a priest is doing. If the meter does not reliably measure absorption, the priest's contribution to the raid is not being measured correctly.

But absorption also raises a crucial question of validity. In *World of Warcraft*, absorption is not technically healing. Absorption prevents damage from occurring rather than healing after damage has occurred. Should absorption be counted toward *healing*? Most meters do not count it. But priests rely on absorption for a good deal of their performance in keeping raid members alive. So are the meters making the correct measurements if the goal is to understand how effective a priest is? Other healing classes rely much less or not at all on absorption, so the priest's contribution may be undervalued.

Given these problems with reliability and validity, it is no surprise that many priests are quite skeptical of meters. A priest on Elitist Jerks wrote in response to a forum discussion of "stupid meters":

On the stupid meters topic…

If a boss output during a fight is say 40k raid damage per second (including tanks), [some priests]…are passively healing 1,200 hps due to renewed hope effect! That is not covered by any meter. I don't think anyone thinks about it either.

The poster observes that a "passive healing" effect of one of the priest's abilities, Renewed Hope, is not measured by any meter because the data are not made available by Blizzard. But Renewed Hope is a raid-wide effect providing substantial healing. A priest's position on the meters certainly would rise if this passive healing were counted. Thus the priest's effectiveness as indicated by meter position lacks validity when considering the effect of Renewed Hope.

These complexities move some priests to comical despair. A poster on Plusheal wrote:

Healing CANNOT be measured correctly by ANY meters!

After this caps-enhanced outburst, the poster went on to more analytical treatment of the topic:

[Analysis]…begins with PoM [a powerful priest spell] and includes a number of other spells that the meters just have trouble getting. I went through the complete combat log once, and PoM had healed around 33% more than any meters (Skada, Recount, DamageMeters (the original)...) showed.

Again, we find a theorycrafting priest undertaking extensive comparative numerical analysis to show that the player-created meters do not capture all the healing a priest is actually doing. In some cases, the mechanics of the tools themselves are incorrect, as the poster notes in the comment about "other spells the meters just have trouble getting." The poster analyzed a complete "combat log" from the game – a line-by-line report of each spell cast (as well as other information). The meters attempt to digest and process this information, but they do not always do it correctly because it is difficult to parse the data as Blizzard presents them. The data can be painstakingly recovered from the line-by-line combat log, as this priest did, but not easily captured in real time for the meters. This priest looked at several meters – Skada, Recount, and DamageMeters – finding that none of them correctly measured the healing generated by the Prayer of Mending (POM) spell.

This poster concluded:

The only effective means of measuring healing is to check weather the group is still alive.

Educating Others About Interpreting Tools

We have alluded to the difficulties priests encounter when other classes do not understand differences between healing meters and damage meters. The problem is particularly acute for "discipline" priests. Priests have two talent builds, or *specs*, for healing (see Choontanom, 2008), meaning that certain abilities are more powerful in a particular spec. Each build requires its own unique interpretive readings of the meters. The discipline spec is centered on absorption and passive healing, so discipline priests will occupy a lower rank in the meters, as this poster on Elitist Jerks wrote:

[Discipline priests who are]...tank healers are not going to be near the top. But, holy [priests] should show up on meters a lot more than disc does.

Another poster counseled:

If you care about big healing meter numbers, you should go holy and raid heal. Otherwise, tank heal as disc and let PoM bounce around and throw out PoH [another spell] during raid spike damage.

But many raid leaders do not understand these game mechanics. After a look at the meters, they may ask discipline priests to change to a holy spec or chide them for poor performance (Taylor, 2008; Wine, 2008; Nardi, 2010). It often falls to priests themselves to explain how meters work through careful exposition of the effects of passive healing and absorption. While such discourse may be tiresome and frustrating in the context of entertainment, it presents an opportunity in a school setting for students to develop communication skills through practice in explaining.

Discussion

Work

The activities of theorycrafting are complex, sophisticated, intellectual endeavors that may possibly have value in training applications at work or in school. Experience with theorycrafting gives players healthy skepticism about quantification and the tools with which it is achieved. Theorycrafting demands the deployment of skills of rhetoric and writing. Our main task in this chapter was to expose the nature of theorycrafting, but we also want to point to how it might connect to activities in school and at work.

Drawing on the first author's work experience, we present an example of the use of metrics in a manufacturing company that raised many of the same issues theorycrafters contend with. (We deploy this example at an abstract level to anonymize the company.) In the company, which we will call Steampunk Products, performance metrics are calculated for profits made each day. These metrics depend largely on the number of suitable (those which pass quality assurance) products produced. The ratio of suitable products to defective products is one factor. The reason why a product unit is defective is another factor. Some metrics will vary from department to department, but the practice of quantifying and analyzing the factors that contribute to daily profit is much like theorycrafting.

First, the correct data need to be captured. This means devising valid measures. Valid measurement is crucial in a business setting in order to assess why a company is doing well or poorly. Capturing the "correct" data may depend on a variety of factors, including the fact that the desired measurement may be a subset of the data that can be collected – what separates data that is nice-to-know from data that are need-to-know. Using Recount as an example, the mod uses raw data from the combat log and separates the damage data from the healing data. DPS players may be interested only in the damage data and healers interested only in the healing data.

Raw data usually are not enough. Some kind of processing needs to occur to produce meaningful metrics. Similar questions apply: Is this processing method measuring what it is supposed to? Is this processing method reliable across time and tools? Again using Recount, a few examples of processed data are total damage done per player, damage per second done per player, total heals done per player, and heals per second done per player. Recount parses through the combat log line by line to calculate these numbers.

Metrics also can be used to measure trends over time. If the measurement method changes for some reason, this change should be noted and explained. Much as theorycrafting tools need to be kept up to date owing to changes in game mechanics, metrics and methods of measurement may change as a company grows over time. For example, at Steampunk Products, new products may be added to the production line and older products removed. The new products may take more time to produce but have more profit for each unit sold. Or the new products take the same amount of time to produce but have a higher cost when defective units are produced. The practice of gathering the correct data must be maintained as company changes take place. A processing method that worked one year may not apply the next year.

It is also important to keep in mind when analyzing data over long time periods that the interpretation of metrics may need to change. For example, when introducing a new product into the market, a higher sales metric may be desirable for that product. However, a year or two later, when introducing a newer product into the market, a lower sales metric may be desirable for the older product when the company wants customers to switch to using the new product. This example reinforces that just as theorycrafters discover, context is important. A new employee who did not know that the company was trying to phase out the first product may view the result as negative. Comparing reports of the two products may provide additional context. Communication with veteran employees will give him or her the context he or she needs to understand that the drop in sales at that time actually was positive. A simple, obvious interpretation – more sales is better – may not always be the case.

Managers may use metrics much like raid leaders use data from meters. They use them in a specific social context, with particular collective aims and goals in mind. Managers must be alert to the context of the data and should not forget the subtleties when evaluating the meaning of numbers, charts, and graphs. Communication between managers and employees can help not only with understanding what the numbers mean but also with how to interpret them correctly to make decisions. Much as meters do not calculate or display the value of discipline priests adequately, workplace metrics may obscure certain aspects of group or individual work. Additional questions may be asked, such as, What are the data not telling me? We admire the open discourse in communities such as Elitist Jerks and can imagine that the presentation of analytical work that takes place in its public forums may find a home in the workplace, as least in some version of such activity tailored to workplace needs.

School

The structure of schools and their transmission of information has not kept pace with participatory media (Steinkuehler and Johnson, 2009). Theorycrafting, an exemplary form of engagement with participatory media, entails the use of mathematics, logic, experimental design, and writing. These are, of course, exactly the skills we strive to teach secondary students. Instead of working with textbooks and tests, theorycrafters create and present the results of their activities on websites and blogs.

Theorycrafting is inherently social and collaborative – like real science (see Olson et al., 2008). Not only are the results of experiments presented, but they are also discussed and interpreted. Websites and blogs form a natural medium in which deep analytical work flourishes. By comparison, the mechanics of textbooks and tests appear unbending and one-sided. Textbooks neither invite nor permit participation. They (generally) do not promote deep engagement with subject matter, nor the sharing and discussion that participatory media yield. With participatory media, students control the means with which to present and store the results of their activities and thoughts. Within the space of a single website or blog, students can publish, comment, edit, and update.

Textbooks and tests contribute to the passivity that permeates classroom experience. Steinkuehler and Johnson (2009) describe students as passive recipients of curricular materials. Students are urged to acquire "tool knowledge" without understanding why the tools may be useful. Lacking a motivated experience within which tools fit, much classroom work is an exercise in discipline rather than an intellectual engagement.

Word problems, for example, are couched in scenarios that have little meaning to many students. Susie is ten years older than George. In two years Susie will be twice as old as George. How old are Susie and George? While a minority of students can connect directly to the math in such a problem, many are left wondering, "Why do we care how old two anonymous people are? How does it affect our daily lives?"

In theorycrafting, word problems emerge as an outcome of motivated activity. Players want to know the answer. The way to find out is with word problems! Zaltu's word problem was formulated to calculate how gems and bonuses affect performance, something players cared about.

In theorycrafting, the word problem is turned on its head. The motivating concept – that of determining the effect of gems and bonuses – is tangible and real for players; it precedes the construction of the word problem. Zaltu applied the same concepts as in a traditional word problem. However, instead of gaining a skill they might use someday (but how? – this is unspecified in a traditional word problem), players were drawn into analysis of a problem they wanted to solve immediately. They grasped the problem through their own activity and were positioned to apply math skills to determine the answer. Similarly, spreadsheets and meters were understood to be quantified measures of game performance. Players approached these tools through self-interest in improving performance.

Theorycrafting generates understandings about the need to move beyond simplistic conceptions of the "right answer" – a notion that is an unfortunate by-product of too much testing. As an analytical activity occurring in a social context, theorycrafting endorses an encounter with numbers understood in relation to a wider community of actors and their interests. A poster on Elitist Jerks said:

> Getting numbers…is often needed to back your claims, I acknowledge it. But numbers [are]…not enough: you need to "show" why they are correct, pertinent and useful.

The poster argued against unreflective acquisition of a right answer – often the sole outcome of the use of classroom tools and skills. The creator suggests that numbers become interesting only when we formulate "why they are correct, pertinent and useful." It is necessary to "show" these interpretations to others, communicating results and ideas to a wider community.[1]

Theorycrafting creates a social space in which players ask questions. Questioning affords practice in articulating complex questions so that others understand what is meant. When Fae wanted to determine an upgrade to his armor but encountered conflicting results, he explained his question, including his original hypothesis and the perceived discrepancy. Theorycrafting activity presents opportunities for students to formulate questions of "evaluative epistemology" (Steinkuehler and Duncan, 2009), that is, why would a player choose *A* over *B*, and is what is gained more advantageous than what is lost? Does this make sense, and why? These fundamental reasoning skills are essential to a good education.

Much writing in secondary school is seen only by the teacher. When a community of readers who are truly interested in each other's writing emerges, so do rules of good writing. They are the same rules learned in school, now made compelling through the authority of a community's shared interests. While certainly not all blog comments and forum posts are models of good writing, the higher-end forums such as Elitist Jerks evidence care for writing. Rules are posted, and forum threads are monitored for content and style. Violators are reprimanded publicly. They subject to the "Banhammer" after too many infractions. Here are some of the ElitistJerks rules:

> All posters are to make an effort to comSmunicate clearly.
> Do not post unless you have something new and worthwhile to say.
> Whining in any form is forbidden.
> Is your shift key broken?

One poster whose "shift key was broken" was told:

> Apparently it is, because this is the second post you've made without capitalization or punctuation. Time for a short break from posting for you.

The schoolmarm is with us yet, incarnated as a theorycrafter. Many teachers can surely relate to the moderator's frustration with improper capitalization and punctuation. It is heartening to see video gamers taking these matters seriously. The development and enforcement of forum rules require no small amount of effort, effort made worthwhile by the community's authentic need for clear communication.

While commercial games have given rise to theorycrafting and they are a congenial venue for theorycrafting activities, it is also possible that students *writing their own games* could learn mathematical modeling, the use of spreadsheets, and so on through game creation. In a blog discussion of theorycrafting, one commenter wrote:

> [B]eing a mathematician, I totally get enjoying the theorycraft part. Some years ago, I tried designing a RPG-esque system [role-playing game], balancing stats and results, [and] boy were the equations difficult [Mike, 2009].

Of course, students may not need to design full-blown role-playing games to acquire educational benefits. For example, in a cooking game where experience points are gained by cooking dishes and money is obtained by selling dishes, students could learn to model which dishes are optimal for cooking, which are optimal for selling, and what combination of dishes yields the highest experience and money. Students could work in groups to manage tasks. They could individually gather data and then collaborate on processing the raw data into a form that others could use. This activity could take place in a classroom as a project or as an after-school activity to reinforce skill sets.[2] As in typical after-school programs, opportunities for mentoring (by college students, for example) and peer learning are plentiful.

Conclusion

Theorycrafting is a multifaceted activity where the role a player plays determines which aspects of theorycrafting the player engages. Rogues focus on the spreadsheet metagame to determine how to gear. Interpretation of meters is a straightforward measure of their performance. As healers, priests do not take the meters at face value but debate how to interpret the numbers to assess their performance. There are multiple contextual variables to consider, including who the healer is assigned to heal and the difficulties of measuring absorption.

Theorycrafting encourages community participation and contribution. Asking questions about spreadsheets or interpreting meters results in intellectual discussions in which participants formulate problems of math and logic. The seriousness and formality of discussions are encouraged by community rules, such as those of Elitist Jerks, who encourage players to follow conventions including proper capitalization, clear communication, and responsible discussion. These rules are actively enforced, causing players to practice their communication skills to get their questions, problems, or solutions clearly across to others.

Future research directions include the origins of theorycrafting, the use of theorycrafting in other games outside the role-playing genre, the amount of complexity, if measurable, a game must incorporate in order to support theorycrafting, and more in-depth study of the collaborative practices of theorycrafting communities.

Notes

[1]   We are not sure why the poster put "show" in quotes. The creator may have been alluding to the difficulties of interpretive activity and/or the impossibility of final demonstrations of scientific reality.

²   See also Seed (2007) on using game creation to teach history. Seed's aim was to teach skills in historical interpretation. While not quite theorycrafting, she found game creation a good way to teach skills because students loved creating the games so much.

References

Byrt. (2009). *Discussion combat and mutilate spreadsheets (updated for 3.3)*. Available at http://elitistjerks.com/f78/t39136-combat_mutilate_spreadsheets_ updated_3_3_a/p51/.

Choontanom, T. (2008). *Build theory in Guild Wars and World of Warcraft.* Undergraduate Honors Thesis, University of California, Irvine. Available at http://uci.triaer.net/papers/H198_Final4.5.pdf.

Fae. (2009). *Discussion combat and mutilate spreadsheets (Updated for 3.3)*. Available at http://elitistjerks.com/f78/t39136-combat_mutilate_spreadsheets_updated_3_3_a/ p51/.

Kow, Y. M., & Nardi, B. (2009). Culture and Creativity: *World of Warcraft* Modding in China and the U.S. In B. Bainbridge (ed.), *Online worlds: Convergence of the real and the virtual* (pp. 21–41). New York: Springer.

Mike. (2009). *Breakfast topic: Nobody understands me. Comment by Mike.* Available at http://www.wow.com/2009/06/01/breakfast-topic-nobody-understands-me/.

Nardi, B. (2010). *My life as a night elf priest: An anthropological account of World of Warcraft.* Ann Arbor, MI: University of Michigan Press.

Nonmagical. (2009). *Discussion combat and mutilate spreadsheets (updated for 3.3)*. Available at http://elitistjerks.com/f78/t39136-combat_mutilate_spreadsheets_ updated_3_3_a/p51/.

Olson, G., Zimmerman, A., Bos, N., & Wulf, W. (2008). *Scientific collaboration on the Internet.* Cambridge, MA: MIT Press.

Paul, C. (2009). *Theorycraft: Structuring World of Warcraft from outside the game.* Paper presented at 2009 AoIR Conference, Milwaukee, WI.

Perini. (2009). *Pocket guide to WOTLK (updated for 3.3)*. Available at http://elitistjerks.com/f78/t37183-pocket_guide_wotlk_updated_3_3_a/p17/.

Seed, P. (2007). Looking Back: A Decade of Using Games to Teach History, 1996–2006. In *Proceedings of the First International Humanities, Arts, Science and Technology Advanced Collaboratory Conference* (pp. 193–200). Available at: http://hastac.org/informationyear/ET/BreakoutSessions/9/Seed

Steinkuehler, C., & Chmiel, M. (2006). Fostering Scientific Habits of Mind in the Context of Online Play. In S. A. Barab, K. E. Hay, N. B. Songer, & D. T. Hickey (eds.), *Proceedings of the International Conference of the Learning Sciences* (pp. 723–9). Mahwah NJ: Erlbuam.

Steinkuehler, C. & Duncan, S. (2009). Scientific Habits of Mind in Virtual Worlds. *Journal of Science Education & Technology*, 17(6), 530–43. DOI: 10.1007/s10956-008-9120-8.

Steinkuehler, C. & Johnson, B. Z. (2009). Computational Literacy in Online Games: The Social Life of a Mod. *The International Journal of Gaming and Computer Mediated Simulations*, 1(1), 53–65.

Taylor, T. L. (2008). Does *World of Warcraft* Change Everything? In Corneliussen, H., & Rettberg, J. (eds.), *Digital culture, play, and identity: A World of Warcraft reader* (pp. 187–201). Cambridge, MA: MIT Press.

Wine, C. (2008). *How big is your epeen? A study of hegemonic masculinity in communication on the World of Warcraft forums*. Women's' Studies Honors Thesis, University of Massachusetts, Boston.

Wytryszek.(2009).*Discussioncombatandmutilatespreadsheets(updatedfor3.3)*.Availableat http://elitistjerks.com/f78/t39136-combat_mutilate_spreadsheets_updated _3_3_a/p51/.

Zaltu. (2009). *Let's talk about socket bonuses*. Available at http://oneroguesjourney. com/2009/08/27/lets-talk-about-socket-bonuses/.

14 Culture and Community in a Virtual World for Young Children

Rebecca W. Black and Stephanie M. Reich

As evidenced by many of the chapters in this volume, robust research is emerging that explores the role of video games and virtual worlds in young people's learning. However, far fewer studies have looked at the role of culture and community in relation to learning not only within these virtual spaces but also in the fan communities that surround them. Moreover, there are even fewer, if any, studies that explore these topics in the context of virtual worlds for very young children. This chapter addresses this gap through a focus on culture and community within and surrounding *Webkinz World* (*WW*), a virtual environment designed for children between the ages of six and thirteen.

While video games such as *World of Warcraft* and virtual worlds such as *Second Life* that target adolescents and adults have been popular for years, online environments aimed at preteen populations (between the ages of six and twelve) are a relatively new phenomenon. Recently, there has been a marked increase in the development of such spaces, with *Webkinz World* (www.webkinz.com), *Club Penguin* (www.clubpenguin.com), *Neopets* (www.neopets.com), and *Barbie Girls* (www.barbiegirls.com) among the most popular. These sites garner a significant number of monthly visitors, with *Webkinz World* attracting approximately twenty-eight million monthly visits in June 2009, *Club Penguin* and *Neopets* boasting approximately ten and ten and a half million, respectively, and *Barbie Girls* attracting nearly eight hundred and fifty thousand (Compete, Inc., 2009). Despite the rampant popularity of such sites, we know very little about children's activities in these spaces at present.

Shared virtual environments (SVEs), such as *Webkinz World* (*WW*), are immersive digital spaces in which players, represented by avatars or digital characters, interact with the virtual world as well as with other players' characters. Unlike massively multiplayer online games (MMOs), which rely on fixed narratives and graded progression through activities (levels), SVEs allow players the freedom to construct their own play narratives and engage in activities in a less constrained format. Thus players in SVEs often spend a great deal of time engaging in activities that mirror offline day-to-day life, such as furnishing homes, gardening, buying clothes, playing games, developing relationships, and caring for virtual pets.

Studying SVEs that target children is important because younger users are more likely to be influenced by the content than adult users and therefore are more vulnerable to messages, activities, and interactions on these sites. Childhood is a time of intense socialization, in which children learn to navigate their social context and develop tools for successful interactions with others. Because of this intense period of learning, there is a need to better understand how SVEs mediate children's development, as well as how children engage with these sites. Such a focus would provide information about the risks and benefits of SVEs for children as well as which aspects of these spaces may capitalize on children's emerging interests and abilities.

In this chapter we look at the world of *Webkinz* and attempt to understand (1) how print-based and graphic renderings both within and surrounding *WW* contribute to *Webkinz* culture and (2) how the designed activities and systems of meaning within *WW* might enable or hinder the development of community in this SVE. These questions are approached from a developmental perspective that considers the complex interaction between learners and learning contexts, thus maintaining a focus on issues that can affect learning, not just in *WW*, but across technological platforms and other designed learning environments.

It is worth noting that while we began our exploration of *WW* with some expectation of encountering aspects of shared knowledge and culture and a sense of community similar to those reported in teen- and adult-oriented virtual worlds (Boellstorff, 2008; Fields & Kafai, 2009; Steinkuehler, 2006), our findings revealed some significant differences between this particular SVE and other popular online spaces. One of the most striking aspects of our findings may very well be the ways in which Internet safety has "gone wild" (Tynes, 2007) in this space, thereby preventing users from engaging in the sort of content creation and sustained communication that are hallmarks of online community. Instead, the culture and content of *WW* are contrived and controlled by the Ganz Corporation and thus reflect adults' idealized notions about children's behavior, as well as the corporation's interest in this early-childhood demographic as a marketing niche. Unfortunately, these concerns for safety, coupled with design choices for the site, curtail children's opportunities for learning as well as for the development of community in *WW*. Thus, as we will discuss in our analysis, many users instead turn to external fan websites for the sorts of social connections, collaborative problem solving, and "playful engagement with the reading and writing of multimodal texts" (Marsh, 2008, p. 1), that are valuable aspects of children's learning and participation in online spaces.

Sociocultural Theory, Learning, and Culture in Virtual Worlds

This chapter is grounded in a sociocultural perspective of learning that recognizes the relationship between human mental processes and social, cultural, and institutional contexts (Wertsch, 1991). Through this lens, children's interactions with people and objects in their immediate social environments play a crucial role in how they learn and develop higher-order functions. To date, the majority of socioculturally oriented theory and research has focused on the influence of culture in offline spaces. However, for the purposes of this chapter, culture is viewed as a "system of meaning" (Goncu & Katsarou, 2000, p. 223) that is shared by a social group. From this perspective, the signs, artifacts, social norms, and communicative practices shared by a group of children in an online space may be considered a culture, and children's learning and development are in part a process of socialization into these online cultures and systems of meaning (Goncu & Katsarou, 2000).

In this chapter, *mind*, or *cognition*, is viewed "as something that 'extends beyond the skin' in at least two senses: it is often socially distributed and it is connected to the notion of mediation" (Wertsch, 1991, p. 14). Thus we will look at both *WW* and the external fan communities of *WW* in terms of how they both might promote collective thinking and socially distributed learning on the topic of *Webkinz*. Such a lens also helps to draw our attention to the fact that children playing SVEs such as *WW* are participating in a cultural activity with guidance that involves "interactions" (Rogoff, 1995, p. 147) with other users as well as profit-driven corporations, game designers, and content consultants, to name just a few. In modern societies, many of these interactions are mediated through print artifacts and literacy-related activities, as well as through the multimodal representations supported by new media and technologies. Thus this chapter will pay particular attention to the role of linguistic, semiotic, and technical mediation in creating culture in virtual worlds.

Related Research

Research suggests that many popular virtual worlds (Boellstorff, 2008) as well as MMOs (Steinkuehler, 2006) allow for the development of robust communities and foster a sense of connection among players. For example, in his ethnographic exploration of *Second Life*, Boellstorff (2008) described the role of *events* and *groups* in enabling "residents" to conjure a sense of community and social relatedness. *Events*, defined as "conjunction[s] of place, time, and sociality" (Boellstorff, 2008, p. 182) ranged from concerts and religious meetings all the way to round-robin storytelling gatherings. These events gave the virtual *Second Life* landscape a social component by providing a time and location for structured interaction. Conversely, *groups*, which were either "named networks of residents" (Boellstorff, 2008, p. 183) or more informal collectivities, provided a social connection that existed independent of time or location. According to Boellstorff, membership in such groups became a significant form of socialization within the virtual world. Group membership also offered residents the means for publicly exhibiting their affiliations by choosing to display the titles of their group membership above their avatars, much like a guild name appearing above players' names in an MMO.

As another example, Steinkuehler's (2005) ethnographic exploration of the MMO *Lineage* described how players developed "sociocultural norms and…shared practices" (Steinkuehler, 2007, p. 301) through membership in *guilds*. These shared practices included scaffolding newcomers into successful participation, sharing insider knowledge about game play, and collaborative problem solving. Steinkuehler's study also outlined an array of "literacy practices" that constituted social events within the game, including poetry readings and storytelling sessions, debates, and games such as "ritual insult," as well as literate practices beyond the in-game environment, including fan sites and blogs, discussion boards, and annotated fan art and cartoons, to name just a few (Steinkuehler, 2007, p. 301).

A common finding in Boellstorff's and Steinkuehler's studies is how language and other forms of semiotic mediation, such as images, movement, and sound, served as "cultural tool[s] that empowered human action in essential ways" (Wertsch, 1998, p. 39). For instance, printed and spoken language played a crucial role in planning, publicizing, and enacting the group and guild events that were significant "instantiations of sociality" (Boellstorff, 2008, p. 183) in these worlds. Also, members used multiple forms of media to create artifacts (e.g., videos, virtual clothing, designs for guild tabards, printed lore) that contributed to the social and cultural landscape of these spaces. In addition, through their avatars, members used image, movement, artifacts, and group or guild titles for "identity work" (Goffman, 1959), which allowed them to demonstrate certain elements of their identity in various social situations. Thus the affordances and constraints of the available cultural tools shaped the communicative practices, social meanings, and cultural landscapes that were possible in these worlds.

In studying young children's immersion in shared virtual environments, it is reasonable to expect some aspects of shared culture and sense of community, largely mediated through semiotics and other tool use, to be salient for these sites. Therefore, it is with this focus that the case study and content analysis of the *WW* and the fan communities surrounding the SVE were directed.

Methods

This chapter uses a case-study approach and is based on data stemming from participant observation and a qualitative content analysis of the SVE *Webkinz World* (www.webkinz.com). This work is part of a larger cross-case analysis of the literacy and developmental features of several SVEs targeting early-childhood populations. Data collection, while still in the preliminary stages, has focused on creating a map of the site contents (e.g., rules, FAQs, and tutorials), activities, and spaces, as well as the collection of artifacts (e.g., in-game texts and screenshots). The content analysis was conducted using an open-ended, qualitative protocol that focused on the design features (i.e., technical and aesthetic) and the literacy-related artifacts and activities of the site. At this point in the project, participant observation and data collection did not involve any interaction with or recording of children's activities. The researchers' observations instead were aimed at gaining a robust sense of navigation, communication, and game play in the SVE.

Webkinz World

Webkinz

Webkinz are stuffed animals with corresponding digital counterparts that were released by the Ganz company in April 2005. Each stuffed Webkinz pet comes with an exclusive code that allows the owner access to *WW*, a SVE in which children participate by adopting the digital version of their stuffed Webkinz toy. After visiting the adoption center, players receive a room for their pet and 2,000 *kinzcash*, a monetary unit that allows them to participate in the *WW* economy. At the W Shop, players can purchase items to furnish their pets' rooms as well as food, toys, and clothes. These highly anthropomorphized pets – their outfits and actions – are children's primary form of self-representation and thus mediate many of their experiences as they navigate *WW.*

In theory, the *WW* site offers opportunities for different styles of individual or social game play. For example, players who prefer more individualized activities can focus on furnishing their pets' rooms, cultivating an outdoor garden, getting a job at the Employment Center, sending their pets on a trip through the Travel Agency, signing their pet up for classes at the Kinzville Academy, entering their pets in competitions (e.g., cooking and beauty pageants) at the Webkinz Stadium, or playing games in the Arcade. For more social forms of engagement within *WW*, players have the option of pitting their skills against other players in the Tournament Arena games, inviting another Webkinz over to their virtual room to visit with their pet, or visiting the Webkinz Clubhouse or Park, where players can communicate with other *WW* members. However, discussion in this chapter will highlight the many limitations placed on communication and self-expression in *WW* and how this hinders social forms of game play and thwarts the development of an in-game community.

Kindness, Caring, and Consumption: Culture in Webkinz World

Players in *WW* navigate the site primarily through the avatars of their virtual pets; consequently, many site activities center on caring for and even indulging these pets. For example, the main user interface, known as the *dock*, uses a mixture of text and icons to help players monitor their pet's happiness (represented by a smiley face), health (represented by a heart), and hunger (represented by a fork). The dock also contains players' in-game inventories, used for storing clothes, foodstuff, games, and toys for pets, as well as the menu for navigating the various spaces and activities of *WW.* Activities such as feeding, bathing, and exercising pets are mandatory in the sense that if a pet does not receive an adequate level of care, it will become sick and require a visit to Dr. Quack (a duck physician) and perhaps some medicine to become well again.

Unfortunately, food in *WW* does not grow freely on trees. Thus children must find ways to feed and care for their pets. Options for earning kinzcash to pay for food include taking jobs at the Employment Center, answering academic and trivia questions at Quizzy's Question Corner, playing games in the Arcade, or special (e.g., Wheel of Yum) and regularly occurring (e.g., Wishing Well 2) activities. Of these activities, those which involve academic knowledge are more lucrative, such that Quizzy's Question Corner pays more than Arcade games, and games within the Arcade that involve math or spelling pay more than those involving typical game play. Another option is for children to purchase a garden and seeds, which allows them to grow enough food to feed their pets and sell any surplus in the W Shop. This option, however, comes with an additional level of responsibility because players must cultivate crops on a regular basis. This includes watering, weeding, and harvesting to keep the crops from dying.

The design choices around food shape the social norms and expectations for players' behavior in *WW*. The mandatory nature of pet care and the ongoing cultivation of crops contribute potentially to a culture of caring that may help to teach children responsibility. These activities also encourage children to take on the identity of a dependable and loving pet owner. However, there is a level of consumerism that is engendered in which money to spend on your pet is necessary to make the pet happy and healthy.

Above and beyond any necessary pet care activities, players also have the option of pampering their pets by buying them fancy clothing, toys, and furniture. Unlike many video games in which there is some functional value in purchasing most in-game items (i.e., specialized armor that adds attack or protection bonuses, food or drink items that heal), there is little practical value to the majority of items that can be purchased in *WW*. However, the designed culture of *WW* promotes this sort of consumption in several ways. For example, the site actively encourages children to associate the purchase of such "material" goods with caring for a Webkinz pet. This is done through various texts in *WW*, such as pets' automated utterances thanking the player for "being so good to me" and saying, "I'm so glad you bought this for me" after purchases are made. Shopping and buying also result in increased happiness and health scores for the pet on the dock interface. Furthermore, W Shop advertisements such as, "A totally rad black hat will make your Webkinz pet feel like one cool dude!" and "For a sophisticated look, you need these chic shades!" also encourage users toward materialism. Other examples include advertisements from the Travel Agency encouraging players to "Send all your pets on a great getaway! Your pets will go on a short trip to the spa and will come back happier, healthier, and less hungry! Wait here while your pet gets pampered!" Even the Ganz-created *Music Starz* uses animated music videos to promote consumptive values by depicting Webkinz pets that are yearning to take a vacation at the Travel Agency, showing off their fancy outfits, and expressing appreciation for all their favorite furniture.

On the one hand, this culture of purchasing validates common concerns about consumption-oriented values and the use of immersive advertising (Grimes & Shade, 2005) in virtual worlds for young children because children are encouraged to take on the identity of consumers. On the other hand, through this type of play, children also have the opportunity to learn about responsibility and saving and spending money because they must balance their desire to purchase in-game luxury items with the need to care for their pets adequately. Thus, despite design choices that encourage consumptive forms of participation, children have the opportunity to shape their own experience of play within the confines of ensuring the health and happiness of their Webkinz.

In considering the presence, development, and rationale for the cultural norms within *WW*, it is clear that concerns about children's safety while using the Internet (Grimes & Shade, 2005) are paramount. As such, site content is designed to minimize risk and consequently reduces users' abilities to interact with one another and contribute meaningfully to the structure and activities on the site. For example, in *WW*, the shared social meanings of the game space are communicated through a variety of media. However, unlike virtual worlds such as *Second Life*, in which members are largely responsible for creating these media, the graphic and print environment of *WW* is designed and maintained exclusively by Ganz. This allows Ganz to create a purported "safe, educational, and fun online community" (Ganz, 2009a, p. "Take a Tour") and makes the corporation rather than site members the main purveyors of shared social meanings within this space.

In many cases, the messages of site texts are explicit. For example, immersive in-game advertising urges young players to "adopt" (aka purchase) more pets, to visit parts of the site that require the purchase of Webkinz products to enter, and to become deluxe members for a forty-nine-dollar annual fee. The social meanings conveyed through some of the other site texts, however, are less explicit. For instance, the majority of female nonplayer characters (NPCs) in *WW* wear cardigans, blazers, scarves, and pearls. Pets go for vacations to tropical islands and spend days at the spa. With the purchase of an outside yard, users can see large green spaces between the backs of neighboring houses. Thus the prevailing aesthetic in *WW* is suburban, with manicured lawns, tree houses, and white picket fences that children can paint in order to earn money.

Collectively, these texts create a culture that is undeniably aligned with white, upper-middle-class values. Moreover, many aspects of the game underscore the consumerist focus of *WW* because the only way for players to receive access to many rare game items and exclusive parts of the virtual world is through real-life financial expenditures (i.e., the aforementioned deluxe membership). This can be contrasted with many other video games and virtual worlds in which players attain such items and access through merit (e.g., gaming skill and time spent trying) or pure luck (i.e., rare items drop at random intervals). Furthermore, access to *WW* is maintained only by purchasing a new Webkinz annually. If no new pet is adopted within twelve months, the user's account is terminated. By tying game access and many game activities to money rather than merit, Ganz essentially is creating a culture of consumption in which children from lower socioeconomic backgrounds are excluded from full participation.

Comparing events in *WW* with those in other SVEs such as *Second Life* illustrates the designed nature of social meanings and culture in these worlds and how cultural tools are accessed and used. For example, the events from Boellstorff's (2008) study were facilitated by the affordances of the *Second Life* software as a cultural tool. According to Wertsch (1998), "When trying to develop new cultural tools, the focus naturally tends to be on how they will overcome some perceived problem or restriction inherent in existing forms of mediated action" (Wertsch, 1998, p. 39). As a cultural tool, the *Second Life* software addresses the problem of making meaningful social connections across geographic borders by allowing for embodied, authentic interactions between residents. According to Boellstorff's study, the affordances of the software allowed residents to plan (via IM), attend (via their avatars), and freely communicate (via chat) at gatherings of their choice, making such events significant "instantiations of sociality" (2008, p. 183) and purveyors of shared social norms and meanings in this online community.

Conversely, as a cultural tool, the *WW* software addresses the problem of how to provide safe, online spaces for children; therefore, all "social" activities and spaces in *WW* are either fabricated by or carefully mediated through constraints of the game software. For example, the Webkinz Stadium, where players compete against each other in beauty pageants and cooking contests, is both attended and judged by an audience of NPCs, and real players are not permitted any authentic interaction. Also, the only "group" available in *WW* is the deluxe membership, which gives players a special gold chat channel, special gifts each month, and an exclusive gold hat "to let everyone know that you're deluxe" (Ganz, 2009b). Unlike the events and groups from *Second Life* that reflect residents' affinities and serve as part of their identity work on the site, the events and groups on *WW* are all fabricated and reflect the corporation's and designers' assumptions about children's culture and their interests.

Communication in Webkinz World

Just as language and the printed word provided the centers around which nonvirtual communities and nations could be imagined (Anderson, 1983), technologies of communication also have been central to the development and maintenance of online communities and their shared cultural practices (see, for example, Baym, 1995; Jones, 1995). As Boellstorff (2008) puts it, "[I]f what makes virtual worlds 'worlds' is that they are places, what makes them sites of culture – and thus amenable to ethnographic investigation – is that people interact in them" (p. 180). Unfortunately, as will be discussed in this section, concerns about Internet safety have seriously curtailed the extent to which people are able to interact and thus contribute to the shared social meanings of *WW.*

KinzChat is an in-game messaging tool that serves as a primary means of communication within *WW.* KinzChat content is strictly controlled through formulaic messaging and thus does not require parental permission. The system allows players to choose from a set of topically organized, preconstructed sentences and phrases. For example, children can choose from the categories "Ask," "Say," and "Rap." The "Ask" category includes subcategories such as "About You," "About *Webkinz World*," "About Stuff to Do." These subcategories then include questions such as, "How was your day?" "How many Webkinz pets do you have?" and "Are you having fun?" Unfortunately, the system is glitchy (e.g., frequent disconnects), cumbersome to use (e.g., slow, necessitates searching through a list of phrases, requires previous coordination because players must be on the same channel in order to chat), is poorly planned (e.g., not all questions have appropriate answers within the menu of response options), and is developmentally inappropriate for young children (e.g., based on adult-created taxonomies rather than interlocutors' expressive wishes and do not consider that most young children lack class inclusion abilities, which are needed to identify in which higher-order category a question or response is located). Thus KinzChat is ineffective as a tool for mediating authentic interaction and utterly useless for facilitating the sorts of shared social practices – participating in events, scaffolding new players' participation, sharing insider knowledge about game activities, and engaging in literate "play" – described in Boellstorff's and Steinkuehler's studies. This structure is unfortunate because sociocultural theory posits that learning is less "the socially facilitated acquisition of knowledge and skill and more…a matter of participation in a social process of knowledge construction" (Salomon & Perkins, 1998, p. 4). Thus children's inability to construct language or freely generate written responses hinders their ability to request or offer help and to participate in socially scaffolded learning activities.

KinzPost is an in-game messaging system in which users can send letters or packages to other users for a price. As with KinzChat, KinzPost relies on lists of preselected categories from which users can select, such as "Birthday," "Friendship," and "Have a great day!" Within these eleven categories are four to ten statements for children to select. This feature, like KinzChat, relies on children having sophisticated class inclusion abilities to determine which higher-order category will contain the statement wanted for the message and prohibits any communication that is not specified in these categories. For instance, while there is a "Thank You" category, there are no other response options in which a child receiving a letter could reply appropriately – other than to state, "Thanks for the letter!" However, KinzPost does provide a way for users to send gifts to other users and somewhat personalize their packaging and stationary for an additional fee (e.g., selecting wrapping paper, adding a heart or other shape to the letter). Thus, like KinzChat, the postal service does not provide an effective mechanism for authentic interaction between users or methods for shaping the norms and culture of the site. While the postal features of the site do not support emergent literacy and communication, as free typing would, they do provide opportunities for reading printed text and may offer a mechanism for users to feel more connected to others by giving and receiving messages and gifts.

KinzChatPlus (KCP) is another in-game messaging system that requires parental approval and can be used only in certain areas of *WW*, such as the Clubhouse and the Park. KCP is what is known as a dictionary messaging system, meaning that children can type their own messages as long as the words are not "on the list of excluded words and phrases" (Ganz, 2009c). Excluded words include profanity, proper names, numbers (to prevent children from disclosing personal information), and misspellings. Unfortunately, the exclusion of misspelled words and certain words and phrases (e.g., *baby, on you*) makes it difficult for young writers to use invented, phonetic spelling and their emerging literacy skills to communicate in this space. In addition, as Grimes (2008) has argued, there has been little to no discussion in the research literature of how decisions are made about what words and phrases to include and exclude from these messaging system dictionaries. An in-depth discussion of this topic is beyond the scope of this chapter; however, it is worth noting that the content of messaging systems underscores how the social and cultural contexts in which SVEs are designed and the carefully mediated nature of communication in such spaces can have a significant impact on the cultural meanings and forms of expression available to children in their play. Nonetheless, KCP is much less restrictive than KinzChat and KinzPost and thus allows children greater freedom for interacting and contributing to the shared social meanings of the game space.

Searching for Community in *Webkinz World*

Through our content analysis, it is clear that cultural values, norms, and practices exist in this virtual world. As studies have consistently found, it is culture that provides a dynamic and contextual (Dean, 2001) "way of thinking and interacting" (Nanda, 1991, p. 67) that individuals can use to navigate their social worlds and solve different sorts of challenges (Reich & Reich, 2006). On *WW*, these cultural norms for in-game play define the goals of the site, the values of activities and interactions, and the ways in which children should engage with the site. In exploring these aspects of culture, it is clear that value is placed on materialism (in-game advertising and need for offline and in-game purchases to continue and upgrade access to the site, ensure Webkinz's health, and use the bulk of the *WW* features) and middle-class values (for normative dress, home structure, employment, and budgeting). However, some aspects of the SVE support nurturing, giving, and interacting (albeit in limited capacity) with others. Users are encouraged to care for their Webkinz's health, happiness, and hunger; interact positively with others users (because only kind and upbeat statements are possible in KinzChat and KinzPost), and visit *WW* features that other users frequent (e.g., Kinzville Clubhouse, and Park).

While these cultural and communicative elements are clearly present on *WW*, there is little evidence of the establishment of a sense of community on this site. Such a finding reminds us that while culture and communication are foundational to the existence and functioning of a community, they alone are not sufficient for establishing social connections or ensuring that members have a sense of investment and belonging in a space. As Foster (1996) pointed out, "[Alt]hough communication serves as the basis of community, it must not be equated with it. One can communicate with another individual without considering that person to be a member of one's own community" (p. 24). The same can be said for culture. Although community members may share cultural values, norms, and behaviors, culture is not the same as community (Jones, 1997). Perhaps a key difference between culture and community is that while it is possible, through the sorts of design choices discussed in the preceding section, to impose culture in an SVE such as *WW*, it is nearly impossible to impose community. This is due in part to the fact that community members have collective needs and wants for the group (Heller, 1989) and provide vital input in the functioning of the group (McMillan & Chavis, 1986). Unfortunately, the design of *WW* does not allow for these aspects of member participation to manifest in any significant way. Nonetheless, while meaningful communication and a sense of community may be lacking on *WW*, as we will discuss in the following section, it can be found in the fan websites that surround the site.

Community Beyond Webkinz World

According to Rheingold (2001), "*Virtual communities* are social aggregations that emerge from the Net when enough people carry on those public discussions long enough, with sufficient human feeling, to form webs of personal relationships in cyberspace" (p. 276). Unfortunately, aside from dressing their pets, furnishing their pets' rooms, and using restrictive chat systems, players have few options for affecting the world of Webkinz or contributing to public spaces and discussions in any significant way. As a result, external fan websites are the only option for forming the sort of "webs of personal relationships" that make up the sorts of online communities to which Rheingold is referring.

For example, *Webkinz* Insider, with approximately eighty-three thousand members, is a popular destination for *WW* fans. While geographically distant, these fans use imagination, creativity, and multiple modes of text to extend their participation and form what Anderson (1983) calls an *imagined community* around *WW*. Much like the *Lineage* guild members in Steinkuehler's (2007) study, the members of *Webkinz* Insider develop a sense of community through offering help for newcomers to *WW*, sharing insider knowledge about the SVE through a forum and Twitter updates, and collaboratively solving problems. To illustrate, the following post appeared on the *Webkinz* Insider home page not long after members began experiencing trouble with a specific part of *WW*:

> If you are experiencing Magical Forest problems on your account, please visit the Glitch Report section of our forum. Our members are getting together and comparing notes to see if they can figure out what triggers these glitches. Hopefully we can collect information that will be useful to the Ganz programmers as they hunt for solutions to these problems.

This post and the responses it generated are a clear demonstration of the distributed nature of knowledge in the *Webkinz* Insider community. By collecting examples of instances of these problems, members are helping each other to avoid triggering these glitches in their game play and attempting to provide Ganz with feedback on how to fix these issues. Such posts, as well as forum threads and articles posted on the *Webkinz* Insider Wiki, cover topics ranging from how to earn more kinzcash and how to make certain desirable clothing items all the way to how to navigate specific parts of the game; moreover, they provide clear examples of the culture of collaborative problem solving and social nature of learning in this space. Members take pride in sharing their knowledge about *WW*, and the *Webkinz* Insider site provides the cultural tools needed for easily and effectively communicating such information.

As another example, the site Everything *Webkinz*, with approximately twenty-one thousand members, is another popular destination for *WW* fans. Created by three mothers, the site's goal – "to provide a fun and safe place for Webkinz lovers of all ages to play and learn and talk about their Webkinz!" – is similar to that of *WW*; however, as a not-for-profit and less restrictive space, Everything *Webkinz* offers far more opportunities for creating a sense of community around *WW*. The site hosts virtual events, such as room decorating contests, raffles, holiday parties, and scavenger hunts, that foster interaction among members. Similar to Boellstorff's (2008) study, these events are a significant source of socialization within this space, yielding artifacts (e.g., screenshots, artwork, contest entries) and shared memories that help members to "conjure an image of their communion" and social connection (Anderson, 1983, p. 5) In addition, the site administrators solicit member input on what these events should be and how they should be structured, thus allowing members to shape the social and cultural landscape of the site.

Conclusion: Sociocultural Theories of Learning and *WW*

Sociocultural theory is predicated on the belief that cultural components are foundational for learning and that learning is supported by social connections and interactions with others. As such, social partners (e.g., siblings, parents, and community members) are active participants in the learning process, and learning is facilitated in the space between people (interpsychological), where culture resides, prior to being internalized (intrapsychological) (Vygotsky, 1978). Thus the social precedes the psychological (John-Steiner & Mahn, 1996). In studying the cultural and community aspects of *WW* and how they might facilitate learning, it is clear that the absence of community, especially in terms of limited communication and user input, impedes the capacity of the SVE to support children's developing intellectual and emotional abilities.

In the absence of direct interaction and feedback, users are constrained in their internalization capacities. While scaffolded learning is possible at some level through the semiotic mediation of *WW* [the SVE is rich with printed (and some spoken) language, sounds, and images], the social aspects of learning are limited because users have few meaningful interactions with others and receive little feedback from site activities (other than gratitude for purchases made for one's Webkinz). Thus the "potential development as determined through problem solving under adult guidance [or site feedback] or in collaboration with more capable peers" (Vygotsky, 1978, p. 86) is lacking. This lack of dialectic processes (Bidell, 1999) minimizes the learning capacity of this SVE.

Furthermore, a core component of sociocultural theory is that learning is an actively supported endeavor and that this scaffolding enables learners to grow from their actual level of ability to their potential level (Vygotsky, 1978). Sadly, this awareness of children's zone of proximal development is missing on *WW* because feedback after errors is missing and responses are often discouraging in their tone. For instance, the Jelly Bean Challenge, a special activity in which users are presented with a partially filled jar of jellybeans and asked to guess how many jellybeans are inside, does not support improvement after errors. Instead, feedback for incorrect guesses include statements such as, "Wow, you were way off!" without any information as to whether the guess was too high or too low. While users get four chances, the user can get the same response four times with no mention of whether any guesses were closer than others. Thus users have no way to improve from one guess or challenge to the next. Interestingly, the fan communities surrounding *WW* do provide feedback that supports learning by listing the maximum capacity of the jar and translating the meaning of responses (e.g., "Wow, you were way off!" means that a guess was off by a thousand or more jellybeans, whereas "Oooo, that was close" means that the guess was off by two hundred or fewer jellybeans). These sites also provide chat and/or bulletin board features in which users can post comments and answer others' questions. Thus users can be the scaffolded learner or the more competent peer – roles that are both supportive of learning.

From a sociocultural standpoint, the design features of *WW* and the concern for users' safety limit the capacity of the site to support learning because meaningful interactions are minimal. Users cannot communicate freely, share ideas, or contribute to the design, activities, or structure of the site. This is unfortunate because learning theories highlight that learning is "a matter of participation in a social process of knowledge construction" (Salomon & Perkins, 1998, p. 4). Thus *WW* is a SVE in which users can be exposed to and possibly internalize cultural norms and values (e.g., materialism, caring) but in no way contribute to them. It is worth noting, however, that in a recent *Webkinz Newz* article, Ganz announced its intention to improve the community aspects of *WW*. At the moment, efforts in this direction include (1) "enhanc[ing] the community aspects of *Webkinz Newz*" (Ganz, 2010, n.p.) through the addition of something called Feedback Fridays in which Ganz solicits feedback about site content from members, (2) "improv[ing] the biggest social area in *WW*, the Kinzville Park, with some great new features to get more people meeting and chatting with one another" (Ganz, 2010), and (3) implementing communal contests that "require players to work together toward a common goal [e.g., 'collectively score 1.7 billion points in Cash Cow 2 (an arcade game)'" (Ganz, 2010, n.p.). It is not yet clear if these efforts actually will help members to develop closer social ties and a sense of investment in the site, but they are indicators that Ganz is aware of shortcomings in this area and is attempting to redesign the space to give members more ownership and influence in *WW*.

While at present *WW* appears limited in its capacity to provide scaffolded learning opportunities and offer members a sense of community within the game site, it remains a compelling space for young children that can offer opportunities for learning along with other fronts. For example, the site affords young children the opportunity to develop a range of technological competencies, such as using a mouse, operating a computer, typing, reading icons, using an avatar to navigate virtual space, and searching for online information. *WW* also engages children in literacy-related practices, such as reading environmental and functional print and deciphering messages via text, audio, and image (Black, 2010). The site also encourages children to play academically oriented games and provides a space for experimenting with online social roles by dressing Webkinz and decorating rooms. In addition, children's engagement with sites such as *WW* inspires the development of ancillary fan sites such as those discussed in this chapter that do provide mechanisms for children's input, scaffolded learning, and a sense of connection with others. Moreover, the site can be used as a motivating factor in classroom activities, such as literacy centers in which children write stories, plays, or poems about their Webkinz pets or research projects that involve exploring the habitat and particularities of the various animals found in *WW*, to name just a few. Also, the virtual world, used in conjunction with face-to-face interactions, could be a resource for scaffolded learning in which feedback and suggestions for improvement are provided by social partners such as siblings, parents, teachers, and peers.

Collectively, the findings and discussion from this chapter suggest that SVEs for young children are significant sites of culture that warrant further exploration. In addition, analyses emphasize the risks to learning and the creation of community when communication and social interactions are limited. This content analysis of *WW* and the fan sites surrounding it underscore the benefits of facilitating a sense of belonging and investment when designing learning spaces. While virtual worlds may create cultural norms, values, and practices, the absence of communication and users' ability to influence the site limits the establishment of online community as well as learning potentials. From a sociocultural perspective, learning is a highly social and mediated process (Vygotsky, 1978). Thus, combining the engaging graphics and play of shared virtual worlds with opportunities for authentic communication, literacy development, and scaffolded learning (as those in the fan sites surrounding *WW*) can provide exciting opportunities for children's learning and development.

Acknowledgments

We would like to thank Reena Shah for her contributions to this chapter.

References

Anderson, B. (1983). *Imagined communities: Reflections on the origins and spread of nationalism*. London: Verso.

Baym, N. K. (1995). The Emergence of Community in Computer-Mediated Communication. In S. G. Jones (Ed.) *Cybersociety* (pp. 138–63). Thousand Oaks, CA: Sage.

Bidell, T. (1999). Vygotsky, Piaget, and the Dialectic of Development. In P. Loyd & C. Fernyhough (eds.), *Lev Vygotsky: Critical assessment*, vol. 1 (pp. 262–81). London: Taylor & Francis.

Black, R. W. (2010). The Language of Webkinz: Early Childhood Literacy in an Online Virtual World. *Journal of Digital Culture and Education*, 2(1), 7–24.

Boellstorff, T. (2008). *Coming of age in Second Life: An anthropologist explores the virtually human*. Princeton, NJ: Princeton University Press.

Compete, Inc. (2009). Site comparison of www.webkinz.com, www.clubpenguin.com, www.barbiegirls.com, www.neopets.com, www.secondlife.com Compete. *http://siteanalytics.com*. Retrieved July 17, 2009, from http://siteanalytics.compete.com/www.webkinz.com+www.clubpenguin.com+www.barbiegirls.com+www.neopets.com+www.secondlife.com/.

Dean, R. (2001). The Myth of Cross-Cultural Competence. *Families in Society: Journal of Contemporary Human Services*, 82(6), 623–30.

Fields, D., & Kafai, Y. B. (2009). "U wanna Go to the Moon?" A Connective Ethnography of Peer Knowledge Sharing and Diffusion in a Teen Virtual World. *International Journal of Computer-Supported Collaborative Learning*, 4(1), 47–68.

Foster, D. (1996). Community and Identity in the Electronic Village. In D. Porter (ed.), *Internet Culture* (pp. 23–37). New York: Routledge.

Ganz. (2009a). Welcome to Webkinz – A Ganz website. Retrieved July 17, 2009, from http://www.webkinz.com/us_en/.

(2009b). Webkinz – Webkinz Deluxe Membership. Retrieved July 17, 2009, from http://www.webkinz.com/us_en/deluxe_membership.html.

(2009c). Webkinz – For Parents – Frequently Asked Questions. Retrieved July 17, 2009, from http://www.webkinz.com/us_en/faq_parents.html.

(2010, February 11). Preview: Communal Contests – *Webkinz* Newz – Webkinz Information. Retrieved February 25, 2010, from http://www.webkinznewz. com/wp-mu/2010/02/preview-communal-contests/.

Goffman, E. (1959). *The presentation of self in everyday life*, 1st ed. New York: Doubleday Anchor Books.

Goncu, A., & Katsarou, E. (2000). Commentary: Constructing Sociocultural Approaches to Literacy Education. In K. A. Roskos & J. F. Christie (eds.), *Play and literacy in early childhood: Research from multiple perspectives* (pp. 221–30). Mahwah, NJ: Lawrence Erlbaum Associates.

Grimes, S. M. (2008, September 2). I'm a Barbie Girl, in a BarbieGirls World. *The Escapist*. Retrieved July 9, 2009, from http://www.escapistmagazine.com/articles/view/issues/issue_165/5187-Im-a-Barbie-Girl-in-a-BarbieGirls-World.3.

Grimes, S. M., & Shade, L. R. (2005). Neopian Economics of Play: Children's Cyberpets and Online Communities as Immersive Advertising in NeoPets. com. *International Journal of Media and Cultural Politics*, 1(2), 181–98.

Heller, K. (1989). The Return to Community. *American Journal of Community Psychology*, 17(1), 1–14.

John-Steiner, V., & Mahn, H. (1996). Sociocultural Approaches to Learning and Development: A Vygotskian Framework. *Educational Psychologist*, 31(3–4), 191–206.

Jones, S. G. (1995). Understanding Community in the Information Age. In S. G. Jones (Ed.) *Cybersociety* (pp. 10–35). Thousand Oaks, CA: Sage.

Jones, Q. (1997). Virtual Communities, Virtual Settlements and Cyber-archeology: A Theoretical Outline. *Journal of Computer-Mediated Communication*, 3(3). Available at http://jcmc.indiana.edu/vol3/issue3/jones.html

Marsh, J. (2008). *Out-of-school play in online virtual worlds and the implications for literacy learning*. Paper presented at the Center for the Studies in Literacy, Policy and Learning Cultures, University of South Australia. Available at http://www.unisa.edu.au/hawkeinstitute/cslplc/documents/JackieMarsh.pdf.

McMillan, D. W., & Chavis, D. M. (1986). Sense of Community: A Definition and Theory. *Journal of Community Psychology*, 14(1), 6–23.

Nanda, S. (1991). *Cultural anthropology*. 4th ed. Belmont, MA: Wadsworth.

Reich, S. M., & Reich, J. (2006). Cultural Competence in Interdisciplinary Collaborations: A Method for Respecting Diversity in Research Partnerships. *American Journal of Community Psychology*, 38, 51–62.

Rheingold, H. (2001). The Virtual Community. In D. Trend (ed.), *Reading digital culture* (pp. 272–80). Malden, MA: Blackwell.

Rogoff, B. (1995). Observing Sociocultural Activity on Three Planes: Participatory Appropriation, Guided Participation, and Apprenticeship. In J. Wertsch, P. Del Rio, & A. Alvarez (eds.), *Sociocultural studies of mind* (pp. 139–64). New York: Cambridge University Press.

Salomon, G., & Perkins, D. N. (1998). Individual and social aspects of learning. *Review of Research in Education*, 23, 1–24.

Steinkuehler, C. A. (2005). *Cognition and learning in massively multiplayer online games: A critical approach*. Unpublished Dissertation, University of Wisconsin–Madison.

(2006). Massively Multiplayer Online Videogaming as Participation in a Discourse. *Mind, Culture, and Activity*, 13(1), 38–52.

(2007). Massively Multiplayer Online Gaming as a Constellation of Literacy Practices. *E-Learning*, 4(3), 297–318.

Tynes, B. M. (2007). Internet Safety Gone Wild? Sacrificing the Educational and Psychological Benefits of Online Social Environments. *Journal of Adolescent Research*, 22, 575–84.

Vygotsky, L. S. (1978). *Mind in society: The development of higher psychological processes*. Cambridge, MA: Harvard University Press.

Wertsch, J. V. (1991). *Voices of the mind: A sociocultural approach to mediated action*. Cambridge, MA: Harvard University Press.

(1998). *Mind as action*, illustrated ed. New York: Oxford University Press.

15   Culture versus Architecture: *Second Life,*
         Sociality, and the Human

Thomas M. Malaby

While the emergence of virtual worlds as viable sites for the generation of economic value and exchange has been central to their broader acceptance as domains where real stakes accumulate (Malaby, 2006a), their capacity as sites for the generation of social ties and for learning – fundamental forms of social exchange beyond the market – has received secondary interest outside of a few forward-thinking disciplines. *Second Life* has demonstrated a substantial such capacity and saw a great amount of growth in both educational use and sociality more generally since its appearance in 2003.[1] That is, *Second Life*'s users accumulated both social capital within the world through the reciprocal cultivation of social ties and cultural capital in the form of competencies as a result of learning within the world, whether formally or informally.

Such success makes it perhaps too easy to assume that *Second Life*'s design – its architecture – presupposed such use and supported it in a thoroughgoing manner. Remarkably, however, the rise of social and cultural capital within *Second Life* has happened in many respects *despite Second Life*'s architecture. In this chapter I argue that *Second Life* was built in fundamental ways on an asocial imagining of the human, one grounded in a techno-liberal sensibility. On this view, human beings are resolutely individuals, at root motivated by the challenge to act within and gain mastery of complex and open-ended systems (not coincidentally, this is also a construction of a specific kind of gamer). Correspondingly, social effects (the creation of exclusionary groups, lobbying and other political activity, and others) are ideally at best minimized or at worst excluded by system design, an issue that I have explored at length in the context of Linden Lab's internal decision making (Malaby, 2009a). The imagined user of *Second Life* was in many respects not supposed to be social except in a very narrow sense, and this raised a number of challenges for users of *Second Life* as well as for the employees of Linden Lab (*Lindens*), who struggled to support the emergent uses of the world that challenged their expectations. I suggest that this has important implications for the kinds of learning that are architecturally recognized within *Second Life*, even if in practice users to a certain extent can transcend these promptings and achieve learning in the social and collaborative sense.

In the increasing rush to celebrate and explore the possibilities that digital games present for learning – which are worthy pursuits and in which this volume seeks to play a large part – it is possible that we will overlook the deeper forces at work that shape many of the largest and most prominent games today. Because of their success, and also because of the ways they reflect a peculiarly American understanding of what gaming – and maybe the human itself – is (more on this below), we are in danger of seeing *World of Warcraft*, *Halo*, or *Second Life* as games or gamelike in a generic sense, as if their characteristics stand for the essential qualities of all games, with no further specification necessary. In a related way, we may be in danger of seeing learning itself through a similarly narrow lens. I suggest in what follows that we consider whether the sociality and learning taking place in and through major commercial games today are themselves not generic but rather to some degree reflective of (or in response to) this same peculiar picture of the human as a gamer of a particular kind.

To explore these issues, I begin by tracing the early conceptual history of *Second Life* and how it was ideologically grounded in the technoliberal worldview of Silicon Valley and practically grounded in the techniques of game design. I then explore how these assumptions found their way into *Second Life*'s architecture, even as in some ways the design of the world nonetheless left certain doors open to social use. The concept of mastery enables us to see links between the assumptions that informed *Second Life*'s architecture; a broader history of American ideas about individuals, authority, and technology; and perhaps certain ideas about learning itself. I close with an account of why it is vitally important for both research in virtual worlds and the development of learning applications for them to recognize the multiple ways in which architecture deeply shapes but does not determine what is possible within these complex and open-ended spaces.

Second Life's First Beginnings

The research that forms the basis for the ideas in this chapter consisted of more than a year of ethnographic field work at Linden Lab, during which time I engaged in extensive observations of Linden Lab's work practice, interviewed dozens of present and past employees at length, and also did work tasks for the company to understand how the company used a variety of technological affordances to build, maintain, and add new features to *Second Life*. As such, this work inevitably focuses on the site of *Second Life*'s cultural production as a piece of software and less on the perspectives of users themselves, who have encountered and engaged *Second Life*'s architecture in surprising ways (see Boellstorff, 2008, and Au, 2008). My primary interest is in how Lindens imagined the human in a very fundamental way and how this imagining found its way into *Second Life*'s architecture (and their own architecture within their office and digital work domains).

In collaboration with Wagner James Au, a journalist also working at Linden Lab at the time, in 2005 I created an online wiki for Lindens, inviting them to contribute to their own history of the company. It became clear from this wiki and from many of my interviews that while the idea for the company sprang specifically from the mind of Philip Rosedale, founder of Linden Lab, his own inspiration was itself rooted in ideas about technology, humanity, and creativity that are part of a specific history in America, one that found fertile ground in the San Francisco Bay Area. It is a set of primarily practical (rather than discursive; see Kelty, 2005) assumptions and ideological commitments that continue to shape the dispositions of those who architect our increasingly digital lives and that I refer to as *technoliberalism*. Like liberalism, in technoliberalism, there is an emphasis on the positive social effects that can emerge from a multitude of individual acts, but technoliberalism extends liberalism's ideas beyond the market and also places technology at center stage (Malaby, 2009a, pp. 16, 59–61, 133). Technoliberalism entails an intense suspicion of vertical authority, a commitment to making technology universally accessible and beyond institutional control, and a deep faith in the positive aggregate effects that follow from individual use of this technology for the purposes of creative expression. The possibility and promise of *contriving* the complex systems within which this individual expressive mastery takes place energizes not only Linden Lab but also other projects that shape our digital lives (such as Amazon's Mechanical Turk).

Rosedale was fascinated by complexity after encountering the ideas of Stephen Wolfram concerning single-cell simulations. Wolfram sought to demonstrate how complexity could evolve in nature through the reproduction of a single-cell organism following a small set of simple rules. Rosedale successfully produced a version of this simulation that he coded himself on an Apple computer in 1982 when he was fourteen years old (see Au, 2008, pp. 15–16). He was again inspired ten years later by Neal Stephenson's

Snow Crash (1992) to create a similarly complex networked simulation of a world with evolving flora and fauna. In the mid-1990s, he, as he put it in the wiki, "entered the dreamless sleep" of a high-technology dotcom startup, working at Real Networks (where he was hired as chief technology officer after selling Real a technology he created for streaming video over low-bandwidth dial-up Internet connections). While his description of these years suggests that during them his dreams of creating a complex, evolving ecology were on hold, nonetheless the experience with network technologies and streaming specifically contributed as well to his vision for the early version of *Second Life* called *Linden World*.

Linden World is worth taking some time to describe because in important ways it both reflects these early inspirations and also stands in marked contrast to *Second Life* as it came to be. As Au characterizes it in his brief but effective discussion of it (2008, pp. 23–9), "Rosedale saw this as an Eden that he and Linden Lab would shape, and only then allow users to interact in. '[Y]ou would wander around in it as an avatar,' Rosedale recalls imagining, 'and you'd come across animals – maybe they'd try to eat you or something – that no one had ever seen.'" Creating first (in true demiurgic fashion) an ocean that flowed across two servers, the Lindens added land and creatures because they aimed to create a complex, evolving, networked system on a massive scale. Their imagined users' relationship with it would be essentially adventurous, whether in the opportunity to observe an accurate astronomical simulation above or in battling the world's denizens and each other in virtual battle-capable robots below. The conception of the world in this gaming-oriented way is at least partly attributable to the arrival of Cory Ondrejka in November 2000; Ondrejka came from a video-game programming background and, more broadly, from training in advanced weaponry technology via the U.S. military. The Lindens added ruined bridges and other seemingly human-made obstacles to the landscape, raising the tactical possibilities of these *battle bots* even further. The idea of the avatar, so central to *Second Life*'s experience, was not a part of this world's appeal. It was envisioned as a Hobbesian landscape of human against human and human against "nature," but with a keen emphasis on emergence and complexity – this open-ended world would surprise and challenge these individual pilots of virtual robots.

All this changed in the midst of a presentation to Linden Lab's investors shortly thereafter. It is a moment I heard referred to repeatedly around Linden Lab, although I could not specify the exact time frame (the best guess would be early 2001). During the demonstration, a live feed of *Linden World* included Lindens using the in-world tools – that had been coded into the program specifically for Linden developer use – to create objects. This caught the attention of Mitch Kapor and others around the table, who pushed Rosedale and Ondrejka to make those tools available to users, to shift the world fundamentally from a complex system the Lindens created themselves and which users explored to one in which the users themselves would create.

In video-game industry terms, Linden Lab in this moment effectively turned over the production of *Second Life*'s "content" to its users. The term *content* in the industry is used to connote, loosely speaking, the "stuff" that is in the games and that their users encounter, use, or interact with. It is at the center of discourse and practice about virtual worlds for both their makers and their users because the "quality" of a world's content is often seen as an index of its appeal. In the first years of *Second Life*'s existence through the time of this writing, Linden limited its own creation of content to showpieces meant to provide examples of content to users, some infrastructure (roads for user-created land vehicles), and more landmass – bringing additional land (and with it, more servers) online to accommodate the growing population of users ("residents"). Residents in *Second Life* can buy this land and not only build on it but also literally reshape it themselves (raising hills, adding lakes and trees, etc.), meaning that the production of content in *Second Life* does not stop at ground level.

Much followed from this change in approach, including the abandonment of battle bots and the development of avatars, and the focus shifted from users encountering a complex world to enlisting the actions of users to generate something like the same kind of complexity that had interested Rosedale for so long. On this view, and it is reflected in many dimensions in *Second Life*'s architecture, the users were assumed to be motivated by a desire to express themselves individually using the content-creation tools provided in the client software to make things in the world. In these early years of *Second Life*, the content-creation tools, not surprisingly, perfectly mirrored the same tools that a more conventional gaming company would use internally to create the stuff that fills the world. The three basic tools are 3D modeling (the ability to create 3D objects in the world), scripting (programming objects so that they can be interactive and perform actions in the world), and texture mapping (the wrapping of objects in "textures" to create a sense of different materials and surfaces in *Second Life*).

Lindens tended to imagine, even through 2005, that the "content" created by users was *only* that which was modeled, scripted, or texture mapped (see Malaby, 2006b), and this practical (not necessarily intentional) bias reflected a limited view of creativity, but one that was sensible when read against the computer gaming development backgrounds of many of Linden Lab's developers. The demiurgic quality of world creation that complex computer game development engenders, especially within the context of 3D, graphically intensive "first-person shooters" (such as *Halo*), follows from the creation of not only a world but also the very physics that operates within it. For most Linden Lab developers, such first-person shooters (FPSs) were the epitome of online games, and they fervently sought to demonstrate that *Second Life* could be a viable platform for their development (that is, that *Second Life* users would create FPSs within *Second Life* – certain zones had health bars and the possibility of avatar "death" specifically for this purpose). The substantial Linden Lab support of such a project, USL: Chinatown, reflected the primacy Lindens gave FPSs as the ultimate index of *Second Life*'s viability and value (see Malaby, 2009a, pp. 101–4).

Game development in fact typically splits these two in-house processes into the development of the game *engine* (which defines such deep characteristics as the physics of the world and how calculations for its objects and their movement or collision will be handled and rendered) and the development of the game *content* (the specific "look" of the world, its narrative or backstory – if any – and the topography, objects, and avatars that fill the space). As this distinction unfolded in Linden Lab, the lab effectively assumed responsibility only for the *game engine* – the physics of *Second Life* itself – and for the hosting and maintenance of a giant world with continents and islands and some infrastructure but left to a great extent otherwise undefined. One can notice even here an extremely important implicit distinction inherited from the computer game industry between those with the ability to create and control the very system within which content creation takes place and those empowered to create that content but not empowered to get "under the hood" and manipulate what the engine controls. In a conventional computer game company, these would be two different departments (the engine developers and the content team; often game engines are in fact licensed from other companies that make them). For *Second Life*, Linden Lab controls the engine, and the users are effectively the content team.

The bias toward seeing *Second Life* content only in what users made with the conventional content-creation tools (as opposed to, for example, content in the form of support groups or other kinds of social networks in *Second Life*) does not reflect only the practicalities of computer game development. In a number of interviews with Linden Lab developers, the creation tools were referenced as having a limitless quality, as themselves sufficient for the creation of *anything* a user could possibly imagine. This was even more powerfully represented in *Second Life*'s marketing materials, which stressed the limitless quality of *Second Life* and one's ability to create whatever one desired: "Your world. Your imagination." Users in *Second Life* were imagined (and represented) – through the included tools – as having all the agency they would ever need, eliding the very real constraints they faced in two directions. First, users were not able to manipulate the engine, the very terms on which *Second Life* was built (under the hood; for an extensive discussion of the implications, see Malaby, 2009a). Second, the tools they were provided could not be used to create anything the users wanted (as in the case of social groups for any of a number of different purposes). To understand why they could not reveals more deeply how asocial *Second Life* was architected to be.

A representation of the demiurgic, even magical, quality of (computer game) creation was intentionally architected into *Second Life*. Every time a resident works with the tools of *Second Life*, whether doing something as common and simple as engaging in text-based chat or changing clothes or appearance, but most obviously and grandly when scripting or building, the resident's activity is represented in gestures and actions of the avatar itself. What is more, if an object is being worked on, the changes to that object are observable by others in the world in real time, even down to click-to-click changes in, say, the object's color as the user tries different points on the building tool's color wheel. (This level of detail does not extend to the production of text for chat; other users see one's avatar "typing" but do not see the production of text letter by letter.)

This publicly visible creation was an intentional decision by the developers of *Second Life*, and according to one engineer who had direct responsibility for coding this part of the client, it ran counter to a number of users' preferences. It was, however, consistent with, as he put it, the promotion of "shared experience," the idea that while "in world" the users would be able to be in touch with what others were doing. We must note, however, that the activity that the code highlights for others' observation is the making of content in the conventional programmer sense. This engineer commented that one of the most remarkable experiences he had in world was watching a master builder (who before participating in *Second Life* had had no prior 3D modeling experience) sculpt a dinosaur in real time. The emphasis, deeply inscribed in *Second Life*'s code, is on representing *individual* content creation activity to others and, again, with a conception of content that gives pride of place to the technical activities of content creation, especially building and scripting. Sociality here is the restricted sociality of appreciating or experiencing the content someone else has made. In this way, the cultural capital of effective building performance is valorized, whereas the social capital mediated through deeper social exchanges is strongly deemphasized. The contribution of many other kinds of content to *Second Life*, such as the organization of a regular meeting group for victims of domestic abuse or establishing oneself as a charismatic socialite in dance clubs, is not distinctively represented in one's avatar's actions; mastery of these kinds of social creation finds little purchase on *Second Life*'s architecture. The social in *Second Life*'s architecture over its first years was, to the extent that it existed at all, architecturally restricted to an expressive individualism, where what one creates is conceived not only as content in a specific sense but furthermore as the realization of an individual user's creative desires.

In *Second Life: The Official Guide*, produced by Linden Lab in 2007, this emphasis on *Second Life* as a space for creative individuals is strong (Rymaszewski et al., 2007). Two of its chapters are devoted exclusively to profiles of individual users in *Second Life*, totaling forty-two such profiles. The second of these chapters, with thirty profiles, is titled "Real Residents" and focuses on very well-known residents of *Second Life*. It introduces each resident with a distinctive label (e.g., "The Scripter," "The Game God," "The Fashionista") that highlights the individual nature of the resident's accomplishments. These are the masters of *Second Life*, the users who have engaged this complex system and achieved a degree of mastery over it. Other marketing materials from Linden Lab during my time there pursued the same course. Linden Lab created trading cards, distributed at gaming industry conferences and similar venues, that each profiled a famous *Second Life* user (see Malaby, 2006a), and they also highlighted individual users in their online marketing (see Malaby, 2009a, pp. 113–14).

Another area where this limited picture of sociality manifested itself was in the group tools provided to users within *Second Life*. In late 2005, Linden Lab was in the midst of a massive rewriting of the code for the group tools because users had complained for some time that they were "flat," reflecting an idea of groups as limited to the idea of a number of people with a shared interest. This made certain kinds of collaboration and organization clumsy at best. Those running businesses in *Second Life*, for example, were frustrated by the lack of hierarchy in the tools, that is, in the ability to create different ranks of members with different rights and privileges. Linden Lab not only did not see groups as a site for collaborative creation (the emphasis on collaboration in their marketing materials can be dated to the involvement of investor Pierre Omidyar, well after the architecture was in place; see Malaby, 2006b), but they also inscribed their own wariness of vertical authority, especially in organizational form, into the software itself. The widely voiced concerns on the part of several Linden Lab developers about the "balkanization" of *Second Life* – of the assumedly negative consequences of people forming exclusive and inwardly focused social groups – found expression in the limited nature of the group tools.

Rosedale's approach to *Second Life*, and that of many of the developers at the company, was one characterized by a technoliberal sensibility; he was interested in aggregate effects of individual actions when access to technology was unconstrained (although within a system the company created and ultimately controlled). This meant that once the shift to a networked space for user creation happened in 2001, Rosedale imagined *Second Life* (the Linden World) as needing many, many people but still did not see making *Second Life* as making a society, with all that that would entail. In an interview in 2005, he told me:

> Given my background there was always a tendency to focus a little bit on the technical because I found the technical problems to be so fascinating involved with creating this. But I think as a person who had a lot of passion for the idea, *I was always struck by the expressive and, not so much societal elements*, although I have to say: I think that a lot of the enthusiasm that I have now for the kind of social change or societal change that might result from something like *Second Life* getting global, or getting a lot bigger – to where it matters…. I think a lot of that stuff I kind of came to understand more as we went along. *I didn't go in feeling like we're going to make people's lives better. But I did go into it feeling like none of it was interesting unless there were a lot of people involved….*
>
> I think that it was more emergent as we saw things start to happen and we saw people be affected by *Second Life*. It was then that we said, "Well, you know, it might be that an environment that has this really, sort of, super-enhanced projective, creative element to it could actually be a kind of a bandwidth-increasing thing between people in general." And then we started writing – I can't remember, maybe in 2003 or 2004 – started writing about – and Cory [Ondrejka] as well – about how if you grossly, *if you just increase the communicative bandwidth between individuals that there's almost no arguing, unless you're really taking a contrarian position, you know, that that probably makes them better…. The whole sort of combination of creative self-expression and the transparent society* [emphasis added].

But this dream of increased bandwidth through many individuals expressing themselves through technology required another element. It was not enough that users have individual desires waiting to be expressed. To create this content in *Second Life*, especially the impressive content creation of crafting a dinosaur in real time, requires *mastery* of those content tools. Mastery is an important concept for understanding the ideological under-pinnings of *Second Life*'s architecture because it points in another way to the status of the individual and furthermore helps us to identify what kind of learning *Second Life* prompts architecturally and what kind it ignores.

Master Narratives

Recent work has charted how some of the most important developments in computing and networking technology in the United States were inex-tricably linked to political and more broadly ideological interests. Works by journalists (Hiltzik, 2000; Kidder, 1981; Markoff, 2005; Waldrop, 2001) and, more recently, academics (Thomas, 2003; Turner, 2006) are helpful in filling out the cultural-historical landscape from which computers emerged, particularly in the San Francisco Bay Area. Specifically, these works reveal how the development of these technologies and their makers' aspirations for them were inextricably linked to general attitudes about authority that characterized the postwar period.

In these works there is a common theme, one that I have developed into the concept of technoliberalism. Among this emerging culture one finds a remarkable and mutually confirming combination of a deeply held skepti-cism toward "top-down" decision making – with a corresponding resistance to (and even resentment of) the institutional control of technology – and a deep faith in the ability of technology to provide solutions when made widely available. The contrast here is with computing as it existed in insti-tutions through the 1960s: Mainframe computing demanded specialized and controlled access to the most powerful tool in an institution, and its enduring image is that of the mainframe in the glass room, accessible only by a priesthood of those empowered to tend it. The attitude that arose in reaction against this image, these books suggest, reflects the antiestablish-ment politics of the period and found purchase in the distinctive disposi-tion of engineers toward new technologies, corporate organizations, and a particular version of libertarianism. As Coleman put it (2004, pp. 511–12):

> Programmers over decades of intense interaction come to viscerally expe-rience the computer as a general purpose machine that can be infinitely programmed to achieve any task through the medium of software writ-ten by humans with a computer language. The technological potential

for unlimited programmable capabilities melds with what is seen as the expansive ability for programmers to create. For programmers, computing in a dual sense, as a technology and as an activity, becomes a total realm for the freedom of creation and expression.

The issue of creation and engineering is central to Linden Lab's project in particular because the making *of* the world of *Second Life* stands in a strange and mutually constructive relationship with the making *in* the world on the part of its users.

This line of thinking about programming as a kind of individual mastery can be linked to an important thinker about play, Mihalyi Csikszentmihalyi (1990). For Csikszentmihalyi, play can be found wherever people face an ongoing mixture of pattern and unpredictability that demands a practiced mastery of performance (what he calls "flow"), such as for the factory worker who happens to confront the properly engaging mixture of constraint and (perhaps dangerous) possibility in manipulating multiple machines and objects. Practiced makers of cedar shingles, for example, deftly handle the slight variations in every piece of wood that comes their way as they coordinate their bodily movements in extremely close proximity to two open and spinning saws. Csikszentmihalyi's focus on a state of mastery aligns well with the ideas of Wiener and others, who saw individuals as active and performative participants in complex systems. To a certain extent, then, when many Lindens imagined their users, they imagined game players in this way. This is not a conception of play or gaming that holds universally (see Malaby, 2009b, 2009c). Instead, it is a particular conception of gaming that fits with the broader postwar American technoliberal ideals, but the cultural-historical situatedness of this imagining is not acknowledged by technoliberals – it is imagined as the essence of being human. All people are seen as gamers in a limited and highly individualistic sense. For many Lindens, a game constituted, at root, a challenge to an *individual* to act within an open-ended system, whether that game involved other players or not.

It is interesting to consider how Linden Lab's decisions to architect for individual creation and shared experience worked together to create a strong emphasis on individual mastery. In many important respects, it is possible to fail in *Second Life* and to fail quite publicly. One of my early encounters with what this means in practice came after buying my first land. Having upgraded my account from the one-time fee version (US$9.95 – later this basic subscription became completely free) to the monthly subscription (US$9.95 per month), I enjoyed some of the benefits of a premium account, including the right to own land, and I shopped around until I found a small plot on the corner of one of the many squares that make up the "grid" of *Second Life*. Each of these squares is called a *sim* (short for "simulator"), and each corresponds to an actual server that controls that square. My plot of land had a beautiful vista: a nice water view (waterfront properties in *Second Life*, as offline, are always more valuable). With an effective size of 512 square meters, this was not a large piece of *Second Life* by any stretch, but it was big enough that I began to think that I ought to put something on it – a place where I could invite others to sit down for a chat. And here we confront what is strangely familiar yet unfamiliar about *Second Life*. What does it mean to sit down in *Second Life*? It means that you sit your avatar (your virtual body) down, and the object you sit on (if it is programmed to be sat on) actually will contain a bit of software that tells your avatar *how* to sit, whether to lounge, to sit upright, to cross your legs, or what have you.

Much of the conversation in *Second Life* in 2005 (long before the ability to speak in *Second Life* and hear others was introduced) was text-based "chat" (typed comments that were visible to every avatar close enough to "hear" them). In thinking about providing a social space on my land, I had already learned (from my own interactions with other users) that sitting down was preferred for this kind conversation – perhaps it was the familiar sight lines or the familiar arrangement of virtual bodies that suggested intimacy and focused attention. It takes very little time for a user to come to identify strongly as the avatar. With it, you can take meaningful actions in the virtual world, and more important, you can fail while trying. It may seem a bit strange for me to tie these two things together – meaning and failure – and even to discuss failure in *Second Life* at all. With no preset goals, what is failure in *Second Life*?

To answer this question, we should begin by recognizing the place of failure in our everyday social experience. As sociologist Erving Goffman showed (Goffman, 1959), the way we present ourselves is always related to the particular domain in which we act, and furthermore, we seek to put forth certain impressions while avoiding others. A server in a fine restaurant manages the front of the house like a stage set (Goffman's "frontstage"), protecting from view or other discernment any messy contingencies that may befall the "backstage." At a job interview, the applicant strives to project a specific version of himself or herself, one that is an apt fit with the open position. Social differentiation (status) trades to a certain extent on those who can perform these roles with élan, with mastery, and it is the possibility of failure that makes success meaningful (and vice versa); thus are the culturally masterful (and this often informs class differences) separable from those who are, well, not. Social expectations for successful performance are ever-present (Bauman, 1977), even when there are no specific goals; often the only goal is to be seen as a competent member of a social group in the circumstances at hand.

In *Second Life*, not to have a space of this sort risked such failure for me. In having one, I would be more likely to present myself as a knowledgeable, competent user of *Second Life* – something other than a "newbie" (or "noob"; see Boellstorff, 2008, pp. 72–5, 134–6). I found a nice, tower-like structure from a "free content" area (a place where other users drop modifiable objects that others can grab copies of for free) and proceeded to tweak it (and my land) a bit until I had a nice bridge attached to a domed sitting area on the top of the tower. Now I could invite others to my land and appear the thoughtful (or at least minimally competent) host. I could respond proudly to inquiries about how I managed to make the roof appear to be hammered copper by alluding to creative use of a Spanish tile texture, wrapping one tile over the entirety of the dome (in fact, this happy outcome was very much an accident – I expected to see a full-fledged tile roof when I applied the texture). In this respect, even the social in *Second Life* is deeply shaped by the display of cultural capital in the form of building mastery. What is more, the social is again narrowly defined – it is restricted to the narrow, and horizontal, shared experience of chat among avatars.

Through the first few years of *Second Life*'s existence, this pressure to display mastery of *Second Life*'s environment also was architected into a rating system. Every user could rate any other user in three categories: behavior, appearance, and building. The latter two categories reflect precisely the technoliberal approach to individuals as desirous of mastering complex systems; the rating of appearance pointed to how well one had mastered the creation of one's avatar, whereas the rating of building indexed one's skills with the three primary content-creation tools (which also could be used to make entirely new avatars).

Conclusion

The architecture of *Second Life*, based on a peculiarly asocial human imaginary, does not in any way utterly determine the scope of social actions possible within it. It is vital when discussing virtual worlds and other deeply contrived arenas for social action that we recognize the open-endedness that always remains and the always remarkable extent to which users "make do" (Certeau, 1984) amid such constraints, often circumventing them practically. *Second Life* users pushed the in-world secondary affordances – the group tools, note cards, and messaging – to the limit and have drawn on out-of-world, often web-based resources as well. But the scholarship on virtual worlds, in its enthusiasm to recognize and celebrate that ingenuity, often has neglected questions of the extent to which the architecture of these contrived spaces shapes the human activity within them.

In the case of *Second Life*, the particular idea of the human embedded in the software not only reflects technoliberal attitudes that we can locate in the history of American ideas and practices about technology and authority, but it also, I have sought to suggest here, connects with ideas about learning through the concept of mastery. This raises potentially challenging questions about the scholarship on games and learning. To what extent does the interest in how computer games promote learning – often explored in rightful contrast to the kinds of learning that largely have characterized conventional schooling in America and elsewhere – perhaps itself remain unaware of its own potential connection to technoliberal ideals? In the rush to discover what kinds of learning take place in the gaining of player mastery over *Pokemon, Civilization,* or *World of Warcraft,* are we ready to recognize what may be deeply shared and historically contingent ideas about the human informing *both* the scholarship *and* the software? Is our interest in learning through digitally mediated games attentive enough to how deep such assumptions may go such that even an open-ended virtual world such as *Second Life,* which has no foundational game objectives, reveals itself as nonetheless deeply *gamelike* in this emphasis on individual mastery? While the limitations of first-person shooters as the epitome of gaming mastery have been recognized by academics, if not by many game developers, and interest in other kinds of game play has increased, this work would gain a great deal of depth and significance if the broader landscape of ideas about the humans, games, and technology that inform our digital environs were incorporated into our inquiries.

Note

[1]   See the extensive and regularly updated list of resources on *Second Life* and its use by educators at http://web.ics.purdue.edu/~mpepper/slbib (accessed March 14, 2010).

References

Au, W. J. (2008). *The making of Second Life*. New York: HarperCollins.
Bauman, R. (1977). Verbal Art as Performance. In R. Bauman (ed.), *Verbal art as performance* (pp. 3–58). Prospect Heights, IL: Waveland Press.

Boellstorff, T. (2008). *Coming of age in Second Life: An anthropologist explores the virtual human.* Princeton, NJ: Princeton University Press.

Certeau, M. de. (1984). *The practice of everyday life* (Steven Rendall, trans.). Berkeley, CA: University of California Press.

Coleman, G. (2004). The Political Agnosticism of Free and Open-Source Software and the Inadvertent Politics of Contrast. *Anthropological Quarterly*, 77(3), 507–19.

Csikszentmihalyi, M. (1990). *Flow: The psychology of optimal experience.* New York: Harper & Row.

Goffman, E. (1959). *The presentation of self in everyday life.* Garden City, NY: Doubleday.

Hiltzik, M. (2000). *Dealers of lightning: Xerox parc and the dawn of the computer age.* New York: Harper Collins.

Kelty, C. (2005). Geeks, Social Imaginaries, and Recursive Publics. *Cultural Anthropology*, 20(2), 185–214.

Kidder, T. (1981). *The soul of a new machine.* Boston: Little, Brown.

Malaby, T. M. (2006a). Parlaying Value: Forms of Capital in and Beyond Virtual Worlds. *Games & Culture*, 1(2), 141–62.

(2006b). Coding Control: Governance and Contingency in the Production of Online Worlds. *First Monday*, special issue no. 7.

(2009a). *Making virtual worlds: Linden Lab and Second Life.* Ithaca, NY: Cornell University Press.

(2009b). Anthropology and Play: The Contours of Playful Experience. *New Literary History*, 40(1), 205–18.

(2009c). These Great Urbanist Games: *New Babylon* and *Second Life. Artifact* 2(3), 1–7.

Markoff, J. (2005). *What the dormouse said: How the 60s counterculture shaped the personal computer.* New York: Viking Adult.

Rymaszewski, M., Au, W. J., Wallace, M., Winters, C., Ondrejka, C., Batstone-Cunningham, B., & Second Life Residents from Around the World (2007). *Second Life: The official guide.* Indianapolis: Wiley.

Stephenson, N. (1992). *Snow crash.* New York: Bantam Books.

Thomas, D. (2003). *Hacker culture.* Minneapolis: University of Minnesota Press.

Turner, F. (2006). *From counterculture to cyberculture: Stewart Brand, the Whole Earth Network, and the rise of digital utopianism.* Chicago: The University of Chicago Press.

Waldrop, M. (2001). *The dream machine: J. C. R. Licklider and the revolution that made computing personal.* New York: Viking Adult.

16 Participatory Media Spaces: A Design Perspective on Learning with Media and Technology in the Twenty-First Century

Erica Rosenfeld Halverson

The learning sciences distinguish itself as a field within education research by their attention to how insights about the cognitive and socio-cultural nature of thinking and learning can be applied to the design of learning environments. As a learning scientist, an artist, and a digital media scholar, I am drawn to questions of how to design spaces for young people so that they can participate successfully in media arts–based production activities. I call these *participatory media spaces*,[1] an extension of Jenkins, Purushotma, Clinton, Weigel, and Robison's (2007) framing of digital spaces for artistic production and civic engagement as *participatory cultures*. The rhetorical shift from participatory cultures to participatory media spaces means changing our focus from documenting what happens in these spaces and how people participate to insights about how to design learning environments with specific learning goals in mind. While prior work has focused on what people learn from their engagement in participatory cultures (Gee, 2007; Ito et al., 2010; Jenkins et al., 2007), I consider design from the perspective of intentional learning. There is no doubt that learning happens as a result of engagement in participatory cultures. Learning happens no matter what we do (Wenger, 1998). However, learning *something* is an entirely different matter. In this chapter I shift the focus from an understanding of learning in participatory media spaces to how to design participatory media spaces so that young people can engage successfully in artistic production processes.

One of the reasons this shift in framing is challenging is that what is learned through membership in participatory cultures is not a settled question. One way to think about learning outcomes is in terms of skills acquired through participation. Jenkins et al. (2007) present a list that includes concrete skills such as the construction of and appropriate use of simulations, as well as abstract skills, such as the ability to multitask and to understand that knowledge is distributed across people and tools. Squire (2006) takes a more sociocultural perspective; he describes learning in these environments as becoming a legitimate, contributing member of the community, along the way acquiring the requisite skills needed for successful participation. Thinking about participatory cultures as designed spaces requires operationalizing these learning outcomes. Instructional designers Wiggins and McTighe (2005) propose that we transform outcomes into learning goals by asking the question: "What do you want students to be able to know and to do?" At the risk of oversimplifying meaningful engagement in participatory cultures, I would argue that fundamentally, designers of participatory media spaces want participants to *mindfully create digital artifacts that are meaningful to the community.* Embedded within this basic goal are the twenty-first-century skills Jenkins et al. (2007) argue for and the identity-related outcomes associated with becoming a contributing community member (Squire, 2006).

Working from this basic learning goal, the primary focus of this chapter is the articulation of three design principles for participatory cultures that, when taken together, represent the design of *participatory media spaces*. I focus on learning environments where young people engage in artistic production, drawing primarily from my research on youth media arts organizations (YMAOs) across the United States and how young people learn to produce digital art about their own life stories. Using data collected from two years of case-study field work with four YMAOs, as well as research on digital story production, video-game play, and massively multiplayer online games as "designed experiences" (Squire, 2006), I outline the following principles for the design of participatory media spaces:

- The learning environment must be structured for participants to engage in a cycle of conceiving, representing, and sharing a piece of digital art.
- Assessment is intentionally embedded into both the process and the product.
- Digital technologies must play an integral role across the conceiving, representing, and sharing process.

I will begin by reviewing our current understanding of participatory cultures and then describe each of these design principles in depth using examples, where appropriate, from my own research on youth media arts organizations. Finally, I will conclude with thoughts on why we need to think of participatory media spaces and design in the context of the games, learning, and society movement.

Participatory Cultures as Learning Environments

In their seminal white paper, "Confronting the Challenges of Participatory Culture: Media Education for the Twenty-first Century," Henry Jenkins and his colleagues (2007) define *participatory cultures* as spaces for artistic production and civic engagement that people have easy access to and where their contributions matter:

> A participatory culture is a culture with relatively low barriers to artistic expression and civic engagement, strong support for creating and sharing one's creations, and some type of informal mentorship whereby what is known by the most experienced is passed along to novices. A participatory culture is also one in which members believe their contributions matter, and feel some degree of social connection with one another [p. 3].

Participatory cultures have been given other names – "affinity groups" (Gee, 2000, 2003), "passion communities" (Collins, Joseph, & Bielaczyc, 2004), "interest-driven networks" (Ito et al., 2010) – but all point to similar ways for understanding how people participate in legitimate social networks that revolve around production. In this chapter I use *participatory cultures* as the umbrella term to describe production spaces, although I believe that these terms are functionally equivalent.

While not explicit in the definition, Jenkins et al.'s description of the skills needed for a new media culture belies the important role that technology plays in participatory cultures. First, Internet technologies connect people across time and space so that communities are not limited by location but rather are organized around interest and passion (Gee, 2003; Ito et al., 2010). Second, cheap and easy-to-use tools and software lower barriers for entry into the practices of participatory cultures. Jenkins et al. (2007) describe this affordance as a shift from the digital divide to the participation gap – what separates the haves from the have-nots is not access to tools but an understanding of how to use them. Finally, easy information storage and retrieval mean that the production of content is truly distributed across people and tools. Mimi Ito and her colleagues (2008) have argued that this distribution has resulted in new forms of production, including remix and mashup; at a broader level, it requires us to rethink what it means to produce something.

While *participatory cultures* describes the way people live in modern, technologically rich, social spaces, as a learning scientist, I am interested not just in characterizing these spaces but also in understanding how to design these experiences for learners. I aim to provide insights for those interested in how to design experiences for learners so that they may become successful producers of digital artifacts that matter.[2] In order to consider design principles for participatory cultures, it is crucial to understand the role of design more generally. The terms *design* and *learning environments* taken together most readily conjure up images of classrooms (Bransford, Brown, & Cocking, 2000) extending perhaps, more recently, to formal online spaces. There are, however, many less traditional spaces that could be considered designed learning environments. Squire (2006) describes video games as *designed experiences* – "experiences resulting from the intersection of design constraints and players' intentions" (p. 26). Considering games as designed experiences acknowledges that participants' motivations and goals have a legitimate role in the environment and that learning is constructed between designers' intentions and affordances for participants. Despite the emergent nature of learning between designers and players, video games, like classrooms, are highly designed learning environments. Some participatory cultures are more emergent; communities of people form around media sharing, from videos to online journaling to fan fiction, without a central designer (or designers) to create a set of a priori goals for members. Robust learning communities do not stay emergent for long; these communities become designed environments when rules for participation are made explicit in terms of both engagement with the process and what counts as a quality product either within the genre or as it pushes the boundaries of the genre.

My research focuses on learning environments that sit in between the highly designed worlds of classrooms and video games and the emergent designs of communities that engage in "everyday media production" (Lange & Ito, 2010). Youth media arts organizations (YMAOs) are out-of-school learning contexts that engage participants in a digital media production process. They mirror some aspects of formal schooling environments – they have explicitly stated learning goals, and there is often a curriculum and set of scaffolded tasks to guide production work. Unlike in digital arts–focused classrooms, however, YMAO participants are not constrained by external assessments, demonstrations of mastery that serve to compare learners with all other learners like them (Sefton-Green & Sinker, 2000). It is within these contexts that I describe design principles for participatory media spaces.

Design Principles for Participatory Media Spaces

The sociocultural turn in research on how people learn has framed learning as an ongoing process rather than a discreet activity that happens when other activities do not. Wenger (1998) notes: "Learning is something we can assume – whether we see it or not, whether we like the way it goes or not, whether what we are learning is to repeat the past or to shake it off" (p. 9). However, when it comes to learning *something*, we have to turn our attention to how we structure the learning environment and the principles that guide participation toward specific outcomes. I have already stated that the central learning goal for participatory media spaces is to mindfully create digital artifacts that are meaningful to the community. By *mindful*, I mean that participants are engaged in a production process where they come to understand how digital artifacts are created, what the representational medium affords them, and why they make the representational choices they do to create meaning. Drawing on my own work with YMAOs across the United States, as well as others' research on how youth engage in digital media production across a range of highly designed (Chávez & Soep, 2005; Hull & Nelson, 2005; Sefton-Green & Sinker, 2000) and emergent learning environments (Lange & Ito, 2010), I propose the following design principles for participatory media spaces:

- *The learning environment must be structured for participants to engage in a cycle of conceiving, representing, and sharing a piece of digital art.* *Conceiving* refers to the generation and explication of an idea, *representing* refers to the mindful and appropriate use of the tools of a medium to express that idea, and *sharing* refers to having an authentic, legitimate audience for the work produced.
- *Assessment is intentionally embedded into both the process and the product.* Considering participatory media spaces as designed learning environments requires attention to evidence that participants have achieved desired outcomes (Wiggins & McTighe, 2005). Here, assessment is an integral part of the production cycle and includes both formative and summative components.
- *Digital technologies play an integral role in the conceiving, representing, and sharing process.* Participatory media spaces are distinguished from other production-oriented activities in that the medium of expression requires digital media technologies.

The Learning Environment Must Be Structured for Participants to Engage in a Cycle of Conceiving, Representing, and Sharing a Piece of Digital Art

Participatory media spaces as designed environments are grounded in a shift from thinking about "literacy" as a print-based, consumptive practice to a multimodal, productive practice known as the *new literacies* (New London Group, 1996). Lankshear and Knobel (2003) argue for both a paradigmatic shift and an ontological shift in our conceptualization of literacy. As a paradigm, the new literacies move away from a traditional psychological understanding of reading and writing as context-free, internal, individualized acts toward "a body of work that argues that reading and writing should be viewed not only as a mental achievements going on inside people's heads but also as social and cultural practices with economic, historical, and political implications" (Gee, 2003, p. 8). Ontologically, the new literacies broaden the range of what counts as literacy from reading and writing printed text to include a broad array of modalities. Current modalities include the interpretation and creation of wikis, video games, mash ups, and movies, although this ontological shift also means that any cataloguing of relevant artifact types is necessarily situated in a moment in time (Ito et al., 2010). In addition to a shift in what counts as literacy artifacts, a change in how we understand the literacy process is also required. *Reading and writing* is redefined as "understanding and competent control of the representational forms that are becoming increasingly significant in the overall communications environment" (New London Group, 1996, p. 61). I operationalize this perspective by proposing conceiving, representing, and sharing digital art as the core process of participatory media spaces.

In my previous work I have described learning environments where young people learn to produce art about the stories of their lives as participation in the *dramaturgical process* – the telling, adapting, and performing of narratives of personal experience (Halverson, 2007, 2008, 2009). From the perspective of design principles, each of these phases is a unique and necessary component of the art-making process. Taken together, they capture the basic structural features of how youth engage in a narrative and performance process. The dramaturgical process idea was developed to describe the production of theatrical plays from autobiographical material (Halverson, 2007; Wiley & Feiner, 2001), although I also have discussed this process in terms of artistic production more broadly (Halverson, 2009).

Table 16.1. *Comparison of the dramaturgical process with the design of participatory media spaces*

Dramaturgical process	Participatory media spaces
Telling stories	Conceiving ideas
Adapting stories	Representing ideas using digital media production tools
Performing stories	Sharing final products with legitimate audience

Here, I adapt the dramaturgical process in two ways: (1) to refer explicitly to participatory media spaces, with an emphasis on how to consider the role of digital media, and (2) to expand what counts as material for the process beyond narratives of personal experience. Table 16.1 highlights the parallels and differences between these descriptions of process.

Chávez and Soep (2005) also have described this process as "cycles of production that pass through periods of planning, practice, performance, and reflection" (p. 417); they depict a variety of learning environments from out-of-school organizations to more progressive classroom environments that are working with young people in this way. In my work with YMAOs, I have documented this cycle and the myriad ways young people and their adult and peer mentors engage in each part of the process.

Conceiving digital art. Fundamentally, participatory media spaces serve as environments where people express ideas. A process that focuses at the start on developing an idea acknowledges that literacy is a design-based process (New London Group, 1996). Becoming literate means learning to communicate – in order to do that, we have to have something to communicate. The production portion of participatory media spaces focuses on the development of ideas that eventually will be represented using the available tools of the medium.

Where do ideas come from? In our work, we are interested in the role production processes played in identity development, so we selected YMAOs for study that explicitly attended to narratives of personal experience (Halverson et al., 2009). As a result, most of the idea generation was focused on experiences that were directly relevant to individual participants or to the communities to which they belonged. However, across participatory media spaces more broadly, the production focus is not necessarily on narratives of personal experience. Chávez and Soep (2005) describe youth as becoming engaged with topics "about which [they] feel passion and develop serious expertise" (p. 417) that could range from local and global political issues to fan culture topics such as *Harry Potter*, *Pokémon*, and *Survivor* (Jenkins et al., 2007). While I will discuss conceiving in terms of narratives of personal experience, these design components easily could apply to the development of interest-based topics more broadly.

At the YMAOs I observed, youth participants worked to develop ideas focused on autobiographical narratives and/or topics that had personal meaning to the youth and the communities to which they belong. This story-generation process often began before youth started their process work; three of the four organizations required youth to submit a written application, including answers to a series of guiding questions such as what stories they might like to tell using digital art and what reasons they had for joining the organization (Halverson, 2010; Halverson & Gibbons, 2010). While I would not argue that having a competitive application process is a principle for the design of participatory media spaces, I would argue that early emphasis on "finding the story" is.

Youth came to the YMAOs I studied primarily for one of two reasons: (1) They had a story they wanted to tell, or (2) they wanted to have a career in digital art. For those who had a story to tell, the initial story-development process was easy; this is what drove them to the organization in the first place. For those who wanted to be professional digital artists, they began with a series of ideas or a general aesthetic sense that they wanted to hone. In both cases, youth were not locked into their initial ideas, nor were the ideas abandoned if what they wanted to produce was not clear from day one. YMAOs provided youth a range of opportunities to craft ideas, including individual, private writing time, one-on-one consulting sessions, group brainstorm discussions, and a variety of "warm-up ideas" where youth wrote short essays, responded to writing prompts, and produced minifilms in an accelerated production cycle. The early emphasis on "finding a story" was universal across the organizations with which I worked and extends to performing arts organizations more broadly.

How do ideas come to be? Youth participants engaged in one of three processes for crafting ideas or stories: (1) Each participant produced an individual piece of work from a personal story, (2) individuals "pitched" stories and found a group of people to work with them to craft a piece of digital art, and (3) groups of youth worked together to develop an idea that had relevance for them and their community. We found that the process in use by each organization was reflective of the conception of identity held by the community in which the organization was situated. For organizations situated in communities with a collectivist perspective on identity, groups of youth worked together to craft ideas; for organizations situated in communities with an individualistic perspective on identity, individual youth made their own films or lobbied for their idea and worked with a group to realize their personal vision (Halverson et al., 2009). As a result, stories can be conceptualized as "my story" – that is, what it means to be a modern Muslim American teenager (Halverson, 2010) – or "our story" – that is, a representation of life on the Ochikadaagweg Reservation (Halverson et al., 2009). There are in-between stories as well; at one organization, a group of participants encouraged one of their members to tell her personal story as the granddaughter of a famous local musician who is himself a large part of the community's musical heritage. Since we focused on YMAOs that work with youth to produce autobiographical art, beliefs about the nature of identity played a role in how the art-making process was structured. It will be interesting to explore whether this relationship would hold for production processes not centered on narratives of personal experience.

The role of artifacts in conceiving ideas? Over the course of crafting their ideas, youth produce a wide variety of artifacts, using a variety of modalities, all leading up to what youth are going to "make." We identified four types of artifacts produced in our YMAOs that ready participants for representing their ideas using digital art as a medium for expression:

- *Applications.* Initial thoughts on what story youth want to tell in the form of written text and/or conversations with adult mentors.
- *Warm-ups.* Youth produced a variety of written and multimodal artifacts, usually in response to adult-generated prompts from structured worksheets to less structured "community interview" projects.
- *The pitch.* Youth were required to sell their ideas to a critical group, either within their community or some outside group. Youth produced a wide variety of artifacts during the pitch depending on the nature of the task as structured by the organization.
- *The first treatment.* Before participants began the production process, they created a representation of their plan, referred to as a *first treatment*, *shot list*, *essay*, or *proposal*, that includes who they will interview, a shot list, ideas for b-roll footage, why they want to make the film, and its importance (for a more in-depth description of artifacts and tasks, see Halverson, 2010).

The importance of having a clear idea before beginning the production process was true across the organizations we studied; in fact, there were several cases of youth who never quite clarified what story they wanted to tell. These youth either never finished their pieces or relied heavily on artist-mentors to help them complete their projects. From a design perspective, scaffolding the idea generation and refinement process in a way that makes sense for the community in which the work is situated encourages all participants to become successful producers rather than relying on personal vision or passion throughout the process.

Representing digital art. Representation involves transforming personal narratives constructed during the telling-stories phase into artistic representations. Youth must express the core ideas of their stories using the tools of the artistic medium in which they are working. In a digital story, for example, representation involves creating a script and choosing images and music to accompany the script (Hull & Katz, 2006; Nelson, Hull, & Roche-Smith, 2008). Digital art production includes a variety of media: digital story, sound (radio and stand-alone sound pieces), video, multimedia, and digital images. The YMAOs we studied worked primarily with documentary filmmaking as a subgenre of digital video, although at one organization youth chose from among a variety of digital representations. In terms of documentary filmmaking, representation is a process of collecting raw footage (either original or available) in the form of video, still images, music, and ambient sound, editing down this large corpus of raw footage, creating transitions between scenes, and determining how the different modes of film interact with each other. The primary learning goal here is for participants to understand how the tools of digital media afford representation. This can be understood at both the macro-level – what a particular genre of digital art affords – and at the micro-level – what the tools of that genre afford in terms of meaning making.

Macro-level representation. The macro-level maps onto to what the New London Group (1996) termed "available designs – the 'grammars' of various semiotic systems" (p. 74) that are used to make meaning. Here, the grammars serve as tools for production, and artist-mentors work with youth to understand what the tools afford them as producers. There is some debate over how closely learners should adhere to the conventions of the medium for representation. Sefton-Green (2000) describes this as the "paradox of genre…student's work is regularly praised and vilified for the same reason: it can either be too imitative and therefore not original, or so idiosyncratic that it doesn't follow a recognised pattern" (p. 219).

We saw evidence of this tension in the YMAOs we studied. Each organization managed genre differently. In one organization, youth were required to produce three-act, short-form documentaries and to provide audio or video transitions between acts that reveal the filmmaker's point of view. At another organization, artist-mentors presented examples of what they considered to be innovative digital art and asked participants to research and share a biography of an artist they respected. These activities

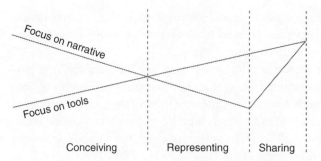

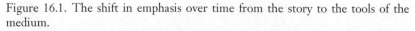

| Conceiving | Representing | Sharing |

Figure 16.1. The shift in emphasis over time from the story to the tools of the medium.

paved the way for youth to make mindful choices about the selection of a genre and what this "design grammar" afforded them. The other two organizations relied primarily on past works produced in the organization itself and on the organization's artist-mentors helping youth determine what representational medium and genre they would choose. The group engaged in critique sessions of prior work, blurring the line between what is often considered the cognitive act of evaluating art and the manual act of creating art (Sefton-Green & Sinker, 2000). Regardless of how organizations worked with youth to select, evaluate, and understand genre, it is clear that from a design-of-learning-environments perspective, several features must be made explicit: (1) Genre or design grammar plays a huge role in transforming an idea into a piece of digital art, (2) in order to work with the design grammar, producers must pay attention to what the genre affords producers, and (3) as producers attend to genre, they will transition from a focus on their story to a focus on the tools for representation. Figure 16.1 marks the shift in emphasis over time from the story to the tools of the medium.

Micro-level representation. At the micro-level, youth also work with the features of their chosen representational medium to best represent their ideas. In my work, the idea to be represented almost always was "identity," so consideration of features focused on how to communicate complex representations of individual or community selves. For example, *The Mizz Perception of Roro!* is an autobiographical film about a young African American woman who seeks to "tackle the misperceptions people have about tall women" (ListenUp! n.d.). The film centers on her peers' initial impressions of her, how those perceptions have changed over time, and how those perceptions are connected to her own sense of herself. Overall, the film is focused on the exploration of a viable social identity (Côté &

Levine, 2002) because Roro describes how she sees herself, how other people see her, how she fits into this community of teen media makers, and importantly, how these versions of self merge together. The filmmaker's use of cinematography as a tool for meaning making is especially apparent in this ten-second clip of the film.[3] The filmmaker explores the use of extreme angles, first with a bird's-eye view shot from the point of view of Roro, followed immediately by an upward-tilt shot from the point of view of the person passing Roro on the street. Even without sound or the visual reactions of the onscreen personalities, the filmmaker conveys her perspective of others and how others see her using exaggerated camera angles.

When we add sound into the interpretation, the filmmaker's voiceover provides additional meaning to the shot choices. She first asks, "Why do people view me like that or ... you know what I'm sayin'? What goes through people's minds when they see me?" This question is in direct response to the prior scene, where an interviewee tells Roro that people think that she is "mean" and "tough" when they first meet her. The first person, bird's-eye view shot gives the impression that Roro is much bigger than the person in the frame, providing explicit evidence that Roro's size may be intimidating to others. When we consider the mis-en-scene, that is, what is inside the frame of the camera, Roro's wave to the camera in the second upward-tilt shot provides a direct counterpoint both to the interviewees descriptions of her as mean and tough and to the prior bird's-eye view shot that can appear visually intimidating.

The ability to understand and use the macro-design grammar and the micro-level tools of a specific genre requires that youth requires that youth develop a variety of skills such as interviewing, camera work, and critique. These skills do not come easy; they require many hours of practice and work with experts. Participatory culture scholars have noted the importance the acquisition of genre knowledge to expertise as emergent in successful online spaces (Jenkins et al., 2007; Steinkuehler, 2008). When designed into participatory media spaces, the acquisition of genre-related expertise is intentional and can help to ensure a consistent, meaningful experience for all.

Sharing digital art. Sharing representations is an inextricable part of the production process; it is not an extra step that can be done if there is time. Sefton-Green (2000) describes the crucial role audiences play in the production process:

> The feedback from the experience of public production is crucial for all forms of cultural production and, again, a key theme across [a variety of

media] is the need to draw on the real context for pupils' work as part of the evaluative process (p. 228).

Constructing and sharing an artistic representation allows youth to realize the power and value of what they have built. The design of a participatory media space must include attention to how the work will be shared, with whom, and in what context. For organizations that work with young people to produce art, attention to how external audiences will receive the final products is always at the forefront of conversations (Halverson 2008; Halverson et al., 2009; Heath, 2004; Wiley & Feiner, 2001). The questions when determining what to create and how to represent it using the available tools of the chosen medium are: How will the product be received? What will the audience understand about this concept? Is the audience likely to be familiar with the concept, or is part of the challenge for representation to create something that will both introduce an idea and make it complex? This last question is an issue raised in Nicole Fleetwood's (2005) work with African America youth who employ visual tropes – "racialized" stereotyped images that make their social identities easily identifiable to an external audience. Visual tropes, while potentially offensive to community insiders, serve a function for unfamiliar outsiders and thus have a place in the representation. The audience, then, serves as a mediator between producers and their ideas (Magnifico, 2010).

I want to make a further distinction between the presence of an audience and the presence of an *authentic* audience. A classroom teacher is an audience; so is a parent. However, in these environments, it is not enough to have a teacher evaluate the product (Cohen & Riel, 1989) unless the teacher is seen as a legitimate expert practitioner in representational media. Motivation to make difficult representational decisions come from the knowledge that those who will be viewing the work have a legitimate reason for judging it (Purcell-Gates, Duke, & Martineau, 2007). The popularization of electronic media for written communication has made clear the crucial role an authentic audience plays in the production of ideas. Magnifico (2010) describes the role that Internet technologies have played in making authentic audiences available and in highlighting the importance of these audiences: "Seen in this way, electronic media not only democratize publication and content creation, [but] they also make it possible for writers to speak with, ask questions of, and be influenced by an audience of readers" (n.p.).

Authentic audience is present across a range of designed participatory media spaces, including classroom environments (e.g., Cohen & Riel, 1989;

Purcell-Gates et al., 2007; Sefton-Green & Sinker, 2000), out-of-school youth organizations (Fleetwood, 2005; Halverson & Gibbons, 2010; Hull & Nelson, 2005), and online environments (Ito et al., 2010; Jenkins et al., 2007; Magnifico, 2010). In fact, the raison d'être for many of these spaces is to share youth-created representations such as fan fiction web communities (Black, 2008; Jenkins et al., 2007), game design sites (Duncan, 2010; Games, 2010), and YMAOs. While Internet technologies make possible a wide range of audiences, particularly interest-based community audiences that transcend physical space (Ito et al., 2010), authentic audiences also can be face to face, as in the presentation of youth films at a gallery show or a film festival. Boyd (2008) even describes hybrid audiences where, through social networking, young people engage with their "real-life" peers in virtual space.

Primarily, this emphasis on authentic audience is in contrast to the media production activities that happen in schools; as evaluators, teachers are often the primary audience rather than collaborators in a "pedagogy of collegiality," where the work is bound for "an audience beyond themselves" (Chávez & Soep, 2005, p. 431). This also may be a contrast, however, with participatory cultures that are emergent and therefore find audiences more by chance. YMAOs build in opportunities for youth to share their work with an authentic audience rather than relying on participants' social capital in an online community. Audiences, like explicit access to and work with the design grammar of the medium, are built into the process.

Assessment Is Embedded Naturally into Both the Process and the Product

The shift from participatory cultures to participatory media spaces, from learning to learning *something*, means that we have to consider the issue of assessment. If the claim is that we can design environments with specific learning goals in mind, then ideas about how to assess learning must be up for consideration. Participatory media spaces are by nature environments where participants learn by doing. Squire (2006) describes these environments as built on a "*functional* epistemology, where one learns through doing, through performance" (p. 22). Learning *is* participation in and successful completion of the tasks embedded in the space. In his synthesis of the assessment of creativity across artistic disciplines, Sefton-Green (2000) describes a tension between assessing the value of a creative product and using that creative product to assess other participant outcomes. The problem, he argues, is not that these two goals are always at odds; sometimes skill and content knowledge are embedded into the product; sometimes social knowledge is embedded in the process itself (see, for example, Soep (2006) for a discussion of the role of critique in learning). Rather, Sefton-Green points out that students are best served when the criteria for assessment are made explicit and are part of the production process. In fact, an understanding of the criteria that is being used to evaluate quality becomes part of the learning process. This avoids "romanticizing" the production process to the point where all creativity is good and products cannot be assessed critically.

I want to describe two forms of assessment that, though intertwined (Sefton-Green, 2000), can be considered separately: Assessment of the production process and assessment of the products themselves. I will describe how to consider learning in YMAOs at both the product and the process level to generate a broader theory of assessment in participatory media spaces.

Assessment of product. In some sense, the successful creation and completion of a product is an assessment in and of itself; that participants complete a cycle of conceiving, representing, and sharing is a performance assessment, where learning is measured through successful completion of an authentic project (Lankshear & Knobel, 2003; Office of Education Research and Improvement, 1993) involving multimodal communication (Kalantzis, Cope, & Harvey, 2003). However, there also must be a consideration of the quality of the product, some assessment of whether what is produced is any good. Determining what counts as quality in the context of creative production is not trivial. Creative endeavors in the context of educational settings suffer from a tension between those who want to reduce production to its technical components and those who romanticize creativity to the point where any critical impulse is read as impinging on a young person's inherent capacity to express himself or herself (Sefton-Green, 2000).

There are two ways to address this dilemma: to rely on external audience assessments of quality and to develop an internal set of measures. As I discussed in the preceding section, having an authentic audience for youth-produced work is an essential component of the conceiving, representing, and sharing cycle. At the YMAOs I researched, a key feature of their artistic process was the public sharing of final work. Research on youth arts organizations more generally has demonstrated the importance of the public performance for youth participation, motivation, learning, and development (Halverson, 2005; Heath, 2000; McLaughlin, Irby, & Langman, 1994). Lange and Ito (2010) found that seeking and gaining audience for work was a key component of independent creative production. The YMAOs I studied were no different. The production cycle always culminated in some form of public sharing, including standing gallery installations, internal community screenings, and public screenings. Beyond these initial presentations, YMAOs also worked toward bringing their digital art to a broader audience through submissions to film festivals across the country, additional art gallery shows, and online forums such as ListenUp!,[4] YouTube, and Facebook. In many of these forums, youth are given the opportunity to publicly reflect on the meaning of their work through artist statements and postscreening talk-backs. These opportunities fit nicely into Sefton-Green's (2000) description of audience as a key feature of assessment: "Indeed, showing work in [creative] subjects to an audience is probably the most important way of beginning evaluation" (pp. 228–9).

In addition to audience feedback, the development and use of an internal set of criteria for evaluating the quality of products constitute an important method of assessment. It is important to acknowledge that these criteria and standards are culturally situated and therefore often changing (Ito et al., 2008). However, to deny young people the opportunity to access, understand, critique, and apply these standards to their own work is akin to denying them access to academic discourses of power (Purcell-Gates et al., 2007). Rather than eliminating evaluative criteria, the development and understanding of culturally bound assessments of quality are an integral part of the learning environment. From a design perspective, the logical question to ask here is: "What belongs in these evaluative criteria?"

In addition to recognition of the cultural nature of these criteria, assessments are also bound by genre. And just as I considered representation at both the macro-level of design grammar and the micro-level of the tools of the representational medium, evaluative criteria exist at both these levels. At the macro-level, there has been some discussion about the development and use of evaluative criteria for judging a variety of product genres, most notably video games (Games, 2010; Peppler, Warschauer, & Diazgranados, 2010). At the micro-level, assessment of products must include attention to how youth use the tools for expression in digital media. In my work with YMAOs that focus on the production of autobiographical digital art, what is being constructed is a representation of self. I use the formal elements of film, coupled with the tools of multimodal analysis, to construct an explanation of how youth accomplish this work (Halverson, 2010). The example I provided earlier of the use of representational tools in *The Mizz Perception of Roro!* is a brief illustration of this analysis at work. While I have used this framework as a method of data analysis, others have labeled it critique or assessment. In fact, this approach has been used in formal learning settings to critically evaluate professional films (Muller, 2006) and informally in online communities (Lange & Ito, 2010) – I would propose that this process be formalized in the design of participatory media spaces.

An interesting feature of these evaluative criteria, and one that is currently underexplored, is what Sefton-Green (2000) calls the "paradox of genre" – where work is both praised and criticized for sticking too close to the conventions of a given genre. If it is too close, then the work is considered unoriginal. If it is too far away, then it is unrecognizable. I have found in the creative production of autobiographical narratives that quality products have reportability, a uniqueness that makes the story worth listening to, and credibility, a believability that makes the story recognizable to an audience (Halverson, 2008). The development of evaluative criteria that reflect both the reportability and the credibility of creative products might help to resolve the paradox of genre and provide a framework for the constantly changing cultural values.

Assessment of process. While the assessment of products provides an authentic and robust measure of learning, one of the features that sets designed learning environments apart from informal, emergent settings is attention to how learners get to the final product and what it is they understand differently as a result. This requires the development of mechanisms to assess the production process. There are several approaches to the assessment of process in participatory media spaces worth mentioning. Elisabeth Soep (2006) traces learning by identifying moments in production processes where youth engage in critiquing others' works in progress, thereby demonstrating that they understand how to use the language of art critique and production to negotiate the construction of an authentic product. Although Soep has identified the conditions under which critique among youth is promoted, the appearance of critiques as "episodes of learning" is neither predictable nor regulated in the way assessment typically is built into a designed learning experience. Glynda Hull and her colleagues in the DUSTY project, an afterschool program focused on the creation of digital stories, use the evolution of the product itself to document process. Drawing from individuals' "folders of work," including dictated scripts and revisions, storyboards, and reflections on others' work, they document the evolution of a digital story from initial idea to final product. They also use ethnographic descriptions of work sessions to understand how authorial decisions are made over time and how those decisions affect the final products (Nelson, Hull, & Roche-Smith, 2008).

In my work with YMAOs, I explored a balance between the emergent opportunities for assessment that Soep identifies and the overly formalized system found in many media education classrooms (Buckingham, Fraser, & Sefton-Green, 2000). I have described a series of key moments throughout the production process in which youth must articulate the relationship between the idea they intend to represent in their video and the tools of the digital video medium that afford representation. These moments serve as checkpoints in which youth make informal, formative assessments before continuing on with the process. By highlighting these key moments, we can both describe the core features of the YMAO organizational process and offer a mechanism for tracing participant learning over time (Halverson & Gibbons, 2010). There is much work to be done in the field of assessment of learning in participatory media spaces. Often assessment is either overly technical in the form of a checklist of skills that participants can complete to demonstrate competence or overly romanticized, where any expression of creative thought by a young person is considered invaluable (Sefton-Green, 2000). Recognizing participatory media spaces as designed environments where participants work to achieve learning goals is the first step toward the development of robust assessments systems of the creative production process.

Digital Technologies Play an Integral Role in the Conceiving, Representing, and Sharing Process

I want to spend some time talking about the importance of digital technologies because much of what has been described in the preceding two sections, in theory, could be applied to any creative process and therefore is nothing especially new. Unlike nondigital creative production processes, participatory media spaces involve the use of digital technologies for conceiving, representing, and sharing multimodal artifacts. Digital media technologies are *tools*, parts of a distributed cognitive system that work together to create an artifact that communicates a core set of ideas. It is important to keep in mind that the tools are not synonymous with the learning environment. A YMAO may create a Ning in order to communicate when its members are not meeting face to face, to store and share information, and to have a record of its process, but the Ning is only a small part of the work of creating digital videos. Likewise, just because students search the web in their history class as a way to engage with digital media tools does not mean they are engaged in a participatory media space.

The suite of digital tools involving the production tasks of participatory media spaces is often referred to as *Web 2.0*, defined by Fahser-Herro and Steinkuehler (2010) as tools that have "a capacity for high user engagement, intellectual rigor, frequent updating, and collective knowledge sharing based on an underlying technological infrastructure of blogs, wikis, podcasts, photo sharing, RSS feeds, social bookmarks, and the like" (p. 56). These tools are distinguished by the ability of users to create content rather than simply retrieve and consume information (Fahser-Herro & Steinkuehler, 2010). Digital technologies that afford users the capacity to represent their ideas are a crucial component of participatory media spaces.

Since the Internet is the primary mechanism for sharing digital media products with both public and more private audiences, digital media technologies are often considered synonymous with Web 2.0. However, there are many non-web-based production-oriented digital media technologies such as digital recording equipment (audio and video), editing software, and modeling tools that do not involve web-based interactions. Given the important role that audience plays in participatory media spaces, Web 2.0 technologies are important tools; however, the appropriate tools for use in these spaces is determined by the task the user needs to accomplish.

In the context of YMAOs, youth participants engaged with a wide variety of digital technologies. A few key features to note about these technologies: (1) They were not optional for participation. In fact, youth were not able to get their creative work done without them. (2) Digital technologies were not used exclusively in the video production process. Many low-tech tools were used as well, including paper and pencil journaling, storyboarding, and face-to-face conversation. The point is that digital technologies are an integral part of the conceiving, representing, and sharing process without being the exclusive means for work. Digital technologies are used when they afford participants the capacity to complete the work they need to complete and solve the problem they need to solve Norman (1993) argues that one cannot separate technologies – what he calls "cognitive artifacts" – from their affordances for users: "When a technology attempts to force a medium into a use that violates its affordances, then the medium gets in the way" (p. 107). Table 16.2 outlines the suite of digital tools used in the YMAOs I studied.

Web 2.0 technologies are most prominent in the sharing phase of the process – youth used a variety of means of communication to ensure that their products were available to a public audience. To produce a

Table 16.2. *Digital media technologies used in YMAOs*

	Conceiving	Representing	Sharing
Web 2.0 technologies	Ning.com E-mail	E-mail Internet search and download	Youth film-sharing websites YouTube Social networking sites
Hardware	Digital video cameras Sound recording equipment Computers TVs and DVD players	Digital video cameras Sound recording equipment Computers	DVDs DVD burners and players Computers
Software		Digital editing software (video and audio) "Ripping" software Graphic design software	

digital video requires a variety of hardware; these tools were prominent throughout the process. Finally, specific software plays a huge role in digital video production, especially as youth work through how to represent their ideas using the digital video medium. In fact, the tools are inextricable from the representation; it is in determining what the software affords that youth can make decisions about how to represent their stories.

While many of these technologies are in use across a variety of learning environments, digital technologies in participatory media spaces are distinguished through their patterns of use. Halverson and Smith (2010) describe two different use patterns for technologies in learning environments: technologies for *learning* and technologies for *learners*. Technologies for learning are designed to work at scale – to be employed in learning situations regardless of the skill set or desire of the learner. In contrast, technologies for learners "put the learner in control of the instructional process. Learning goals are determined by the learner, and the learner decides when goals are satisfied and when new goals are in order" (p. 51).

Participatory media spaces are predicated on the idea that people will use the tools that are appropriate to the task they need to accomplish. Just as Gee (2003) describes one of the design principles of good video games as the "explicit information on-demand and just-in-time principle," participatory media spaces afford people the opportunity to engage with digital technologies when they need to. In the case of YMAOs, this is when the particular technologies help them to achieve a goal within the production, representation, and sharing process. This is not to say that every person's process within a participatory media space is completely idiosyncratic and requires that they learn to use a completely unique set of digital technologies. Unlike in the video games Gee describes where players learn to play games primarily on their own, YMAOs create learning settings where youth filmmakers constantly work with peers, instructors, and artist-mentors throughout the process. Sometimes instructors provide lessons to the whole group that they know from experience youth will need and be ready for at a certain time. For example, all the organizations I studied gave a formal lesson on all aspects of the documentary interviewing process, from options for shooting video footage to the development of interview questions to the positionality of the interviewer. Other group lessons were spontaneous, based on the needs of participants that arose. For example, one organization decided to share its final work in a gallery-style production, prompting artist-mentors to work with youth to understand the relationship between their digital art and the gallery space. They watched films that were presented in nontraditional ways and talked in depth about the role environment can play in representing a concept. The result was a wide variety of final products including the use of video projection on a large wall and audience interactive audio projects.

Finally, some just-in-time lessons happen one on one between youth and artist-mentors or more experienced peers as youth discover that they need to be familiar with a particular piece of hardware or software in order to realize their vision for representation. These are not predesigned lessons, nor are they predictable in advance of the process. Rather, these instructional moments are made possible by the just-in-time and on-demand nature of the process in these participatory media spaces (Gee, 2003). Participatory media spaces rely on technologies for learners where the task drives tool use, not the other way around.

Why the Shift to Participatory Media Spaces Matters

As an artist turned artist-educator turned academic, I often have been frustrated by the cavalier attitude with which artistic production is treated. The idea that if you give a child a camera, magic will happen; what Sefton-Green (2000) refers to as the "romanticizing of creativity" has stopped us from theorizing the depth and complexity of learning to create and share a piece of digital art. Since any critique around creativity is off-limits, schools have turned to the technical aspects of production as learning goals for students.

As a result, the work that young people do in their lives outside school in the participatory cultures to which they belong is left out almost entirely from formal learning situations (Ito et al., 2010). These systems exist in parallel, although many educators acknowledge that the skills and habits of mind young people who are successful in participatory cultures acquire are crucial to their advancement in society. What I have tried to do here is to create a bridge between the powerful insights of participatory cultures and the intentional design of formal learning environments. We may never want our schools to look like the interest-driven networks in which young people voluntarily participate. Likewise, once these networks start to look too much like school, young people likely will flee from them in droves. However, the motivational power of participatory cultures coupled with the intentional design of learning goals and assessments may allow more learners to engage successfully in creative production. And, as Don Norman points out, the ability to represent an idea in some medium other than its original form is "the essence of intelligence, for if the representation and the process are just right, then new experiences, insights, and creations can emerge" (p. 47). As educators, I think this is what we ought to be after.

Notes

[1]   I have made references to this term in some earlier writing; see Halverson (2009) and Halverson & Halverson (2008).
[2]   This learning goal is also present in the work on twenty-first-century skills (http://www.p21.org).
[3]   http://www.transana.org/halversonbasswoods2010/.
[4]   http://www.listenup.org.

References

Boyd, D. (2008). Why Youth (Heart) Social Network Sites: The Role of Networked Publics in Teenage Social Life. In D. Buckingham (ed.), *MacArthur Foundation series on digital learning: Identity volume* (pp. 119–42). Cambridge, MA: MIT Press.

Black, R. (2008). *Adolescents and online fan fiction.* New York: Peter Lang.

Bransford, J. D., Brown, A. L., & Cocking, R. R. (2000). *How people learn: Brain, mind, experience, and school.* Washington, DC: National Academy Press.

Buckingham, D., Fraser, P., & Sefton-Green, J. (2000). Making the Grade: Evaluating Student Production in Media Studies. In J. Sefton-Green & R. Sinker (eds.), *Evaluating creativity: Making and learning by young people* (pp. 129–53). London: Routledge.

Chávez, V., & Soep, E. (2005). Youth Radio and the Pedagogy of Collegiality. *Harvard Educational Review,* 75(4), 409–34.

Cohen, M., & Riel, M. (1989). The Effect of Distal Audiences on Students' Writing. *American Education Research Journal*, 26(2), 143–59.

Collins, A., Joseph, D., & Bielaczyc, K. (2004). Design Research: Theoretical and Methodological Issues. *Journal of the Learning Sciences*, 13(1), 15–42.

Côté, J. E., & Levine, C. G. (2002). *Identity formation, agency, and culture: A social psychological synthesis*. Mahwah, NJ: Erlbaum.

Duncan, S. C. (2010). Gamers as Designers: A Framework for Investigating Design in Gaming Affinity Spaces. *E-Learning and Digital Media*, 7(1), 21–34.

Fahser-Herro, D., & Steinkuehler, C. (2010). Web 2.0 Literacy and Secondary Teacher Education. *Journal of Computing and Teacher Education*, 26(2), 55–62.

Fleetwood, N. (2005). Authenticating Practices: Producing Realness, Performing Youth. In S. Maira and E. Soep (eds.), *Youthscapes: The popular, the national, the global* (pp. 155–72). Philadelphia: University of Pennsylvania Press.

Games, A. (2010). Bug or Feature: The Role of *Gamestar Mechanic's* Material Dialog on the Metacognitive Game Design Strategies of Players. *E-Learning and Digital Media*, 7(1), 49–66.

Gee, J. P. (2000). Identity as an Analytic Lens for Research in Education. *Review of Research in Education*, 25, 99–125.

(2003/2007). *What videogames can teach us about language and literacy*. New York: Palgrave MacMillan.

Halverson, E. R. (2005). InsideOut: Facilitating Gay Youth Identity Development Through a Performance-Based Youth Organization. *Identity: An International Journal of Theory and Research*, 5(1), 67–90.

(2007). Listening to the Voices of Queer Youth: The Dramaturgical Process as Identity Exploration. In M. V. Blackburn and C. Clark (eds.), *Literacy Research for Political Action and Social Change* (pp. 153–175). New York: Peter Lang Publishing.

(2008). From One Woman to Everyman: The Reportability Paradox in Publicly Performed Narratives. *Narrative Inquiry*, 18(1), 29–52.

(2009). Artistic Production Processes as Venues for Positive Youth Development. *Revista Interuniversitaria de Formacion del Profesorado*, 23(3), 181–202.

(2010). Film as Identity Exploration: A Multimodal Analysis of Youth-Produced Films. *Teachers College Record*, 112(9), 2352–78.

Halverson, E. R., & Gibbons, D. (2010). "Key Moments" as Pedagogical Windows into the Digital Video Production Process. *Journal of Computing in Teacher Education*, 26(2), 69–74.

Halverson, E. R., & Halverson, R. R. (2010). Competitive fandom: The case for fantasy baseball. *Games and Culture*, 3(3–4), 286–308.

Halverson, E. R., & Smith, A. (2010). How New Technologies Have (and Have Not) Changed Teaching and learning in Schools. *Journal of Computing and Teacher Education*, 26(2), 49–54.

Halverson, E. R., Lowenhaupt, R., Gibbons, D., & Bass, M. (2009). Conceptualizing Identity in Youth Media Arts Organizations: A Comparative Case Study. *E-Learning*, 6(1), 23–42.

Heath, S. B. (2000). Seeing Our Way into learning. *Cambridge Journal of Education*, 30(1), 121–132.

(2004). Risks, Rules, and Roles: Youth Perspectives on the Work of Learning for Community Development. In A. Perret-Clermont, C. Pontecorvo, L. Resnick, T. Zittoun, & B. Burge (eds.), *Joining society: Social interaction and learning in adolescence and youth* (pp. 41–70). New York: Cambridge University Press.

Hull, G. A., & Katz, M. (2006). Crafting an Agentive Self: Case Studies of Digital Storytelling. *Research in the Teaching of English*, 4(1), 43–81.

Hull, G. A., & Nelson, M. E. (2005). Locating the Semiotic Power of Multimodality. *Written Communication*, 22(2), 224–61.

Ito, M., Baumer, S., Bittanti, M., et al. (2010). *Hanging out, messing around, and geeking out: Kids living and learning with new media*. Cambridge, MA: MIT Press.

Ito, M., Horst, H., Bittani, M., Boyd, D., Herr-Stephenson, B., Lange, P. G., Pascoe, C. J., & Robinson, L. (2008). *Living and learning with new media: Summary of findings from the Digital Youth Project*. The John D. and Catherine T. MacArthur Foundation Reports on Digital Media and Learning. Chicago, IL: MacArthur Foundation.

Jenkins, H., Purushotma, R., Clinton, K., Weigel, M., & Robison, A. (2007). *Confronting the challenges of participatory culture: Media education for the 21st century. Building the field of digital media and learning*. Retrieved September 1, 2009, from http://newmedialiteracies.org/files/working/NMLWhitePaper.pdf.

Kalantzis, M., Cope, B., & Harvey, A. (2003). Assessing Multiliteracies and the New Basics. *Assessment in Education*, 10(1), 15–26.

Lange, P. G., & Ito, M. (2010). Creative Production. In M. Ito et al. (eds.), *Hanging out, messing around, and geeking out: Kids living and learning with new media* (pp. 243–93). Cambridge, MA: MIT Press.

Lankshear, C., & Knobel, M. (2003). *New literacies: Changing knowledge and classroom learning*. Berkshire, England: Open University Press.

ListenUp! (n.d.). *The Mizz Perception of Roro!* Available at: http://listenup.org/screeningroom/index.php?view=a4dcd000c6dc5c7bb20a753f117c447f

Magnifico, A. (2010). Writing for Whom?: Cognition, Motivation, and a Writer's Audience. *Educational Psychologist* 45(3), 167–84.

McLaughlin, M. W., Irby, M. A., & Langman, J. (1994). *Urban sanctuaries: Neighborhood organizations in the lives and futures of inner-city youth*. San Francisco: Jossey-Bass.

Muller, V. (2006). Film as *Film*: Using Movies to Help Students Visualize Literary Theory. *English Journal*, 95(3), 32–8.

Nelson, M. E., Hull, G., & Roche-Smith, J. (2008). Challenges of Multimedia Self-Presentation: Taking, and Mistaking, the Show on the Road. *Written Communication*, 25(4), 415–40.

New London Group (1996). A Pedagogy of Multiliteracies: Designing Social Futures. *Harvard Educational Review*, 66(1), 60–92.

Norman, D. (1993). *Things that make us smart*. Garden City, NY: Double Day.

Office of Education Research and Improvement, U.S. Department of Education (1993). *Performance assessment*. Retrieved March 25, 2009, from http://www.ed.gov/OR/ConsumerGuides/perfasse.html.

Peppler, K., Warschauer, M., & Diazgranados, A. (2010). Game Critics: Exploring the Role of Critique in Game-Design Literacies. *E-learning and Digital Media*, 7(1), 35–48.

Purcell-Gates, V., Duke, N. K., & Martineau, J. A. (2007). Learning to Read and Write in Genre-Specific Text: Roles of Authentic Experience and Explicit Teaching. *Reading Research Quarterly*, 42(1), 8–45.

Sefton-Green, J. (2000). From Creativity to Cultural Production: Shared Perspectives. In J. Sefton-Green & R. Sinker (eds.), *Evaluating creativity: Making and learning by young people* (pp. 216–31). London: Routledge.

Sefton-Green, J., & Sinker, R. (2000). *Evaluating creativity: Making and learning by young people*. London: Routledge.

Soep, E. (2006). Critique: Assessment and the production of learning. *Teachers College Record*, 108(4), 748–77.

Squire, K. D. (2006). From Content to Context: Videogames as Designed Experience. *Educational Researcher*, 35(8), 19–29.

Steinkuehler, C. (2008). Cognition and Literacy in Massively Multiplayer Online Games. In J. Coiro, M. Knobel, C. Lankshear, & D. Leu (Eds.), *Handbook of research on new literacies*, (pp. 611–34). Mahwah, NJ: Erlbaum.

Wenger, E. (1998). *Communities of practice: Learning, meaning, and identity*. New York: Cambridge University Press.

Wiggins, G., & McTighe, J. (2005). *Understanding by Design*, 2nd ed. New York: Prentice Hall.

Wiley, L., & Feiner, D. (2001). Making a Scene: Representational Authority and a Community-Centered Process of Script Development. In S. C. Haedicke & T. Nellhaus (eds.), *Performing democracy: International perspectives on urban community-based performance* (pp. 121–42). Ann Arbor, MI: University of Michigan Press.

Games as Twenty-First-Century Curriculum

17   Introduction to Section III

Sasha Barab

Over the last decade we have seen video games grow in popularity, becoming one of the most influential forms of entertainment in the last century. According to the Entertainment Software Association (2009), at least 68 percent of American households play computer and video games, and the number of years that adults have played video games averages 12 years. Other surveys also have demonstrated that video gaming as a leisurely pursuit is pervasive: 97 percent of youth play video games and 53 percent of adults also play video games (Lenhart, Jones, & Macgill, 2008; Lenhart et al., 2008). Clearly, video games are engaging to diverse populations, and for this reason alone, many educators are interested in leveraging technologies and methodologies to support learning. However, games are more than fun, and Gee (2003/2007) argues that it is their potential to support meaningful learning that makes them truly of interest to educators. There are many reasons that educators should care about video games, including their noted discursive richness, depth of collaborative inquiry, complexity of game play, opportunities for consequentiality, rich perception-action cycles, exploration of situated identities, and the complex forms of learning and participation that can occur during game play (Gee, 2003/2007; Salen & Zimmerman, 2004; Shaffer et al., 2005; Squire, 2006; Steinkuehler 2006; Shaffer, 2007; Thomas & Brown, 2006).

Beyond documenting the complex learning that occurs when playing commercial games, we are seeing the emergence of game spaces designed to intentionally support the teaching and learning of academic content as valued in schools, and this is the focus of this chapter (see, for example, Barab et al., 2007; Barab, Gresalfi, & Ingram-Goble, forthcoming; Rosenbaum, Klopfer, & Perry, 2007; Squire & Jan, 2007; for a review, see Clark et al., 2009). Toward illuminating the potential of these game spaces as a twenty-first-century curriculum, the collection of chapters in this section is not intended to provide

an exhaustive review but rather to illuminate potential designs and to discuss
the challenges involved in repurposing a successful entertainment methodology and technology and using it explicitly to achieve educational purposes
(see Barab et al., Chapter 19 in this volume). In pondering these challenges,
I am reminded of one interview with a ten-year old who was using my *Quest
Atlantis* educational video game (http://QuestAtlantis.Org) both in his classroom and at an after-school center. When interviewed at school, he referred
to *Quest Atlantis* as a "game," but three days later, when interviewed at the
after-school center, he referred to it as "school work." This highlights what
Squire (Chapter 2 of this volume) and others have been arguing that games
are contextually bound and that their meanings are as much determined by
the context of use and individual players as they are by some inherent features hardcoded into their bits and bytes.

More generally, society seems be questioning less and less as to
whether learning occurs in games, whether the type of learning is significant, whether educators should be attempting to create educational
games, and whether it is possible to create a game and have it used in
schools. Instead, there seems to be numerous federal initiatives (see recent
requests for proposals from the National Sciences Foundation, Institute
of Educational Sciences, National Institute of Mental Health) and private
foundation initiatives (see recent requests for proposals from the MacArthur
Foundation, the Gates Foundation, and the Hewlett Foundation) designed
to foster the research and development of educationally useful games. This
section includes six research and design projects, with authors first describing their assumptions in viewing their designs or potential designs and
illuminating in particular the opportunities and challenges associated with
both the design and the implementation of these innovative curricula. In
this manner, this section is about advancing possibility, not attempting to
settle arguments on the value of these designs, but to illuminate the vast
potential at the same time acknowledging that we are still in our infancy
in understanding how to use games to support the learning of particular
academic content.

Of particular interest is how these projects have both infused pedagogical potential into the games they are providing to learners and, just
as significantly, how they are managing to get their spaces used, both in
terms of engaging children in rich experiences and in terms of gaining
the approval of adult gatekeepers. In terms of the game-play experience,
this involves ensuring not only that the pedagogical focus does not overwhelm the player's immersion in the activity but also that the activity does
indeed have pedagogical value. I am reminded that when we start inserting

progress-oriented goals and adult values into students' play spaces, they might unknowingly produce a sort of micropolitical resistance from the very people we are trying to engage. This challenge is exacerbated only when teachers leverage these spaces in their classrooms and make play a mandatory activity with assessment implications. The projects in this section operate within this tension, neither shying away from the challenges nor blindly moving forward in their designs. In a very real way, this section is about advancing what Christensen (2009) refers to as "disruptive technologies."

Taking on this exciting challenge of using video games to support academic learning, Chapter 18 illuminates the power of video games for supporting science learning. In this chapter, Clark and Martinez-Garza discuss the potential of video games from the perspective of science educators interested in supporting conceptual change and fostering model-based thinking. They begin with an overview of other efforts and use this reviews as a springboard to clarify important distinctions that are central to their chapter goals. One important distinction is between science games in which the core content is "conceptually embedded" as opposed to those in which the ideas are "conceptually integrated" into the game play. In the former, the game provides a conceptual framing for appreciating or "situating" the meaning and value of the ideas, whereas in the latter games the concepts are the core game mechanics. Another important distinction highlighted in this chapter is between what others have referred to as model-based versus constraint-based reasoning. Simply, it is one thing to play a game where one simply responds to the local cues provided by the game and quite another to build a more general model that one uses to think about the underlying dynamics of the game. I am reminded of my first experience playing *Half-Life*, in which I shamefully never strayed far from a game FAQ, and as a result, I found myself completing the game challenges without really getting better at playing the game. It wasn't until I abandoned the security of the FAQ that I really began to play the game in a meaningful way, and what became so entertaining at this point (beyond using the gravity gun) was how the game continually expanded on this model in interesting ways. Returning to the chapter, the authors then discuss the relevance of the predict-observe-explain model for science education, advancing a vision of a conceptually integrated game that would leverages this framework to support model-based thinking.

Barab, Pettyjohn, Gresalfi, and Solomou, in an attempt to highlight the tension of inserting educational goals within play spaces, discuss in Chapter 19 the notion of transformational play, a theory meant to highlight the importance of games as providing a form of dramatic agency that, if designed properly, meaningfully positions the person with intentionality, content with legitimacy, and context with consequentiality. More than a theoretical discussion, the authory situate these ideas in the design and implementation trajectory of their *Modern Prometheus* game. In their example, the important point is that the game positions content having use value in that the only way to advance the game storyline is to engage the elements of persuasive writing in a consequential form, in this case, to build an argument either for or against the town doctor being able to run ethically questionable tests on his or her creation. Importantly, in the curriculum design, the game *context* evolves and changes based on the doctor's efforts and decisions (if the player decides that it is illegal for Dr. Frankenstein to continue, the doctor may be arrested, and the plague spreads). At the same time, the *player* himself or herself also evolves, because he or she is treated differently by other in-game characters and real-world players based on his or her accomplishments and decisions. In addition, his or her *actual tasks* in the game change and grow more challenging because the more advanced investigative reporter is now able to take on more difficult assignments. This transactive potential, they argue, is one significant affordance of games with the potential to transform education occurring in the classroom from a contextually desolate experience to one that is personally meaningful and situationally consequential.

In Chapter 20, Coulter, Klopfer, Sheldon, and Perry overview their work using augmented reality to connect players to familiar places. In particular, they discuss the work they have been doing with mobile games, in which they develop rich experiences that help players to rediscover the areas around them from a new perspective. Beyond describing their games, they connect the kinds of experiences players are having when playing their games with the National Research Council framework for learning science in informal environments. This analytic lens illuminates the value of these spaces as they relate the six strands to moments they have observed their players engage through their designs. While designing video games to teach others is quite a challenge, Chapter 20 goes farther and shares the authors' experiences in placing these design tools into the hands of players. More than providing a sandbox, they release these tools in the context of educational curriculum such that in the second half of their chapter, they are able to again connect the NRC framework with the observed experiences of players using their design tools. Of particular importance is the way in which these tools can help younger students see the "horizons of science they can aspire toward" and the way they overlay the virtual and the real.

Directly interested in providing players with design tools, Chapter 21, by Kafai and Peppler, overviews their research on Scratch, highlighting how, through the use of design tools, youth develop gaming fluencies. Grounded in their treatment of games as a form of interactive art, this discussion begins with an overview of the three dimensions that they theorize are central to game production: technical, critical, and creative. This addition of the artistic and creative dimensions, along with an appreciation for how through social review designers become more critical with their work, is an important contribution to the conception that constitutes gaming fluencies. These ideas are used to examine two years of research on inner-city youth as they used the scratch game design tools to design games that other youth used, remixed, and critiqued. Their research shows that youth are quite motivated to design games in their free time without any requirement to do so and that the affordance of the Scratch platform to easily remix other media as part of game design seemed to make it quite accessible and engaging for this population. Also of interest is that youth gaming fluencies improved overtime without any explicit scaffolds or instruction to support this evolution in thinking. Lastly, they found that despite the sophisticated creations and even their increasing sophistication over time, developing criticality was quite difficult to cultivate in the after-school setting. This chapter demonstrates the realized potential when design tools are placed in youth hands and the further need for mechanisms that also facilitate the development of a necessary critical stance if youth are to maximize this potential.

Continuing this theme, Macklin and Sharp, in Chapter 22, also focus on the use of game design, but with a particular interest in having youth use game design as a means of exploring civic issues. Their work is focused on bringing together issues – literacy, civic engagement, and systems fluency – with the belief that designing games has a rich potential for uncovering the systems at play in the content a game contains. Therefore, supporting youth in using game design to explore big concepts such as what it is like to be a Hutu woman keeping a baby silent to protect him from approaching soldiers or, on a different note, the contrast between navigating the dark alleys of New York City and being at a friend's birthday party. While designing games to develop deeper insight may seem like an interesting possibility on the surface, part of what the authors reveal in this chapter is the shear complexity of what one has to know to design a game (e.g., storytelling, visual art, systems thinking, sound design, interactive rules, and the core content that the game is to be about). Therefore, an important component of this chapter is to overview projects that have leveraged game design successfully, and especially those which used game design to promote insight into socially significant issues. As part of this journey, the authors share research from classes using the Grow-a-Game deck, where players are able to use a deck of cards to connect game mechanics, values, social issues, and actions as they brainstorm a game concept. They also look at *Playing for Keeps*, which emphasizes the research, understanding, and ideation parts of game design and then works to support collaborations among youth and game designers. And they look at the *Quest to Learn* school, which has been built on the belief that game design is a legitimate and valuable process, one in which an entire curriculum can be modeled around. Lastly, the lessons from these various project are incorporated into the Activate! Project, where youth engage a website to complete stages of expertise where they design, share, and critique each other's projects. This chapter leaves the reader with a rich appreciation of both the challenges and opportunities that game design provides for fostering deep and critical engagement with significant societal issues.

This section closes with Shaffer discussing, in Chapter 23, the problem of transfer and how experiences players have in a game relate to their lives outside the game. Quite usefully, he reconceptualizes in this chapter what it means to know as a process of situated action; a perspective that has important implications for how he characterizes the phenomenon of transfer. Central to his argument is that transfer is not about the application of a particular skill or conceptual understanding learned in one setting to another. Instead, he argues for a view of participation that is a cultural practice or what he refers to as the "engagement of an epistemic frame." While knowledge or even procedural skill is a component of this frame, so are values, skills, epistemologies, and even one's identities. In his conception, to understand what one knows or how one participates, the observer first needs to build models of situated action, and he sees this less of a thing and more of a network of interacting pieces that collectively come to define and constitute participation. Therefore, to understand transfer, one must first build an epistemic network of the situation in which we want people to function eventually, and understand the overlap with the network that they are being asked to function within the game world. Returning to the task of answering the question of whether transfer occurs from games, he then describes the application of a methodological approach that he refers to as epistemic network analysis. Using this approach, he compares player's participation in the games he has designed with those of the authentic communities. As such, this chapter quite meaningfully illuminates the complexity of the transfer question and provides a methodologic lens for measuring it.

Collectively, these chapters provide a lens into the challenges and opportunities associated with designing games to support the teaching and learning of academic content. Importantly, beyond theoretical critiques or simple discussions of what might be possible, they grounded their ideas in a rich body of works that create a pragmatic utility to this chapter that is often missing from discussions of educational games. Further, the authors share their success and failures, creating more than an aspirational account, instead providing a realistic vision of what are the possibilities of educational games and challenges in getting there. As a collection of work, this section provides a hopeful vision for future learning and the role that games might come to play as a form of twenty-first-century curriculum that even has the potential to bridge the problematic divides of content from context, of the cognitive from the personal, of required versus elected participation, and of what is actual and what is possible. In general, I believe that in the "no child left behind" legislation there has been an attempt to ensure that all children earn a particular test score, and this has done little to inspire curriculum that helps children to see and desire futures that call on disciplinary content knowledge. An important focus of this work is to fill that gap, both positioning existing content in new learning platforms and expanding our understanding of what it means to be literate. All of this in a manner that creates a vision of the future that can begin today.

References

Barab, S. A., Gresalfi, M. S., & Ingram-Goble, A. (forthcoming). Transformational Play: Using Games to Position Person, Content, and Context. *Educational Researcher*.

Barab, S. A., Zuiker, S., Warren, S., et al. (2007). Situationally embodied curriculum: Relating formalisms and contexts. *Science Education*, 91(5), 750–82.

Christensen, M. (2009). *Pedagogical reforms of digital signal processing education*. Unpublished doctoral dissertation, University of Florida, Gainesville, FL.

Clark, D. B., Nelson, B., Sengupta, P., & D'Angelo, C. M. (2009). Rethinking Science Learning Through Digital Games and Simulations: Genres, Examples, and Evidence. Invited Topic Paper in the *Proceedings of the National Academies Board on Science Education Workshop on Learning Science: Computer Games, Simulations, and Education*, Washington, DC.

Entertainment Software Association (ESA) (2009). *Essential facts about the computer and videogame industry*. Washington, DC: ESA.

Gee, J. P. (2003/2007). *What videogames have to teach us about learning*. New York: Palgrave.

Lenhart, A., Jones, S., & Macgill, A. (2008, December 7). *Adults and videogames*. Washington, DC: Pew Internet and American Life Project.

18 Prediction and Explanation as Design Mechanics in Conceptually Integrated Digital Games to Help Players Articulate the Tacit Understandings They Build through Game Play

Douglas B. Clark and Mario Martinez-Garza

Well-designed digital games are exceptionally successful at helping learners to build accurate intuitive understandings of the concepts and processes at the heart of those games owing to the situated and enacted nature of good game play (e.g., Gee, 2003/2007). Most commercial games fall short as platforms for learning because they do not help people articulate and connect their evolving intuitive understandings to more explicit formalized structures that would support transfer of knowledge to other contexts. Games hold the potential, however, to support learners in integrating their tacit spontaneous concepts with instructed concepts, thus preparing learners for future learning through a flexible and powerful foundation of conceptual understanding and skills (Clark et al., 2009a). The integration of prediction and explanation mechanics into game play potentially provides tools for supporting this extension from tacit to explicit by helping players articulate and explore the connections between the science-based dynamics present in the game and the formalized scientific principles they instantiate. This chapter explores these possibilities and proposes an example of how this might be accomplished in a physics-based game.

Background: Digital Games for Science Learning

This perspective that games provide significant potential affordances for science learning is not idiosyncratic. In 2006, the Federation of American Scientists issued a widely publicized report stating their belief that games offer a powerful new tool to support education and encouraging governmental and private organizational support for expanded funded research into the application of complex gaming environments for learning. In 2009, a special issue of *Science* (Hines, Jasny, & Merris, 2009) echoed and expanded this call. Later in 2009, the National Research Council convened a committee and workshop to explore this potential of games and simulations for science learning in greater depth.

Clark and colleagues (2009b) wrote the first of the five topic papers for this workshop, focusing on the evidence for the value of simulations and games for science learning. That review discusses several studies providing evidence for the potential of digital games to support science proficiency. These studies, for example, demonstrate potential in terms of conceptual understanding and process skills to operate on that understanding (e.g., Annetta et al., 2009; Barab et al., 2007a; Clark et al., 2009b; Dieterle, 2009; Hickey et al., 2009; Holbert & Wilensky, 2010; Ketelhut et al., 2006; Klopfer et al., 2009; Steinkuehler & Duncan, 2009). These studies also show that games can support players' epistemologic understanding of nature and development of science knowledge (e.g., Barab et al., 2007b; Clarke & Dede, 2005; Neulight et al., 2007; Squire & Jan, 2007; Squire & Klopfer, 2007) and players' attitudes, identity, and habits of mind in terms of their willingness to engage and participate productively in scientific practices and discourse (e.g., Anderson, 2009; Barab, Gresalfi, & Ingram-Goble, forthcoming; Barab et al., 2009; Dede & Ketelhut, 2003; Galas, 2006; McQuiggan, Rowe, & Lester, 2008).

Several of these games cast players as scientists or investigators (e.g., *Quest Atlantis*, *River City*, and *Operation: Resilient Planet*). In these games, the player learns science by moving through the game world to specific locations and engaging in explicit inquiry activities at those locations. This chapter will refer to this genre of games as *conceptually embedded games*, where science processes are embedded within the game world. This approach has the advantage of directly making the science learning and processes explicit. Furthermore, these types of games have the potential to be very transformative in terms of the players' identities. The players can view the world as a scientist, using scientific tools, seeing how and why it's interesting, and using science to have a direct impact on the world (Gee, 2003/2007; Squire, Chapter 2 of this volume).

Another smaller set of games focuses on science learning directly within the motion and mechanics of the game world itself, such as *Supercharged* (Squire et al., 2004; Anderson and Barnett, 2011;), *SURGE* (Clark et al., 2009a, 2010a; D'Angelo & Clark, forthcoming; D'Angelo et al., 2009), and *FormulaT Racing* (Holbert & Wilensky, 2010). This chapter will refer to this genre of games as *"conceptually integrated" games*,[1] where the science concepts of focus are integrated directly into the core mechanics that operate in the game environment. These games have the potential advantage of engaging the player with the science ideas targeted in the game a higher percentage of the play time (potentially the vast majority of play time), whereas conceptually embedded games involve other interactions while moving and exploring the world between specific inquiry locations and activities or as backdrop for those activities. The disadvantage of integrating the science learning goals directly within the motion and mechanics of the game world, however, is that while the players may spend the vast majority of game-play time interacting with the core ideas as a means of navigating through the world, making the core ideas and relationships explicit rather than tacit is a much bigger challenge than in the conceptually embedded approach.

Essentially, even though playing a conceptually integrated game engages the player constantly in the targeted relationships, the player may never articulate or even identify those relationships. For example, in a study on *Enigmo*, researchers found that while players of this commercial physics-based projectile-motion game developed some tacit understanding that led to higher performance on an immediate post-test in terms of predicting trajectories, they didn't demonstrate gains on other aspects of Newtonian mechanics on the immediate post-test and showed no gains compared with a control group after subsequent traditional instruction (Masson, Bub, & Lalonde, 2010). Thus, while *Enigmo* provides students with a strong intuitive "feel" for physics concepts, it doesn't appear to help students make the leap from tacit understanding to more formalized knowledge. Specifically, Masson, Bub, and Lalonde found that students "improved their ability to generate realistic trajectories" (p. 1). However, the game did not help them learn more from a direct instruction "tutorial" when compared with a control group.

These findings suggest that simply having players engage with physics-based games is not sufficient to help them learn physics. This result is not overly surprising; few people would suggest that playing soccer, for example, will teach people physics, even though soccer is clearly a physics-based game in many ways. *Enigmo* was developed as a commercial recreational game rather than as a learning experience and thus unsurprisingly follows along this path. Soccer and *Enigmo*, however, potentially could be re-envisioned or redesigned in a manner that would support explicit articulation and exploration of the core physics implicit in their game experience.

Paralleling these findings, *Super-Charged* research has emphasized the importance of supports for metacognition (Squire et al., 2004; Anderson & Barnett, 2011). Squire and colleagues, for example, report that the teacher collaborating in their research created activity structures outside the game to engage students in predicting and explaining what was happening in the game and reflecting on connections. Similarly, research with *SURGE* has demonstrated some learning gains on questions based on or drawn from the Force Concept Inventory, but that further supports helping players explicitly articulate and explore the core relationships that would be of significant pedagogical value (Clark et al., 2009a, 2010a; D'Angelo, 2010; D'Angelo et al., 2009). *SURGE* research further suggests that the players' learning was heavily related to their embodied experience in the game and raised the possibility that whatever learning gains the players were making remained inchoate and contextually rooted in the game experience (Clark et al., 2010a, forthcoming).

What needs to happen to support an explicit articulation and exploration of the relationships in a physics-based game?

Framing the Challenge: Learning Occurs but Remains at an Intuitive Level

We propose that the learning challenge of conceptually integrated game mechanics can be framed in terms of the distinction that Parnafes and diSessa (2004) make between model-based reasoning and constraint-based reasoning. Parnafes and diSessa explored players' thinking in a gamelike simulation called *NumberSpeed*. In *NumberSpeed*, players designate the position, velocity, and acceleration for two different turtles to solve a series of challenges (e.g., get Turtle A to a distance of 20 first while getting Turtle B to a distance of 40 first). Parnafes and diSessa observed that players sometimes engaged in thinking very locally through simple processes of covariation (constraint-based reasoning) and sometimes engaged in thinking more deeply about the underlying relationships and components to make more principled or model-based accounts of the challenge and what needed to happen to solve the challenge (model-based reasoning).

Essentially, constraint-based reasoning involves "using a set of heuristics to meet the problem constraints, usually using simple co-variation" (Parnafes & diSessa, 2004, p. 265). It involves means-ends strategies focusing on local comparisons, simple motion principles, or pure covariation focusing on a small number of the problem constraints or parameters at a time. Model-based reasoning, however, involves "creating a mental model of the whole scenario of motion, and mentally running the model to reason about the motion situation" (p. 268). It involves examining plans and modifying or considering alternative plans in pursuit of an integrated qualitative solution based on complex motion principles and multiple parameters.

From the perspective of science learning, constraint-based thinking is fine because it supports the development of model-based thinking about phenomena, ultimately the latter type of thinking being necessary for lasting understanding. In a game, for example, if players never progress beyond reactively adjusting their avatar's motion through the game space in a constraint-based manner (e.g., just a bit more to the right or a bit more to the left), it would seem surprising if those players exhibited understanding deeper than that level of reflexive compensation on transfer or assessment tasks subsequent to the game. Thus we might expect the player to be able to predict how a specific minor action component (e.g., clicking the "left arrow" key) might affect the trajectory of an object, for example, but more global understandings would seem unlikely. This is so because more global understandings would involve model-based thinking about the relationships in the game rather than simple constraint satisfaction, which even may reside primarily at an even lower unarticulated tacit or instinctive level "in the thumbs" of the player.

We can characterize the differences in learning in terms of elemental perspectives on conceptual change (e.g., Clark, 2006; Clark, D'Angelo, & Schleigh, forthcoming; diSessa, 1993; diSessa, Gillespie & Esterly, 2004; Parnafes, 2007; Wagner, 2006). These perspectives hypothesize that students' conceptual ecologies include a wide range of elements such as subconceptual p-prims,[2] beliefs, facts, facets,[3] and mental models, among others. These elements are cued by context and interact with one another in a network of positive and negative connections. These core mechanisms and interactions result in the potential for conflicts between ideas, sensitivity to contexts, differential weighting of ideas, and the systematicities created by the interaction of prominent elements. Learning according to these perspectives occurs as people sort through and revise their ideas as they build and revise connections between those ideas. The ultimate goal is that the learners hopefully will develop a more parsimonious and coherent understanding of normative theory-like character over time through these process. The goal for education, then, is to facilitate these processes of revision and reorganization.

The challenge for games with conceptually integrated core mechanics is that if the games demand only constraint-based reasoning of the player, very little substantial reorganization and revision of the player's ideas are required. People's understanding of physics situations is often not at an articulated level [e.g., diSessa's (1993) discussion of phenomenological primitives or Clark's (2006) account of students' thinking about heat and temperature). Game play that allows or incentivizes players simply to react through constraint-based reasoning or for game play to remain in the player's "thumbs," neither pushes players to articulate the components of their thinking (e.g., p-prims) nor the overarching relationships and connections between the multiple components relevant to the phenomenon at hand. Turkle argues this in terms of learning in *SimCity*, for example, which focuses on learning simple heuristics (Turkle, 1997). Squire (forthcoming) argues that this kind of shallow understanding transforms into model-based reasoning as people become more expert. The focus of this chapter is on how we might design game play that specifically incentivizes this model-based thinking at a higher level of conceptual awareness and articulation (e.g., mental models rather than p-prims) that involves closer consideration of the nature of the components and the overarching relationships between them.

Possible Solutions: Prediction and Explanation Mechanics

If encouraging model-based reasoning is the goal, how can we incentivize it? In simulations and hands-on science labs, students often use trial and error as opposed to mindful strategies (Chang & Tsai, 2010). Parnafes and diSessa argue that certain representations provide more ready affordances for one form of reasoning or the other. Research has shown that contexts can be structured or queued in a manner that the students are more likely to view their goals in an epistemological manner, encouraging pursuit of explanatory coherence (e.g., Ranney & Schank, 1998; Rosenberg, Hammer, & Phelan, 2006; Thagard, 1989, 2007; Thagard & Verbeurgt, 1998). Research also suggests that coupling highly interactive visualizations with meta-level learning activities, such as self- or peer evaluation (Chang, Quintana, & Krajcik, 2010; Moreno and Valdez, 2005) or critique (Chang, 2009; Chang & Linn, submitted; Clark et al., 2011) can help students to reflect on and refine ideas (Linn et al., 2011).

A further challenge for conceptually integrated games involves building in these exterior supports while preserving the immersive and engaging properties of the game itself. We propose that engaging players in prediction through the navigation interface and explanation through their dialog with the game's nonplayer characters or entities can provide metacognitive supports for model-based reasoning.

A growing body of research and scholarship on games and cognition emphasizes cycles of prediction, observation, and refinement as being a core mechanic of game-play processes (Salen & Zimmerman, 2003; Squire et al., 2003; Wright, 2006). We propose to leverage these ideas with research from psychology on self-explanation and research from science education on prediction and explanation to operationalize and refine the potential of prediction and explanation mechanics in conceptually integrated games to support science learning. Even if players do engage in reflective cycles of hypothesis formation and revision, few games provide structures for externalizing and reflecting on these cycles. More often such articulation and reflection occurs *outside* the game, through discussion among players or participation in online forums (Gee, 2003/2007; Squire, 2005; Steinkuehler & Duncan, 2009). Developing methods to integrate such articulation and reflection into the game experience and extending them so as to promote broader application are challenges for contemporary educational design.

The focus on prediction and explanation is central to many curricula in science education. The predict-observe-explain model developed by Champagne, Klopfer, and Anderson (1980), for example, has seen wide practical application as pedagogical practice in science classrooms and school laboratories. Broadly described, predict-observe-explain is a classroom or laboratory activity with three distinct stages. In the prediction stage, students are shown a situation or system at rest in which a given science principle applies, and students are prompted to predict the outcome of setting the situation or system into motion. In the observation stage, students see the phenomenon unfold (or perform the experiment themselves) and are asked to describe the outcome. Finally, in the explanation stage, students are asked to compare their observations with their predictions and explain their agreement or disagreement. The predict-observe-explain process has long been recommended by science educators (e.g., Grant, Johnson, & Sanders, 1990; reviewed more generally in Scott, Asoko, & Driver, 1991; Mazur, 1996) as a classroom activity that is epistemologically similar to real-world scientific inquiry. Many studies show predict-observe-explain to be effective at promoting learning and reflection on concepts of science (e.g., Baird & Mitchell, 1986; Borges, Tecnico & Gilbert, 1998; Cosgrove & Osborne, 1985; Palmer, 1995; Rickey & Stacy 2000; Shepardson, Moje & Kennard-McClelland, 1994) and also as a useful tool for probing and diagnosing students' conceptions of science facts as well as monitoring conceptual change (Liew & Treagust, 1995, 1998; Searle & Gunstone, 1990; White & Gunstone, 1992).

Along with general demonstrations and arguments in favor of the efficacy of predict-observe-explain, several other lines of research have probed more deeply into the connections of predict-observe-explain to constructivist, conceptual change, and metacognition literatures. From a constructivist perspective (e.g., Liew & Treagust, 1998), the predict-observe-explain teaching/learning sequence draws on the Piagetian concept of accommodation (Piaget, 1964), whereby learners become aware of conflicts between their conceptions and physical reality. Thus later works on predict-observe-explain (e.g., Kearney, 2004; Kearney & Treagust, 2000) have highlighted the importance of the explanation stage of predict-observe-explain as being the moment where learning is most likely to occur. Some didactic approaches similar to predict-observe-explain (e.g., ideational confrontation, as described in Champagne, Gunstone, & Klopfer, 1985) involve a more social dynamic, evocative of Vygotsky, by asking students in the explanation stage of predict-observe-explain to convince each other of the validity of their ideas. Many of these constructivist perspectives fit well with the elemental perspectives on conceptual change that guide this research. Other lines of research have supported the predict-observe-explain sequence from a cognitive perspective by grounding it in metacognition (Champagne, Klopfer, & Gunstone, 1982) and conceptual change (Tao & Gunstone, 1999). According to these perspectives, the process driving learning in predict-observe-explain is the prediction stage, where students not only must articulate their naive concepts but also marshal explicit support for those concepts, underscoring the importance of the monitoring and regulatory aspects of metacognition (White, 1988; White & Gunstone, 1992). Other work in science education has focused more broadly on the value of prompting reflection. Work by White and Fredericksen (1998, 2000) demonstrates the value of asking students to reflect on their learning during inquiry with physics simulations, for example, and Lin and Lehman (1999) demonstrated similar high learning gains by prompting for reflection in a computer-based biology environment.

In addition to research in science education, work on self-explanation by Chi and others provides clarity into the value of explanation for learning (e.g., Chi et al., 1989; Roy & Chi, 2005; Chi & VanLehn, forthcoming). That work began by demonstrating that students who explained their answers and worked to themselves perform better on post-tests. The work went on to demonstrate that students who are prompted to provide explanations of their answers perform better on post-tests. A recent review of research on self-explanation by students reports that self-explanation results in average learning gains of 22 percent for learning from text, 44 percent for learning from diagrams, and 20 percent for learning from multimedia presentations (Roy & Chi, 2005). Encouragingly, research by Bielaczyc, Pirolli, & Brown (1995) showed that instruction that stresses generating explanations improves performance even after the prompts are discontinued.

In terms of implementation in gamelike environments, Mayer and Johnson (2010) implemented a self-explanation condition using an explanation selection format based on work by Hausmann and Chi (2002) showing that a computer-based multimedia learning environment reduced self-explanation effects when learners were required to type rather than verbalize their thoughts. Similarly, work by Atkinson, Renkl, and Merrill (2003) showed that performance on computer-based worked-out examples improved when learners chose explanations for each step from a pull-down menu. Mayer and Johnson (2010) found significant gains on a transfer task following game play for participants in the self-explanation condition in comparison with the control condition. These results suggest the potential value of building this functionality into conceptually integrated games.

The inclusion of prediction and explanation into game environments for learning is not a trivial challenge. Although already rich with interaction schema that support learning (Gee, 2003/2007), video games do not regularly ask players to predict or explain in-game phenomena at the level of general principles. At a more localized level of interactivity, however, prediction and (self) explanation exist throughout game play, framed as internal responses to moments of choice (Salen & Zimmerman, 2003). A central task of our research plan is to highlight these moments of choice for the player-learner and turn them into opportunities for reflection and learning.

Example: What Might Prediction and Explanation Look Like in a Conceptually Integrated Physics Game?

In some game formats, integration of explicit prediction and explanation can be envisioned more easily. In a conceptually embedded game, such as a role-playing game where the player is cast explicitly as a scientist, the game could include prediction and explanation in a relatively straightforward manner. Physics-based games, however, are potentially less obvious in this regard. To explore what this might look like in a physics game, we now outline a game design to implement these into the game mechanics in a manner that might support the explicit articulation of model-based thinking in a conceptually integrated physics game. We first describe a simple core game mechanic as a context and then describe how prediction and explanation might be integrated.

Game Description: *Cup Racer*

To provide a context for these proposed prediction and explanation mechanics, we first outline a hypothetical physics game context, which we will refer to as *Cup Racer*. Essentially, players in *Cup Racer* need to navigate their avatar (a small but very intelligent gecko who has equipped a coffee mug with rocket engines) through the play area to pick up food and friends and deliver them to safe locations while avoiding obstacles and enemies. The player in *Cup Racer* uses the rocket engines to navigate through levels that correspond initially to areas of a kitchen filled with food, friends, and dangers. Levels in *Cup Racer* are very short and puzzle-like in nature. Levels involve executing a small number of navigation maneuvers to solve specific challenges. From a content perspective, *Cup Racer* focuses on Newton's second law (force = mass × acceleration) and basic kinematics in terms of the relationships among distance, velocity, acceleration, and friction, with some emphasis on how forces can change motion in a new direction.

Prediction. How might prediction be integrated into a physics game? We propose that the navigation interface provides an excellent opportunity for prediction. Essentially, while real-time and just-in-time navigation formats are common in games such as *Cup Racer*, formats supporting prediction are also not uncommon and could be developed within the "magic circle" of the game without breaking the game aspects of *Cup Racer*. Furthermore, a game such as *Cup Racer* provides excellent opportunities for research on the integration of prediction into games because of the range of interface formats afforded along a prediction/real-time format.

Essentially, real-time or just-in-time navigation formats engage the player in making decisions during the flow of the level, often in a reflexive manner mirroring constraint-based thinking (e.g., the player continually microadjusts direction and velocity as it becomes apparent that adjustments are required). Examples of such interfaces might include

- **Real-time constant velocity.** Clicking and holding down arrow keys on the keyboard to move the avatar at constant velocity in the direction of the arrow key. This is a standard navigation interface in many games, ranging from casual platform-style games to massively multiplayer online games. This interface requires no prediction in terms of result of pressing a key – push the key and move in that direction at a fixed velocity no matter what motion you may have been involved in the moment before. This is the core control condition for our pilots.
- **Real-time constant acceleration.** Clicking and holding down arrow keys to apply a constant acceleration in the direction of the arrow key. The classic arcade game *Asteroids* made this interface popular

long ago. This interface requires a higher level of prediction and model-based thinking because it requires more planning in terms of what you will need to do to maneuver into a location or vector of motion because you are just adjusting your velocity in terms of speed and direction rather than directly mandating your velocity simultaneous with your keystrokes.

- *Real-time tilting for constant velocity or constant acceleration.* Tilting a controlling device, such as the controller of the Nintendo Wii game console, or the entire device in the case of a smaller digital device such as the iPad or Sony PSP portable game player to recreate any of the interface formats described earlier. Such an approach could create a more embodied and physical connection to the navigation, and even more embodied options are becoming available, such as the upcoming Microsoft Natal system.
- *Real-time key-based variable magnitude acceleration.* Clicking arrow keys multiple times to increase the magnitude of acceleration or magnitude of force being applied along an axis (up-down or side-to-side). A rocket burst could begin and end when increasing above 0 and returning to 0, or a rocket burst could be defined as beginning and ending with clicks on another key (e.g., the spacebar) for an interface version that counted or limited the number of rocket bursts. This is similar to the preceding interface but involves more planning about longer-term navigation goals.
- *Real-time mouse-based variable magnitude acceleration.* Moving the mouse across a vector representation to choose direction and magnitude of force or acceleration. The player might click the mouse to begin and terminate a rocket burst or might click another key, such as the spacebar, to initiate and terminate a rocket burst. This would provide a more visual representation and connect the player's navigation more directly onto a formal representation format from the physics discipline. The vector could be constrained to one of the four cardinal directions or even just to single axis (e.g., up-down) depending on the level. Alternatively, the vector could be allowed to span the full 360-degree range of possible motions.

Some of these interface formats incentivize a higher degree of prediction and model-based thinking than others. In a predictive interface, the player needs to think ahead more systematically about what the outcomes will be for a possible action. The more aspects of mechanics the interface requires the player to consider in making a successful prediction for solving the challenge at hand, the more that interface would seem to require and incentivize model-based thinking versus constraint-based thinking, and the further we would align that type of interface along the prediction end of the spectrum.

In the interfaces just outlined, for example, the constant-velocity interface requires the least prediction, whereas constant acceleration requires a bit more. Similarly, the vector interfaces that only allow thrusts along the up-down and side-to-side axes require more prediction than the vector interfaces that allow free 360-degree manipulation of direction. Adding fuel limits or other resource limits further pushes toward the prediction end, whereas allowing unlimited resources moves the challenge and experience more toward the real-time end (e.g., allowing a limited number of rocket bursts incentivizes players to plan and think more carefully about the outcomes of each burst than an interface that allows unlimited bursts because in the latter interface the player can keep applying bursts to micro-adjust navigation in pursuit of a burst rather than needing to get "the most" out of each one). The examples below highlight some possible interfaces further along the prediction end of the spectrum.

- *Predictive table-based pause and program.* Pausing the game and programming direction of force, magnitude of force, and duration of force into a table for the next rocket burst and then pressing a key to initiate the burst. This process then would be repeated for each subsequent burst, allowing the player to consider and plan carefully the impact of each decision, which might be further incentivized by tying the score or success to minimizing the number of bursts required to succeed. This programming approach for each "move" hearkens back to early projectile-motion games, such as *Scorched Earth*, where the player programmed each cannon shot in a race with the opposing player. This interface format simply adds the duration of the rocket burst to the process and transforms the planning format into a sequence of rocket bursts rather than a series of independent projectile launches.

- *Predictive vector-based pause and program.* Pausing the game and using a vector interface for the magnitude and direction of the next rocket burst, entering a duration, then pressing a key to initiate the launch, and then pausing the game for each sequential burst. This transforms the preceding format into a graphic user interface (GUI) and is a standard approach in many current projectile-motion games, such as *Gravitee 2* on Kongregate.com.

- **Predictive table-based full program.** Programming the direction of force, magnitude of force, starting time, and duration of force for each rocket burst in a planned sequence of rocket bursts in a data table using numbers and then pressing a key to launch the plan and put it into action. This interface format requires the most prediction and model-based thinking because it requires the player to project and predict the results of subsequent rocket bursts in a chain to achieve a goal rather than executing one burst and then engaging in planning the next to adjust toward the goal in a manner mirroring more constraint-based thinking or the simple hill-climbing approach to problem solving.
- **Predictive vector-based full program.** Programming visual or GUI approach mirroring the preceding approach, but rather than using numbers in a data table, this GUI approach might place blocks to represent duration and magnitude of rocket bursts along timeline tracks representing the direction of the burst, with distance along the track representing the timeline for when the bursts initiate. As above, the player eventually would press a key to initiate the program. This GUI version might prove easier for players to use in visualizing the nature of the program they are creating, facilitating model-based thinking and prediction. These more predictive interfaces, we would argue, should support a higher level of model-based thinking than constraint-based thinking, as well as a higher percentage of explicit articulation of thinking versus implicit intuitive thinking that might stay at the level of unaware application of p-prims.

Explanation Mechanisms. Explanation seems more tricky to integrate within the "magic circle" of the game play for single-player conceptually integrated game, but the literature supporting the role of explanation in learning is so compelling that further exploration for games seems very promising. We see numerous examples of players working collaboratively outside and inside the game as part of collaborative raids (Thomas & Brown, 2009), guild membership debriefs (Steinkuehler, 2007), forum discussions (Steinkuehler & Duncan, 2009), affinity groups (Gee, 2003/2007), emergent universities (Squire, Chapter 2 of this volume), and such. Two challenges for integrating explanation into single-player conceptually integrated games include (1) providing a format for the player to provide an explanation that is not cumbersome and stays within the game play and (2) doing so in a manner that allows the software within the game to assess and react to the explanation. Generally, most approaches to explanation likely would shift toward a conceptually embedded approach but still could complement and synergize with the core conceptually integrated game mechanics.

One surface possibility for *Cup Racer* or other games could involve having the player explain how to overcome a certain type of challenge to a hypothetical nonplayer character (NPC) in the game so that the NPC theoretically could engage in that activity successfully. Similarly, the NPC actually might need to try and accomplish the task, and the player could see the result and adjust the explanation.

This latter mechanic is central to the *Betty's Brain* software (Biswas et al., 2005), where a student creates a concept map to teach Betty about the relationships between various factors in problem context. *Betty's Brain* then allows the player to give Betty a test to see what she actually knows. By adopting this concept map format for explanations, Betty's brain allows the player to provide explanations that the software can interpret and act on.

A simpler approach to explanations might involve adopting the standard conversation format from many role-playing playing games, where the player is given a list of possible responses and chooses one from that list. Rather than choosing "I'd like to hire you as a guide to show me where the hidden cavern is," the player might have choices such as "When you double your mass, you halve your acceleration." The computer then could give feedback, such as "I have input your explanation into the computer's flight simulator, and it looks like we would still crash. Do you have other suggestions we might try?" This role-playing game convention is essentially just multiple choice, but it does allow the game to anticipate answers and provide targeted feedback to those explanations.

Another possibility involves integrating argumentation into the process so that players include explanations as well as evidence for their choices. *Operation: Resilient Planet*, for example, has players include icons representing pieces of evidence that they have collected in support of the multiple-choice claim. This approach to claims and evidence has been extended and enhanced in other games, such as *Citizen Science*, *Phoenix Wright*, *Our Courts*, and *Policy World*. In these games, evidence generally involves the completion of a specific activity or reading a specific piece of text. These pieces of evidence generally are attached to claims. *Citizen Science* and *Our Courts* move a step further by including other components of arguments. In *Quest Atlantis*, players upload scientific reports that are then reviewed, and feedback is provided by teachers often signing their critiques as in-game characters (Barab et al., 2007b). Or, as another form of reflection, players in *Quest Atlantis* are expected to interpret a water-quality problem and implement an in-game solution, after which they are required to travel to the future and, as a form of reflection, analyze the outcome of their solution.

All these are excellent approaches for game settings where other artifacts and readings make sense within the context of the game (e.g., reading a policy brief in *Policy World* or checking the contents of a shark's stomach in *Operation: Resilient Planet*). In this section we propose a structure that would allow the player to more flexibly create and choose claims, qualifiers, and evidence in direct connection with the mechanics of a physics game. We first outline an iconic explanation creator that could allow players to flexibly create explanations that the game might assess and act on. We then explain an approach for allowing players to flexibly identify evidence gathered through the game engine that the game could assess and act on. A game might include only the iconic explanation creator, or it might also include the evidence/argumentation component to extend the iconic explanations.

Iconic Explanation Creator. Figure 18.1 below shows a possible interface for an iconic explanation creator. Explanations are represented in a manner that can be read as text and symbolically to clarify the structure. Essentially, explanations involve an independent variable, a dependent variable, modifiers for each variable that define their relationship (e.g., "Increasing" for the independent variable and "Decreases" for the dependent variable in the figure), and any relevant conditions that define or limit the domain across which the explanation applies. Conditions (also called *qualifiers* in the argumentation literature) thus are essentially modifications to the explanation about the range of the domain in which the explanation holds true. These conditions are stated in terms of ranges for specific variables. These ranges can be stated verbally for some general relationships (e.g., "Independent of…" or "For a constant…") or as ranges of values (e.g., "If velocity is greater than 80 m/s" or "If velocity is between 80 and 130 m/s").

Players create explanations by clicking on boxes in the explanation that open a set of pull-down menus where the players choose the independent and dependent variables, modifiers for each, condition variables, and modifiers for each. Using this basic format, the game updates the player's explanation. If the player adds or deletes a condition, the game resizes the explanation appropriately. Available options in each pull-down menu would be increased from a small number of choices initially to larger numbers of choices as the game progressed. Examples of modifiers and explanations are as follows:

- Modifiers for independent variables
  - Increasing
  - Decreasing

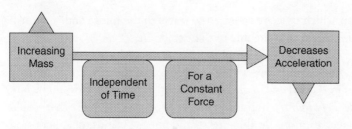

Figure 18.1. Iconic explanation creator provides students pull-down menus to select components of their explanations and displays the relationships in natural language and symbolically.

- Doubling
- Halving
- Modifiers for dependent variables
  - Increases
  - Decreases
  - Doesn't affect
  - Doubles
  - Halves
- Modifiers for qualifiers
  - For a constant...
  - Independent of...
  - If "Variable" is greater than, less than, between...
- Example explanations
  - Increasing time increases velocity if acceleration is greater than 0.
  - Increasing velocity increases distance independent of mass.
  - Increasing time doesn't affect mass.
  - Increasing mass decreases acceleration for a constant force if time is greater than 0.

Players would use the iconic explanation creator to create explanations for various phenomena or situations in the game posed by an NPC. For example, between levels in *Cup Racer*, a friend of the gecko might show a short segment of play and ask why something happened the way it did (e.g., "Does the mass of the people you pick up in your cup affect your velocity?"). The player then might create an explanation in answer that the game might assess, with the friend of the gecko responding (e.g., The friend might respond in the next frame by saying, "I tried it myself, and it works. Thanks for explaining!" or "I tried using that explanation, but it doesn't seem to help me get the strawberry. Do you have any other ideas?").

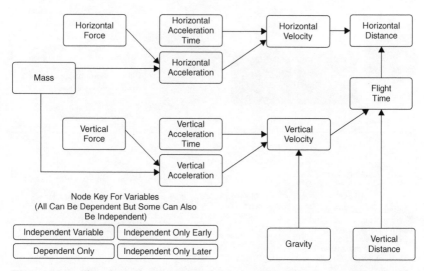

Figure 18.2. Flowchart showing logical relationships between variables for the iconic explanation creator that would allow software to interpret both the accuracy and relevance of a student's explanation.

The game could assess players' explanations using a causal map of the variables potentially involved in a scenario (which would be a matrix but that is displayed here visually for clarity). The links would specify the relationship between the variables. Figure 18.2 displays such a map that would address the relationship between all possible independent and dependent variables that the player might choose to include a complex projectile-motion scenario late in the game (the player chooses only one independent and one dependent variable for an explanation, but the matrix needs to be able to account for all possible pairs). For simpler scenarios, a simpler matrix of pairs and relationships would suffice. In the map in the figure, any dependent variable that is not "downstream" of the independent variable would be considered as "Doesn't affect" from the modifier list. Conversely, any dependent variable that is downstream is affected, although potentially only with qualifiers (e.g., Increasing horizontal acceleration time increases horizontal velocity only if horizontal launch acceleration is greater than 0). The color codings in the map suggest possible relationships to consider as valuable to have the player explore from the perspective of the physics content.

Evidence and Argumentation Components. This explanation system could be woven into the story between play levels, and players could earn additional points, unlock new levels, or gain other incentives, such as customization options for their appearance. A more elaborate and potentially

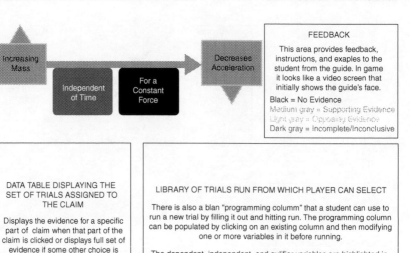

Figure 18.3. Integrating the iconic explanation creator with data collection and selection to warrant or rebut explanations.

intrusive system that would shift the player more into the player-as-scientist role in alignment might engage the player in further argumentation around the explanation by incorporating evidence. The nature of conceptually integrated game mechanics actually would allow the player to collect and identify evidence more fluidly and organically than is typical of argumentation-based games. Whereas evidence in most argumentation games tends to be predefined by the game authors, conceptually integrated games might allow the player to identify and select evidence created through interaction with the game engine. In programming/prediction interface versions of *Cup Racer*, for example, the player experiments with different maneuvers or relationships in the game and then selects sets of these trials as evidence for or against an explanation or parts of an explanation (see Figure 18.3).

In the figure, parts of the explanation can be clicked on to highlight the attached evidence in the data table, and there is an option to click on the trials to see them run. For cases where the players are given an explanation by an NPC to critique, they would present both supporting and opposing evidence. For explanations the players create, the focus likely will be on supporting evidence because they would modify the model to adjust aspects

of the arguments that they found evidence against (or they would add quali-
fications). The core relationship of the argument, as well as the individual
qualifiers, changes color as evidence is connected to support or refute. All
components start gray until evidence is attached, become red until a set of
evidence is selected that supports or refutes the relationship or qualifier, and
then turn green if the evidence effectively supports or blue if it contradicts.

Players experiment to find a combination of trials that supports or
refutes specific claims. The data table stores their trials, and they select sets
of trials from the table. Players can delete trials if they wish and possibly
annotate trials. Clicking on a trial can rerun it to the environment. At the
most basic level, the player can select two trials as supporting the claim. The
software then can determine if the trials support the claim, refute it, or are
neutral/not connected to the claim and provide this feedback to the player.
Essentially, the software can check the trials to determine if the independent
variable was varied, if the dependent variable responded in the manner indicated, if other variables were controlled, and if other stated conditions of the
qualifiers were met. Potentially more feedback could be provided.

More complex arguments could require two or more claims and trials
to support the combined claims. At the easiest level, two trials could be
selected for each subclaim. There might be more complex relationships
that could be chosen. The software could, for example, incorporate simple logical operators (e.g., AND, OR, and IF) to allow the player to make
more complex claims composed of separate subordinate claims. Similarly,
a 2 × 2 experimental design could be implemented. Thus this approach to
argumentation and experimentation could allow the player to flexibly and
organically create and identify evidence in support or opposition of explanations provided by NPCs or explanations that they themselves had created regarding mechanics within the game, thus incentivizing model-based
thinking and scaffolding the explicit articulation of this thinking.

Generalizability of Approach and Final Thoughts

These ideas about prediction and explanation mechanics would seem
better suited to some domains and game formats than others. Generally
speaking, games with extended levels might be less amenable than games
with shorter, focused levels. Similarly, games that focus on reflex speed
(or *twitch* speed) are less amenable than games that are more strategic or
puzzle-based. Essentially, the challenge needs to be in deciding on a set
of choices to make rather than on the dexterity or speed with which the
player can implement those choices. That said, however, even in twitch

games, specific levels might be added to focus on core mechanics within the game.

Along these lines, the game mechanics need to be amenable to programming, preplanning, or segmenting play in some way to capitalize on the prediction qualities of the plan. The explanation components, however, are more open for implementation because they simply ask the player to explain relationships within game play. It is relatively easy to imagine, for example, a first-person immersive game that involves ongoing play where the player is asked to explain why sometimes his or her movement is slower than at other times (e.g., perhaps the player might create an explanation about the relationship of mass to acceleration). Integrating evidence and argumentation components with their explanations, however, also would require some way of programming, preplanning, or segmenting play so that trials could be identified as evidence.

The easiest explanations to address in the proposed evidence/argumentation functionality would seem to be ones of direct and indirect proportionality in systems that reach a final state in the model or a steady state. It would seem that systems that involve a very dynamic equilibrium process (such as ecology models) or where the issues of interest occur and fluctuate during the motion of the model would be difficult to handle this way, but phenomena where the equilibrium is more smoothly reached and is more constant, such as many gas law relationships, would work well (i.e., even though properties of the gaseous system are emergent properties of the independent individual interactions of the particles, a steady-state equilibrium condition is smoothly arrived at, with the end result being the object of interest more than any fluctuations observed in achieving that equilibrium).

The challenge is in finding game mechanics that include these characteristics. *Supercharged* involves very amenable characteristics in the domain of electrostatics, and *Cup Racer* would fit well in the domain of mechanics. These domains are not, however, the only such domains for conceptually integrated learning games. We now need to think inventively. Not so long ago, the wild popularity of matching pitch or rhythm to a visual analogue in the music games *Dance Dance Revolution*, *Frequency*, and *Rock Band* was far from obvious. We now need to locate and leverage these opportunities for learning. Prediction and explanation mechanics seem to provide excellent opportunities for incentivizing model-based thinking and scaffolding players in explicitly articulating the intuitive understandings they develop about the underlying relationships in these conceptually integrated learning games. Then, if a game is more than a simulation, we need also to ensure that the game play itself, especially with these extra layers of participation, remains fun.

Notes

[1]   In making this distinction between *conceptually embedded* and *conceptually integrated* games, we certainly are not diminishing the power of conceptually embedded games. Our purposes is simply to highlight differences in affordances and challenges for conceptually integrated games, which generally have received less focus in games for learning research.

[2]   p-Prims (or *phenomenological primitives*) are inarticulate explanatory primitives in a student's conceptual ecology that provide the basis for many of that student's explanations about science phenomena (e.g., diSessa, 1993).

[3]   Facets are independent explanatory facts or "rules of thumb" that students use to understand and explain situations and phenomena (e.g., Hunt & Minstrell, 1994).

References

Anderson, J. (2009). Real Conversations in Virtual Worlds: The Impact of Student Conversations on Understanding Science Knowledge in Elementary Classrooms. Paper presented at the American Educational Research Association Annual Meeting, April 13–17, 2009, San Diego, CA.

Anderson, J., & Barnett, M. (2011). Using Video Games to Support Pre-Service Elementary Teachers Learning of Basic Physics Principles. *Journal of science education and technology*, 20(4), 347–62.

Annetta, L. A., Minogue, J., Holmes, S. Y., & Cheng, M.-T. (2009). Investigating the Impact of Video Games on High School Students' Engagement and Learning about Genetics. *Computers and Education*, 53(1), 74–85.

Atkinson, R. K., Renkl, A., & Merrill, M. M. (2003). Transitioning from Studying Examples to Solving Problems: Effects of Self-Explaining Prompts and Fading Worked-Out Example Steps. *Journal of Educational Psychology*, 95, 774–83.

Baird, J. R., and Mitchell, I. J. (eds) (1986). *Improving the quality of teaching and learning: An Australian case study – The PEEL project*. Melbourne, Australia: Monash University Press.

Barab, S. A., Gresalfi, M. S., & Ingram-Goble, A. (forthcoming). Transformational Play: Using Games to Position Person, Content, and Context. *Educational Researcher*.

Barab, S. A., Sadler, T., Heiselt, C., Hickey, D., & Zuiker, S. (2007a). Relating Narrative, Inquiry, and Inscriptions: A Framework for Socio-Scientific Inquiry. *Journal of Science Education and Technology*, 16(1), 59–82.

Barab, S. A., Scott, B., Siyahhan, S., Goldstone, R., Ingram-Goble, A., Zuiker, S., & Warrant, S. (2009). Transformational Play as a Curricular Scaffold: Using Videogames to Support Science Education. *Journal of Science Education and Technology*, 18, 305–20.

Barab, S. A., Zuiker, S., Warren, S., Hickey, D., Ingram-Goble, A., Kwon, E-J., et al. (2007b). Situationally Embodied Curriculum: Relating Formalisms and Contexts. *Science Education*, 91(5), 750–82.

Bielaczyc, K., Pirolli, P., & Brown, A. L. (1995). Training in Self-Explanation and Self-Regulation Strategies: Investigating the Effects of Knowledge Acquisition Activities on Problem Solving. *Cognition and Instruction*, 13(2), 221–52.

Biswas, G., Leelawong, K., Schwartz, D., & Vye, N. (2005). Learning by Teaching: A New Agent Paradigm for Educational Software. *Applied Artificial Intelligence*, 19, 363–92.

Borges, A. T., Tecnico, C., & Gilbert, J. K. (1998). Models of Magnetism. *International Journal of Science Education*, 20(3), 361.

Champagne, A. B., Gunstone, R. F., & Klopfer, L. E. (1985). Effecting Changes in Cognitive Structures Among Physics Students. In L. H. T. West and A. L. Pines (eds.), *Cognitive structure and conceptual change*. Orlando, FL: Academic Press.

Champagne, A. B., Klopfer, L. E., & Anderson, J. H. (1980). Factors Influencing the Learning of Classical Mechanics. *American Journal of Physics*, 48(12), 1074–9.

Champagne, A. B., Klopfer, L. E., & Gunstone, R. F. (1982). Cognitive Research and the Design of Science Instruction. *Educational Psychologist*, 17(1), 31.

Chang, H.-Y. (2009). Use of Critique to Enhance Learning with an Interactive Molecular Visualization of Thermal Conductivity. Poster presented at the Annual Meeting of National Association for Research in Science Teaching (NARST), 2009, Garden Grove, CA.

Chang, H.-Y., & Linn, M. C. (submitted). Learning from a Molecular Visualization: Observe, Interact or Critique? *Journal of Research in Science Teaching*.

Chang, H.-Y., Quintana, C., & Krajcik, J. (2010). The Impact of Designing and Evaluating Molecular Animations on How Well Middle School Students Understand the Particulate Nature of Matter. *Science Education*, 94(1), 73–94.

Chang, H.-Y., & Tsai, K. C. (2010, June). Investigating the Role of Physical and Virtual Experiments in Developing Integrated Understanding of Thermal Conductivity and Equilibrium. Paper presented at the symposium "Using Visualization to Link Abstract Science and Everyday Experience," International Conference for the Learning Sciences, 2010.

Chi, M. T. H., Bassok, M., Lewis, M. W., Reimann, P., & Glaser, R. (1989). Self-explanations: How Students Study and Use Examples in Learning to Solve Problems. *Cognitive Science*, 13(2), 145–82. DOI: 10.1016/0364-0213(89)90002-5

Chi, M. T. H., & VanLehn, K. A. (forthcoming). The Content of Physics Self-Explanations. *Journal of the Learning Sciences*.

Clark, D. B. (2006). Longitudinal Conceptual Change in Students' Understanding of Thermal Equilibrium: An Examination of the Process of Conceptual Restructuring. *Cognition and Instruction*, 24(4), 467–563.

Clark, D. B., D'Angelo, C., & Schleigh S. (forthcoming). Multinational Comparison of Students' Knowledge Structure Coherence. *Journal of the Learning Sciences*.

Clark, D. B., Nelson, B., D'Angelo, C. M., & Menekse, M. (2009a). Integrating Critique to Support Learning about Physics in Video Games. Poster presented as part of a structured session at the National Association of Research in Science Teaching (NARST) 2009 Meeting, Garden Grove, CA.

Clark, D. B., Nelson, B., D'Angelo, C. M., Slack, K., & Martinez-Garza, M. (2010a). *SURGE:* Integrating Vygotsky's Spontaneous and Instructed Concepts in a

Digital Game. In *Proceedings of the Ninth International Conference of the Learning Sciences* (pp. 384–5), Chicago, IL.

Clark, D. B., Nelson, B., D'Angelo, C. M., Slack, K., & Martinez-Garza, M. (forthcoming). *SURGE:* Exploration and Inquiry-Related Learning About Mechanics in a Digital Game. *Journal of Research and Practice in Technology Enhanced Learning.*

Clark, D. B., Nelson, B., Sengupta, P., & D'Angelo, C. M. (2009b). Rethinking Science Learning Through Digital Games and Simulations: Genres, Examples, and Evidence. Invited topic paper presented at the National Academies Board on Science Education Workshop on Learning Science: Computer Games, Simulations, and Education. Washington, DC.

Clark, D. B., Nelson, B., D'Angelo, C. M., Slack, K., Martinez-Garza, M., & Menekse, M. (2010b). SURGE: Assessing students' intuitive and formalized understandings about kinematics and Newtonian mechanics through immersive game play. Paper presented as part of a structured poster session at the American Educational Research Association (AERA) 2010 Meeting, Denver, CO.

Clark, D. B., Sampson, V. D., Chang, H., Zhang, H., Tate, E., & Schwendimann, B. (2011). Research on Critique and Argumentation from the Technology Enhanced Learning in Science Center. In M. Khine (ed.) *Perspectives on scientific argumentation: Theory, practice and research* (pp. 157–200). Amsterdam: Springer.

Clarke, J., & Dede, C. (2005). Making Learning Meaningful: An Exploratory Study of Using Multi-User Environments (Muves) in Middle School Science. Paper presented at the American Educational Research Association Conference, Montreal, Canada.

Cosgrove, M., and Osborne, R. (1985). Lesson Frameworks for Changing Children's Ideas. In R. Osborne & P. Freyberg (eds.), *Learning in science: The implications of children's science*(pp. 101–111). Boston: Heinemann.

D'Angelo, C. M. (2010). *Scaffolding vector representations for student learning inside a physics game.* Unpublished Ph.D. dissertation. Arizona State University.

D'Angelo, C. M., & Clark, D. B. (forthcoming). Scaffolding Vector Representations for Student Learning Inside a Physics Game.

D'Angelo, C. M., Clark, D. B., Nelson, B. C., Slack, K., & Menekse, M. (2009). The Effect of Vector Representations on Students' Understanding of Motion. Poster presented at the Physics Education Research Conference (PERC)/American Association of Physics Teachers (AAPT) 2009 Meeting. Ann Arbor, MI.

Dede, C., & Ketelhut, D. J. (2003). Designing for Motivation and Usability in a Museum-Based Multi-User Virtual Environment. Paper presented at the American Educational Research Association Conference, Chicago, IL.

Dieterle, E. (2009). Neomillennial learning styles and River City. *Children, Youth and Environments,* 19(1), 245–278.

diSessa, A. A. (1993). Toward an Epistemology of Physics. *Cognition and Instruction,* 10(2 & 3), 105–225.

diSessa, A. A., Gillespie, N., & Esterly, J. (2004). Coherence versus Fragmentation in the Development of the Concept of Force. *Cognitive Science,* 28, 843–900.

Galas, C. (2006). Why Whyville? *Learning and Leading with Technology,* 34(6), 30–3.

Gee, J. P. (2003/2007). *What video games have to teach us about learning and literacy.* New York: Palgrave Macmillan.

Grant, P., Johnson, L., & Sanders, Y. (1990). *Better links: Teaching strategies in the science classroom*. Melbourne, Australia: STAV Publication.

Hausmann, R. G. M., & Chi, M. T. H. (2002). Can a Computer Interface Support Self-Explaining? *International Journal of Cognitive Technology*, 7, 4–14.

Hickey, D., Ingram-Goble, A., & Jameson, E. (2009). Designing Assessments and Assessing Designs in Virtual Educational Environments. *Journal of Science Education and Technology*, 18(2), 187–208. doi:10.1007/s10956-008-9143-1

Hines, P. J., Jasny, B. R., & Merris, J. (2009). Adding a T to the Three R's. *Science*, 323, 53.

Holbert, N. R., & Wilensky, U. (2010). FormulaT Racing: Combining Gaming Culture and Intuitive Sense of Mechanism for Video Game Design. In K. Gomez, L. Lyons, & J. Radinsky (eds.), *Learning in the disciplines: Proceedings of the 9th International Conference of the Learning Sciences* (ICLS 2010), Vol. 2: *Short papers, symposia, and selected abstracts* (pp. 268–9). Chicago: International Society of the Learning Sciences.

Hunt, E., & Minstrell, J. (1994). A Cognitive Approach to the Teaching of Physics. In K. McGilly (ed.), *Classroom lessons: Integrating cognitive theory and classroom practice* (pp. 51–74). Cambridge, MA: MIT Press.

Kearney, M. (2004). Classroom Use of Multimedia-Supported Predict-Observe-Explain Tasks in a Social Constructivist Learning Environment. *Research in Science Education*, 34(4), 427–53.

Kearney, M., & Treagust, D. (2000). An Investigation of the Classroom Use of Prediction-Observation-Explanation Computer Tasks Designed to Elicit and Promote Discussion of Students' Conceptions of Force and Motion. Presented at the National Association for Research in Science Teaching, New Orleans, LA.

Ketelhut, D. J., Dede, C., Clarke, J., & Nelson, B. (2006). A Multi-User Virtual Environment for Building and Assessing Higher Order Inquiry Skills in Science.

Klopfer, E., Osterweil, S., & Salen, K. (2009). Moving learning games forward. *The Education Arcade*, 1–58.

Liew, C. W., & Treagust, D. F. (1995). A Predict-Observe-Explain Teaching Sequence for Learning about Students' Understanding of Heat and Expansion Liquids. *Australian Science Teachers Journal*, 41.

  (1998). The Effectiveness of predict-Observe-Explain Tasks in Diagnosing Students' Understanding of Science and in Identifying Their Levels of Achievement. Presented at the American Educational Research Association, San Diego, CA.

Lin, X. D., & Lehman, J. (1999). Supporting Learning of Variable Control in a Computer-Based Biology Environment: Effects of Prompting College Students to Reflect on Their Own Thinking. *Journal of Research in Science Teaching*, 36(7), 837–58.

Linn, M. C., Chang, H.-Y., Chiu, J. L., Zhang, Z., & McElhaney, K. (2011). Can Desirable Difficulties Overcome Deceptive Clarity in Scientific Visualizations? In A. S. Benjamin (ed.), *Successful remembering and successful forgetting: a Festschrift in honor of Robert A. Bjork* (pp. 235–58). New York: Psychology Press.

Masson, M. E. J., Bub, D. N., & Lalonde, C. E. (2010). Video-game training and naive reasoning about object motion. *Applied Cognitive Psychology*. DOI: 10.1002/acp.1658.

Mayer, R. E., & Johnson, C. I. (2010). Adding Instructional Features That Promote Learning in a Game-Like Environment. *Journal of Educational Computing Research*, 42(3), 241–65.

Mazur, E. (1996). *Peer Instruction: A User's Manual* (Pap/Dskt.). New York: Benjamin Cummings.

McQuiggan, S., Rowe, J., & Lester, J. (2008). The Effects of Empathetic Virtual Characters on Presence in Narrative-Centered Learning Environments. In *Proceedings of the 2008 SIGCHI Conference on Human Factors in Computing Systems*, Florence, Italy, pp. 1511–20.

Moreno, R., & Valdez, A. (2005). Cognitive Load and Learning Effects of Having Students Organize Pictures and Words in Multimedia Environments: The Role of Student Interactivity and Feedback. *Educational Technology Research and Development*, 53(3), 35–45.

Neulight, N., Kafai, Y. B., Kao, L., Foley, B., and Galas, C. (2007). Children's Participation in a Virtual Epidemic in the Science Classroom: Making Connections to Natural Infectious Diseases. *Journal of Science Education and Technology*, 16(1), 47–58.

Palmer, D. (1995). The POE in the Primary School: An Evaluation. *Research in Science Education*, 25(3), 323–32.

Parnafes, O. (2007). What Does "Fast" Mean? Understanding the Physical World Through Computational Representations. *Journal of the Learning Sciences*, 16(3) 415–50.

Parnafes, O., & diSessa, A. A. (2004). Relations Between Types of Reasoning and Computational Representations. *International Journal of Computers for Mathematical Learning*, 9, 251–80.

Piaget, J. (1964). Development and Learning. In R. E. Ripple & V. N. Rockcastle (eds.), *Piaget Rediscovered* (pp. 7–20). Ithaca, NY: Cornell University Press.

Ranney, M., & Schank, P. (1998). Toward an Integration of the Social and the Scientific: Observing, Modeling, and Promoting the Explanatory Coherence of Reasoning. In S. Read & L. Miller (eds.), *Connectionist models of social reasoning and social behavior* (pp. 245–74). Mahwah, NJ: Erlbaum.

Rickey, D., & Stacy, A. M. (2000). The Role of Metacognition in Learning Chemistry. *Journal of Chemical Education*, 77(7), 915.

Rosenberg, S., Hammer, D., & Phelan, J. (2006). Multiple Epistemological Coherences in an Eighth-Grade Discussion of the Rock Cycle. *Journal of the Learning Sciences*, 15(2), 261–92.

Roy, M., & Chi, M. T. H. (2005). The Self-Explanation Principle in Multimedia Learning. In R. E. Mayer (ed.), *The Cambridge handbook of multimedia learning* (pp. 271–86). New York: Cambridge University Press.

Salen, K., & Zimmerman, E. (2003). *Rules of play: Game design fundamentals* (illustrated edition). Cambridge, MA: MIT Press.

Scott, P. H., Asoko, H. M., and Driver, R. H. (1991) Teaching for Conceptual Change: A Review of Strategies. In R. Duit, F. Goldberg, & H. Niederer (eds.),

Research in physics learning: Theoretical issues and empirical studies. Proceedings of an International Workshop, March 1991, IPN 131, ISBN 3-89088-062-2.

Searle, P., & Gunstone, R. (1990). Conceptual Change and Physics Instruction: A Longitudinal Study. Paper presented at the American Educational Research Association, Boston, MA.

Shepardson, D. P., Moje, E. B., & Kennard-McClelland, A. M. (1994). The Impact of a Science Demonstration on Children's Understandings of Air Pressure. *Journal of Research in Science Teaching*, 31(3), 243–58.

Squire, K. (2005). Toward a Theory of Games Literacy. *Telemedium*, 52(1–2), 9–15.

(2011). *Video games and learning*. New York: Teachers College Press.

Squire, K., & Jan, M. (2007). Mad City Mystery: Developing Scientific Argumentation Skills with a Place-Based Augmented Reality Game on Handheld Computers. *Journal of Science Education and Technology*, 16(1) 5–29.

Squire, K., & Klopfer, E. (2007). Augmented Reality Simulations on Handheld Computers. *Journal of the Learning Sciences*, 16(3), 371–413.

Squire, K., Barnett, M., Grant, J. M., & Higginbotham, T. (2004). Electromagnetism Supercharged! Learning Physics with Digital Simulation Games. In Y. B. Kafai, W. A. Sandoval, N. Enyedy, A. S. Nixon, & F. Herrera (eds.), *Proceedings of the 6th International Conference on Learning Sciences* (pp. 513–20). Los Angeles: UCLA Press.

Squire, K., Jenkins, H., Holland, W., Miller, H., O'Driscoll, A., Tan, K. P., & Todd, K. (2003). Design Principles of Next-Generation Digital Gaming for Education. *Educational Technology*, 43(5), 17–23.

Steinkuehler, C. (2007). Massively Multiplayer Online Gaming as a Constellation of Literacy Practices. *eLearning*, 4(3) 297–318.

Steinkuehler, C., & Duncan, S. (2009). Scientific Habits of the Mind in Virtual Worlds. *Journal of Science Education & Technology*, 17(6), 530–43.

Tao, P., & Gunstone, R. F. (1999). The Process of Conceptual Change in Force and Motion During Computer-Supported Physics Instruction. *Journal of Research in Science Teaching*, 36(7), 859–82.

Thagard, P. (1989). Explanatory Coherence. *Behavioral and Brain Sciences*, 12, 435–66.

(2005). Coherence, truth, and the development of scientific knowledge. *Philosophy of Science*, 74(1), 28–47.

Thagard, P., & Verbeurgt, K. (1998). Coherence as Constraint Satisfaction. *Cognitive Science*, 22, 1–24.

Thomas, D., & Brown, J. S. (2009). Why Virtual Worlds Can Matter. *International Journal of Learning and Media*, 1(1), 37–49.

Turkle, S. (1997). Seeing Through Computers: Education in a Culture of Simulation. *The American Prospect*, 31(March–April), 76–82.

Wagner, J. F. (2006). Transfer in Pieces. *Cognition and Instruction*, 24(1), 1–71.

White, B. C., and Frederiksen, J. R. (1998). Inquiry, Modeling, and Metacognition: Making Science Accessible to All Students. *Cognition and Instruction*, 16(1), 3–117.

(2000). Technological Tools and Instructional Approaches for Making Scientific Inquiry Accessible to All. In M. J. Jacobson and R. B. Kozma (eds.), *Innovations in science and mathematics education* (pp. 321–59). Mahwah, NJ: Erlbaum.

White, R. T. (1988). *Learning science*. Oxford, England: Basil Blackwell.
White, R. T., & Gunstone, R. F. (1992). *Probing understanding*. New York: Routledge.
Wright, W. (2006). Dream Machines. *Wired*, 14(4). Available at http://www.wired.com/wired/archive/14.04/wright.html.

19 Game-Based Curricula, Personal Engagement, and the *Modern Prometheus* Design Project

Sasha Barab, Patrick Pettyjohn, Melissa Gresalfi, and Maria Solomou

> Once understood in the context of the narratives that give it meaning, law becomes not merely a system of rules to be observed, but a world in which to live.
>
> —Bruner, 1990, p. x

We have reached a challenging junction at which, on the one hand, teachers and schools face increased pressure to prepare students for standardized tests, whereas, on the other hand, they face a generation of students who regard the school curriculum as largely irrelevant to their own lives. It has become all too common to develop curricula and teach domain content distinct from the people, places, and situations through which the content has meaning. While it is expected that the information learned will somehow, later, be connected to those situations in which it is useful and meaningful, this is rarely what occurs. All too often the knowledge students "acquire" in schools remains inert (Whitehead, 1929), something demonstrated on a test in a school context where it can be traded for a grade but not applied to a situation in which it has intrinsic worth (Lave, 1991, 1997; Wenger, 1998).

> The irony is that we then wonder why children appear unmotivated to learn after we have disconnected meaning from the learning situation, assuming that the learner somehow will attribute the same functional value to the information as the teacher does [Barab & Roth, 2006, p. 3].

Unless we begin to engage youth in rich situations that add meaning to disciplinary concepts – as part of the learning process – the content of schools will be perceived as a thing to be acquired and exchanged for a test score (having *exchange value*) and not as a useful tool that has direct functional value in the world or to the learner.

The purpose of this chapter is to present a theoretical rationale for the design of a game-based curriculum, showing the relevance of this theory to the research and design of one particular curricular unit being used in fifth- to eighth-grade classrooms around the world. Instead of a lesson plan designed to impart some ready-made expert description of a concept (a thing), we argue that by leveraging video-game technologies and methodologies (discussed by Squire, 2006; Gee, 2003; Shaffer, 2007), it becomes possible within school-based classrooms to provide students *a world in which to live* – a world in which their decisions and the content of schools matters. Toward this end, we present a design story of one specific unit in our curriculum offering, with the goal of illuminating the tensions that arise when attempting to design game-based learning environments that meaningfully position person, content, and context to be functionally bound in that they are dependent on each other.

The curriculum we describe involves trajectories or missions that include rich story lines, multiple tasks (e.g., talking to different people, collecting data, becoming proficient with relevant tools, implementing solutions, reflecting on the consequences of chosen actions), and interactive objects (i.e., people, places, and things) that require the player to make conceptually informed choices. The important point is that the learner playing the game, the content to be learned, and the game-based environment are *transactively engaged* such that, at some level, there exists a sense of *intentionality*, with user actions occurring in relation to a situationally meaningfully goal; *legitimacy*, with academic content becoming conceptual tools for acting on the world; and *consequentiality*, because user actions have an effect on the virtual world (Barab, Gresalfi, & Arici, 2009; Barab, Gresalfi, & Ingram-Goble, 2010a). Collectively, we refer to this type of consequential participation as a form of *transactive engagement*. We enlist Dewey and Bentley's (1949) notion of transactive[1] here to capture the phenomena central to well-designed games, where each component is influencing the other, with changes in one necessarily affecting future opportunities for and bringing about changes in the other.

In the most powerful cases, supporting transactive engagement involves fostering a deep sense of immersion in which the learner enters into a situation conceptually and perceptually, has a goal, has a legitimate role, and engages in actions that have consequence – whereby both the learner and the situation with which he or she is engaged become transformed (Barab, Gresalfi, & Arici, 2009; Barab, Gresalfi, & Ingram-Goble, 2010a). Such curricular designs require a learning context that is less a set of information to be attained and more what Bruner (1990) referred to as *a world to be lived.* Learning in such dynamic environments becomes a way of seeing the world or of being in the world, one that in our designs requires enlisting disciplinary content as tools for understanding and transforming particular contexts. And while the types of curricular designs that we develop are meant to immerse learners within a rich context, our interest is not simply in supporting knowledgeable participation within the one context but in crafting storylines and experiences that have metaphorical loft in that the learner appreciates both the immediate situation and the underlying content as having value in both the fictional and real worlds (see Shaffer, Chapter 23 of this volume).

We refer to games that integrate person, content, and context in such transactive ways as *transformative play spaces,* and our goal is to design such spaces such that the content being enlisted is academically meaningful and relevant to the accountability structures of schools. In this way, we are bringing together what is known about how people learn (e.g., Bransford, Brown, and Cocking, 2002), the metaphorical power of narratives (e.g., Bruner, 2002), and game-design methodologies (e.g., Gee, 2003; Salen and Zimmerman, 2004) to establish an educational, entertaining, and personally transformative learning experience. Melding these various methodologies and agendas is not necessarily a straightforward process, as Ito (2005) makes clear when she discusses the tensions arising when adults insert their agendas into children's play spaces (cf. Sutton-Smith, 1997). At some level, the power of these play spaces is that participation is interest-driven and not a mandatory activity imposed on the player by adults. In fact, play itself is often a form of transgressive behavior, where players take on roles that are unavailable or inappropriate in their real lives (Squire, 2006; Steinkuehler, 2007). At the same time, educators are facing a generation of students who more than in any other time are opting out of school (e.g., reports of dropout rates of over 50 percent in some major U.S. cities), and when we look at what youth are doing, video games are a central form of engagement in their lives (Lenhart et al., 2008). As such, our goal is to leverage the engaging power of video games in part because they are fun but also because of their potential to foster transactive engagement. The challenge has been to establish transactive experiences in a form that provides teachers with tools that they can leverage in working with their students.

Theory of Transformational Play

It is one thing to argue about the power of learning in video games yet quite another to use video-game methodologies to design curriculum that establishes a rich learning opportunity for K–12 students in the context of schools and all the constraints they bring (Fishman et al., 2004). Toward this end, we have been designing environments to support rich and complex forms of participation and attunement and, given our role as design-based researchers (Barab and Squire, 2004), evolving theories about the value of these designs. At its core, in our thinking, this involves rich narrative frames and learners who have agency in determining how those narratives unfold. At the same time, in order to be pedagogically useful, students' agency is carefully framed such that success in our games requires that students employ disciplinary concepts (e.g., water-quality concepts, measures of center, persuasive writing skills) to transform a problematic situation embodied within a game-based fictional world.

In particular, our challenge is to design fictional worlds that allow for the positioning of a person with a reason for learning, content with a use value, and context as pedagogically consequential in that it provides the learner with information about the implications of his or her understandings and practices. Supporting experiences that connect person, content, and context is central to our theory of transformational play. According to Barab, Gresalfi, and Ingram-Goble (2010a, p. 5):

> Playing transformationally involves (a) taking on the role of a protagonist (b) who must employ conceptual understandings (c) to make choices (d) that have the potential to transform (e) a problem-based fictional context and ultimately (f) the player's understanding of the content as well as of (g) herself [or himself] as someone who has used academic content to address a socially significant problem. Playing transformationally integrates person, content, and context as part of a transactive system in which each type of positioning motivates and is motivated by the other types.

Supporting transformational play involves the design of spaces that position *person with intentionality* (the player becomes the protagonist equipped with dramatic agency in making choices that determine the direction of the unfolding storyline), *content with legitimacy* (making academic content necessary if one is to usefully understand and resolve the game-world dilemma), and *context with consequentiality* (embedding the context with interactive rules and game-world states that are responsive to player choices). Essential to the design of our transformational play spaces are that they are transactive and reflexive.

Building on the preceding, *transactivity* is an idea advanced by Dewey (1938), who argued that genuine experience involves a dynamic that

Figure 19.1. Screenshot from *Modern Prometheus* showing a darker context with player walking toward graveyard where she may choose to steal grave parts to help the doctor.

effectively couples individual with environment. In his thinking, "every experience enacted and undergone modifies the one who acts and…changes in some degree the…conditions under which experiences are had" (p. 39). Our work has attempted to create such dynamic and transactive couplings by developing worlds in which players have agency in affecting the world and at the same time are changed over time as their game character (and real self) evolve in their understanding and, therefore, change the game-world possibilities for action. However, our design and implementation challenges go beyond simply engineering such dynamic couplings but also are intended to support reflexive engagement with these dynamics as players negotiate with themselves, the world, their peers, and their teacher what counts as meaningful action within the game. As such, an essential aspect of our theory of transactive engagement concerns the designs for *reflexive* action: opportunities for the player to introspect on his or her participation and consider feedback from his or her choices, ultimately recognizing the role these choices have played in framing his or her identity (Barab et al., 2010a).

Building on these ideas, in this section we discuss our work building a game-based version of Shelley's *Frankenstein* (1831). We describe our design evolution of the *Modern Prometheus* game-based curriculum (see Figure 19.1 for a screenshot from the game). The *Modern Prometheus* unit was developed with the goal of better understanding the potential of converting a classic piece of literature into a transformational play space (see Barab et al., 2010b and the worked example hosted at http://workedexamples.org/ projects/plague-world-a-modern-prometheus). The unit focuses on persuasive writing because students are asked to convince others to share their perspective on particular ethical dilemmas. Students grapple with ethical dilemmas with respect to science and technology and whether and when ends justify means. Of particular interest in our designing process was investigating the elements of transformational play and how they affect student learning and engagement. In what follows, we present two rounds of design and implementation that varied with respect to our attention to the elements of transformational play. By sharing the changes across two iterations of design, we hope to ground the theoretical conjectures discussed here and at the same time provide empirical support for our thesis regarding the value of these designs.

Modern Prometheus **Game-Based Curricular Drama**

Elsewhere we have presented data demonstrating that students learn academic content through completing our designed units, whether it is science content (Arici, 2009; Barab et al., 2007; Hickey, Ingram-Goble, & Jameson, 2009), mathematics content (Gresalfi & Barab, 2011), or persuasive writing (Barab et al., 2010c). In terms of this unit in particular, we also have collected data showing that students using version two of this curriculum had statistically significant learning gains from pretest ($M = 8.55$, $SD = 3.77$) to post-test ($M = 14.67$, $SD = 3.52$), $[t(32) = 14.85$, $p < .001]$ and learned more than students using a control curriculum $[f(32, 31) = 11.03$, $p < .001$; effect sizes: control = 1.22; experimental = 1.83]. Here, our focus is to use the design iterations to illuminate the theory and mechanism of transformational play. The specific research question addressed in this study was

> *RQ1: Did our designed changes across iterations, made in response to the model of transformational play, support deeper content engagement and do so without undermining personal engagement?*

Below we begin with a discussion of the methods used in this particular study, followed by the quantitative results and then a more in-depth description of the design iterations and data from their implementations. Following a close discussion of these findings, we then share tensions in balancing personal engagement and adult-sanctioned agendas all in the context of an educational game.

Methods

Given our motivation of engaging underrepresented youth, a group that consistently resists deep engagement with academic content, we conducted this research in inner-city, seventh-grade classrooms with over 90 percent of the students receiving free- or reduced-cost lunch. All data come from the classroom of one teacher; one class from the spring of 2008 (implementation 1) and one class from the spring of 2009 (implementation 2). The year one classroom had twenty-six students, with twelve boys and fourteen girls who completed the necessary assignment for this analysis. The year two classroom had fifteen boys and fifteen girls who completed the final essay. All students across both years had already received previous lessons on persuasive writing as part of the regular language arts curriculum.

We implemented the first version of the unit in year one, and as part of that work, we collected and analyzed data. These data were used to inform design changes that were integrated into the second version of the unit and implemented by the same teacher in year two. Both versions of the unit were conducted during students' regular language arts time and were used at the end of the year as enrichment to support students' persuasive writing abilities and to prepare them for the upcoming end-of-year exam. Students worked independently, each controlling his or her own avatar and submitting individual work. The teacher would intermittently gather the students together for whole-class conversations, where they would discuss the storyline of the unit. Students' work was submitted online, reviewed by the teacher, and then (sometimes) returned for revision. In this comparative analysis, the final culminating essay was coded to capture students' engagement with person, content, and context. The essays had a few structural changes across iterations, but the basic content remained the same and so was deemed valid for comparison purposes. Two researchers coded each individual essay separately and then worked to resolve any differences in order to ensure 100 percent agreement.

The coding process involved leveraging a priori codes, with the goal of classifying student engagement in terms of person, content, and context. Specifically, essays were analyzed for *context* by examining whether students used their experiences and knowledge of the game-world storyline

and dynamics as specific narrative details and narrative inferences to create
a persuasive article. Essays were analyzed for *person* by considering how
the student positioned himself or herself in the article. Analysis focused
on whether students were detached, giving general solutions without
mentioning personal role, or personally involved, using their personal experiences and opinions from their involvement in the narrative as a means of
persuasion. Finally, essays were analyzed for *content* by examining how well
students grasped the procedural and conceptual elements of persuasive
writing. Procedural elements included whether students had a thesis, reason, and evidence in their essays. We measured conceptual understanding
by assessing the relationships between evidence and reasons and reasons
to the thesis.

Below is an excerpt of an essay that was scored high on content and
context but low on person (content = 5; context = 4; person = 1). The essay
received a 5 for content because throughout the essay the student offered
reasons to support his claim and evidence to support and develop those
reasons. As an example, the student opened the essay with a clear thesis,
"The doctor should be allowed to continue trying to find a cure for the
plague" and provided a clear rationale to support his claim:

> The doctor should be allowed to continue trying to find a cure for
> the…[plague]. If the doctor doesn't stop then you will all end up like poor
> Henry who has the…[plague] as we speak. If Dr. Frank dose find a cure
> then Henry (and others) won't be in this predicament….
>
> Lastly the doctor cares about Ingolstadt and is determined to find the cure.
> He is rich enough to get on a train and leave, but he decided to stay and
> he knows that he can catch the…[plague]. Now that takes a lot of commit-
> ment. He lost his sister to the…[plague] and he is trying so that is not your
> fate. If he did not care then he would be gone.

The essay was scored 4 for context because the student specifically leveraged
details from the characters in the game to support his claim that the doctor cares about Ingolstadt and should be trusted. These strong connections
between reasons and context-relevant evidence were evident through the
entire essay. In addition, the student made inferences from his experience in
the narrative to add emotion and pressure to his arguments. For example,
the student made an inferred evaluative statement after his given example
of why the doctor cares about Ingolstadt, "Now, that takes a lot of commitment." Such a statement requires understanding the dynamics and conflict
of the narrative. In contrast, there is no sense of the student himself in the

essay because he wrote as a distant third person. There was no mention of his work or interaction in Ingolstadt; thus he received a 1 for person.

Design Iterations

Design 1

The first iteration of the unit emphasized the ethical dilemma of whether the ends justify the means. Our goal was to position the player in the narrative so that he or she came to develop an empathic relationship with the context and motives of the characters in the space. Based on the hypothesis that deeper empathy would be likely to support more robust engagement and thus superior persuasive writing (seen through more sophisticated justification), we focused on portraying the tensions that different characters with competing agendas and commitments are likely to face. Students' response to the Plague unit confirmed that the narrative and the space indeed were engaging and captivating. Students debated with each other about whether the monster had a right to live, and some students seemed to take their role in the game quite seriously. Although it is clear that they were aware that the game was fictional, debates at times got quite heated.

However, in examining the student-submitted essays, it was clear that although students were personally engaged, they were not disposed to realize their engagement in a disciplinary important way. Essays indicated that students quite enthusiastically took up the role of trying to save the town from an impending plague (see iteration 1 person scores below). Additionally, they struggled with issues of humanity and whether it was acceptable to create life for the service of others. However, although students had strong opinions, they were not enlisting disciplinary content to support those opinions in a convincing manner. In sum, what failed in our first round of implementation was positioning the disciplinary content as having an important role in this world and on their actions. For example, while children consistently reported that they were struggling with ethical dilemmas and the feeling of responsibility that they felt from having the fate of the town in their hands, not one student in our analysis of the final essays reported below associated his or her success as depending on constructing a persuasive argument.

We also observed little usage of persuasive writing techniques, especially with respect to particular skills or the general notion of what makes an argument compelling and persuasive. This limitation of our design was made especially apparent as our theory around transformational play became solidified and we applied it as a frame for analysis of this project. Looking at our initial work through this lens, it is clear that while we had positioned the player successfully with an intention in relation to a context, we had done little to legitimize the content or help players to see their potential impact as depending on the application of persuasive writing. Armed with this appreciation, we revised the *Modern Prometheus* world such that the experience did a better job of positioning the player in such a way that disciplinary content would be central to the player's role; in this case, not simply as a child but also as investigative reporter working for a newspaper.

Design 2

Consistent with notions central to design-based research (Barab & Squire, 2004), our goal in revising the curriculum was both practical and theoretical – practical in that one can see change directly in the curriculum itself and theoretical in that investigating implementation experiences helped to inform the advancement of more general theoretical claims. As such, it is necessary to articulate our revisions in relation to the underlying theory being advanced in this chapter. Our revisions included changes that drew on all elements of transformational play: intentionality, legitimacy, and consequentiality. To support intentionality, we began with a change in the framing dilemma that begins the unit. In the first iteration, we highlighted the students' agency by ensuring that their game play had an explicit purpose – to make good decisions. We hypothesized, following implementation 1, that this framing was too broad and did not help to create a need for the disciplinary content the unit was targeting. In implementation 2, we transitioned from positioning the player as a *compassionate person* to an *investigative reporter.* In so doing, we sought to bind the student's role (player intention) with content expertise as opposed to personal investment only. An example of the change can be seen in the first lines of the letter that is sent to the students:

> **Design 1:** I have to ask a favor of you – an adventure of great importance. You are the only one who can do this! As your mother, I have seen you grow *into an independent, compassionate person* who makes morally responsible choices.

> **Design 2:** As your mother, I have seen you grow into a thoughtful person who makes good choices. *I am so proud of your work as an investigative reporter* – your skills in gathering facts, examining the evidence, and writing persuasive articles to convince others have helped so many people.

It also was clear that in our first design, students did not see persuasive writing as a *legitimate* means of accomplishing their goals. We realized that we had not given students opportunities to learn about and experience the potential of persuasive writing techniques to accomplish desired ends. With this goal in mind, we developed an evidence-analysis tool and a transition tool that students could use to analyze quotes and write articles. This tool served two key purposes. First, it created a scaffold to help students think about the difference between evidence and opinion and whether and why different forms of evidence are more or less persuasive. Second, it allowed for formative feedback as students played and experimented with different sources of evidence in order to see for themselves why different pieces of evidence are more or less persuasive based on their particular thesis. To use this tool, as students interview different characters in the space, they collected quotes that they thought were particularly meaningful. Students then assembled these quotes based on their selected thesis and received a score based on their relevance to their chosen thesis. The latter tool was designed such that each quote could be applied to one of three reasons in support of a particular thesis; thus a quote might earn 5 points if it was aligned with one reason and thesis and only 1 point if it was positioned in support of a different reason and/or thesis. As a form of formative feedback, students were provided an opportunity to purchase quotes from other reporters to increase their score if the first time they approached the evidence-analysis tool they failed to collect the relevant quotes.

Finally, we wanted to ensure that students came to associate their decisions and actions in the game with actual *consequences*, thus reinforcing the importance of being an effective persuasive writer. Improving students' experience of consequentiality was accomplished in several ways. First, game-based characters treat players differently based on the alignment between players' decisions and the characters' personal agendas. For example, the policeman is unfriendly to the player if he or she chooses to allow the doctor to continue his work, whereas the fabric lady is grateful. In addition, players' core thesis statements also produce a new narrative ending. Students who decide to support the work of the doctor produce a world in which there is plague, but the monster remains unhappily manacled to the doctor's table, and many people are disparaging of the ethical choices made by the player. In contrast, if the player chose to stop the doctor, then the town is overrun by the plague with only a couple of survivors, including a happy creature who has been able to build a farm on the vacated land (see Figure 19.2). Importantly, while in the first version many of the narratives were communicated by a follow-up e-mail, the revised

Figure 19.2. Screenshot of different consequences based on choices. The top represents the plagued world if the monster is freed, and the bottom involves the manacled monster but the town freed of the plague. Note the darker sky and hospital beds in top world and the lighter world, except for the dark laboratory, in the bottom world. In iteration one, these differences simply were described in an e-mail to the player.

version involves world changes such that the final narrative is experienced perceptually rather than simply described narratively. Our observations of students suggested that these consequential changes were significant: In contrast to observations of some students giggling in round one, students' responses in round two involved audible gasps when they witnessed the consequences of their choices.

Quantitative Results

The final essays between the two implementations were compared in terms of the elements of transformational play: person, content, and context. First, a multivariate analysis of variance was run showing significant differences between conditions with respect to the multivariate composite of the three element scores [$f(31) = 3.10, p < .05$, Wilks' lamba = 0.75]. Given our desire to inform design, our interest also was in the individual elements (content, context, and person) and, in particular, whether the persuasive writing (content) was of a higher quality. An independent-sample t test comparing *content* scores revealed that the students who used the revised curriculum (implementation 2) scored significantly higher ($M = 3.40, SD = 1.68$) than the students receiving the first iteration of the design (implementation 1)

[M = 1.83, SD = 1.42; $t(31)$ = 2.91, p < .01], representing a large effect size. Similarly, we found *context* to be greater for implementation 2 (M = 3.60, SD = 0.91) than for implementation 1 [M = 2.50, SD = 1.47; $t(31)$ = 2.53, p < .01]. Positioning of *person* did not change significantly, which was gratifying in that we feared revising the unit to support higher levels of content engagement might undermine person engagement.

As a final analysis of these data, we wanted to ensure that the increase in the persuasive writing quality was not simply because students in the subsequent version were receiving more or better feedback on initial submissions than those in the first version. The *t* test comparison results showed that students did significantly more revisions in the 2008 version, with only 13 percent requiring revision in the 2009 class, as opposed to over 61 percent in the 2008 version, with 42 percent requiring more than one revision in the earlier classes. Comparing classrooms in terms of numbers of revisions, the work of students in implementation 1 required significantly more revisions than those in implementation 2 [$t(31)$ = 3.10, p < .01]. While these quantitative results were gratifying in terms of the quality of our work, they provide little insight into the theory. As such, below we describe the design decisions and empirical findings related to both designs with the broader goal of revealing the utility and mechanism of transformational play.

Discussion

These results indicate that the second iteration of the *Modern Prometheus* unit resulted in significantly stronger student essays. This was especially evident when one examined the quality of the essays in terms of using standard elements of persuasive writing, as evident in the higher content scores. Relating this to the design decisions, we specifically added in the reporter tool and the requirement that students had to collect evidence in support of their argument before they even could submit their work. While this did not ensure conceptual understanding, it did guarantee that students, at the very least, recruited the standard persuasive writing trope of ensuring that the article has a core thesis with three supporting reasons and three types of supporting evidence for each reason. The utility of this for the classroom teacher was further evident in the fact that students did significantly fewer revisions in the second iteration, possibly owing to the fact that they could not submit essays until they had the necessary components of a high-quality essay.

While the teacher requiring fewer revisions does not necessarily mean better work, in this case, when we couple it with the fact that these students also had higher-quality essays, the data become additional evidence of the quality of the design iterations. Elsewhere, Gresalfi and colleagues (2009) distinguished among procedural (knowing *what* to do), conceptual (understanding *why* a process works), and consequential (applying the content to *solve a particular problem*) understanding of a particular content. We view the support of procedural understanding with the content to be an important affordance that video games can provide teachers. In this case, designing a tool that ensured correct procedural engagement with persuasive writing provided important scaffolding to students as they composed their essays.

Interviews with the teacher suggested that she had spent more time supporting students' writing when using the first implementation than she did in the second implementation. In fact, she was quite surprised at how much better the first iterations of the essay were in the second year, crediting this to the use of the editor's notebook and the strong positioning of persuasive writing more generally. In a postinterview with the research team, the teacher stated: "The unit did a much better job of teaching and making sure students' used the correct elements of persuasive writing." Of significance to this study was the fact that such positioning of content did not, according to the data reported earlier, appear to undermine personal engagement. However, there were significant differences in context positioning, with more students explicitly referring to the need to affect the situation in the second essays, indicating a resonance with the game narrative and their positioning as individuals whose work would change the storyline – an outcome that was emphasized perceptually because they saw the world change based on the quality and direction of their essay.

Design Tensions

In closing, we wish to highlight some of the design tensions that we struggled with as educators who were enlisting gaming methodologies in the service of teaching academic content. As stated previously, our goal in deigning this curriculum was to balance students' personal engagement and meaning making with the demands of learning particular academic content. Balancing these often-contradictory goals was a challenge, and we struggled with particular decision points in our designs. We have described some of the more general tensions associated with supporting transformational play elsewhere (Barab, Gresalfi, & Ingram-Goble, 2010a). Here, however, the explicit focus is on illuminating the challenges associated with maintaining student engagement yet inserting an educational agenda. When we refer to tensions, similar to Barab, Barnett, and Squire (2002, p.

491), "We are referring to conflicting, and frequently overlapping, needs that drive a system and that need to be balanced – not minimized." In fact, we find ourselves with each new design continually aligning design decisions with both sides, privileging neither one nor the other, but instead treating the tension as a duality whose complementarity drives innovative design (Wenger, 1998). Three key tensions we have found as central to educational game-design efforts in which one is attempting to balance interest-driven participation with the progress-oriented goals of the designs are knowing versus being, lesson versus story, and assigned versus elective.

Knowing versus Being

The first tension that is central to our work involves knowing versus being. Traditionally, our school systems have been somewhat preoccupied with information retrieval, prioritizing content acquisition over engaged participation (Lave & Wenger, 1991). This is motivated in part by the misguided belief that context-free understandings are more robust and transferable than learning that is more contextually bound, which is less generalizable and transferable (see Shaffer, Chapter 23 of this volume for an alternative view of transfer). More pervasively, this can be traced back to Descartes, who treated the world of a person's ideas, beliefs, and (intellectual) knowledge as somehow distinct and disconnected from the bodily experience, giving rise to a series of problematic dualisms, with mind–body, individual–environment, and content–context separation being some of the most pervasive and problematic (Barab et al., 1999). However, we also have been witnessing a move away from such coldly cognitive perspectives and instead are witnessing more and more learning theorists advocating that cognition is fundamentally situated and designing learning opportunities accordingly (CTGV, 1990; Kirshner & Whitson, 1997).

In our games, we go beyond the situating of content in a context and instead additionally argue for the importance of situating the learner, developing games that also engage the person (Barab, Gresalfi, & Arici, 2009). As argued elsewhere, the games we design offer entire worlds where learners are central, important participants and in which *what you know* is directly related to *what you are able to do* and, ultimately, *who you become*. Thus, while our *Taiga Park* unit supports the learning of water-quality content, it does so by letting the player become an environmental scientist. Or, in our *Ander City* game, students learn about measures of center, but they become a statistical analysis, and in the *Modern Prometheus* game, they learn persuasive writing, but they become an investigative reporter. However, just telling the player that he or she is an investigative reporter is not convincing or believable unless he or she also believes that he or she has the expertise to take on that role meaningfully. It is in this way that we support knowing and being, providing moments of game play where the players level up their skills, but in the service of becoming a skilled individual who uses those skills to affect change. And, if designed properly, we approach Gadamer's (1975) vision of play as offering the player the opportunity not simply to play the game but also to "play out self." Elsewhere we have documented how game play tends to bind itself into students' personal lifeworlds (Dodge et al., 2008).

Lesson versus Story

A distinct challenge that we face as educators is how to ensure that the content students engage is meaningful, particularly in a school climate where information is often distanced from the contexts in which it is useful. Unless we begin to engage youth in rich situations that add meaning to disciplinary concepts, the content of schools will be a perceived as a thing to be acquired and exchanged for a test score (having *exchange value*) and not a useful tool that has direct functional value in the world (Lave, 1988). So clearly illustrated in Gee's (2003) critique of schools is that we provide children the manual but not the situations in which the concepts in the manual can be used. In a very real way, our textbook manuals have created a crises of meaning, and we believe that video games are one very powerful means of connecting content back into spaces in which it can be a tool and students can begin to see themselves as individuals who have used content toward personally engaging and situationally meaningful ends. To this end, we have stated elsewhere that video games have the potential to narratize the curriculum (Barab et al., 2010a), reconnecting the content into those situations in which it has meaning so that learners can appreciate why the content has value.

For us, this has involved building rich stories, and to make the roles convincing to the youth who play our games, we have found utility in evoking the fiction. This is so because in a fictional story it makes sense that a young child can be a scientist or an investigative reporter with the fate of a community in their hands. We have found that fiction can be quite educational and, within the context of a properly designed game world, can be created to place the learner in situations in which enlisting academic content becomes necessary for advancing the storyline. We can do this because in a game, the player has a form of dramatic agency in which his or her actions can determine the direction of the unfolding story (Murray, 1997). And while providing such consequentiality to a child can be quite transformative personally, when we bind up the player's potential to have influence by placing him or her in a professional role that requires conceptual expertise, it also can be cognitively illuminating and quite motivating (Barab et al., 2010b). This involves a tight dance between freedom and constraint, with play operating right in between the two (Salen & Zimmerman, 2004). More generally, balancing the explicit teaching of the underlying lessons and the immersion within an engaging storyline is difficult and a task that, in our work, *always* has involved multiple iterations of design (see Barab et al., 2007).

Assigned versus Elective

The final tension we discuss here is related to Ito et al's., (2010) findings that much of the motivation and high levels of participation observed around the use of new media (including games) by youth is so because it is interest-driven. Thus one must ask if it is even possible to develop a game that captures the engagement of children. Squire (2006), Ito et al., (2010), and Sutton-Smith (1997) to different degrees and for different reasons have argued that these spaces are so motivating in part because they are subtly or blatantly transgressive and not adult-sanctioned. What happens when we start inserting our educational aspirations and making participation required? While for some players such direct adult appropriation of these interest-driven spaces might feel problematic and be met with resistance, if done overtly and with respect, it can be quite powerful. In our own work, we have found students to be quite enthusiastic about our designs and teachers to be willing to explore spaces in the service of education. We believe that this is so in part because playing one of our games, even those assigned by the teacher, supports what D'Amato (1992) calls a situational rationale for engaging and not a structural rationale that most often directs participation. The former occurs when engaging in classroom activities comes to have value in itself because it gives rise to experiences of mastery and accomplishment, as opposed to much of current educational practice, in which achieving is either required by the teacher or is a means of attaining future educational and economic opportunities.

This is not to say that simply providing a situational rationale makes participation in these spaces interest-driven and equivalent to participation in peer-owned spaces. In fact, within our own designs we see the richest forms of participation to be occurring when students engage in activities not required by their teacher. For example, in one of our player-owned worlds, where players can rent property and build spaces for their peers to play, we see upwards of a hundred pages of collaborative chat each week as opposed to ten to twenty pages in the teacher-assigned worlds. Another more subtle form of personal positioning occurs given that players have agency with respect to the unfolding drama and types of activities in which they engage in our designed spaces. Simply providing critical decisions both within a story (e.g., Do we stop the doctor or not?) seems to foster commitment to the activities in ways that narratively immutable curriculum does not. As an example, when we interview children about their motivation for completing the unit, we routinely find the majority of students in control curricula saying they learned because it was required and see the reverse with students in the Quest Atlantis group – most saying they perseverated because they wanted to solve the game task. The important point, from our perspective, is not that it is wrong to insert adult-sanctioned agendas and progress-oriented goals but rather that we need to make salient and personal their value. In games, we can build an entire world that does just that.

Implications

It was our starting conviction that academic content devoid of some applied contextualization has little meaning, especially to learners who do not already appreciate potential contexts of use for the content. And such, contextualization should involve more than seeing a concept or even a context of use; it requires a projective stance that involves *being in* the context and recognizing the value of the tools in terms of the context. One of the core problems of school learning is that when domain concepts, practices, methods, and principles are stripped of the legitimate situational frames in which they have meaning and value, they run the likely risk of becoming facts to be memorized rather than useful tools for operating in the world (Brown, Collins, and Duguid, 1989). While formal definitions abstracted from a particular context of use may be useful in that they can mitigate contextual ambiguity about core conceptual meanings, help reveal the common deep structure underlying different contextual phenomena, and provide an organizing role for a discipline, they are less useful for facilitating the conceptual development of an individual who is learning the discipline or recognizing the value of disciplinary formalisms for meaningfully interacting with the world (Nathan, 2005). In contrast, the central thesis of this chapter was that video games provide a powerful opportunity to position person, content, and context meaningfully as part of a learning system.

Central to this work has been a focus on understanding the value of transformational play. Students who play transformationally become agents of change who use real-world knowledge, skills, and concepts to make sense of a situation and then make choices that actually transform the play space and themselves. More generally, we conceive of education as inciting children's passions, their evolving conceptions of and relation with the world, and their growing capacity to discover, sustain, and transform the world they inhabit. Somewhat ironically, it is in the fantastical world of games that we have been able to find such opportunities, for our experience is that through games we can increase the likelihood that the learning experience is deeply immersive, highly interactive, and experientially consequential. This, we have argued, is so because when you operate within the designed world of a video game, *what you know* is directly related to *what you are able to do* and, ultimately, to *who you become*. We hold hope that in the future we will see a rich set of curricular opportunities available to teachers that allow students to try on and develop a desire to become doctors, scientists, engineers, and even game designers. It is a passion for these experiences, not simply the ability to pass a standardized test, that should tell us whether a child has been left behind.

Note

[1]   Dewey and Bentley (1949) introduced the transactional perspective to characterize the inseparable and mutually constitutive nature of subject and object. A *transaction*, according to *Merriam-Webster's Dictionary*, is "a communicative action or activity involving two parties or things that reciprocally affect or influence each other."

References

Arici, A. (2009). *Meeting kids at their own game: A comparison of learning and engagement in traditional and 3D MUVE educational-gaming contexts.* Unpublished Ph.D Dissertation, Indiana University, Bloomington.

Barab, S. A., & Roth, W.-M. (2006). Curricular-Based Ecosystems: Supporting Knowing from an Ecological Perspective. *Educational Researcher*, 35(5), 3–13.

Barab, S. A., & Squire, K. D. (2004). Design-Based Research: Putting a Stake in the Ground. *Journal of the Learning Sciences*, 13(1), 1–14.

Barab, S. A., Barnett, M. G., & Squire, K. (2002). Building a community of teachers: Navigating the essential tensions in practice. *The Journal of The Learning Sciences*, 11(4), 489–542.

Barab, S. A., Gresalfi, M. S., & Arici, A. (2009). Transformational Play: Why Educators Should Care About Games. *Educational Leadership*, 67(1), 76–80.

Barab, S. A., Gresalfi, M. S., & Ingram-Goble, A. (2010). Transformational Play: Using Games to Position Person, Content, and Context. *Educational Researcher*, 39(7), 525–36.

Barab, S. A., Dodge, T., & Ingram-Goble, A. (2010a). Narratizing Disciplines and Disciplinizing Narratives: Games as 21st Century Curriculum. *International Journal of Gaming and Computer-Mediated Simulations*, 2(1), 17–30.

Barab, S. A., Cherkes-Julkowski, M., Swenson, R., Garrett. S., Shaw, R. E., & Young, M. (1999). Principles of Self-Organization: Ecologizing the Learner–Facilitator System. *Journal of the Learning Sciences*, 8, 349–90.

Barab, S. A., Pettyjohn, P., Gresalfi, M., Volk, C., & Solomou, M. (2010b). *Designing a 21st-century story: The Modern Prometheus game*. Unpublished manuscript.

Barab, S. A., Dodge, T., Ingram-Goble, A., Peppler, K., Pettyjohn, P., Volk, C., et al. (2010c). Pedagogical Dramas and Transformational Play: Narratively Rich Games for Learning. *Mind, Culture, and Activity*, 17(3), 235–64.

Barab, S. A., Zuiker, S., Warren, S., Hickey, D., Ingram-Goble, A., Kwon, E.-J., et al. (2007). Situationally Embodied Curriculum: Relating Formalisms and Contexts. *Science Education*, 91(5), 750–82.

Bransford, J. D., Brown, A. L., & Cocking, R. R. (eds). (2002). *How people learn: Brain, mind, experience, and School*. Washington, DC: National Academy Press.

Bruner, J. (2002). *Making stories: Law, literature, life*. New York: Farrar, Straus and Giroux.

Brown, J. S., Collins, A., & Duguid, P. (1989). Situated Cognition and the Culture of Learning. *Educational Researcher*, 18(1), 32–42.

D'Amato, J. (1992). Resistance and complice in minority classrooms. In E. Jacobs & C. Jordan (eds.), *Minority education: Anthropological perspectives* (pp. 181–207) Norwood, NJ: Ablex.

Dewey, J. (1938). *Experience & education*. New York: Collier Macmillan.

Dewey, J., & Bentley, A. F. (1949). *Knowing and the known*. Boston: Beacon Press.

Dodge, T., Barab, S. A., Stuckey, B., Warren, S., Heiselt, C., & Stein, R. (2008). Children's Sense of Self: Learning and Meaning in the Digital Age. *Journal of Interactive Learning Research*, 19(2): 225–49.

Fishman, B., Marx, R., Blumenfeld, P., Krajcik, J. S., & Soloway, E. (2004). Creating a Framework for Research on Systemic Technology Innovations. *Journal of the Learning Sciences*, 13(1), 43–76.

Gadamer, H.-G. (1975). Hermeneutics and Social Science. *Philosophy Social Criticism/Cultural Hermeneutics*, 2, 307–16.

Gee, J. P. (2003). *What video games have to teach us about learning*. New York: Palgrave.

Gresalfi, M. S., & Barab, S. A. (2011). Learning for a Reason: Supporting Forms of Engagement by Designing Tasks and Orchestrating Environments. *Theory and Practice*, 50, 300–10.

Gresalfi, M. S., Martin, T., Hand, V., & Greeno, J. G. (2009). Constructing Competence: An Analysis of Students' Participation in the Activity System of Mathematics Classrooms. *Educational Studies in Mathematics*, 70, 49–70.

Hickey, D., Ingram-Goble, A., & Jameson, E. M. (2009). Designing Assessments and Assessing Designs in Virtual Educational Environments. *Journal of Science Education and Technology*, 18(2), 187–208.

Ito, M. (2005). Mobilizing Fun in the Production and Consumption of Children's Software. *Annals of the American Academy of Political and Social Science*, 597, 82–102.

Ito, M., Baumer, S., Bittanti, M., et al. (2010). *Hanging out, messing around, and geeking out: Kids living and learning with new media*. Cambridge, MA: MIT Press.

Lave, J. (1988). *Cognition in practice: Mind, mathematics, and culture in everyday life*. Cambridge, England: Cambridge University Press.

(1991). Situating Learning in Communities of Practice. In L. B. Resnick, J. M. Levine, & S. D. Teasley (eds.), *Perspectives on socially shared cognition* (pp. 63–82). Washington, DC: American Psychological Association.

(1997). The Culture of Acquisition and the Practice of Understanding. In D. Kirshner & J. A. Whitson (eds.), *Situated cognition: Social, semiotic, and psychological perspectives* (pp. 17–36). Mahwah, NJ: Erlbaum.

Lave, J., and Wenger, E. (1991). *Situated learning: Legitimate peripheral participation*. New York: Cambridge University Press.

Lenhart, A., Kahne, J., Middaugh, E., Macgill, A. R., Evans, C. & Vitak, J. (2008). *Teens, Video Games, and Civics*. Available at http://www.pewinternet.org/PPF/r/263/report_display.asp.

Kirshner, D., & Whitson, J. A. (1997). *Situated cognition: Social, semiotic, and psychological perspectives*. Mahwah, NJ: Erlbaum.

Murray, J. (1997). *Hamlet on the Holodeck: The future of narrative in cyberspace*. New York: Free Press.

Nathan, M. J. (2005). *Rethinking formalisms in formal education*. WCER Working Paper Series No. 2005–11. Madison, WI: Wisconsin Center for Educational Research.

Salen, K., & Zimmerman, E. (2004). *Rules of play*. Cambridge, MA: MIT Press.

Shaffer, D. W. (2007). *How computer games help children learn*. New York: Palgrave Macmillan.

Squire, K. (2006). From Content to Context: Videogames as Designed Experiences. *Educational Researcher*, 35(8), 19–29.

Steinkuehler, C. (2007). Massively multiplayer online games as a constellation of literacy practices. *e-Learning and Digital Media*, 4(3), 297–318.

Sutton-Smith, B. (1997). *The ambiguity of play*. Cambridge, MA: Harvard University Press.

Wenger, E. (1998). *Communities of practice: Learning, meaning, and identity*. Cambridge, England: Cambridge University Press.

Whitehead, A. N. (1929). *The aims of education and other essays*. New York: Free Press.

20   Discovering Familiar Places: Learning through Mobile Place-Based Games

Bob Coulter, Eric Klopfer, Josh Sheldon, and Judy Perry

February 12, 2100: Walking down by the river's shore it is hard to believe that as recently as a hundred years ago this bank of the river was dry land. Today all of this land is frequently under water as a result of increasingly wild weather events. Looking across the river you see the steady red light on the tower indicating that yet again, rain is in the forecast and people need to be ready to move to higher ground.

Traveling back a hundred years as a TimeLab researcher, you are surprised to learn that the risk of flooding was rather low in the past. Concerned for your family and friends, you think it would be great if the river didn't have to rise – if this land could still be as dry as it was back then. Perhaps that is unrealistic and it is best to use this experience to prepare for still worse conditions in the future. But…perhaps it is possible that you can convince your ancestors to make a few small changes that will make your home in the year 2100 better.

This scenario is part of the experience that players have during the augmented reality (AR) game *TimeLab 2100* developed at Massachusetts Institute of Technology (MIT) as part of a series of research and development initiatives referred to as *MITAR*. The goal of MITAR is to provide experiences that merge the best of real and virtual in order to involve learners of all ages in games that are engaging, thought-provoking, and fun.

MITAR has its origins in a series of AR games developed at MIT and rooted in environmental science and public health. In games such as *Environmental Detectives* (Squire and Klopfer, 2007) and *Mystery@MIT* (Klopfer, 2008), players role-play as scientists, engineers, and other members of the scientific enterprise as they try to solve local environmental problems through active research. This research consists of interviewing virtual experts and witnesses, reviewing primary documents and background research, and using virtual sampling equipment to obtain readings for possible contaminants in the air, water, and soil. Since this game is AR, it takes place in real space such that if a player wants to interview the mayor, he or she would need to stand outside town hall to obtain that interview on his or her mobile device. If the player wants to take a reading of the bacteria in a lake, he or she would need to walk down to the shore of that lake to use his or her virtual sampling equipment.

Players in these games need to integrate the virtual information they get on their mobile devices with their own observations in the real world. What is the slope of the terrain as it heads to the lake? How close is the nuclear reactor to the hot spot of contamination? Players role-play in different roles that typically characterize particular professions – environmental scientist, civil engineer, medical technician, etc. The use of roles in these games promotes players individually making these connections and also as team members collectively and collaboratively solving the problem at hand through data sharing, exchange of complementary information, and creative problem solving.

While games such as *Environmental Detectives* and *Mystery@MIT* were designed to require players to observe, understand, interpret, and integrate virtual and real experiences, it turned out that many players incorporated unintentional information from the real world. In taking action and making decisions, players often would cite the concerns of the real people they observed boating on the river, walking by the fictional "environmental disaster," driving nearby, or simply known to have concerns in the community. In essence, they turned what was designed to be a "purely" scientific or engineering activity into one that incorporated both social and scientific concerns, which is a more complex, more realistic, and more engaging scenario.

The appropriation of additional real-world data into the games sparked the creation of new MITAR games that explicitly incorporated both social and scientific considerations. AR in many ways (as detailed in the rest of this chapter) is an ideal medium for creating challenging and compelling experiences in which players must learn and understand socioscientific issues, combining science, engineering, social science, and twenty-first-century learning.

Later games have been designed explicitly to incorporate this balance of social and scientific – resulting in games that can be used for learning science, contextualizing research, and informing the public. In one of the more recent games, the aforementioned *TimeLab 2100*, players role-play as inhabitants of the early twenty-second century in Cambridge, Massachusetts. As with previous MITAR games, the game is designed around a central theme that is real and relevant to players. Global climate

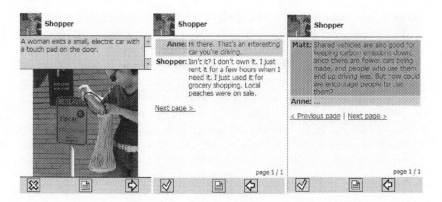

Figure 20.1. A sequence in the *TimeLab 2100* game. When players arrive at the Zipcar station, their virtual guides Matt and Anne enter into dialog that describes the sociopolitical and scientific impacts of practices around shared transportation.

change is out of control, and players are given the opportunity to go back a hundred years in time (roughly to our present day) to try and make changes that will ameliorate the situation. The catch is that the only thing the players can do is make small changes in the past in the form of getting items on the local ballot. Those items may be measures either to decrease global warming (e.g., provide incentives for improving home energy efficiency) or to decrease the inevitable impacts of global warming (e.g., raise roads out of a flood plain so that they will remain usable).

As the players are sent back in time to our present day, they are split into teams that cover different territories. Players are also paired with each other, and each member of the pair is accompanied by a digital guide (Matt or Anne) who provides them with expertise in the scientific (Matt) or sociopolitical (Anne) implications of the potential laws. In order to promote collaboration, players only receive half the dialog between Matt and Anne (Figure 20.1), which they then must share with their partners. This collaborative mechanism enforces a simple jigsawing of information between the two players. Using the combined information players need to estimate the impact (high, medium, or low) of a particular measure, as well as the likelihood (also high, medium, or low) of that measure passing. Matt and Anne also offer their opinion on these factors.

Players in *TimeLab 2100* head out into their community to gather and weigh their options. A typical player experience starts out with everyone gathered in a classroom or meeting space. An incoming video transmission sets up the scenario.

Hello and welcome to TimeLab, where our employees are never late. We're thrilled that you could be here with us today. As you know global warming has greatly changed the world as we know it. You are here to help us improve our world. At the TimeLab we go back and make small changes in the past. For this mission a few carefully chosen laws will be placed on the ballot in Cambridge, Massachusetts way back in the 21st century. We can't force the voters to make good decisions. We're not magic or anything like that. But we can hope that they make good decisions. If they do, TimeLab research has shown this can have a domino effect creating positive change around the world. As historical researchers you decide which laws will be placed on the ballot. As you walk around here today consider two factors. 1) Which laws if they were passed would have the greatest benefit to society. 2) Which laws would be mostly likely to be passed in the first place. Then after you consider these two factors you will have a group discussion and make recommendations to us on which laws should be placed on the ballot. We'll take care of it from there. That's all. I'm going to send you off to meet some more of my colleagues from the TimeLab. Good luck. We're all counting on you.

Players then receive their roles, including both whether they are guided by Matt or Anne and which subsection of points they need to investigate. Matt and Anne are graduate students who understand the issues well and can explain things clearly. Players are told that they have a fixed amount of time to gather the necessary information, after which they will come back inside and debate which three measures should be placed on the ballot. They then head outside together as a group, where everyone sees the same small set of possible destinations on their screens and their current real-world location marked with a constantly updating icon. After visiting the initial location with their partners, they are presented with some background information on the scenario, primarily what their guides will tell them. Matt and Anne describe a two-factor rating scale for the possible measures they will encounter. One factor is the likelihood of the measure passing, and the other is the impact that the measure would have if it did pass. Each station that they visit will need to be rated on these factors based on the information they receive.

After this initial point, each group is provided with six to eight additional destinations, each associated with a possible ballot measure. The points are clustered but situated in places that make them contextually relevant. The player also may click on each of the points for a brief description of what he or she will be investigating at that point, allowing the player to plan convenient pathways, as well as pathways that explore a particular line of investigation.

For example, some players head to a Zipcar station, where they learn about possibilities for expanding shared transportation options. When they arrive at the station, Matt and Anne describe possible models for car sharing that could be expanded, including possible legislation that would reserve parking spaces for shared vehicles. They describe the models in some detail, along with how people might react to such plans on the impact that the plans would have on carbon emissions. After reviewing the information, the players rate the likelihood of passing and the impact of the measure, during which Matt and Anne provide feedback. The feedback from Matt and Anne is filled with real research that is designed to help guide the players in understanding the issues around climate change. Understanding this information is the key to success in the game – getting the measures with the largest and most likely impact passed.

Continuing the line of reasoning around automotive transportation, the pair heads to another location, down by the river, where they learn that the road and sidewalk that they see are underwater in the future and need to consider what they could do to avoid losing that road. As the pair considers this measure, which assumes that climate change is inevitable and must be prepared for, they note its contrast with the previous measure, which tried to prevent climate change. The players discuss where they should place their emphasis – prevention or preparedness. Some of this conversation is generic, but much of it pertains to the particular circumstances in which they are situated. They consider whether the road that they are on could be relocated and what the impact might be on the local community. They talk about the local citizens and what they think would be possible to pass in this particular community.

After considering these measures and where they might rank them, they head off to explore a few more possible measures. In the end, they gather and consider six or seven different options relating to climate change before heading back inside to debate. Each of the other groups has done similar investigations and brings their information to the table in the form of a thirty-second pitch for their most important measures. The "augmentation" slips out of the way as players debate the science and policy surrounding the measures, recalling the information they received from Matt and Anne but also their own personal feelings and expertise.

After playing *TimeLab 2100*, one student commented, "It really scares me to think that the place I call home might someday be underwater." This shows that he connected the game world with his own community. *TimeLab 2100* isn't a game just about global climate change; it is a game about global climate change in the players' city – what it will do to their city and what they can do about it. Similarly, another player said that she most enjoyed "… running around and seeing new things, the way ordinary stuff was imagined as futuristic." Feedback such as this shows that players were able to connect the digitally represented future world with the real world of their own experience.

AR and Science Education

AR games in use today can be found most often in a variety of semi-structured learning environments, including after-school programs and at "informal" institutions such as zoos and ecology centers. While these settings don't carry the same testing and accountability requirements that schools typically do, there is still an overarching concern with what participants are learning. More generally, AR is being developed in a climate that is increasingly recognizing that learning is an ongoing continual process, with schooling or education representing only a small part of that endeavor (e.g., Collins and Halverson, 2009; National Research Council, 2009).

In their recently published *Learning Science in Informal Environments*, the National Research Council (2009) has offered a framework for what the NRC characterizes as "long," "wide," and "deep" learning in a range of situations and across the lifespan. While the report specifically focuses on science, it could just as easily be talking about learning in other academic fields with only modest adjustments. These strands are quite useful for understanding the value of AR games, both the ones we design (elaborated next) and for thinking through the potential power of putting design tools in the hands of youth (discussed later in this chapter).

Strand 1: Sparking and Developing Interest and Excitement

Our experience with using AR games with teachers and kids makes it clear that the game platform certainly sparks near-universal interest and excitement. While some of this no doubt is attributable to something of a Hawthorne effect because the participants use unfamiliar tools (handheld computers with embedded GPS), we have seen even comparatively jaded adolescents become animated as they take on the personas embedded in game characters. Given the research base (e.g., Athman and Monroe, 2004) on how learning correlates with strong interest, this enthusiasm can only help in promoting interest and excitement. In *TimeLab 2100*, part of this interest and excitement comes from the theme of the game itself – climate change and the role of your own community. But part of it is somewhat more generic – understanding relevant scientific issues through a blend of the familiar and the unfamiliar.

Strand 2: Understanding Scientific Knowledge

Well-designed AR games can embed accurate and useful scientific information within the game scenario and clues. More important, the game scenario itself can model knowledge structures that are more helpful and appropriate. In *TimeLab 2100*, players are challenged with understanding the scientific information that Matt and Anne provided to them to make decisions on measures that will be put on the ballot. This understanding comes from reading the dialog with their partner and evaluating the evidence that they are presented with for the later debate.

Another example of this strand can be seen in a recent ecology simulation one of the authors helped to develop. In this game, fifth graders "interviewed" a variety of plants and animals found in the forest, with the challenge of settling an argument over who rules the forest. As the students proceeded through the game, they repeatedly encountered the interdependencies that members of an ecosystem must live with. While the kids already "knew" interdependence as an abstract concept, playing the game modeled how these connections work in a real ecosystem much more than did their textbook food-web diagrams. The students were also able to draw on what they knew of Missouri bottomland forests to fill in their mental images of who eats what, leading to a richer overall learning experience.

Strand 3: Engaging in Scientific Explanation and Argument

AR games offer opportunities to engage players in scientific explanation and argument, both in the design of the game and in moving toward a resolution of the challenge embedded in the game. As players encounter nonplayer characters, these NPCs can be used to model effective scientific thinking (or perhaps even model ineffective thinking with the ensuing lack of success). This might involve the NPC showing how to think about data, what to observe, and how to draw conclusions based on evidence. In turn, a well-structured AR game will require that the "live" players collaborate in developing a proposed solution to whatever the problem situation is for the game. As they do this, they will be engaging in scientific explanation and argument as they debate the relevance of various field observations and data points players have accumulated over the course of the game.

The culmination of *TimeLab 2100* is explicitly designed to encourage debate and argument around the elements that will be placed on the ballot. Players need to prepare their arguments individually for the debate, backing up their opinions with the evidence they have gathered in the game (as well as legitimate outside evidence). As in real science, there isn't necessarily a single answer, so the players must evaluate and weigh the evidence they have.

Strand 4: Understanding the Scientific Enterprise

In conjunction with the previous strand promoting scientific explanation and argument, game players come to understand the larger scientific enterprise as it is modeled for them by the NPCs and in the tasks the players undertake. For example, in the previously mentioned *Environmental Detectives*, players come to understand how environmental scientists monitor creek health through analysis of biotic and abiotic water-quality data and field observations. But they also understand that equally important in such an investigation are background research in the library and laboratory, as well as conversations with other experts and witnesses. Later games, such as *Mystery@MIT*, integrate role-play – scientists, engineers, reporters, analysts, doctors, and technicians. They get the experience of walking a mile in each of those professions' shoes while also figuring out how they all work together as part of a larger investigation. Given persistent misconceptions among students as to who a scientist is or what one "looks like" (e.g., Chambers, 2006), a well-crafted game environment will engage players in seeing and doing "real" science.

Strand 5: Engaging in the Scientific Process

Using the Tools and Language of Science

Continuing in this vein, players in a well-crafted AR game use simulated and/or real data-collection tools as they pursue investigations. Since many of these tools are too expensive, sophisticated, or dangerous for use by younger students, virtual tools help players to see the horizons of science they can aspire to. Likewise, the NPCs model the language of science as they use key terms such as *hypothesis, experiment, data*, and *conclusion*, each in a meaningful way that helps to move the game along. In turn, players (by themselves and with the guidance of teachers or group leaders) practice the use of this language as they interpret what they observe, discuss alternative strategies, and propose solutions to the underlying challenge of the game.

For example, in *Mystery@MIT*, players need to draw various AR samples from the air, water, and soil. Rather than having perfect information about the extent of contamination, they are limited in their tests by their resources and thus need to figure out where and when they should be sampling. When they receive samples back, they need to be able to interpret them, not only understanding their units but also understanding their variability (in both what they are testing and how they are testing) as well as what is "normal" for those samples.

Strand 6: Identifying with the Scientific Enterprise

Given the importance of students' building scientific interest and literacy, it is essential that steps be taken to build a greater affiliation with the scientific enterprise. While only a portion of today's students actually will go on to be scientists, all of us need to vote on emerging issues that affect climate change, medical research, and other domains. Whether it is used professionally or not, disengaging with a scientific worldview is in some ways tantamount to disenfranchising one's self. A more pressing consideration for younger people is the necessity of not limiting potential career options. Given the extent to which certain classes such as Algebra I serve as "gatekeepers" (U.S. Department of Education, 2008), youth need to be encouraged to keep their options open in their course selections. "Moving up" in levels of science and mathematics classes becomes difficult both in high school and college once a track has been settled into. Motivating an interest in science, technology, engineering, and mathematics (STEM)–related fields through engaging learning environments such as an AR game is an essential component of building and maintaining identification with science as a possible career choice.

AR games such as *TimeLab 2100* make this connection through the use of real-world issues of concern presented in an understandable and often humorous way. The guides Matt and Anne provide a sense of humanity in the context of the scientific investigation. They, like the other NPCs in *Environmental Detectives* and *Mystery@MIT*, represent the diversity of science and engineering fields (including the intersection with social science) as well as scientists. The AR delivery, whether it is through text, images, or video shot onsite, makes the scientists and engineers relevant and accessible.

AR and Place-Based Education

AR games or simulations offer a number of potential educational benefits, but the overarching and comparatively distinct affordances derive from the capacity AR has to overlay the virtual on the real. Doing this, AR games promote and extend an educational approach commonly known as *place-based education*. In a place-based approach, a student's own community serves as the setting and the motivation for wanting to learn more (Sobel, 2004). That is to say, students are more likely to care about the investigation if it's in a space that matters to them. Water quality in the creek my dog drinks out of is more important to me than an abstraction such as water quality in the Gulf of Mexico's "dead zone." This isn't to say that all learning should be local only; however, it is true that if a project affects people or places close to me, I'm more likely to care. Research data drawn from a national collaborative of place-based projects (PEEC, 2010) documents enhanced teacher motivation as well as improved student learning, stewardship interests, and community involvement. As they become part of the subsoil of school culture, place-based projects have been shown to transform school culture and to foster lasting connections between schools and their community.

From a gaming perspective, the primary benefit of embedding the project in the player's own community is seen in the fact that the player with local knowledge has intimate personal experience with the space, which allows a much greater degree of context and nuance to be brought to bear on the problem or investigation at hand. At the very least, this improves the authenticity of the experience because even the most richly developed virtual world is still at its core a model, lacking in those details. If you've ever taken a guided tour of an unfamiliar city, you've experienced how a locally informed guide can fill in the spaces between highlights, bringing your attention to the fascinating details that otherwise would be overlooked. As you gain experience from repeated visits to that new city and become more of a "local," you too will build a network of meaningful observations and associations. Not all of these can be fully articulated, but to paraphrase Michael Polanyi (1974), we all have spaces where we "know" more than we can tell about. Our tacit knowledge of familiar places is unquestionably an aid to understanding.

The risk here, of course, is that things that are too familiar may be overlooked, so it is incumbent on the AR game designer to leverage this local knowledge effectively. Attention must be drawn to key features, in a sense "activating" them in the player's mind. What does that drainpipe carry? Where does it come from? Once activated, that pipe can serve as a talisman pointing implicitly to a range of understandings about community geography and local environmental issues. In the case of the drainpipe, knowing that there is a golf course and a mulch pile upstream may help a player to solve an environmental mystery. A good AR game can, in the words of anthropologist Clifford Geertz's classic aphorism, "make the familiar strange," enhancing appreciation and intrigue while at the same time drawing on things we have known all along. For those who prefer a more poetic ring, T. S. Eliot (1968) offered these words of advice that can be valuable for an AR game designer:

> We shall not cease from exploration
> And the end of all our exploring
> Will be to arrive where we started
> And know the place for the first time.

Brought forward to the cognitive level, this web of personal experience in the space allows facts, observations, and prior experiences to be used in solving the underlying puzzle or mystery, filling in the gaps around the information provided by the game.

More generally, players who actually are positioned in a real-world space have to "read" a much more complex landscape to determine what is relevant or not. This filtering of the relevant from the nonrelevant helps to develop players' cognitive sophistication as they learn to discriminate what is a useful clue. Does it bear on the issue at hand? How can I use this to solve the mystery? When the AR game encourages or requires collaboration among players (e.g., by embedding multiple roles into the game), this benefit of drawing on knowledge of the community has the potential to increase understanding considerably because each participant brings his or her own local experience to the pooled effort. As the colloquialism says, all of us know more than any one of us. The "mental game space" increases with more players, as does the opportunity for productive communication, collaboration, and cooperation.

A traditional video game (whether it is software, web-based, or a hybrid) will provide requisite clues and perhaps some red herrings, but it won't be able to activate a player's web of tacit and explicit local knowledge because ultimately it is an abstracted representation. While virtual environments certainly are becoming much richer and more realistic, there is still an air of artificiality and, ultimately, of simplification. Observing what is real brings layers of authenticity that can support players' broader learning. A rock could be represented as a set of pixels on a screen, but a real rock that has bulk, size, texture, and a broader palette of colors provides a multisensory experience. Even the most complex of virtual game spaces is limited to what the designer chose to place in the game, inevitably constraining choices to a set of prearranged options. These can be diverse and just as challenging, but inevitably they will be limited to a finite number.

Of course, this constrained palette can be beneficial in a game environment, particularly with younger or less experienced players. At some point, too much choice can be paralyzing because minor variations serve to confuse more than they help (Schwartz, 2005). These are ultimately choices for the game designer; our point here is simply that there are certain benefits to be derived from experiencing the real world, both for the game play and for broader educational development. All too often, young people have limited contact with nature (Louv, 2005); AR gaming is a means to get kids outdoors to expand their range of experience.

AR and Community Stewardship

In addition to the technological innovation described later in this chapter, a major strand of our work with AR games seeks to leverage gaming to promote community stewardship because this is the logical outgrowth of a place-based learning experience. If I care about a place and come to know it, I'll want to make a difference. Our two major collaborations – Local Investigations of Natural Science (LIONS) and Community Science Investigators (CSI) – are each funded by the National Science Foundation to investigate the educational benefits of technologically rich out-of-school-time (OST) learning environments.[1] Both projects run after-school and summer programs for upper elementary and middle school students, led by classroom teachers hired by the project for the extra duty. Students use AR as one component of a larger effort to link games, computer mapping tools (GIS and GPS), and stewardship projects. Thus, for example, students might play a game that introduces them to water-quality issues in the local stream, map out pollution sources, and engage in a stream-bank stabilization project to mitigate the pollution they found. Closing the loop, students might create an original AR game to engage others with local aquatic ecology.

In each project, we are testing the premise that the AR game serves as a catalyst to enhance interest and build understanding of key conceptual elements of the general topic being investigated. Thus, for example, imagine Eric – a sixth grader in suburban St. Louis participating in a LIONS project – playing an AR game built around a pretty typical environmental mystery: What is causing pollution to appear in the stream? The key difference provided by the AR environment is the awareness it builds in Eric of the potential sources of pollution in his neighborhood, including a dog park that he didn't pay any attention to previously. As he noted, "I probably never noticed it before" (Crawford, 2008). A well-designed game has this potential to bring forward aspects of the community that are often over-looked – an educational version of "making the familiar strange" and notic-ing what is all too often taken for granted. By the end of the game, Eric and his partner were drawing plausible conclusions about what might be caus-ing the pollution in his local park, considering their own observations, the data provided in the game, the spatial locations of the sites, and the time sequence of events (such as a rain storm and an imaginary dog show that potentially would increase the fecal coliform load in the creek) relative to when the pollution was documented. This orientation supplied by the AR game provided useful context for subsequent water testing in the park done by the LIONS group, and it motivated them to participate in stewardship projects to improve the park.

Combining AR with stewardship projects has the potential to create fusion between two major youth motivators. As readers of this volume are well aware, substantial numbers of young people find game play enticing. Add to this the motivation many young people feel to be involved in the community (Hart, 1997), and there is a potentially powerful combina-tion drawing on different interests. The game environment that may be appealing to a more technologically oriented youth can lead him or her to increased interest in community involvement, whereas a civic-minded youth who may not see himself or herself as much of a game player can expand his or her technological horizons as he or she engages in AR play through the larger project. Motivation through community engage-ment, in turn, links back to academic achievement, as documented in a recent Environmental Protection Agency (EPA) study (Duffin, Murphy, and Johnson, 2008) comparing learning outcomes in projects that have an action component with ones that have only an academic base.

Students as AR Game Designers

It should be clear at this point that playing an AR game offers consider-able potential for engaging students in learning about their community and then using what they know to make a difference through steward-ship projects. In our experience, students can go even further when they become game designers. Using a continuum from playing to modifying and then designing original games, we have scaffolded students as young as fourth grade in the creation of original AR games. This work promotes development in a number of academic areas, including spatial thinking (as they work with aerial photos representing the game site) and language development (as characters are created and background information is drafted). Logical thinking is also promoted as the young game designers plot out the sequential flow of the game.

Beyond these general academic growth opportunities, game design supports growth in computational thinking – an increasingly important skill in a technological world. Computational thinking (CT) describes an approach to framing problems or issues that relies on two main pillars: abstraction and automation (Wing, 2008). Or, as Dave Moursund (2009) describes it, "the underlying idea in computational thinking is developing models and simulations of problems that one is trying to study and solve." In an AR context, this plays out as designers create a series of abstract iconic representations of NPCs and objects and then develop hierarchical branching "rules" for how they interact (e.g., which follows which sequentially and planning out when individual items appear on the screen). The software automates these intentions, leading to a finished game in relatively short order.

An additional benefit of students serving as game designers is seen in the ways that game design enhances students' awareness of their neighborhood. In terms of developing a sense of place, AR designers need to be intimately aware of the game space. Simply dropping points down on an aerial photo won't suffice. Instead, a detailed study of the game site is critical. Where can players observe key sites that might be affecting water quality? In which order should they be explored? Or, for a historical mystery, What clues in the community "speak" to the past? Is there an old building foundation nearby? What used to be there? Who used to live here? All these make the local community real and relevant to the game designers (and, in turn, to the players). Effective designers need to get out of Mom's minivan and start walking around because the best AR games make creative use of the neighborhood. Their mentors can support this process through guided exploration, looking for potential sites. Many of these sites will be left on the cutting room floor, so to speak, but the process of seeing the neighborhood as a game space provides students with a new lens on where they live. The familiar becomes strange as a sequence of possible sites and artifacts is considered for possible inclusion in the emerging game.

Over the last five years, we have observed hundreds of children engage with the various versions of our design tools to develop AR games. While we still have much to learn in terms of how to empower novices to use these tools effectively, here we provide an aspirational vision to further illuminate the power of positioning youth to design with these tools. We have examples of designs that are both less and more productive than the synthesized account we present here. The following scenario, synthesized from a number of experiences in summer and after-school programs, illustrates the ways in which AR authoring contributes to science learning:

> Small groups of two or three students each dot the park near a middle school just outside of Milwaukee. Michaela and Jenny pore over a paper printout of a map they have from their earlier work in the computer lab, and compare it to the smaller view of the area provided by the handheld computer Jenny is carrying. As they move through the park, they become more and more engrossed in conversation about features of the landscape they plan to use in the MITAR game they are building. Soon they approach a water fountain next to the fenced-in dog run at the far corner of the park. Observing more closely, the girls notice that there are insect larvae growing in the water sitting in a dog bowl near the fountain.
>
> After a quick round of "Ewwwww's," they latch on to an idea for their game. "I bet those are mosquitoes," Michaela comments. "I know!" Jenny exclaims, "Our game can be about mosquitoes bothering people and dogs when they come here for walks!"
>
> Michaela picks up on this thread, adding, "Yeah, all of them are out more in the mornings and evenings. We can even pretend that some players get diseases from the mosquito bites."
>
> With that, they snap a few photos of the larvae, of themselves in front of the dog park sign, and of the school in the distance. Then they head back inside to catch their rides home.
>
> The next week, Jenny and Michaela are even more excited about their game. They've been talking about it with each other and a few adults, but they've been careful not to give anything away to their club-mates, who will be the first audience for the game they're creating.
>
> The pair has a very full hour-and-a-half work session this week. They start by downloading the photos they took the week before onto the computer. After seeing the photo of the larvae and another chorus of "Ewwwww, that's so cool," they search the web for a good photograph of a full-grown mosquito. Having found one, they settle in to write the dialog for one of their main characters, Marvin the Mosquito. At the same time they realize it would be fun to write some of their classmates into the story to make it fun and meaningful to their peers.
>
> Part way through writing the dialog, though, they realize they don't know what diseases mosquitoes in Wisconsin carry. "Ms. Weisman," they shout together, "we have a question!" After a whispered conversation with Ms. Weisman, a teacher from their school running the after-school program,

they look for information about some of the nastier diseases that affect dogs or humans and are carried by mosquitoes in the Midwest. As they do this they are filtering their results mentally, looking for how what they are learning is relevant to their game. This research generates a lot of discussion between the two girls – What density of larvae in the water dish allows the mosquito population to grow? and How long does water need to stand before it becomes a risk for breeding larvae? And most contentiously, "Should the park continue to leave dishes out for thirsty dogs (and mosquitoes)?"

Another couple of busy afternoons later, Michaela and Jenny are back out in the park. They walk carefully through the game they've made and take notes about the relative positioning of game "hotspots" – the water bowl that they had noticed on their first trip out (which now can be virtually "sampled" for larvae), the nearby pond, and the preschool playground on the far side of the park. They also note small spelling errors this time through, and one major "oops" – an important character that doesn't show up when she should.

Finally, after a few tweaks to the game later that afternoon, they're ready to show it off to their fellow club members the following week. All week, they wish for good weather, and to their delight, it's all systems go when Wednesday rolls around. The handhelds all have their game loaded and ready to play, they haven't given away the ending (they hope), and like proud directors, they nervously watch as the first audience starts to play the game they've built. If all goes well, their peers will not only have a fun time playing their game, but will learn something about potential dangers of mosquito-borne illnesses and what they as a community can do about it.

This experience demonstrates some of the many ways that authoring of AR games engages students in science knowledge and practice. Thinking back to the six strands from the National Research Council's *Learning Science in Informal Environments* report, we see how those play out for Jenny and Michaela.

Strand 1: Sparking and Developing Interest and Excitement

This is perhaps one of the greatest strengths of AR authoring, combining real-world kid-friendly issues, game play, and immense levels of personalization and customization. As the girls illustrate, there are many points of engagement in this experience. Finding the "smoking gun" of the dog water bowl, writing dialog for their friends, taking on an issue that they have identified as relevant, and creating work for their peers all combine to create an experience that captured their attention and interest in different ways. This illustrates the potentially broad applicability of game design as an educational hook because it captures the interest of people who like to wander around in the park, do research, write fiction and/or nonfiction, work with digital media, and engage in a range of other tasks. All these are relevant to this experience. Collectively, this range of hooks helps to bring people in and over time develop real interest and excitement about science.

Strand 2: Understanding Scientific Knowledge

The scientific knowledge in this case includes field investigations of potential breeding grounds for mosquitoes, background research on mosquito-borne diseases, construction of plausible data on mosquito larvae densities, and studies of the impacts of different interventions. While these investigations could be as simple as a quick Internet search, creating a scenario that is satisfying to the authors and compelling for their peers will involve much more than that. Just as a movie audience is unsatisfied with an implausible ending to a mystery (How were we supposed to know that?), so too a game's audience will be unsatisfied with disconnected clues and consequences not related to choices they have made within the game space (Barab, Gresalfi, and Arici, 2009). AR authors quickly learn this and construct their game so that it contains the information, challenges, and sequences needed to make the game a better experience for the players.

Strand 3: Engaging in Scientific Explanation and Argument

The girls had many issues to debate, including the evidence that they were embedding in their game and the merit of different actions that could be taken. In the end, the best game experience for players is the one in which they are required to weigh evidence and make meaningful decisions. This means that the authors need to thoroughly consider the nature and amount of evidence they supply in the game for the players. Creating the basis for players to have thoughtful deliberation around the issues requires authors to have an even deeper understanding of the issues and how they relate to each other.

Strand 4: Understanding the Scientific Enterprise

For many students, the scientific enterprise is "bench science," something that individuals in white coats and goggles do in the laboratory.

Students who use a multitude of sources while creating AR games begin to realize that the scientific enterprise is much larger than just bench science. They collect field data through observation and analysis. They do background research on issues at hand using digests and primary research. They see that science is integrated – chemistry, biology, and earth science are all parts of one whole. And they also see that science can be concrete because they use basic science to improve the lives of others in their community.

Strand 5: Engaging in the Scientific Process – Using the Tools and Language of Science

AR games put unlimited tools at the disposal of authors. One can create virtual versions of any kind of scientific sampling or analysis device imaginable. But doing so in a reasonably realistic way involves considerable understanding of those data and the tools used to measure them. In this case, the authors wanted to allow players to "sample" larvae from different water sources that they encounter in the game. They needed to think about what devices they would virtually provide to the players and how those devices would collect and analyze the data. To provide players with a greater understanding, they even wanted to put in scans of microscope slides showing larvae. In terms of the language of science, note that the authors need to write about all this using accurate dialog involving characters of many kinds: medical personnel, community members, and even mosquitoes. In each of these dialogs, they need to consider both what the character's message is and how that message is conveyed.

Strand 6: Identifying with the Scientific Enterprise

The reason why the girls chose to develop this game is because they made a meaningful discovery on their own. While it may seem mundane to us – a standing source of water in the park – it provided meaning and purpose to their game. While the story in the game may be fictional, the experience for them is quite real. Building on that initial spark, they conducted research on a variety of scientific issues and procedures, resulting in a greater understanding of how and why the scientific enterprise is relevant to their lives. And by embedding the work within familiar life spaces, the work itself is more likely to "rub" up against and become a part of their personal life-worlds (Barab & Roth, 2006).

Student-Friendly Tools for AR Game Building

The earliest AR games built in MIT's Scheller Teacher Education Program Lab embedded game objects in an XML file. Readable by only a small number of people, this format required arcane knowledge of the file format to implement a game. To allow broader use of this game format, the need for a game editor usable by a technically savvy nonprogrammer became apparent. And so came the MITAR Editor, a drag-and-drop graphic user interface (GUI) for editing AR game files. The MITAR Editor, currently at version 6.0, enables a game designer to implement all the possible features of MITAR games, including

> Items and NPCs – icons on a game map with which players can interact when they are physically within range of that map location
> Triggering and antitriggering of game objects – allowing the game designer to set game objects to appear or disappear after other game objects are visited
> Roles and chapters – segmentations of the game by time and by fictional player roles
> Spills – virtual gradients of a substance from some epicenter that players of the game can take samples of
> Portals – game objects that allow players to move from one game map to another
> And numerous other features

The MITAR editor's flexibility and rich set of features allow game designers free rein to build complex games. In reality, however, most games built do not take advantage of all or even most of the features available. Furthermore, seemingly simple game-building tasks require the builder to delve several layers deep into the interface. For example, to add text for an NPC requires the builder to double-click on the icon for that NPC to open the Properties dialog box, select the "Info" tab, select whether to specify settings based on role and chapter or not, and then click the "Add" button to add a new page for the NPC, which opens another dialog box within which the builder can type the text for the character, unless, of course, the builder wants formatting for the text, in which case he or she should choose the "File" option. This level of complexity makes a novice designer put too much focus on the software and not enough on game design.

As plans unfolded to have middle-school-aged children build their own games, the desire for a simplified game-building tool grew. And so the MITAR GameBuilder was created. This tool, also a GUI-based tool, edits the same game files as the MITAR Editor but has a much cleaner, simpler, and more intuitive interface. GameBuilder does not allow the designer to use all the features of the MITAR Editor. Instead, it presents the tools to do the most common tasks easily and quickly. For example, to add a character with dialog to the map, the designer simply clicks the "Add Person" button, which leads to a three-step wizard that allows the user to specify the name of the character, a picture to use for the character, what the character says, and then place the character on the map.

Early formative assessment of a version of GameBuilder that did not allow users to trigger or antitrigger (turn on and off) items and characters showed that students easily used the tool to build linear narratives in which players moved from one point to another through the game. In order to promote more complex game play, the current iteration of GameBuilder allows these triggers and antitriggers, which enables students to build games in which their players have to make choices as they move through the game. Work continues as GameBuilder evolves to enable students to design complex games in a supportive software environment.

Looking More Broadly: Using AR Gaming to Build Students' Creative Agency

In addition to the academic and community benefits described so far, AR gaming offers a heightened capacity to develop students' agency as they play and then create sophisticated products valued by their peers. Typical Western school models devalue student ownership of their learning and their ability to make a difference with what they know. Instead, most schools are formed around a banking model (Friere, 1993), where students are expected to make deposits for future benefits. Learn everything, just in case you need it some day.

AR game design projects turn this worldview upside down. Playing a well-crafted game that involves consequential choices creates a space for autonomous mastery. Typical school assignments are highly prescriptive in their scope and deliverables. A game with multiple branching options puts more of a burden on the player to make wise choices and to experience success or failure based on the soundness of those decisions. With experience, the player's success rate improves.

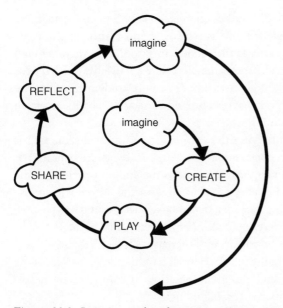

Figure 20.2. Iterative cycle of creation. (*Source*: Mitchel Resnick, MIT Media Lab.)

As players become designers, the possibilities of student ownership of their learning increase considerably. Designing original games allows an iterative cycle of creation to be followed as designers imagine, create, and play games as a shared experience that is followed up by reflection (Resnick, 2007) (see Figure 20.2).

When you contrast this producer/consumer (or "pro-sumer") model with the more typical "learn this because you will need it when you get a job" message that school provides, it's not surprising that many find their out-of-school lives more enriching than school. In terms of autonomous control, self-direction, and sense of efficacy, OST learning is often both more rewarding and more cognitively complex. In light of this gap in approaches to learning, we have found the greatest success in using AR in after-school and summer learning environments, as well as in partnerships with informal science institutions. We do, however, have some formative experiences using AR in regular school classrooms and hope to expand that dimension of our work in the near future.

We noted earlier that a great deal of creative effort is expended in the creation of the games, but there is the potential for as much or more growth in the sharing and reflecting phases of the project. Abstractions are called into question as designers work together to consider the objects and

NPCs: Are they well created? Do they share just enough to create an interesting game scenario? Rule making as a form of automation is also critical to the success of the game: Is the sequencing right? Are there enough plausible alternatives to make the game challenging? Ideally, this happens in a mutually reinforcing studio environment where students can become critical connoisseurs of good design (Hetland et al., 2007) and learn from more experienced peers (Smith, 1987).

At the risk of oversimplifying the distinction, traditional schooling is founded on a stimulus-response mind-set, where students are expected to respond in predictable (and approved) ways to the stimuli provided in the form of lessons, tests, and grades. Contrasted with this stimulus-response approach, AR gaming embraces a sociocultural view where students become competent social actors exerting agency (Emirbayer and Mische, 1998) or the ability to influence the world around them. As Resnick's iterative cycle moves forward, students build an experiential base that informs successive designs. This base likely includes a combination of competencies developed through previous experiences, including

- Technical skills with computers
- Competence with the AR game design software
- Knowledge of the local community where the game will be played
- Understanding of content relevant to the game
- General knowledge of what makes a good game.

Phrased most broadly, each of these elements can be thought of as strands where continuous improvement is both possible and required for any significant growth as a player or designer. Through incremental learning, competence grows. As Dweck (2000) describes it, this "incremental" frame for learning provides a more solid foundation for future learning than the "entity" frame that treats competence as something you either have or don't have.

Returning to the consideration of agency, an AR player or designer draws on an experiential base developed over time to envision future alternatives and make rational decisions about the potential success of each. As he or she gains experience, these projections are increasingly well founded (again, drawing on what has been learned in previous iterations), drawing on visions of what is possible given what he or she knows of the different strands identified earlier. Comparative depth or lack thereof in any of those will inform or constrain the quality of the projections.

Living in this dynamic tension between past iterations and future projections, the player/designer is cast as an active decision maker rather than a passive reactor. As Emirbayer and Mische (1998) frame it, the student is involved in a process of "practical-evaluative" decision making that draws on previous iterations and is guided by the projections. As a creative agent in the process, choices the student makes have an impact on how well he or she succeeds in a task meaningful to the student. In Barab, Gresalfi, and Arici's (2009) terms, the game play is "consequential" in that the choices made have an impact on the player. Good game play builds the player's capacity, which influences future design skills and opportunities to engage in stewardship projects informed by what was learned in the game space.

Augmenting the Already Strange: AR in Informal Learning Settings

While schools and their neighboring communities offer many possibilities for digital augmentation to "make the familiar strange," other locations, by their very nature, are already decidedly "strange." That is to say, they are unusual in that they are places of interest. These places, including museums, zoos, nature centers, botanical gardens, and historic locations, offer special, often unique opportunities to engage visitors with an intrinsically rich physical setting that includes unusual objects, animals, natural phenomena, or other striking features.

Such locations already offer visitors interesting experiences and often use docents or signage to suggest frames through which to understand the exhibits. Still, these locations can benefit from using AR to suggest additional frames through which visitors can see the exhibits. In an AR game developed for Boston's Museum of Science, visitors (many of whom were museum members and therefore self-identified as very familiar with the permanent exhibits) were embedded in a mystery game. To succeed at the game, players needed to view the exhibits through the lens of "codes," prompting players to consider the exhibits in ways they had not previously done. Players were surprised, for example, to find particular exhibits they had never seen before and to see exhibits they "knew" in a different light. In this way, the museum was able to create new experiences by providing a digital lens for visitors, all without significant changes to the artifacts themselves.

In the Museum of Science example, cracking various "codes" became a compelling vehicle to engage visitors with a variety of exhibits. However,

AR games can prompt more thoughtful consideration of weighty issues. In our work with the Columbus Zoo and Aquarium in Dublin, Ohio, we have sought to make AR games that do this, in both an engaging and enjoyable way. In our first zoo game, *Zoo Scene Investigators* or *ZSI*, we targeted fourth to eighth graders, layering content about the illegal wildlife trade within a mystery set in the zoo's Asia Quest exhibit area. Imagine the following scenario, drawn from real observations of students playing *ZSI*:

Shayla and Tasha are sixth graders from Columbus, Ohio, spending the day with their class on a middle-school field trip to the Columbus Zoo and Aquarium. As part of their trip, they are playing an AR game called *Zoo Scene Investigators* (aka *ZSI*, spoofing the popular television series). The pair is seated with four classmates and a chaperone around a round table in the Pavilion building. Shayla and Tasha fasten the badges to their jackets that identify them as the "detective" role to their teammates. They also pick up their handheld computer, which Shayla starts to play around with as Tasha watches closely. The lights dim, and an introductory video begins:

> Last night, something strange happened at the Zoo. A strange man was caught trespassing on the grounds after the zoo had closed to visitors. Before the security guard was able to tackle him, he ran all over the Asia Quest area of the zoo, tossing items he had been carrying. When he was eventually tackled, he had nothing but the clothes on his back. He has no ID and so far has revealed nothing about himself or his motives during questioning. You – the famous Zoo Scene Investigators – have been brought in to gather evidence at zoo, try to figure out what he was up to.

The video ends, and Shayla and Tasha wonder how they're going to solve the mystery. What was that guy up to last night? As zoo staff give some additional instructions about how to play today's game, Shayla and Tasha walk outside, along with their chaperone and teammates, and watch excitedly as their handheld's GPS indicator turns on, showing their current location on an aerial map of the zoo. They then do a brief "walking tutorial" during which they discover various virtual objects and even a talking goose along their path, including a mysterious empty box with a note suggesting that the box used to contain items confiscated because they were part of the illegal wildlife trade. After the tutorial, the zoo staffer sends them off with their teams to investigate.

None of Shayla's team has been to the zoo before, but Jasmine immediately takes on the impromptu role of navigator. Looking down at the map on her handheld's screen, she watches the orange dot that shows her present location move around as she walks down the path, turning the handheld device until she sees herself moving in the same direction that she's walking. "C'mon – it's this way," she yells back over her shoulder as she waves to her teammates.

The students pause when they see a food vendor, but Kenneth quickly corrals his team to stay focused. Kenneth asks his teammates what they've discovered and shares what he knows with them. He tries to keep everyone moving and paying attention to the details.

The students arrive at their first game icon, a sun bear that tells students about the suspicious behavior he saw last night. The detective teammates paraphrase what they learned from the sun bear. Their team chaperone, Mary, a class parent, asks Tasha to repeat what she said so that she can take notes in her printed "Chaperone Guide" (which includes sequential prompts/questions to help the chaperone, who does not use a handheld, keep up with the complex multifaceted activity).

The bear mentions that the man dropped something shiny. One pair of students is now looking for a real shiny object in the bear enclosure. "No, I think we're supposed to look for a clue code." Shayla looks up and sees a clue code posted on the upper beams of the enclosure where they're standing. She points out the special printed card displaying a four-digit "clue code" to her teammates. The students enter the code in their handhelds, and another role learns that the shiny object was in fact a tranquilizer gun. The gun suggests that the man was going to sedate but not kill the sun bears. The students learn that baby sun bears are captured and sold illegally as exotic pets but that they do not in fact make very good pets. People sell bears and other wild animals as pets? Really? That's wrong.

This evidence helps their case against John Doe, and they continue to other locations around Asia Quest, gathering evidence from an elephant, whose evidence suggests that the intruder may have been trading in ivory, illegally poached from elephants, and may have been after the tusks. They also speak with a tiger, who thinks the intruder might have been after his pelt, and the markhor, whose antlers are prized as trophies and are ground up for use in some cultures' traditional medicines.

After gathering all the evidence available in the zoo, the team heads back to the Pavilion. As the students file into the building, the group's chaperone nudges their classroom teacher. She mentions how engaged the group was and her surprise that Kenneth was especially engaged. The teacher concurs, mentioning how Kenneth is typically distracted by his friends and often disinterested in his academics. His leadership role this morning was an unexpected surprise.

The activity wraps up with a discussion of the evidence the teams found throughout the zoo. The facilitator deems the evidence sufficient, and John Doe provides a confession in the form of a video in which he confesses to his various dealings with the illegal wildlife trade.

Concluding Remarks

The potential gains of using location-based gaming in formal education are substantial. AR games can connect formal concepts to concrete realities and motivate student learning through connection with their community. With these connections, this technology naturally also creates service learning opportunities. However, as we have discussed, the limits of the current approaches to schooling frequently inhibit this implementation in schools while still permitting AR to be a fun and useful technology in after-school and informal environments.

If models of schooling evolve toward greater emphasis on sustained inquiry and student-driven investigations, we can envision a bright future for AR in the regular classroom. From a technological point of view, mobile technology (and access to that technology) is changing rapidly. A few years ago it might have been considered absurd to think that everyone would have access to the Internet wherever and whenever they chose via pocket-sized devices. Today, that ubiquity is nearly a reality. Similarly, web-based tools are dramatically simplifying the way that people access applications and their associated data. This increase in ubiquity and broad accessibility of devices, combined with ease of implementation, brings with it an opportunity for innovation in the classroom and beyond.

AR games then could become "just" another form of user-generated content – created by the masses, shared with like-minded peers, and mashed up by many. This removes the technical challenges to implementation in schools, enables students to be able to play games as a part of their daily lives, and puts game creation on par with a host of other Web 2.0 tools that students readily master without extensive instruction. At this point, the teacher could focus on learning and experiential objectives instead of being burdened with device management and technology overload. Students gain because AR games aren't a closed experience done in a few hours or a few days but rather something that becomes a part of their lives – something that they can use to share their own ideas, develop new understanding, and learn from others.

Note

[1]   Local Investigations of Natural Science is funded under NSF Grant 0639638; Community Science Investigators is funded under NSF Grant 0833663. Opinions expressed here are those of the authors and may not be those of the National Science Foundation.

References

Athman, J., & Monroe, M. (2004). The Effects of Environment-Based Education on Students' Achievement Motivation. *Journal of Interpretation Research*, 9(1): 9–25.

Barab, S. A., & Roth, W.-M. (2006). Intentionally-Bound Systems and Curricular-Based Ecosystems: An Ecological Perspective on Knowing. *Educational Researcher*, 35(5), 3–13.

Barab, S. A., Gresalfi, M., and Arici, A. (2009). Why Educators Should Care About Games. *Educational Leadership*, 67(1): 76–80.

Chambers, D. W. (2006). Stereotypic Images of the Scientist: The Draw-a-Scientist Test. *Science Education*, 67(2): 255–65.

Collins, A., and Halverson, R. (2009). *Rethinking education in the age of technology: The digital revolution and schooling in America.* New York: Teachers College Press.

Crawford, J. (2008). Garden's Gamers. *St Louis Post-Dispatch*, November 21, 2008, pp. CC1, C9.

Duffin, M., Murphy, M., & Johnson, B. (2008). Quantifying a Relationship Between Place-Based Learning and Environmental Quality: Final Report. Woodstock, VT: NPS Conservation Study Institute in cooperation with the Environmental Protection Agency and Shelburne Farms. Retrieved February 12, 2010, from http://www.peecworks.org.

Dweck, C. (2000). *Self-theories: Their role in motivation, personality, and development.* New York: Psychology Press.

Eliot, T. S. (1968). *Four quartets.* New York: Harvest Books.

Emirbayer, M., & Mische, A. (1998). What Is Agency? *American Journal of Sociology*, 103(4): 962–1023.

Friere. P. (1993). *Pedagogy of the oppressed.* New York: Continuum Books.

Hart, R. (1997). *Children's participation.* New York: UNICEF.

Hetland, L., Winner, E., Veenema, S., & Sheridan, K. (2007). *Studio thinking: The real benefits of visual arts education.* New York: Teachers College Press.

Klopfer, E. (2008). *Augmented learning: Research and design of mobile educational games.* Cambridge, MA: MIT Press.

Louv, R. (2005). *Last child in the woods: Saving our children from nature deficit disorder.* Chapel Hill, NC: Algonquin Books.

Moursund, D. (2009). *Computational thinking.* Retrieved February 12, 2010, from http://iae-pedia.org/Computational_Thinking.

National Research Council (2009). *Learning science in informal environments: People, places, and pursuits.* Committee on Learning Science and Informal Environments. Philip Bell, Bruce Lewenstein, Andrew W. Shouse, and Michael

A. Feder, eds. Board on Science Education, Center for Education, Division of Behavioral and Social Sciences and Education. Washington, DC: National Academies Press.

PEEC (2010). *The benefits of place-based education*, 2nd ed. Retrieved September 19, 2010, from http://www.promiseofplace.org/Research_Evaluation/ Display?id=105.

Polanyi, M. (1974). *Personal knowledge: Toward a post-critical philosophy*. Chicago: The University of Chicago Press.

Resnick, M. (2007). *All I really need to know (about creative thinking) I learned (by studying how children learn) in kindergarten*. Paper presented at the Creativity and Cognition conference, June 2007. Retrieved February 12, 2010, from http://web.media.mit.edu/~mres/papers.html.

Schwartz, B. (2005). *The paradox of choice: Why less is more?* New York: Harper Perennial.

Smith, F. (1987). *Joining the literacy club*. Portsmouth, NH: Heinemann.

Sobel, D. (2004). *Place-based education: Connecting classrooms and communities*. Great Barrington, MA: Orion Society.

Squire, K., & Klopfer, E. (2007). Case Study Analysis of Augmented Reality Simulations on Handheld Computers. *Journal of the Learning Sciences*, 16(3), 371–413.

U.S. Department of Education (2008). *Foundations for success: The final report of the national mathematics advisory panel report*. Washington, DC: USDOE.

Wing, J. (2008). Computational Thinking and Thinking About Computing. *Philosophical Transactions of the Royal Society A*, 366: 3717–25.

21 Developing Gaming Fluencies with Scratch: Realizing Game Design as an Artistic Process

Yasmin B. Kafai and Kylie A. Peppler

Much of the current games research focuses on how learning to play games can engage players in various valuable practices relevant to and supportive of school learning and literacies (see Gee, 2003). We contend that learning to design games can engage youth in an equally wide range of valuable practices, all of which are complexly intertwined ecologies that help youth to coordinate multiple activities and types of meaning-making systems (Kafai, 2006a). We call this intermix of technology and gaming practices *gaming fluencies* because youth can become fluent not only in game design but also in the creative, critical, and technical aspects of working with new media. We're using game production as a way to promote gaming literacy in the broadest sense as well as to enhance technology fluency, particularly among disadvantaged youth (Kafai, Peppler, & Chiu, 2007). Our approach of gaming fluencies aligns with work in the constructionist tradition (Kafai, 2006b; Papert, 1980) that proposes pedagogies to promote technology fluency and further argues that video games are a form of twenty-first-century art (Mitchell & Clarke, 2003).

To illustrate our view on gaming fluencies, we examine the game artifacts that were designed in a place called the *Computer Clubhouse*, a community technology center located in South Los Angeles (Kafai, Peppler, & Chapman, 2009). Youth in this clubhouse had access to a wide range of design tools, but our attention focuses particularly on their use of Scratch (Resnick et al., 2009), a media-rich software design environment that we introduced beginning in 2005 as part of a larger research project. During the following two years, we documented daily design work in field notes and archived all Scratch projects. Our analyses will focus on an archive of Scratch projects created over a two-year period by clubhouse members. A large percentage of these designs were games that imitated standard game genres or were interactive narratives and are the subject of this chapter (more than 68 percent of the total archive, n = 430) (Peppler & Kafai, 2010). Scratch games were categorized in a wide range of genres, including sports, adventure, and racing games, but also included mazes or puzzles.

The focus of this chapter is to further investigate how these games encapsulate multiple professional practices, including expertise in areas relevant to game design, such as "graphic design (visual design, interface design, information architecture), product design (input and output devices), programming, animation, interactive design (human computer interaction), writing, and audio design" (Salen, 2007, p. 318). We categorize this array of professional practices into three distinct groups of creative, technical, and critical aspects of game design (Peppler & Kafai, 2010). Using a case-based approach (Dyson & Genishi, 2003), we identified various creative, technical, and critical aspects (e.g., design choices, interface features, and narrative elements) used by youth in their creation of original games and examine their development over time by comparing first- and second-year game designs and approaches. These investigations allow us to address the following two questions: What kinds of fluencies do youth engage in while in the process of designing games? and How do these young designers develop over time? Such in-depth analyses of game-making activities and artifacts in informal settings have been rare and will provide a window into the complexities of learning involved in game making. In our discussion, we consider how our approach to gaming fluencies builds on prior conversations about "gaming literacies" (Salen, 2007; Buckingham & Burn, 2007).

Background

Gaming Fluencies

Our efforts to articulate gaming fluencies draw on early work in this area (Kafai, 1995; 2006a) and a series of related studies. A recent review of the research literature (Games & Hayes, 2008) identified four different goals to making games: (1) learning programming (Bruckman, 1997), (2) interesting girls in computer programming (Flanagan, 2006; Denner & Comb, 2008), (3) learning content in other academic domains (Good & Robertson, 2003; Kafai, 1995), and (4) understanding design concepts (Hoyles et al., 2001). All these approaches saw special value in engaging youth as game designers for the sake of developing their interest in and knowledge of technology skills, design thinking, and academic domains. But the proposed distinctions between approaches failed to take into account that making games for learning often incorporates two or more purposes rather than just one. In fact, early studies were specifically designed to leverage the mutually beneficial aspects of game design, emphasizing that learning programming is integrated with the learning of, for instance, mathematics in the design of artifacts and representations and providing motivational benefits through personalization (Kafai, 1995).

More current developments situate game making in the field of new media literacies (Gee, 2010) and emphasize benefits such as system-based thinking (Salen, 2007) and critical engagement with media (Buckingham & Burn, 2007; Pelletier, 2008). Those interested in gaming literacy or literacies have proposed and developed game-specific toolkits such as Missionmaker (Buckingham & Burn, 2007) or Gamestar Mechanic (Salen, 2007) that allow young game designers to focus on design elements and processes. We, in contrast, see game making as part of a larger do-it-yourself (DIY) effort in which youth engage (Guzzetti, Elliot, & Welsch, 2010; Lankshear & Knobel, 2010) and provide a model of observation that expands the palette of previously conceptualized literacies to include a broader spectrum of design activities that are important to youth culture. In particular, we add the artistic and creative ends that games take as well as the critical aims of production that are often left out of the discussion of youth game-production efforts. In this effort, we distinguish three different dimensions that we see as essential to youth game production that comprise of technical, critical, and creative practices.

Technical practices. The technical aspects of game design are what have received the most attention from previous explorations into youth gaming literacies (for an overview, see Games & Hayes, 2008). Youth technical practices when they are engaged in game design include the acquisition of information technology concepts, information technology skills (e.g., sustained reasoning, managing problems and finding solutions, and using graphics and/or artwork packages to express ideas creatively), and high-level skills such as algorithmic thinking and programming. Game design projects often use programming as a means to understand the production and manipulation of familiar media (Kafai, 1996, 2006a). Programming within the context of game design is particularly important because it allows individuals to manipulate the computer as an artistic medium of expression (Reas, 2006). Effective use of the medium and taking advantage of the affordance of digital media for interactivity, immersion, and trans-activity are other important technical practices as game designers learn how to make games more engaging for the player (Saltz, 1997; Ryan, 2001; Jensen, 1998). In an effort to introduce the essentials of software design to youth, we argue that learning to code is important but by no means the only building block for understanding how media games are designed; it can provide an additional venue to originality and expression in digital media.

Critical practices. More recently, several approaches have examined game design as a way to involve youth in critically viewing media and using this understanding when creating original work. As youth began to take advantage of living in a digital world by capitalizing on the wealth of images, sounds, and videos accessible as "materials" to reuse in their own work, media educators grew particularly concerned about the ways in which youth were either reinscribing or questioning existing dominant norms (Buckingham, 2003; Buckingham & Burn, 2007). These critical practices of game production include youth being able to reflect critically on and evaluate media texts, understanding references made in popular texts and deconstructing and interpreting the meaning behind such texts (Buckingham, 2003; Buckingham & Burn, 2007). By observing the critical practices of game designers in this way, we gain an understanding of the extent to which young designers understand and question the popular texts that they incorporate in their work, apart from what they learn about software programming and the arts. For instance, critical choices can take the form of game designers intentionally removing all shooting features and enemies while keeping other features of a run-and-gun game genre intact (e.g., side-scrolling engine, smooth-action animation, core mechanics, etc.) to create a peaceful setting in a once-violent video game (Peppler & Kafai, 2007).

Creative practices. What perhaps has been most conspicuously overlooked in prior research efforts in this area are explorations into how youth participation in game production involves expanding beyond technical and critical considerations toward creative or artistic ends. Many of these creative practices are rooted in the arts but overlap with visual literacy goals, such as the importance of being able to interpret and express original ideas in a variety of modalities (e.g., through music, dance, sculpture, or dramatization) and frequently are able to make meaningful connections between two or more of these modalities (Kress & Van Leeuwen, 1996; Gee, 2003). In observing creative practices as they pertain to youth game design, we are particularly interested in the ways that youth learn about and appreciate artistic principles within any particular modality (e.g., visual, audio, or kinesthetic) or through their connection of multimodal sign systems, which is the practice of crossing between two or more modalities (e.g., visual and sound, visual and movement or gesture, and sound and movement) to convey an artistic idea. For example, choosing an image of a castle and then finding colors to augment the idea that the castle is scary versus making it a friendly space is considered to be working within a single modality. Importing an audio file of "Take Me Out to the Ballgame" into an illustration of a baseball diamond in order to make the scene appear "real" is an example of connecting multimodal sign systems (in this case, visual and sound). While the first practice creates the opportunity for learning traditional skills in any one discipline (e.g., perspective, movement, and melody), the latter practice demonstrates the ability of the youth to depict objects and ideas as a combination of stimuli and is an important aspect of meaning-making and learning how to convey certain ideas across modalities.

Games as Interdisciplinary Practice

We thus propose gaming fluencies as consisting of three interrelated practices (i.e., the technical, critical, and creative practices) in game-making activities rather than having a single disciplinary focus. Building on our prior work, we have represented youth gaming practices in Figure 21.1 through the intersection of three circles. The three inner circles represent the domains that provide a foundation for our conceptualization of the ecosystem of game design based on the observed practices at the Computer Clubhouse (Peppler, 2007, 2010). Any overlap of two or more circles creates an area that best describes the domain of gaming fluencies. This conception grew out of our earlier explorations of youth media arts and design practices (Peppler & Kafai, 2007; Peppler, 2010) and is especially relevant to current perceptions of video games as a form of artistic creation (Mitchell & Clarke, 2003).

We argue, along with others, that video games are a form of twenty-first-century art. Often defined with regard to having an explicit goal and a win/lose state (Salen, 2007), video games are fundamentally expressive creations, representations of worlds real or imagined as seen through a game designer's subjective "lens." Our view of gaming fluencies pays homage to the artistic processes that shape game designers' visions and recognizes that hard-and-fast distinctions between the artistic processes that support game production versus other forms of artistic production are counterproductive because the technical, critical, and creative practices that support the creation of both video games and their related forms of expression in new media are inextricably linked. Furthermore, this conceptualization has resonance with youths' more inclusive definitions of what makes a "game" and expands our definition of games from something that requires a win/lose state to a view of gaming artifacts as a set of rules, core mechanics, components, considerations of space, and goals (Torres, 2009) that are

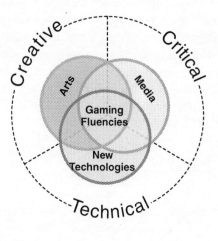

Figure 21.1. Situating *gaming fluencies* as a transdisciplinary field, heavily drawing on our understanding of the arts, media, and new technologies.

deeply rooted in the aesthetics of the medium in which they're produced. Further, as youth engage in game design, they are connecting with the authentic and meaningful practices of experts in professional game design, including graphic designers, programmers, and other professional fields (Peppler, Warschauer, & Diazgranados, 2010).

A key component of this model is the focus on the alignment between the overlapping practices and the authentic practices they reinforce, drawing connections between youth game-design practices and the various professional fields that assign them value. As such, this conceptualization of the field represents a mixture of emic (insider) and etic (outsider) perspectives on the local culture (Erickson, 1979). Although practices that would be recognized by experts in each field are distinct, they also share similarities with the other fields. This is reflected in Figure 21.1 by lines stemming from the outer circle dividing the circle in thirds but not entirely on the boundaries of each field. For example, programmers with design experience and the ability to think critically about interface and relationship to the user help to increase marketability and productivity. Accordingly, creative practices are not entirely the domain of the arts; they can be a part of the practices of those working with new media and technologies.

As stated in our prior work (Peppler & Kafai, 2008), we take a stridently disciplinary approach to understanding literacy and learning in making games by aligning youth game-design practices with professional practices in related fields, namely, those of the arts, media, and new technologies. Youth game-design practices could be described as "authentic practices" (Sawyer, 2006) because they parallel what professional game designers do in all three disciplines. This serves multiple purposes, but aligning youth game practices with current professional practices in closely related fields allows us to identify potential overlaps and envision integrating game production with existing school curricular activities and goals. Although it's somewhat artificial to separate and dissect youth practices and map them onto traditional understandings, much can be learned from this undertaking, such as observing how the entire ecology of game-design practices fits together and not only how youth engage in technical and creative practices but also how those practices can intertwine in interesting ways with other critical practices.

Others have proposed frames for understanding the field by looking at consumption and participation in online spaces (Jenkins et al., 2006), yet these perspectives downplay the role of production in the gaming literacy landscape and instead highlight participating in online social networking spaces. However, this is of limited practical relevance to youth in urban or disenfranchised communities who, although potentially adept at skills pertaining to virtual online networks, are largely unsupported in the post-secondary or professional realm to use those skills to their advantage. By contrast, our framework for understanding youth game-design practices is, to our knowledge, the only known conceptualization rooted in the work currently produced by youth communities while also aligned with professional practices (Maloney et al., 2008; Peppler, 2010; Peppler & Kafai, 2007, 2010). By aligning youth gaming fluencies with professional practices, youth who have specialized in particular practices over time can consider evolving their identities (e.g., in programming) to think about how those practices align with opportunities in computer science, for example.

At the same time, this framework allows for multiple trajectories; others who have developed fluency around making artistic choices by creating unique onscreen characters, for example, then can see how those practices prepare them for pursuing careers in fields such as graphic design. As we align youth practices with authentic participation, we further examine what constitutes participation or learning in each of the individual domains that make up game production (i.e., arts, media, and new technologies). Below we examine how gaming fluencies were developed within a particular after-school community and showcase a range of work created in Scratch, a new tool that is amenable to game design.

For this chapter, we concentrated on the game designs such as sport, adventure, action, and shooting games, as well as puzzles and mazes, produced by youth in the Computer Clubhouse game design studio. We also have included in our analyses what we consider to be *interactive narratives* or *playable fictions* (Barab et al., 2010) that include short animations, choose-your-own adventure stories, and other types of art projects with interactive components. Based on our earlier field work with youth (Peppler, 2007; Peppler, Warschauer & Diazgranados, 2010), youth claimed these projects to be "games," and we felt that they also were the first steps toward narrative-based gaming or interstitials in video games (i.e., short video animations that progress the stories in games).

Scratch Game Design Studio: Participants, Tool, and Context

Participants

Our field work at the Computer Clubhouse in South Los Angeles was driven by a desire to better understand youth media design practices (Peppler & Kafai, 2007). The Computer Clubhouse, which also functioned as a game-design studio, was situated at a storefront location in one of the city's poorest areas and served over a thousand high-poverty African American and Hispanic youth. Youth worked individually and in small groups on projects and ranged from eight to eighteen years of age, but most were between the ages of ten and fourteen. A community of mixed-age and mixed-ability learners consisting of novice and expert youth and an array of local and partnering university mentors supported game-design efforts. It's essential to note that mentors were novices with computer technology and had little to no programming or game-design experience themselves (Kafai et al., 2008). However, many of them were avid game players on console and PC platforms.

Game-Making Tool: Scratch

Our work focuses on Scratch as a tool for game making. It's unique because it uses programming as a means to engage youth in facets of game design. Scratch in particular differs from other visual programming environments (Guzdial, 2004; Kelleher & Pausch, 2006) by using a familiar building-block command structure (Maloney et al., 2004; Resnick, Kafai, & Maeda, 2003),

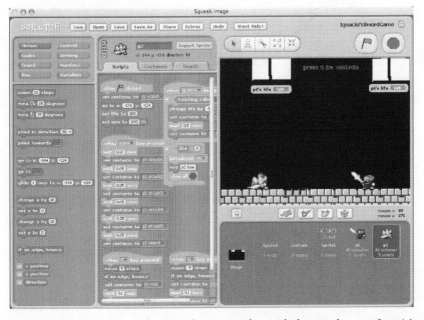

Figure 21.2. Screenshot of the Scratch user interface with the sample game *Ignacio's SwordGame.*

Source: Created by Scratch as a sample game. Scratch image provided under Creative Commons share alike license. Scratch comes from the Lifelong Kindergarten group at MIT.

eliminating thorny debugging processes and the risk of syntax errors that can impede a novice designer from creating games (see Figure 21.2). Programmed objects can be any imported two-dimensional graphic image, hand drawn or chosen from a personal archive. Two-dimensional game design holds several advantages for youth wanting to make their own video games. For example, two-dimensional programming facilitates easy incorporation of third-party images, enabling greater creative expression and allowing for easier entry for novices than three-dimensional programming.

The Scratch vocabulary of roughly ninety commands includes commands for motion, image transformations (i.e., rotation, scaling, and effects such as fish-eye), stop-motion animation (switching between images), recorded-sound playback, musical note and drum sounds, and a programmable pen. From a programming standpoint, Scratch has a number of control structures, including conditionals (*if, if-else*), loops (*repeat, forever, repeat-until*), and event triggers (*when-clicked, when-key-pressed*). Communication is done via named broadcasts. For example, one sprite might broadcast, "You won!" causing another sprite to appear on the stage and play a victory song. One broadcast then can trigger multiple scripts. A variant of the broadcast command waits for all triggered scripts to complete before going on, thus providing a simple form of synchronization. In addition, Scratch supports two kinds of variables. *Sprite variables* are visible only to the scripts within that sprite, whereas *global variables* are visible to all objects. Global variables sometimes are used in conjunction with broadcasting as a way to pass data between sprites.

Figure 21.2 is a full screenshot of the Scratch user interface for game making. On the left side of the screen is the palette of *programming command blocks*, allowing youth to control and manipulate sound, images, motion, and various types of input from the players. In the lower right side of the screen there is a library of *sprites*, which can be any imported or hand-drawn character or object in the game. Above the library of sprites is the *stage*, displaying the games that are in the process of being created or edited. The middle panel contains three tabs with information about the selected sprite. In this screenshot, stacks of commands that the creator has stacked together to control a particular sprite are displayed in the center panel. If the other two tabs at the top of this panel were to be clicked, information about the sprite's costumes (see also Figure 21.2) or sounds would be displayed. The game also can be converted to play mode with the touch of a button. In this mode, the game can no longer be edited or changed by the player.

Context

The Computer Clubhouse provided youth with an impressive variety of software, including the programming environment, Scratch, as well as Microsoft Office, Bryce 5, Painter 7, RPG Maker, and video, photography, and sound-editing software. We know from our observations that the design culture was present before the introduction of Scratch: Seventy percent of all activities were dedicated to design projects (Kafai, Peppler, & Chiu, 2007). The clubhouse coordinator introduced Scratch in the fall of 2004. Although Scratch was loaded on several of the computers at that time, fewer than ten members took advantage and created anything using the new software. Beginning in the winter of 2005, a steady stream of undergraduate mentors joined the clubhouse, and the first explosion of Scratch activity was seen starting in early January 2005 (Kafai et al., 2008). Youth were encouraging one another to try out the program, and mentors worked with youth to create the first Scratch projects. Frequently, mentors would engage youth who had never worked in Scratch before by suggesting they import some of the pictures they had stored in their folders on the clubhouse server. At this point in time, the archive of projects represented a predominance of graphics-only projects with many game ideas that lacked any computer programming, which was due in part to the high volume of youth opening the program without any official orientation.

In the winter of 2006, there was an even greater interest in *Scratch*, and some new things began happening within the clubhouse culture. Printouts of projects quickly began to cover the walls, and Scratch slowly became the leading design activity within a few months of its introduction. Scratch was used among the youth as a measure of membership in the local culture: New members who wanted to establish clear membership in the community had to first create at least one Scratch project and store it for others to play on the central server. For the first time, more expert youth were seen mentoring other youth in Scratch. Scratch experts had a high-status position within the local culture, and some youth emerged as general experts that mentors, coordinators, and other youth consulted for help; other youth had specialized in certain genres or tricks within Scratch, and they too were called on by their peers and mentors. In addition, groups of youth had begun working collaboratively to create projects, posturing together as a unit and creating flashy team names such as DGMM, for the Dang Good Money Makers. Youth also began to work independently of mentoring support, reflective of the high volume of projects beginning in June 2006, on complex projects and problems that they encountered in Scratch.

Documentation of Scratch Game Designs Archive

At the particular clubhouse where this study was conducted, all computers were networked to a central server, where youth had a personal folder that served as an image archive and repository for finished and in-progress game designs. This facilitated long-term projects as well as sharing. Youth game designs in Scratch were collected on a weekly basis from the central server and entered into an archive for further analyses ($n = 430$ games). In addition, field notes that describe literacy events and practices were collected by a team of forty graduate and undergraduate mentors that visited the field site on a regular basis over the period of the study (Kafai et al., 2008).

Analyses of Game Designs

In the following sections we describe in more detail how we selected and analyzed game designs from the archive. We chose to focus on a representative sample of fourteen case studies for further analyses. This selection was analyzed for the creative, critical, and technical dimensions of game designs. In a previous study we had already coded the entire Scratch project archive for game genre (Peppler & Kafai, 2010), as well as for media arts conceptual understanding (Peppler, 2007). We used these analytical codes to illuminate a fuller range of gaming fluencies.

A top-down approach to coding (Chi, 1997) was derived from the literature on game studies to code and categorize the genres of game designs in the archive into several subcategories (e.g., sports, adventure, racing, mazes, puzzles, etc.). We then asked an external panel of five design and media artists to reliably score the projects along five dimensions, including (1) originality of concept, (2) criticality, (3) use of medium, (4) technique, and (5) overall success (see Peppler & Kafai, 2008). The external panel scored all projects on a 0 to 5 scale for each of the criteria (0 = low and 5 = high), and the average scores were used in later analyses. Panel members also were asked to comment briefly on the works via an open-ended response.

These coding categories align with the aforementioned framework for gaming fluencies in the following ways: *Originality of idea concept* refers to the visual or conceptual uniqueness of the piece in relationship to previous works and is related to the creative aspects of game design. In the context of game design, this refers to the originality of the game produced. For example, games produced that imitated (sometimes painstakingly so) existing video games scored low on originality, which prized new games or mods of existing games. *Criticality* is the degree to which the piece makes a critical comment on other art works, theories, genres, and/or pop cultural representations. Panel members assessed the extent to which a work actively questioned standing norms and expectations and whether it addressed, consciously or subconsciously, an issue present in the medium or social strata. Examples of projects that would score high in criticality include games that were a social commentary on violence, race, or class found in commercial video games.

Use of medium is the degree of success in choosing a medium and style to convey the overall game design and is one dimension of the technical aspects of gaming fluencies. This could mean whether the player made good use of human-to-computer or human-to-human interaction. For example, a well-designed game in Scratch takes into account the use of the keyboard and other methods of interaction for game play. In other words, a game that makes good use of the arrow keys for directional controls would score higher than a game that uses a random set of four keys. *Technique/skill* refers to a project's level of technical sophistication and successful skill execution, which is the second technical aspect of gaming fluencies. This goes beyond the programming or code to include issues of visual design and user interactivity, etc. For instance, Scratch game designers often use images found on the web in their designs. A game that would score high on this dimension would have artfully repurposed the image, cleanly cut it out, and perhaps created several frames to make a smooth-action animation. By contrast, designers that chose an image from the web and were sloppy in cutting the image out, losing some of the detail in a nonpurposeful manner, would score lower on this dimension. Finally, *overall success* allows for an overall assessment of the aesthetic success of the project, independent of the measures of the preceding categories, that is a dimension of the artistic or creative aspect of gaming fluencies. As games go beyond each of these elements to include whether they are fun and challenging to play, we included this fifth category, which is inclusive of how the other four elements come together.

To illustrate application of the coding scheme, we present three vignettes of Scratch game designs from the Computer Clubhouse. In addition, we further analyze the work of selected game designers who had produced more than one game over the course of the two years to further explore whether these clubhouse members became more knowledgeable in their gaming fluencies over time. The gaming archive consisted of more than 430 projects (about 68 percent of the total Scratch projects produced in a two-year period), of which we were able to identify fourteen longitudinal case studies of game designers for analyses. Two pieces for each of the fourteen cases were chosen (chronologically, their first and last game that was contained in the gaming archive), serving as a pre- and post score. On average, there were about four months between pre and post assessments. To further determine if there were significant gains in the case study's gaming fluencies, paired-sample t tests were used to determine whether the individual cases demonstrated any growth in their gaming fluencies.

The Creative, Critical, and Technical Dimensions of Gaming Fluencies

In previous analyses of the Scratch game archive (for more detail, see Peppler & Kafai, 2010), we found a range of game genres produced by the youth, but by far the largest group included narrative games (50.8 percent), followed by sports games (7.3 percent) and simulation games (2.3 percent). The remaining games (11.1 percent) were categorized as "other" and included mazes, rhythmic games, role-playing games, interactive shooter games, racing games, and platform games. The remainder of projects (more than 30 percent) defied categorization because they were graphics-only or empty files with titles only and thus could not be coded for game genre. These projects were excluded from the gaming archive because they did not adhere to our expanded definition of *game* and were removed during further analyses.

In order to illustrate the technical, critical, and creative dimensions of gaming fluencies, we begin our report with three vignettes that represent a variety of game designs within the archive. We selected these vignettes because they were representative of the large number of games created in Scratch by Computer Clubhouse members. While in many of these the game designs are not fully fleshed out, in some instances even unfinished, they still provide insight into the game designers' intentions for game genre, mechanics, artistic choices, and critical designs. We have reported previously on a series of more full-fledged game designs implemented by one clubhouse member (see Peppler & Kafai, 2007). We then move on to a general review of game-making activities before expanding on the creative, critical, and technical dimensions of gaming fluencies in a select group of game designers that produced more than one game over the two-year period.

Vignettes of Gaming Fluencies: Three Scratch Designs

The first example comes from a ten-year-old Latino male named Carlos who designed the baseball-themed game depicted in Figure 21.3, which was created in coordination with an older male mentor at the club. At the outset of the game, there is a player standing at home plate, ready to bat and surrounded by a team of opponents in the field. Like a typical baseball game, the object of the game is to hit the ball and round the bases to score when crossing home plate. While this game was not fully finished (e.g., no scoring system was included, and the fielders do not respond to the ball being hit in their direction), there are several features worth noting. At the start of the game, the baseball starts at the pitching mound and is pitched when the player presses down an arrow key. Once the ball is "thrown," the hitter can bat at the ball using the "Enter" key. If the hitter makes contact with the ball, the baseball bat then flies at the umpire standing on the sidelines, and the player rounds the bases to make a home run, using a combination of number keys and arrow keys to direct the runner's movement. This game was categorized as a sports game because of the baseball theme.

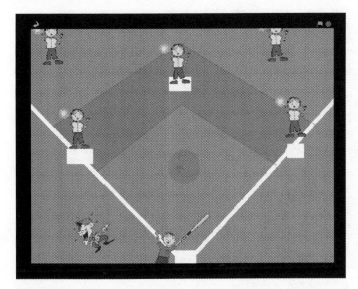

Figure 21.3. Screenshot from the game entitled *Baseball* by Carlos in play mode.

Source: Created by Carlos. Scratch image provided under Creative Commons share alike license. Scratch comes from the Lifelong Kindergarten group at MIT.

When a panel of external raters scored the project along five dimensions on a 0 to 5 scale, the overall success of the piece was rated as emergent (a 2 in the scoring system) because of the quality and thought of the visual regularity of the image and the narrative that was suggested by the piece. Additionally, the project had an undeveloped sense of criticality and seemed to be imitating a scene from a popular sports game and not commenting on other art works, theories, genres, and/or pop cultural representations, which is why it scored a 1 for criticality. By contrast, the originality of idea, the use of medium, and technique/skill (i.e., the technical aspects), scored 3's across the board because the technical difficulty of the piece was high, and the design was slightly better than most projects found in the archive in terms of its originality. In terms of gaming fluencies, this project was strongest in the technical aspects of design, followed by the creative aspects, and then finally scored lowest in the critical aspects of design, which is a pattern that was similar to most of the projects in the archive.

A second example, *Andre's Game*, was created by a nine-year-old African-American male named Andre with limited help from a Computer Clubhouse mentor (see Figure 21.4). This game is based on the fairly well-known game called *Pong*, which was first made popular in the mid-1970s. *Andre's Game* was one of the first *Pong* games to be made in Scratch

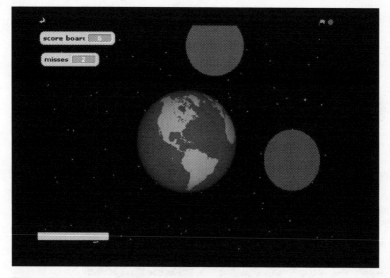

Figure 21.4. Screenshot from the game entitled *Andre's Game* in play mode.

Source: Created by Andre. Scratch image provided under Creative Commons share alike license. Scratch comes from the Lifelong Kindergarten group at MIT.

but was later adopted by the Scratch community, which circulated a similar version of the game (based on the original) among the sample projects that were downloaded with every new version of Scratch. This game was classified as a sports game because it is loosely based on table tennis in the original arcade version of *Pong*. To underscore the relationship to sports, Andre chose sports themes for the other backgrounds of the games that are not depicted in the figure, including a tennis court and a basketball court.

Similar to *Pong*, *Andre's Game* includes a ball that randomly falls from the top of the screen toward the bottom (depicted here as the solid spheres). The player is able to move the paddle at the bottom of the screen using the right and left arrow keys. If the ball hits the paddle at the bottom of the screen, then it disappears, and a new ball falls from the top of the screen from a random position and a point is scored on the board. This is a slight variation on the original owing to the difficulty of programming a bouncing ball. As the number of points increase in the game, the background changes to a new level (of three possible levels), and the size of the paddle decreases, which makes it harder to hit the ball. As the levels increases, the paddle also begins to fade into the background, making it harder to see for the player. If the ball misses the paddle, the number of misses increases

Figure 21.5. Screenshot from the game *Stop* in play mode.

Source: Created by Gerardo. Scratch image provided under Creative Commons share alike license. Scratch comes from the Lifelong Kindergarten group at MIT.

by one. The player has a bonus opportunity to hit a second ball that will decrease the number of misses by one to give the player extra time when the player accrues exactly ten points. Once the player has three misses, a voice announces, "Oops! Game over!" and the game comes to an end.

This game was rated highest in terms of its technique and scored a 4 – the programming, for example, was highly sophisticated and made use of variables in the scoring system as well as conditional statements to create the various levels and interactivity between the balls and the paddles. The project also was rated highly for its overall success and its use of medium, scoring a 3 for both areas. And it scored lowest in terms of criticality and originality, scoring a 2 in both areas because of heavy similarity to the game *Pong* without critically commenting on this history of games. The game did vary slightly from the original, which is why it earned a 2 overall on the scale. Similar to the first example, this game scored highest in its technical aspects of game design, followed by its creative aspects, and it scored lowest in its critical aspects of game design.

The third and last vignette depicts a scene from the unfinished game *Stop*, made by a twelve-year-old Latino male named Gerardo, that is set in outer space (see Figure 21.5). The game is fairly simple because the player controls both the space shuttle and the rocket with keyboard strokes. The

Table 21.1. *Development of fourteen game designers at two different time points*

Scale	14 Case studies		
	N	Mean score	Significance
Originality of idea			*
Pre	14	1.86 (±0.89)	
Post	14	2.71 (±0.78)	
Criticality			
Pre	14	1.11 (±1.16)	
Post	14	1.43 (±1.36)	
Use of medium/ approach			*
Pre	14	2.07 (±1.00)	
Post	14	3.11 (±0.94)	
Technique/skill			*
Pre	14	2.14 (±1.17)	
Post	14	3.18 (±1.09)	
Overall success			*
Pre	14	2.04 (±0.77)	
Post	14	2.93 (±0.92)	

Note: Paired-samples *t* tests were used.
* Significance $p < 0.05$

object of the game is to keep the spacecrafts from colliding, preventing the outer space disaster. As the player pushes the buttons, both spacecrafts move forward on a collision trajectory, and one changes color. When the two spacecrafts touch one another, an explosion should occur. While the visual image for the explosion was pasted into the game, the vehicles were never programmed to react to one another, making the game incomplete. This game was categorized as "other" in the genre analyses because it does not clearly adhere to one particular genre type and is similar in several respects to both a racing game and action games. Because it was unfinished, this project scored a 1 across the board in all aspects of the technical, creative, and critical aspects of gaming fluencies because it did little to advance a critical agenda, to investigate technique, to use the medium successfully, or to have what the panel would call "originality" in the design.

These vignettes illustrate the diversity of game designs found in the Computer Clubhouse community and how technical, creative, and critical criteria apply to them. In order to understand how the quality of designs varied over time, in the next section we examine longitudinal trends across five dimensions – originality of concept, criticality, use of medium, technique, and overall success – that are important to game design and media art more broadly.

Development of Gaming Fluencies in Productive Scratch Game Designers

Within the Scratch game archive, there were fourteen individuals who had authored two or more projects in the random sample. Two designs for each of the fourteen designers were chosen (chronologically, the first and last piece that was contained in the random sample), serving as a pre and post score. On average, there were about four months between pre and post scores (see Table 21.1).

We find that this productive group of game designers gained on all five measures. It's important to note, however, that not all designers partake in *all* the aforementioned practices, and even central participants engage in these practices unevenly. Pre and post scores differed significantly ($p <$ .05) on four of the five measures except criticality. Again, this indicates that critical dimensions of game designs, while not being absent in the archive, were more difficult to develop in the absence of direct instruction.

Over the course of the two years of the study, the Computer Clubhouse game designers significantly increased in their ability to design and create original games. While initially youth began to create games that imitated ones they had experience playing (e.g., versions of *Metal Slug*, *Pong*, *Mortal Kombat*, and basketball), over time, they began to venture out to create more unique games. Second, the youth began to use the Scratch programming environment more effectively over time, employing greater human-to-human and human-to-computer interactions. Additionally, games made greater use of the multimedia features in Scratch (including sound and various forms of animation), as well as use of gaming components (e.g., score boards and timers). Third, technique and skill were seen to increase significantly in the case studies as well as the larger Scratch community. This was due largely to the increased facility that youth had with the Scratch image editor to create clean avatars and smooth animation sequences. Additionally, the case studies became more adept at their use of programming, making better use of a wider array of commands and engaging the big ideas of computer programming over time for effective game play. The gains in these areas also contributed to significant gains in the overall success of the games. This was due largely to better game play over time. In short, the games were becoming more fun to play and more challenging owing to successful use of gaming levels, a balance was struck between games being too hard or too easy, and the games' goals and directions became clearer.

The only category that didn't register significant gains within the case-study work (or the larger community) was that of criticality. While there are certainly wonderful examples of critical games that emerged in the community over time (Peppler & Kafai, 2007), the community as a whole didn't seem to be cultivating criticality over time. This could be due to several reasons. It's difficult to recognize criticality in youth work because it takes some background knowledge both about the individual and about the context of the game that the youth is in the process of designing. In viewing and evaluating a large number of designs and spending only a small amount of time with each game, this often can lead researchers and external evaluators to overlook key features that would indicate project criticality. Second, criticality is something that develops over time in the iterative process of creation and reflection. Prior field work indicates that as youth engage in the process of game design over long periods of time, the work becomes increasingly more critical as the designer has more opportunity to refine the message (see Peppler & Kafai, 2007). Since many of the games in the archive were left unfinished, it's possible that these games never reached the stage where a clear message was being sent. Lastly, it's possible that criticality is something that is better taught within formal educational communities and difficult to cultivate in informal learning communities such as the Computer Clubhouse.

Accumulatively, our analysis of these technical, creative, and critical practices of game production paint a more detailed picture of the types of learning that occurred in our study. These findings mirror results of a prior longitudinal analysis that the clubhouse community as a whole was becoming more sophisticated in their game-design practices over time but particularly in the creative and technical practices of game design (see Maloney et al., 2008). Such outcomes are nontrivial for an after-school community with little or no direct instruction or guidance from professional game designers or artists to observe this type of marked improvement over time.

Discussion

Youth within the Computer Clubhouse space engaged in various aspects of game design. In this process, game production was enacted as a set of interconnected practices that are a mix of established literacies ranging from traditional to visual to media literacies and technology fluencies. While the findings from this particular clubhouse cannot be generalized readily to the entire population of youth game designers, the framework proposed here can be a useful way of looking at any game-design activity across settings. In the following sections we discuss the significant but differential growth in how clubhouse youth gained game-design expertise in gaming fluencies and situate these findings in relation to learning in informal contexts and equity issues.

Our results indicate that individuals within the community were gaining game-design expertise over time – something that could be masked in informal learning communities, where group membership is constantly shifting. These types of individual gains also contributed to the larger community trends aforementioned. The one key difference between examining individuals within the larger community, as opposed to the general community trends, was that technique and skill were something that individuals gained on more so than the community. This suggests that game-design technique and skill are more apt to individual mastery over time as opposed to originality of ideas, use of medium/approach, and overall success, which may be more greatly influenced by the larger community. For example, the community may gain expertise over time by pushing its members to search out more novel solutions and may have ways to showcase existing solutions, contributing to the rise in originality of idea. By contrast, the community may not be as efficacious at teaching particular techniques or new media skills to new members.

Overall, youth seemed to engage less in critical game-design practices, and this was true not only in the community at large but also in our smaller sample of productive game designers. We have argued that critical practices seemed more difficult to cultivate in informal learning communities such as the Computer Clubhouse over time – or perhaps they just develop on a slower time scale than what we were able to examine in this study. It is also possible that many of the adult mentors and coordinators were not as well versed in critical examination and thus may have contributed to steering conversations into technical and creative aspects of game design. It is perhaps much easier to compliment a member on a new design feature or on finding a technical solution than discussing critical aspects. It is also possible that many game designs were not far along or well developed to reach a critical mass that would allow for critical examination.

Unlike in other studies (Pelletier, 2008; Salen, 2007), we did not tell clubhouse members to design games in Scratch or how to design them. In fact, the choice of Scratch designs, whether a game, story, or animation, was left entirely to clubhouse members' own devices. There also was no curriculum or sequence of activities that mapped out designs or structured conversations. In contrast, many designs were in production in the clubhouse – games were just one of them. As such, our study presents much more a case of game design "in the wild," on what youth engage in and practice when the choice is up to them. This allows for a fuller range of gaming fluencies to be seen of value, potentially opening the doors for youth to connect in authentic ways to an array of disciplines. Moreover, the current work has demonstrated that youth – even in informal learning settings – are learning to engage more deeply in this range of gaming fluencies over time. There is, however, one notable exception. Developing criticality seemed to be particularly difficult to cultivate in this after-school setting. While this could be so for a host of reasons, it is certainly worthy of further study. What we captured then in our analyses of technical, critical, and creative aspects is an illustration of youths' informal practices. We found evidence of sophistication, but we also found room for improvement.

Finally, gaming fluencies also present the added benefit of addressing equity issues of participation in the new media literacy landscape. Our study in particular focuses on urban youth as game designers, expanding traditional misconceptions of urban youth as consumers of new media. Thinking and producing like a game designer is a valuable starting point for our conceptualization of equity in a digital age. Historically, women and minorities have been woefully underrepresented in game production. This has been problematic for many reasons, including the lack of representation of women and minority avatars in games, the reduction of these groups to exaggerated stereotypes, and the overabundance of games marketed toward white males (for a review, see Kafai, 2009). By providing opportunities for underrepresented youth to participate in making games similar to those showcased in this study, we allow them to become vehicles of change as both critical consumers and designers in an industry that has an increasing importance for schools and society at large.

Conclusion

In this chapter we addressed how gaming fluencies represent a complementary pathway for learning and participation in today's media culture. We argue that by involving youth in game design in and out of school, we can help to extend their understanding beyond learning about games and connect them with becoming fluent in a wide range of creative, critical, and technical fluencies and, perhaps more important, can establish ties between youth and their communities and out-of-school identities. The data suggest that if we want to improve players' critical engagement with media, we might need to include explicit scaffolds and structures to "push" them to become more critical. Both schools and well-designed multiuser virtual environments seem poised to help youth articulate these understandings. The findings presented here provide a perspective on how urban youths' informal game-making culture and practices can be used to support alternative pathways toward gaming fluencies and, more broadly, the new literacies important to twenty-first-century learning.

Acknowledgments

The research cited in this chapter was supported by a grant from the National Science Foundation (NSF-0325828) awarded to the first author and a Dissertation Year Fellowship from the Spencer Foundation to the second author. We also thank Sasha Barab for comments on earlier drafts of this chapter.

References

Barab, S., Dodge, T., Ingram-Goble, A., Pettyjohn, P., Peppler, K., Volk, C., & Solomou, M. (2010). Pedagogical Dramas and Transformational Play: Narratively Rich Games for Education. *Mind, Culture, and Activity*, 17(3), 1–30.

Bruckman, A. (1997). *MOOSE crossing: Construction, community, and learning in a networked virtual world for kids*. Unpublished Ph.D. Dissertation, Massachusetts Institute of Technology, Cambridge, MA. Retrieved January 12, 2008, from http://www.cc.gatech.edu/~asb/thesis/.

Buckingham, D. (2003). *Media education: Literacy, learning, and contemporary culture*. Cambridge, England: Polity Press.

Buckingham, D., & Burn, A. (2007). Game Literacy in Theory and Practice. *Journal of Educational Multimedia and Hypermedia*, 16(3), 323–49.

Chi, M. T. H. (1997). Quantifying Qualitative Analyses of Verbal Data: A Practical Guide. *Journal of the Learning Sciences*, 6(3), 271–315.

Denner, J., & Comb, S. (2008). What Do Girls Want? What Games Made by Girls Can Tell Us. In Y. B. Kafai, C. Heeter, J. Denner, & J. Sun (eds.), *Beyond Barbie and Mortal Kombat: New perspectives on gender and games* (pp. 129–45). Cambridge MA: MIT Press.

Dyson, A. H., & Genishi, C. (2003). *On the case: Approaches to language and literacy research*. New York: Teachers College Press.

Erickson, E. (1979). *On standards of descriptive validity in studies of classroom activity*. Occasional Paper no 16. East Lansing, MI: Michigan State University, Institute for Research on Teaching.

Flanagan, M. (2006). Design Heuristics for Activist Games. In Y. B. Kafai, C. Heeter, J. Denner, & J. Sun (eds.), *Beyond Barbie and Mortal Kombat: New perspectives on gender and games* (pp. 265–279). Cambridge MA: MIT Press.

Games, I. A., & Hayes, E. R. (2008). Making Computer Games and Design Thinking. *Games & Culture*, 3(3), 309–32.

Gee, J. P. (2003). *What can video games have to teach us about learning and literacy?* New York: Palgrave Macmillan.

(2010). *New digital media and learning as an emerging area and "worked examples" as one way forward.* Cambridge, MA: MIT Press.

Good, J., & Robertson, J. (2003). Using a Collaborative Virtual Role-Play Environment to Foster Characterization in Stories. *Journal of Interactive Learning Research*, 14(1), 5–29.

Guzdial, M. (2004). Programming Environments for Novices. In S. Fincher & M. Petre (eds.), *Computer science education research* (pp. 127–54). London: Routledge Falmer.

Guzzetti, B., Elliot, K., & Welsch D. (2010). *DIY media in the classroom: New literacies across content areas.* New York: Teachers College Press.

Hoyles, C., Noss, R., Adamson, R., & Lowe, S. (2001). Programming Rules: What Do Children Understand? In *Proceedings of the 25th Conference of the Psychology of Mathematics Education*, Vol. 3 (pp. 169 – 76). Utrecht, The Netherlands.

Jenkins, H., Clinton, K., Purushotma, R., Robison, A., & Weigel, M. (2006). *Confronting the challenges of participation culture: Media education for the 21st century.* White paper, The John D. and Catherine T. MacArthur Foundation, Chicago, IL.

Jensen, J. F. (1998). Interactivity: Tracing a New Concept in Media and Communication Studies. *Nordicom Review*, 19(1), 185–204.

Kafai, Y. B. (1995). *Minds in play: Computer game design as a context for children's learning.* Hillsdale, NJ: Erlbaum.

(1996). Learning Through Making Games: Children's Development of Design Strategies in the Creation of a Computational Artifact. In Y. Kafai & M. Resnick (eds.), *Constructionism in practice* (pp. 71–96). Mawhaw, NJ: Erlbaum.

(2006a). Playing and Making Games for Learning: Instructionist and Constructionist Perspectives for Game Studies. *Games and Culture*, 1(1), 34–40.

(2006b). Constructionism. In K. Sawyer (ed.), *Cambridge handbook of the learning sciences* (pp. 35–46). Cambridge, England: Cambridge University Press.

(2009). Serious games for girls? Considering gender in learning with games. In U. Ritterfeld, M. Cody, & P. Vorderer (eds.), *Serious games: Mechanisms and effects* (pp. 219–233). New York: Routledge.

Kafai, Y. B., Peppler, K. A., & Chapman, R. N. (eds.) (2009). *The Computer Clubhouse: Constructionism and creativity in youth communities.* New York: Teachers College Press.

Kafai, Y. B., Peppler, K., & Chiu, G. (2007). High Tech Programmers in Low-Income Communities: Seeding Reform in a Community Technology Center. In C. Steinfeld, B. T. Pentland, M. Ackerman, & N. Contractor (eds.), *Communities and technologies: Proceedings of the Third Communities and Technologies Conference, Michigan State University, 2007* (pp. 545–563). London: Springer.

Kafai, Y. B, Desai, S., Peppler, K., Chiu, G., & Moya, J. (2008). Mentoring Partnerships in a Community Technology Center: A Constructionist Approach for Fostering Equitable Service Learning. *Mentoring & Tutoring*, 16(2), 191–205.

Kelleher, C., & Pausch, R. (2006). Lessons Learned from Designing a Programming System to Support Middle School Girls Creating Animated Stories. *IEEE symposium on visual languages and human-centric computing*, (pp. 165–72). Los Alamitos, CA: IEEE.

Kress, G., & Van Leeuwen, T. (1996). *Reading images: The grammar of visual design*. London: Routledge.

Lankshear, C., & Knobel, M. (2010). *DIY media: Creating, sharing and learning with new technologies*. New York: Peter Lang.

Maloney, J., Burd, L., Kafai, Y., Rusk, N., Silverman, B., & Resnick, M. (2004). Scratch: A sneak preview. In *Second International Conference on Creating, Connecting, and Collaborating Through Computing*, Kyoto, Japan, pp. 104–9.

Maloney, J., Peppler, K., Kafai, Y. B., Resnick, M., and Rusk, N. (2008). *Digital media designs with scratch: What urban youth can learn about programming in a computer clubhouse*. Proceedings published in the 2008 International Conference of the Learning Sciences (ICLS) held at the University of Utrecht, Utrecht, The Netherlands.

Mitchell, G., & Clarke, A. (2003). *Videogame art: Remixing, reworking and other interventions*. Paper presented at the Digital Games Research Association (DiGRA) Meeting, Utrecht University, Utrecht, The Netherlands.

Papert, S. (1980). *Mindstorms: Children, computers, and powerful ideas*. New York: Basic Books.

Pelletier, C. (2008). Producing Difference in Studying and Making Computer Games: How Students Construct Games as Gendered in Order to Construct Themselves as Gendered. In Y. B. Kafai, C. Heeter, J. Denner, & J. Sun (eds.), *Beyond Barbie and Mortal Kombat: New perspectives on gender and games* (pp. 145–61). Cambridge, MA: MIT Press.

Peppler K. (2007). *Creative Bytes: Literacy and Learning in the Media Arts Practices of Urban Youth*. Unpublished dissertation. UCLA: Los Angeles.

(2010). Media Arts: Arts Education for a Digital Age. *Teachers College Record*, 112(8), 2118–53.

Peppler, K., & Kafai, Y. B. (2007). From SuperGoo to Scratch: Exploring Creative Digital Media Production in Informal Learning. *Learning, Media, and Technology*, 32(2), 149–66.

(2008). *Literacy and the learning sciences: Creating a framework for understanding and analyzing youths' media arts practices*. Proceedings published by the 2008 International Conference of the Learning Sciences (ICLS), University of Utrecht, Utrecht, the Netherlands.

(2010). Gaming Fluencies: Pathways into a Participatory Culture in a Community Design Studio. *International Journal of Learning and Media*, 1(4), 1–14.

Peppler, K., Warschauer, M., & Diazgranados, A. (2010). Developing a Culture of Critical Game Design in a Second Grade Classroom. *E-Learning and Digital Media*, 7(1), 35–48.

Reas, C. (2006). Media Literacy: Twenty-First Century Arts Education. *AI & Society*, 20(4), 444–5.

Resnick, M., Kafai, Y., Maeda, J. (2003). *A Networked, Media-Rich Programming Environment to Enhance Technological Fluency at After-School Centers in Economically-Disadvantaged Communities.* Proposal (funded) to National Science Foundation, Washington, DC.

Resnick, M., Maloney, J., Hernandez, A. M., Rusk, N., Eastmond, E., Brennan, K., Millner, A., Roenbaum, E., Silver, J., Silverman, B., & Kafai, Y. B. (2009). Scratch: Programming for everyone. *Communications of the ACM*, 52(11), 60.

Ryan, M.-L. (2001). Narrative as Virtual Reality: Immersion and Interactivity in Literature and Electronic Media. In Nichols, S. G., Prince, G., and Steiner, W. (eds.), *Parallax: Re-visions of culture and society* series. Baltimore: Johns Hopkins University Press.

Salen, K. (2007). Gaming Literacies: A Game-Design Study in Action. *Journal of Educational Multimedia and Hypermedia*, 16(3), 301–22.

Saltz, D. Z. (1997). The Art of Interaction: Interactivity, Performativity, and Computers. *Journal of Aesthetics and Art Criticism*, 55(2), 117–27.

Sawyer, K. (2006). *The Cambridge handbook of the learning sciences.* New York: Cambridge University Press.

Torres, R. (2009). *Learning on a twenty-first-century platform: Gamestar Mechanic as a means to game design and systems thinking within a nodal ecology.* Unpublished Ph.D. dissertation, New York University, New York.

22 "Freakin' Hard": Game Design and Issue Literacy

Colleen Macklin and John Sharp

We had ambitious goals for the Boys & Girls Clubs of America's GameTech Program. We set out to use the lens of game design to expose nine- to thirteen-year-old youth to systems thinking, basic programming skills, the iterative design process, game-design concepts, and understanding the dynamics of real-world issues, something we call *issue literacy*. This was an incredible laundry list of pedagogical goals, each alone presenting its own complexities and together posing a rather daunting curriculum design challenge. The issues we encountered were numerous but can be boiled down to five core challenges: teaching the software tools to the point where they were not the locus of attention, instilling a deep understanding of games and systems thinking, the complexity of finding form-appropriate means of addressing issues in games, creating issue literacy, and the difficulties in assisting teachers and facilitators in teaching all the above.

This chapter is a travelogue of our work in this space, the challenges we faced along the way, and our encounters with other programs and projects pursuing similar goals. In the pages that follow we will explore the challenges in combining active learning through game design with differing forms of issue literacy and civic engagement. While the connections among game play, learning, and civic engagement have been explored and studied widely (Lenhart et al., 2008), using game design, not game play, as an entry point to learning about social and civic concerns is a much less explored pedagogical space. We will look at the difficulties presented by this curricular approach, our investigation of programs with similar pedagogical objectives, and how we refactored our approach in Activate!, a more recent online curriculum we developed for thirteen- to fifteen-year-olds. Framing our discussion is the question: Is learning to make games a natural next step in game-based learning programs, or is it a complete departure from programs based on play?

Like other curricula anchored by game design and production, our work, first with GameTech[1] and then with Activate!,[2] takes the position that the game-design process can create deeper understanding on two levels: learning about how games are designed and produced and learning about the specific subject domain(s) a game might explore. This isn't to say that game design is a conduit through which subjects can be fed; instead, we view the process of designing a game as one possible lens through which youth can explore a subject, find its underlying systems, and then create a game for others to play that, in turn, provides some level of experience with the subject domain. The systemic nature of games serves as a gateway and model for the importance of systems thinking to understanding our world. The design and production of games also expose youth to applied contexts for developing and honing skills as varied as mathematics, technology use, programming, logic, communication, iteration, sound and visual design, and conceptual thinking.

For both GameTech and Activate!, a core learning objective is *issue literacy*, a term we first used during a 2009 Game for Change Festival panel with Mary Flanagan and Jay Bachhuber of Tilt Factor Lab and Barry Joseph of Global Kids. Issue literacy involves developing an empathy and awareness of societal concerns and an understanding of the systemic nature of society and its problems and, in turn, their potential solutions. In many ways, issue literacy is an offshoot of systems thinking and system dynamics – a way of addressing complex problems by approaching them systemically (Forrester, 1958). To design a game about an issue involves the excavation of the systems underlying the issue, which then are represented through the game's rules, core mechanics,[3] and aesthetics. Our goals for both GameTech and Activate! are for youth designers to develop an understanding of and empathy around the subject domain that they embed in their games, which they in turn pass on to the players of their games.

This presents a number of educational subchallenges: game design and its processes, the tool skills necessary to produce digital and nondigital games, and fostering and developing issue literacy and systems thinking. Wrapped around all this is the development of a framework that can allow educators and program facilitators who are not necessarily experts in all (or any) of these areas to guide young people through the program.

Our experiences as we negotiated these challenges with GameTech and, later, Activate! led us to this fundamental question: Is it even possible to teach issue literacy through the design and production of video games?

Looking Closer: Games, Meaning, and Learning

Games, in essence are "meaning machines" (Lantz, 2009). Rather than containing meaning in an innate form (think of this as the engine switched off), games produce meaning when they are activated (or turned on) through play. Games are systems made up of interconnected parts that work together: a combination of rules, goals, narrative content, signs and symbols, interactive design, and the platform through which they are delivered, whether they be a deck of playing cards or a next-generation game console. Game designer Greg Costikyan (2002) has referred to games as producing meaning endogenously: "A game's structure creates its own meaning." Game designers can be thought of as architecting or orchestrating these structures that players eventually inhabit, enliven, and interpret through play. Players are compelled to learn how a game works for the sake of pleasure, discovery, competition, and a whole host of other reasons that are often compressed into the notion of "fun." In games, we learn how systems work, and the system rewards us as we learn. This process of discovery and mastery produces a game's meaning.

Game play as an active-learning approach is borne from the general educational movement away from passive educational methods. Of great influence on our work and that of many of our colleagues is the research, writing, and public speaking of James Paul Gee. Gee (2003) has set forth a convincing argument for the vital role games can play in the education of youth. Much of Gee's focus is on the play act and the cognition and literacy development it facilitates. In a move toward deeper media literacy, curricula such as Tincan's Youth Media initiative, Globaloria's My Global Life, Values at Play's Grow-a-Game Deck, Global Kid's Playing for Keeps, the Institute of Play's Quest to Learn School, and PETLab's GameTech and Activate! extend this thinking about the play of games to the design of them.

From Play to Production

The transition from game play to game design and production entails taking a very large leap. We are asking our learners to go from a consumptive media experience to one that requires conceptualization, design, and media production skills, among others. What are the steps involved in making this transition from play to production? A useful model for thinking about this transition can be found in Scott McCloud's (1993) book, *Understanding Comics*. In the chapter "Six Steps," McCloud suggests the stages of development required for creative expertise in a given form: idea/purpose, form, idiom, structure, craft, and surface. Briefly summarized from the point of entry, *surface* is the ability to imitate examples in the form, such as copying the images from one's favorite comic; *craft* is the development of the basic skills to produce original pieces, such as making one's first comic; *structure* is the ability to understand the organizational structures of a form, how it works systemically; *idiom* is the ability to work within a personal style; *form* is an integrative understanding of the form as a whole; and *idea/purpose* is the ability to communicate in a form-appropriate manner (McCloud, 1993, pp. 162–84).

By asking youth to design and produce games about issues, we are asking them to dive deep into McCloud's continuum, passing through craft, structure, and form all the way to idea/purpose. This process takes a good deal of time, bringing to mind Ericsson, Krampe, and Tesch-Römer's (1993, pp. 363–406) work on the development of expertise that was popularized as the "10,000 Hour Rule" in Malcolm Gladwell's *Outliers* (2008, pp. 35–68). The premise of the "10,000 Hour Rule" is that developing elite-level expertise in a given discipline – playing the violin, competitive chess, athletic performance – requires prolonged, disciplined practice of a minimum of 10,000 hours across a ten-year period.

Of course, time alone does not guarantee mastery. Charness, Krampe, and Mayr (1996, pp. 51–80) outlined five factors that affect skill acquisition: the external social environment, internal motivation, external information and its quality, practice, and the cognitive system of the participant. While elite-level skills are not required to produce games of the scope and scale expected by youth game-design programs, the research of Ericsson, Charness, and their colleagues suggests that the development of even a minimal level of expertise will take a good deal of time, effort, self-motivation, and discipline on the part of the participant *and* a structured, supportive environment.

Programs such as GameTech and Activate! can serve as catalysts and provide a certain amount of the structure and support required to develop a strong interest and skill set around game design and production. However, the educational goals of our curricula and those of our colleagues are not to create world-class violinists (or game designers) but instead creative and engaged citizens of the twenty-first-century using the design and production of games as the educational scaffold. This presents a real challenge: How do you help youth master the process and tools well enough to realize the goal of issue literacy?

This question is best answered with a question: If games are at their essence systems for producing meaning through active experience, then how does a game get made about a societal concern? In order to create a game about climate change, for instance, the game designer needs to understand enough about the dynamics of climate change to create a play model of that system. One of the first tasks in designing a game about climate change is to seek expert knowledge of the subject and the systems at play within it. Often experts can identify the most significant elements of their domain, isolating dynamics and general rules, saving a great deal of time and energy in the design process. In this context, expertise generally is considered to be an understanding of a domain that can be abstracted and adjusted dynamically to suit new problem sets. It is about understanding the underlying systems and rules at play beneath the surface. In essence, game designers – like teachers – must become "miniexperts" on a subject because they need to parse and reverse engineer the subject's underlying systems in order to generate procedural representations of them within the structure of their game.[4]

When using game play as a vehicle for learning, assumptions can be made about *play literacy* – most youth will know how to play a game in both digital and analog forms, so the subject domain can be addressed through well-crafted game design. The transition from game play to game design as a means of considering systems thinking and issue literacy relies on a general game literacy as a starting point. This is not so different from relying on reading skills or the ability to parse a film or TV show. In short, this position treats games as a form of media. Still, jumping from playing to producing games is a quantum leap. The steps between play and design are, considering McCloud's six-step model, multiple and staggeringly challenging. In most cases, the design process and the craft skills necessary to produce games are foreign to participating youth. Further, the process of developing these areas of expertise is time-consuming and arduous, as the research of Charness, Ericsson, and their colleagues have shown. Where game play calls on active participation in order to produce the "content" of the game, game design and production ask the participant to be a "miniexpert" on the content of the game *and* to have a level of mastery of both game design and game production.

The challenge of creating games that model real-world issues is immense, even for professional game developers. To translate the literacies youth need to design games around issues into a form that's accessible and entertaining, without being too arduous and prescriptive, is equally challenging. Programs need to be built around institutional constraints; they need to impart design, technology, and issue expertise to facilitators; and they need to choose the right technology for game making: not too basic, not too complex. In addition, the issues explored need to feel integrated into the learning experience, not foreign or randomly tacked on. In our work negotiating the challenges of issues-based game design and production, we have identified a long list of literacies that need to be addressed:

Issues: Understanding the subject and its underlying system(s).

Game design: From a basic game literacy to an understanding of the dynamics of rules, rewards, aesthetics, and mechanics.

Technology: Choosing a platform and learning how to create assets and program and use game-development tools.

The iterative process: Prototyping, testing, and refining games.

Systems thinking: Understanding the systemic nature of both games and issues.

Storytelling: Taking difficult-to-understand concepts and creating a tangible representation of them.

Visual art: Learning how the visual representation and animation lead players through the experience, as well as drawing and rendering skills.

Sound design: Learning to record and create sounds and how sound serves to cue players and generate a sense of the game space.

In the following examples we will explore the tension – and some solutions – to bridging the play-design-issues literacy gap.

Revisiting GameTech

GameTech is a useful case study for examining the tensions that arise when developing a curriculum that addresses the daunting list of learning goals involved in issues-based game design. Although our first foray into this space, GameTech has, in the months since its release, proved successful for the Boys & Girls Clubs, there are a number of things about the program that we could have done better to achieve our goals.

The first unit of the GameTech curriculum introduced a basic game-design vocabulary (i.e., rules, mechanics, play space, play pieces, etc.) and the process of iterative design. Iterative design functioned as the through-line of the program, with each activity using the iterative cycle of "think, design, play, and change" as its process. These iterative activities can be thought of as the curriculum's *core mechanics* and, in turn, proved to be the most fluid component to teach and learn. Likely this is due to iteration being familiar as the exploratory process found in both game play and learning. The game-design vocabulary and the abstract concepts the vocabulary represented proved to be more difficult. While individual terms found their way into the GameTech participants' vocabulary, the understanding of the systems represented by the terms was not fully formed. Most challenging was the concept of how game mechanics, the actions players repeatedly engage in, are connected to meaning. For example, when asked to make a game whose mechanic represented "haunting," participants at one of the pilot sites incorporated images of ghosts into their game rather than game play that was about the action or the feeling of "haunting." Of course, coming up with a haunting mechanic demands a nuanced understanding not only of what a mechanic is but also of what the word *haunting* elicits. This challenge, converting mechanics into messages, is at the heart of issues-based game design and continues to flummox not just GameTech participants but some the most experienced game designers as well. However, it is also the test for a true understanding of an issue and its underlying dynamics.

Unit two of the GameTech program focused on developing proficiency in Scratch, an open-source media-creation tool developed by MIT's Mitch Resnick and his team.[5] This unit used a series of analog and digital exercises to teach basic programming concepts and the Scratch drag-and-drop puzzle-piece-development environment. A moment from an early pilot session of GameTech is instructive. Before the participants were introduced to Scratch, they estimated that it took a couple of hours to make a game; after an introduction to Scratch, their estimates increased to years, with some wondering how any video games were ever made. As we found in our five-site pilot test of GameTech (Newark, Atlanta, Austin, Chicago, and Santa Monica), when the focus shifts from using game play to game creation as the vehicle for active learning, everything changes about the situation. Suddenly, tool learning dominated all other concerns, pushing systems thinking and game-design methodologies to the background. And while the locus of the curriculum was on the subject domain of the given group of issues, the participant focus was on basic tool skill development. Programming and graphics production were conceptually and practically challenging for youth without prior experience in these areas. In fact, these difficulties were in gaining basic proficiency in the craft, the second in McCloud's six-part process for mastering a creative form.

The third and final part of GameTech introduced social issues as subject matter for games. This was done through a more free-form activity that presumed a certain level of mastery in game design, Scratch programming, and issue literacy. Unit three, called "What's YOUR Game?," used three sets of cards: Game Actions, Scratch Recipes, and Challenges. By combining the Game Actions and Challenge cards, participants could conceive of game ideas that tackled the issues they encountered in their own communities, matching these ideas with implementation in Scratch using the Recipe cards. By the time we got to this material in our pilot sessions, the idea of issues as game subject matter felt out of place and unrelated to the games and skills the participants developed in the first two units. We were suddenly asking them to consider challenging ideas without providing a framework for developing an understanding of the issue and how it might translate into a game.

GameTech's strengths – basic game design processes, the iterative process, and Scratch programming – were maintained in the released curriculum, whereas the decision was made to remove the issues component from the curriculum. In retrospect, this does not come as a great surprise because we had not stitched the exploration of social issues into the introductory processes of designing and producing games. As good a job as we had done in instilling the iterative design process and programming in the fabric of the program, we had utterly failed to embed a framework for developing nuanced understandings of issues and how they might be explored through games.

Case Studies: Projects and Programs in Game Design

To help us think about the challenges of teaching game creation as a vehicle for developing issue literacy, we selected three different programs that address the idea of using game design as a teaching tool. In the case studies we present, the tension between play and production is a real one, raising several questions: How do we help youth transition from the role of game player to game designer? What are the goals in doing this? Is it possible to generate an awareness of games as procedurally rhetorical systems while at the same time exposing youth to social issues? Is the transition from player to designer a necessary step in developing issue literacy?

At one end of our case-study spectrum is the Grow-a-Game deck, which focuses on conceptualization and reorienting participants' thinking about the content of games. Next is Playing for Keeps, an after-school program in which youth participants research, ideate, and engage in early-stage game design. Third is the Quest to Learn School in New York City, which presents educational content and issues through game-based curricula and the play, design, and production of games.

By isolating three core components in these programs – issue literacy, game design, and technology/tools – we hope to illuminate different approaches to the challenges we faced in using an active and design-centric approach to teaching issue literacy.

The Grow-a-Game Deck

The Grow-a-Game deck seeks to answer the question: How might we change thinking about games as a platform for exploring values and social issues? Developed by the Values at Play team,[6] the Grow-a-Game deck is a card game used to generate innovative ideas for games by connecting game mechanics, values, social issues, and actions as the building blocks of a game concept.[7] The deck is built on the idea that games can serve as solutions to or investigations of societal problems and provides a toolkit for developing such game concepts.

The Grow-a-Game deck includes five types of cards: *challenges* (social issues or conflicts such as racism), *games* (from board games such as *Monopoly* to video games such as *Tetris*), *values* (ideals such as "loyalty"), *verbs* (action words such as *smashing*), and *vote* (for giving points to the players with the best ideas). The Grow-a-Game deck addresses the challenge of thinking through the rhetorical power of game mechanics by juxtaposing the mechanics of well-known video games such as *Pac-Man* ("Navigate maze in order to consume dots while avoiding the ghosts") with values such as "justice," challenges such as "disease," and verbs such as *haunting*. The deck reveals the creative and generative potential of putting these seemingly incongruent concepts together. In the same way rules provide the constraints necessary to generate play, the Grow-a-Game cards provide productive constraints for design brainstorming that can lead to innovation, creativity, and ultimately, a reconsideration of the expressive potential of games.

Of the triad of issues literacy, game design, and technology/tools, the Grow-a-Game deck is the most useful tool we have found for connecting issues literacy to game design. The deck focuses on the early concept-development phase of both issues literacy and game design. It does not go beyond brainstorming into actual design prototyping, development, or further subject domain research, which makes it a very flexible tool to use for developing concepts for all kinds of games or simply to think about games as a tool for change. Although designed for college-level use, the Grow-a-Game deck has been implemented successfully in high schools, colleges, conferences, and game studios alike.

One of the primary strengths of the Grow-a-Game cards is that the generative potential of a hand dealt from the deck is equally accessible to designers and nondesigners. We have seen them used successfully by groups composed of different disciplines, generating common topics for discussion and debate that transcend disciplinary boundaries. They provide structure and challenge to brainstorming for game-design "newbies" and veterans. As Mary Flanagan, principle investigator of the Values at Play project and the Grow-a-Game deck's designer, says, "Lots of people want to learn to design, or have more fun, or think out of the box when they're designing games around social issues and this seems to help even professional game designers just think a little bit differently" (personal communication, May 12, 2010). The deck is a catalyst for anyone interested in games to think critically about them, how they create meaning, and what new kinds of games one might make by thinking about them "a little bit differently" (personal communication, May 12, 2010).

Another strength of the deck is its modularity and reconfigurability, prompting different types of brainstorming missions. In many of the use cases we are aware of, the game aspect of the Grow-a-Game cards is not adhered to, and not all card types were always used. Most of the educators and designers we had the chance to talk to use the decks in modular ways to support game ideation, selecting different card types as fit their needs. For instance, one might decide to only draw from verbs and challenges, leading to combinations such as *singing* and *human rights*. Placing these two seemingly incongruous terms together can generate a plethora of ideas about possible game mechanics and how they might be interpreted. In fact, these very terms provoked interesting results for two students from Tracy Fullerton's course in intermediate design in the Interactive Media Program at USC. In the course, teams of graduate and undergraduate students pulled one card each from the verb and challenge sets. One group drew *singing* and *human rights* – a combination that on the surface seemed impossible, leading them to return to Fullerton to ask for a different pair of cards. She encouraged them to spend a little more time with the cards they were dealt and try to explore them as much as they could. The result was a game concept that Fullerton describes as a complete surprise to everyone in the class. The game placed the player in the position of a mother in 1993 Rwanda hiding from the Hutu with her small children. In order to protect them from the soldiers, the mother sings softly to her child to soothe her and keep her quiet. Conceptually, Fullerton knew this was an interesting approach to exploring a difficult subject through a unique game concept and application of the rhythm game genre. Encouraged to develop the idea, the students faced many design and production challenges and were close to giving up on several occasions. However, despite multiple iterations, their initial concept never wavered, and they were able to complete a very simple but powerful Flash-based game called *Hush*,[8] demonstrating the generative capacity of two words and the ability of the Grow-a-Game deck to encourage new ways of thinking about games.

As Fullerton says of the Grow-a-Game deck, "The beauty of the cards is that they create goals students initially don't think they can achieve. These are values that come from our highest aspirations as a culture, so, of course, it's hard to come up with ideas that are fun about something such as human rights. And that's exactly what students should be talking about in their games" (personal communication, May 28, 2010).

The strength of the Grow-a-Game deck is its ability to foster new ideas and integrate issues, values, and mechanics. It places complex social issues right at the beginning of the game-design process, which is a high aspiration in any game-design curriculum. Asking youth between the ages of twelve and sixteen to do so is doubly challenging, as we learn with the following case study, Playing for Keeps. By stopping short of the design process and steering far clear of game development, the Grow-a-Game deck is an excellent tool for considering serious games and starting on the path to designing them.

Global Kids' Playing for Keeps

The Global Kids' Playing for Keeps program uses the Grow-a-Game deck as a key introductory tool. From there, it focuses on a more in-depth investigation of the research and game-design process. The program deliberately leaves out the technological aspects of game development in favor of an emphasis on media literacy, research, and game design. Looking at Playing for Keeps, we hoped to answer the question, If you focus on the design process and remove the development and related technology skills, does issue literacy increase?

The mission of Global Kids is to create empathetic, involved global citizens through the process of creating and designing a variety of media experiences. The organization's strengths and expertise are focused on the idea of aware, active, responsible citizenship through the lens of youth media. As Barry Joseph put it, "The reason we started [Playing for Keeps] was that we saw games as a form of youth media, that they are just another form of communication that young people are experiencing all the time as consumers and that we wanted to put them in the spot to see what would happen if they were the creators" (personal communication, April 26, 2010).

The Global Kids' Playing for Keeps program is the game component of the organization's broad focus on using youth media to encourage responsible global citizenship. Like other Global Kids initiatives, the focus is on using media literacy and media creation to address global awareness and active participation in local concerns. In the case of Playing for Keeps, youth participants research a wide range of issues, brainstorm to identify issues that will make solid game concepts, and develop high-level game designs for a social issue game. The low-level design and production of the games, however, are either handled by outside developers or not done at all. So far this process has produced two well-received games: the GameLab-produced *Ayiti: The Cost of Life*[9] and the Gamepill-produced *Hurricane Katrina: Tempest in Crescent City*.[10]

The basic question Global Kids wanted to ask through Playing for Keeps was simple yet challenging: Could serious issues be addressed through the game-design process? A three-year $500,000 grant from Microsoft allowed Global Kids to develop the program. Early in the funding cycle, Playing for Keeps staff worked with Gamelab to develop a curriculum and process for teaching game design to augment Global Kids' proven approach to teaching media literacy, research techniques, and global awareness. In that first year, Global Kids youth spent their time researching and designing alongside Gamelab designers, finalizing a design for Gamelab artists and programmers to implement. This entailed a year-long commitment on the part of the participating youth and for Gamelab, as the development studio, to be part of the process as much as possible, providing mentoring and feedback on the youths' designs.

Three games were produced during the three-year term of the grant. The first year produced *Ayiti: The Cost of Life*, which explores the role of education in breaking the cycle of poverty in Haiti. The second year resulted in a game built inside *Second Life*, *CONSENT!*, which addressed racism toward African American males in the U.S. prison system, with teens developing the game instead of an outside developer. In the third year of funding, the youth designed and developed *Hurricane Katrina: Tempest in Crescent City* with the development assistance of Gamepill and additional funding from the AMD Foundation. *Hurricane Katrina: Tempest in Crescent City* explores the challenges of life in post-Katrina New Orleans.

Playing for Keeps emphasizes research, understanding, and ideation within the framework of game design. An important factor in the creation of well-designed, serious games is developing a deep understanding of the systems that make up the subject domain. To grasp this, a good deal of research and contemplation are required both to develop the deep understanding of the subject domain and then to identify the subsystems within it that will serve as a backbone of the game design. By keeping the participants focused on developing an understanding of the subject domain through the lens of game design, not game production or programming, Playing for Keeps is able to foster miniexpertise on issues with their youth participants.

Games function as the primary hook in Playing for Keeps. The first third of the program focuses on playing serious games and thinking about game design in general and the design of serious games in particular. From there, Playing for Keeps moves into issue exploration. The program's curriculum recognizes that seeing beyond one's own life and having a broader sense of empathy may not come natural for all youth. The program's strategy, therefore, is to develop issue literacy slowly, beginning with content such as the Universal Declaration of Human Rights. The youth spend time exploring the various points in the declaration and, with the encouragement of the facilitators, look for points of reference in their own lives. Slowly, participants begin to identify more general phenomena in their own lives that they want to research and consider as the subject of a game. Embedded in the research process is media literacy – learning about different online sources, what kinds of materials you will find where, how to vet sources, etc.

As participants think about the issues, facilitators help participants with how the issue can be made into a game using game-play experiences from the early stages of the program as a reference point. As they research, they begin writing a game-design document and making rough prototypes. Prototypes may be acted out by participants or may be roughed out in a tool such as GameStar Mechanic. Some participants work on art assets, some compose music, and some design logos. Participants are allowed to contribute in any way that interests them so long as they are actively producing and furthering the game design.

The three pilot years proved that Playing for Keeps was indeed successful at creating aware, empathetic global citizens (Nudell, Brunner, & Pasnik, 2007). The next step for the program was making it extensible, stand-alone, and feasible for a much smaller financial and resource cost. The decision was made to focus the conclusion of the program not on professionally produced games but instead on the packaging and presentation of game-design concepts in a public forum. In choosing to focus the youth's attention on game design and not development, Barry Joseph says, "We have decided that the young people are not building games. They are building game designs, and building game designs is not only valuable in and of itself but can be emotionally and intellectually rewarding for the young people. So helping the young people understand that is also really key because otherwise they will be like, 'We thought we were going to build a game'" (personal communication, April 26, 2010). Joseph and the other staff believe that the program's success is based in part on the participants' presentation of their ideas in public and to game developers to validate the experience but not necessarily the designs. As Joseph said, "As long as they get to express themselves through the game design process, that's the end goal" (personal communication, April 26, 2010).

An important concern for scaling Playing for Keeps was the education of facilitators in both game design and issue literacy. As Joseph articulated, "How do you take people who aren't even identified as gamers and put them in a position to work with young people who are gamers and to teach them to identify as and effectively work as game designers?" (personal communication, April 26, 2010). Joseph and his team developed a three-tier system to teach: a three-day educator training workshop, a twenty-unit game-design curriculum to use with the participating youth, and online and phone support.

As with other Global Kids initiatives, Playing for Keeps emphasizes the importance of being an empathetic, aware global citizen. The creators have not taken for granted that issue literacy is present in participating youth; as such, they have developed an active-learning curriculum for guiding youth through the process using the lenses of game play and game design. By stopping short of having participating youth produce the games, Playing for Keeps manages to keep the focus on the development of miniexperts capable of ideation and design conceptualization of form-appropriate serious game concepts. And by developing an infrastructure and curriculum for training and supporting the program's facilitators, they have prepared for the program's wider dissemination and use.

Quest to Learn

How can school be transformed through games to activate systems literacy? This is a fundamental question asked by the Quest to Learn School (Q2L), a 6- to 12- grade public school in New York City with game play, game design, and technology as core pedagogical elements. The school was founded in the fall of 2009 with its first six grade class.

Q2L is an experiment in twenty-first-century learning and what school can be. The curriculum, which embeds educational standards in game-based structures, translates course content into quests and missions that lead to "boss levels" and overall metagames. Designed to enhance and reinforce learning, the games students play are digital, physical, and blends of both. Every day, throughout the entire school year, students engage in game play and game design, puzzle-solving and code breaking, and even "traditional" book, lecture, and pencil-based learning activities in pursuit of topics ranging from fluid dynamics and fractions to diversity and artistic expression.

On staff are curriculum and game designers who work closely with teachers to conceive of and design activities – or in Q2L parlance, *quests* – to engage students in the subjects at hand. This connection between pedagogical design and game design is uniquely supported through these collaborations between educators and game designers who work together to design and iterate lessons and games. The Q2L game designer we spoke to, Tracy Gromek, described the process of designing games and quests as "…backwards design, the end goal will be we want the kids to be able to have a serious debate about multiple topics and think on their feet as well as research" (personal communication, May 10, 2010). This approach of designing for active, "on their feet" engagement demands rapid and iterative design. As Gromek remarked, "It's constant, and we're constantly editing everything we're doing" (personal communication, May 10, 2010). She estimates making over seventy unique games in the first year, incorporating everything from fake newspapers to beakers and sponges, objects with sensors, and immersive environments, such as the school's SmallLab. In addition to these exciting environments and approaches, Gromek also described a scene that might seem impossible in traditional educational environments: "It's quite exciting to see forty sixth graders completely silent in a classroom and totally engaged…. it always floors me that that actually happens" (personal communication, May 10, 2010).

While the Q2L curriculum does not have an explicit "issues" focus, it is implicitly about how games as systems can express diverse types of content, including but not limited to social issues. Although traditional educational content and game design at Q2L are addressed in separate classes, students often are asked to translate something they are learning about in one class into a game they are designing in another. In fact, game design is given its own class, "Sports for the Mind," where design principles (brainstorming, iteration, and testing) are linked with technology and media literacy and other twenty-first-century skills. GameStar Mechanic[11] and the 3D game-development platform Atmosphir[12] are used alongside other tools to give students the opportunity to design, produce, and iterate their own games.

Many assignments are meant solely to explore game design itself without specific content but instead with design constraints, such as limits on the number of enemies, levels, and sprites one can use or making the hardest game or easiest game one can. Playtesting is emphasized, and students actively play and comment on one another's games. As far as assessment goes, in addition to teacher feedback, the amount of peer comments and plays one's game gets are an honest measure of how a student's design skills are progressing.

Issues-based games do get made at Q2L, although not always through assignments focused on issues. One Sports for the Mind assignment is to design a game for a friend's birthday that conveys the fun and excitement of a birthday party. The instructor, Al Doyle, was surprised to see that one of the student's games involved a dark journey through a world filled with dangerous obstacles and enemies. Thinking that the student had misinterpreted the assignment, he asked her what happened to the birthday party. She explained that in order to get to the party, the player needed to make it through the tough streets of the city first. Sure enough, the final level was the bright and cheery world of the birthday party.[13] She had designed a game exploring the contrast between navigating dangerous urban streets and finding safety and friendship. While it's just one example, it shows the potential youth have to build games addressing issues they find important. This student's game expressed the real social issues of crime, safety, and everyday urban life without prompting. When students learn the many expressive potentials of games, they have developed a skill that can enable them to think critically of games as a form, reaching McCloud's sixth step, idea/purpose – having enough facility with a medium to be able to express new ideas through it (1993).

Another course at the school, "Wellness," has more explicitly engaged with issues-based game design. The course's primary foci are socioemotional learning, physical education, health, and nutrition. This year an issue arose across the sixth grade class that became a special focus of the Wellness course: diversity. A quintessential NYC public school, Q2L has a very diverse student population. A side effect of this diversity happened to be students forming cliques and exclusive groups. It was clear that some activities fostering inclusion and acceptance needed to be designed. Q2L game designer Tracy Gromek and the Wellness instructor developed quests and interactive environments to allow students to explore their own and each others' cultural backgrounds through the lens of social anthropology. The students learned how anthropologists think and engage in ethnographic practices such as observation, interviewing, and surveying. This enabled role play with a professional identity that operates under different sets of rules and behaviors from their own, allowing them to see their differences as positive traits to be explored. James Paul Gee (2003) has referred to the interplay between real-life role and virtual role (in this case the anthropologist) as a *projective identity*, engaging through play in a dialogue between one's own beliefs and the projected beliefs of one's avatar. In this case, students reimagined themselves by renegotiating their feelings about cultural difference through the practices of an ethnographer. The quest, to identify a "Q2L culture" also asks that students imagine the collective identity of Q2L, observing and participating in it as an anthropologist would. Other features of the cultural investigation included discussions and sharing in the ritual space of SmallLab; an interactive environment with clear rules and connotations for students; a liminal space of play and learning; and definitely not a traditional classroom. By taking an issue that came up unexpectedly and converting it into a learning experience enhanced with responsive game design, interactive environments, and role-playing activities, the teachers and game designers at Q2L developed a practice-based approach to enable issues literacy through-play. One can barely imagine what a sixth grade student six years from now – more than halfway to Ericsson et al.'s ten-year/10,000-hour expert status (1993) – will be able to accomplish in this environment.

Activate!

Our more recent curriculum, Activate!, is in many ways inspired by the Grow-a-Game deck, Playing for Keeps, and Q2L. It attempts to be a useful tool, similar to the Grow-a-Game deck, for youth working alone and in facilitated groups to engage in critical thinking about what games are, how they are made, and how they make meaning. It aims to engage deeply in the design process and consider specific issues in the way that the Playing for Keeps program does. Finally, it asks youth to play, make, and share games with each other, inhabiting the role of game designer, as the students at Q2L do, particularly in the Sports for the Mind class.

Activate!, however, also attempts to deliver its message differently – in bits, through a website open and available to anyone online, with materials targeting use in after-school programs and by individuals alike. The site is composed of three key sections: Games, Game Design Challenges and Codex. Games is the library of participant-created games developed around energy and environmental issues. Game Design Challenges are a set of exercises that teach systems thinking, issue literacy, game design, and game programming. The Codex is a miniature encyclopedia of game design, energy, and environmental issues and game-maker concepts. Together, these three sections create a communal space for youth to play, think about, and make serious games.

The core curriculum of Activate! is embedded in the Game Design Challenges, which are divided into four difficulty levels: rookie, apprentice, master, and ninja. The first three levels scaffold game design, systems thinking, and game-production activities for the participants to tackle. Each challenge ends with a call to produce something – a concept map of an issue, a sketch for a game design, a nondigital game, or a game created in a freely accessible tool such as Game Maker. Game Maker games then are submitted to the site for inclusion in the Games section.

The fourth level, Ninja, is a more free-form level in which a "one-armed bandit"–style application presents participants with a game-design challenge for an energy or environmental issue – a platformer about composting, a maze game addressing embodied energy or a shoot-em-up conceived around photosynthesis. As with the lower-level challenges, the games produced for the Ninja level are submitted for inclusion in the Games section. Games in the library have moderated comment threads in which participants can give each other feedback and encouragement.

A key decision we made in the design of Activate! was to integrate the issues into all activities. We focus the play experience around games made within the Activate! program to provide models for the types of games one might make about topics such as recycling, energy conservation, or solar power. We chose a different development tool from GameTech – Game Maker instead of Scratch – because we felt that it was more age-appropriate for thirteen- to fifteen-year-olds and was a more intuitive development model (it is made for game making, as opposed to Scratch, which covers the more general areas of animation and programming). We also put greater emphasis on the investigation of ideas and research around the issues, focusing on an initial set of games and challenges under topics of sustainability.

To assist in the understanding and use of concepts such as systems thinking, research methods, and game design, we developed a set of nondigital activities that introduce and apply the methods and principles. For example, systems thinking is introduced in a unit in which participants work with the facilitator to break down the systems at work in solar energy. They then take the elements of the system and design to a schoolyard or table top game addressing solar energy. Similar nondigital activities have been developed to introduce basic programming concepts and the Game Maker development environment framework. And like the other core subject domains, successively more difficult challenges are found at the apprentice and master levels.

Activate! is meant to provide an entry point to the tools, systems thinking, game design, and issues. A great deal of effort was spent framing the learning process as a gamelike system and making games that in and of themselves were fun to play. We start participants off by helping them reconstruct and then mod the games on the site. To show quick results, the first game in the first level can be made and changed in fifteen minutes or less. We also attempt to circumvent a certain amount of the production by providing themed sprite packs, including special unlockable sets after completing challenges. The sprite sets reinforce the issues investigated in Activate! and also provide unexpected assets too, elements that begin to conjure ideas for new possible games.

Despite multiple pilots, it's too early to tell whether the casual, online environment of Activate! will convey issues literacy effectively. It's also going to be challenging to assess. In fact, this might be an unattainable goal for one website in a vacuum. It will likely take an ecology of sites, card decks, after-school programs, and schools to foster the kind of issues literacy, civic engagement, and systems fluency that we feel is necessary for a robust and responsive society in the face of today's systemic challenges.

Conclusions

Using game design as a teaching tool has much more in common with teaching carpentry than it does game play. This is so because the skills required to design and produce games range across a vast set of conceptual and tools skills. However, just as carpentry is an element of design – involving at an intimate-level concept such as materials, ergonomics, context, and formal beauty – game design also involves a deeper understanding of the material qualities of video games (code and art), game play, and the message and aesthetics involved. It's understandable why issues get lost in the process. However, just as good carpentry reveals the purpose of the built object, game design has a profound ability to uncover the systems at play in the content it contains.

The early successes of the Grow-a-Game deck, Playing for Keeps, Q2L, GameTech, and Activate! are promising. There indeed does appear to be value in using game design and production as lenses for exposing youth to issues and issues literacy. Still, there is a good deal left to learn and improve within these and other curricula using game design to create empathetic, active learners. The challenges are numerous. At the top of the list is the support required to teach and coach students through the different skill acquisition to the eventual design and production of games. Properly trained facilitators are critical. So is having the right proportion of facilitator to students and having the right amount of time for a given activity given the student-to-facilitator ratio. Extending the role of facilitators are the students themselves. Including opportunities for youth to play and critique each other's games is a major motivator. At Quest 2 Learn, students give each other feedback and encourage each other to make better games. They also learn to make their games more playable through this kind of peer play testing.

Environment and context play a major role in the design of any curriculum, and for game-design programs, this is as relevant. In after-school environments, such as the Boys & Girls Clubs, learning to make games can't feel like more school. Playing games figures into the session as much as making them, and activities are broken up into small, modular units that can be mixed and matched according to a participant's skill level.

Linking issues with game design requires enough time to gain basic competence in making simple games and enough time to realize the rhetorical potential of games. This is aligned with McCloud's (1993) notion of six steps, where it takes all six steps to communicate original ideas and messages through the form. However, it takes connecting to issues at each to generate enough fluency with the concept of issues-based game design to reach the penultimate step of idea/purpose. For example, starting with step one, *surface*, we found that in the Activate! curriculum, copying and modifying already created games was the best way to kick-start tools-based skill development and issues literacy.

In many ways, the lessons we've learned about creating issues literacy through games design are the lessons we are trying to teach. Game-design concepts such as level design come into play as we try to create meaningful transitions between levels of difficulty in the curriculum. We need to consider balance, one of the most important hallmarks of a challenging and fun game, as we try to balance the triad of issues literacy, game design, and technology/tools. One of the most salient parallels is that it is incredibly challenging and entails a great deal of iteration. As Barry Joseph put it so eloquently, developing successful curricula using game design as a vehicle for creating issue literacy is "freakin' hard" (personal communication, April 26, 2010). In both curriculum design and game design, thinking consciously about what we are asking participants to do, and why, is key.

Notes

1. http://myclubmylife.com/Arts_Tech/Pages/gametech.aspx (accessed June 1, 2010). Funding for the curriculum development was provided by the AMD Foundation's Changing the Game initiative.
2. http://www.activategames.org (accessed July 12, 2010). Funding for the curriculum development and project maintenance provided by the AMD Foundation's Changing the Game program.
3. Mechanics are the primary activities involved in playing the game. For instance, dribbling, shooting, running and passing are mechanics found in basketball.
4. It is important to note here that we are not proposing that it is possible to create perfect simulations of real phenomena. Any game about a real-world issue is an interpretation of that issue in the rhetorical space of the game.
5. http://scratch.mit.edu (accessed June 1, 2010)
6. http://www.valuesatplay.org/ (accessed June 1, 2010)
7. http://www.valuesatplay.org/?page_id=6 (accessed June 1, 2010)
8. http://interactive.usc.edu/members/jantonisse/2008/01/hush.html (accessed June 1, 2010)
9. www.costoflife.org (accessed June 1, 2010)
10. tempestincrescentcity.ning.com (accessed June 1, 2010)
11. http://gamestarmechanic.com/ (accessed August 15, 2010)
12. http://www.atmosphir.com/atmosphir/ (accessed August 15, 2010)
13. Al Doyle, Games for Change Festival Panel, May 2010.

References

Bachhuber, J., Flanagan, Joseph, B. M., Macklin, C., & Sharp, J. (2009). *Issue literacy: Teaching games for change.* Games for Change Festival [Conference], The New School University, New York, May 2009.

Charness, N., Krampe, R. T., & Mayr, U. (1996). The Role of Practice and Coaching in Entrepreneurial Skill Domains: An International Comparison of Life-Span Chess Skill Acquisition. In K. A. Ericsson (ed.), *The Road to excellence: The acquisition of expert performance in the arts and sciences, sports and game* (pp. 51–80). Mahwah, NJ: Erlbaum.

Costikyan, G. (2002). I Have No Words and I Must Design: Toward a Critical Vocabulary for Games. In F. Mäyrä (ed.), *Proceedings of Computer Games and Digital Cultures Conference* (pp. 9–33). Tampere, Finland: Tampere University Press.

Ericsson, K. A., Krampe, R. T., & Tesch-Römer, C. (1993). The Role of Deliberate Practice in the Acquisition of Expert Performance." *Psychological Review,* 100(3), 363–406.

Forrester, J. W. (1958). Industrial Dynamics – A Major Breakthrough for Decision Makers. *Harvard Business Review*, 36(4), 37–66.

Gee, J. P. (2003). *What video games have to teach us about learning and literacy*. New York: Palgrave Macmillan.

Gladwell, M. (2008). The 10,000 Hour Rule. In *Outliers* (pp. 35–68). New York: Little, Brown.

Lantz, F. (2009, August 30). Games Are Not Media. *Game Design Advance*; available at http://gamedesignadvance.com/?p=1567; accessed May 25, 2010.

Lenhart, A., Kahne, J., Middaugh, E., Macgill, A., Evans, C., & Vitak, J. (2008, September 16). Teens, Video Games and Civics. *Pew Internet & American Life Project*; available at http://www.pewinternet.org/Reports/2008/Teens-Video-Games-and-Civics.aspx; accessed on August 4, 2010.

McCloud, S. (1993). *Understanding comics: The invisible art*. Northampton, MA: Kitchen Sink Press.

Nudell, H., Brunner, C., & Pasnik, S. (2007). *Playing 4 keeps evaluation report*. EDC, Center for Children and Technology.

23 Models of Situated Action: Computer Games and the Problem of Transfer

David Williamson Shaffer

Any discussion of games and learning has to address a fundamental question: How do we know that players aren't just learning how to play the game? That is, how do we know that what they do in the game will help them do other things in the world around them, the world outside the game?

Answering such questions forces one to come dangerously close to – indeed, to step right on – the third rail in the study of learning today: the problem of *transfer*. No term, no word, no concept is as problematic, as debated, or as contentious. Schema theorists say that it is essential, socio-cultural theorists say that it doesn't exist, and never the twain shall meet, it seems. Debates are held in scholarly journals (see, for example, Anderson, Reder, & Simon, 1996; Greeno, 1997; Hutchins, 2008; Packer, 2001; Seel, 2001). Graduate students and junior faculty avoid the term, knowing that where you stand on transfer determines where you sit in the field, and whatever you say will cast you in a dubious light somewhere.

But the problem of transfer is unavoidable in a field that examines the conditions under which and the processes by which people learn. As Dewey (1938) points out: "Every experience influences in some degree the objective conditions under which further experiences are had" (p. 37). A key question for the design of games for learning has to be: "What are the mechanisms by which one experience influences another?" The premise of education writ large is that it is possible for experience to transfer – in this general sense – from one context to another. Otherwise, there is no education, in games, in school, or anywhere. There is no learning. There is no continuity, no culture, nothing beyond the immediate here and now.

To make matters worse, no currently dominant theory accounts very well for this central problem of how experiences in one context (such as a computer game or a classroom) change the way learners think in other contexts. At the microscopic level of analogical problem schemata (Anderson,

1993), theories of *learning as transformation of an individual* suggest that transfer occurs when a solution developed to address one problem is used to solve an analogically similar problem. The schema view is pervasive (formally or informally) in the current education system, in which isolated facts and problem-solving strategies are taught in classroom settings with the expectation that students will use those pieces of information and tools in other contexts. But nearly a half-century of research suggests that transfer in this sense is rare, difficult to achieve, and limited to problems that are very similar to the original context in which a solution is developed (the phenomenon of *near-transfer*). At the macroscopic level of membership in communities of practice (Lave & Wenger, 1991), theories of *learning as participation by individuals in larger practices* suggest that individuals learn by becoming members of a community, being mentored to do more tasks in different contexts within which the community operates.[1] In this view, however, skills do not transfer between settings; individuals can learn only to accomplish particular tasks within particular settings. Thus neither view accounts very well for how students might be able to take an experience in a game, classroom, or after-school program and use it to accomplish meaningful ends in their lives outside school; so neither view, by itself, is particularly useful for the development and analysis of new technologies and new environments for learning.

In presenting these "two views," I do not mean to suggest that there are no other extant theories of learning. I only argue that the two dominant paradigms for thinking about learning – as exemplified by particular theories – are mutually incompatible and individually incomplete as guides to the analysis and development of learning environments.

This division is particularly problematic in the study of games for learning, a domain in which designers have little – too little – in the way of research and theory to guide them. They can follow one paradigm and emphasize repetition of general principles or the other and build richly immersive environments that encourage situated thinking, with little theoretical framework as to how learning in a virtual situation will lead to action in the real world. This makes it difficult to advance our understanding of how learning takes place in games – and thus what we can do as designers to make games for learning more effective, more powerful, more meaningful, and more useful in the broad curriculum of students' lives.

It does not have to be this way. A new generation of scholars has begun to work in the last decade, after the schism that divided sociocultural and symbolic approaches to the study of learning, trained to think about issues from both points of view. I deliberately include in this generation both those whose training incorporated symbolic and sociocultural perspectives and those who began working from one perspective and have taken up others later in their careers. A great deal of work went into distinguishing a coherent sociocultural science of learning from the orthodoxy of classical cognitive science, and the study of learning is deeply indebted to that work. But that hard-fought distinction having been made, some scholars are increasingly interested less in asking which view is right than in understanding how these views can inform one another – and how together they can advance our understanding of how to design environments for learning. In what follows, I argue that we can understand learning – the transfer of experience from one context to another – as something that can be discussed, analyzed, conceptualized, and supported as both *transformation of an individual* and *participation in a practice*.

One way to start in this direction would be to provide an overview of extant theories, mapping the current landscape, highlighting the strengths and weaknesses of each approach. However, such overviews have already been written (see the particularly lucid and comprehensive Barab & Plucker, 2002) and in any event tend to emphasize the existing dialectic rather than the possible synthesis. Instead, I follow Chi's (1997) example from some years ago, in which she mapped a complex theoretical landscape by providing one particular pathway through it.

In this chapter I begin by framing the problem in both personal and literary terms. I then propose a particular theoretical perspective on the issue. In so doing, I will present some empirical data and refer to studies of computer games that use, explore, and expand this theory; but my purpose is primarily descriptive rather than demonstrative. My purpose is descriptive because my larger goal is less to argue for one particular theory than to provide an example of a broader class of theories that examine learning – and the mechanisms of learning – as simultaneously individual and cultural. I argue that these are the kind of theories that we need to develop to study learning that happens in games: learning that is simultaneously and authentically both symbolic and situated.

The Helmets of "Amsterdam"

I recently had the great pleasure and privilege of spending a year on sabbatical, living with my family in a city in Europe. This city – let's call it Amsterdam for convenience sake, although any similarity to the real city of Amsterdam is purely coincidental – is a city of some three quarters of a million people and, remarkably, over a million bicycles. Everyone in

"Amsterdam," young and old alike, rides a bike.[2] Our seventy-five-year-old neighbor, for example, whose groceries we helped carry upstairs, rode her bicycle every day to the store.

Something like 83 percent of the population of Amsterdam is over the age of fourteen, which makes Amsterdam a city of more than six hundred and twenty thousand adult bike riders. However, in a year of living among six hundred and twenty thousand bicycle-riding adults, I literally *never* saw a Dutch adult riding with a helmet. The six hundred and twenty thousand bicycle-riding adults of Amsterdam certainly know about helmets. They make their children wear them. They use helmets when riding racing bicycles through the countryside. But no adult could be seen – or would be seen – wearing a helmet while riding his or her commuter bike in the city.

This may be purely a practical matter, in the sense that Amsterdam is well planned for bicycle traffic. There are separate lanes for bicycles on most streets, and many are actually physically separated from lanes for other vehicular traffic. Cars and buses – and even pedestrians – reliably give bicycles the right of way. So Amsterdam is arguably a safer city for bicyclists than many, and that certainly could be part of the reason adults do not wear helmets.

However, I argue that this phenomenon is better understood as an aspect of *culture*. In making this claim, I am using the term *culture* following Geertz (1973) (who is himself following Mead and others) as "a traffic in...significant symbols – words for the most part, but also gestures, drawings, musical sounds, mechanical devices like clocks [or, for that matter, bicycles and helmets] or natural objects like jewels – anything, in fact, that is disengaged from its mere actuality and used to impose meaning upon experience" (p. 45). But although Geertz was writing half a century ago (and Mead yet again a half a century before him), current scholarship continues to look at "shared cultural systems of meaning" (Lave & Wenger, 1991, p. 54) and "cultural models" (Gee, 1999), at culture as a system of public symbols through which experience is understood (Sahlins, 2000).

It perhaps requires little convincing that a bicycle helmet – or rather, in this case, the choice someone makes about whether to wear a helmet or not – is a cultural phenomenon, but still I offer as evidence the fact that during my stay in Amsterdam, Dutch friends and colleagues almost without fail commented that wearing a bicycle helmet made me look like a foreigner. Their occasional laughter (good-natured, of course) marked the helmet as the token of an outsider. Carrying a helmet after riding to a meeting led to discussions of the relative skill of Dutch and American bicyclists. And, of course, the pragmatics of cycling in Amsterdam – from the organization of the roads to the habits of drivers – are also part of the cultural *habitus* of Amsterdam's social organization.[3]

I make this point about the cultural nature of bicycle helmets because I want to draw attention to a particular fact about life as an American living in Amsterdam: There were other Americans living there too, and *most of them did not wear bike helmets either*. Or, to be more precise, as in Dutch families, most American children wore bicycle helmets in Amsterdam, and most American adults did not. Being a curious ethnographer, I naturally conducted some informal interviews with a convenient sample of Americans who were living in Amsterdam at the time.[4] In this small survey of American acquaintances, I discovered four interesting results:

1. All the adults I spoke with said they wore helmets when riding a bicycle in the United States.
2. Among those who did not wear a helmet in Amsterdam, the reasons they gave were various: "I feel silly doing it here," "No one else does," "I feel safer here," "I have to take it on and off so many times," "It messes up my hair," and so forth.
3. Those who continued to wear helmets while in Amsterdam gave the same reason every time: "It's safer."
4. The length of time someone had been living in Amsterdam did not seem to make much difference as to whether someone wore a helmet or not. After a few months (or even weeks), recent arrivals were just as likely to be wearing a helmet as those who had been in Amsterdam for longer periods of time.

Now I tell this little story – this small fly of personal experience now preserved in the amber of print – because although the issue is perhaps a small one (except, of course, for those Americans unfortunate enough to be in a bicycle accident while in Amsterdam), it illustrates a central dilemma in the study of learning:

> *If all the Americans living in Amsterdam wore helmets in the United States, why did some of them stop wearing helmets in Amsterdam while others continued to wear them?*

Golding versus Defoe

The wearing of bicycle helmets is a cultural practice: one that is a part of the culture in much of the United States and part of the culture in very little of Amsterdam. This means that the question of who does and does not wear a helmet is a matter of *enculturation*. By this I mean, following Brown, Collins, and Duguid (1989), that wearing (or not wearing) bicycle helmets is one of the ways in which "people, consciously or unconsciously, adopt the behavior and belief systems of new social groups" (p. 34). In other words, we have to ask why some Americans adopted the Dutch behavior and belief system regarding bicycle riding, whereas others did not.

Wertsch (1998) discusses this question of the adoption (or lack of adoption) of cultural practices in terms (following Bakhtin, 2002) of *resistance* and *appropriation*, where, in this case, Americans who continue to wear helmets are resisting the dominant local culture and those who follow local practice are appropriating the local culture. But this theme of selective enculturation is quite universal. Consider, for example, two well-known novels: William Golding's (1954) *Lord of the Flies* and Daniel Defoe's (1996) *The Life and Strange Surprizing Adventures of Robinson Crusoe of York, Mariner: Who Lived Eight and Twenty Years, All Alone in an Un-inhabited Island on the Coast of America, Near the Mouth of the Great River of Oroonoque; Having Been Cast on Shore by Shipwreck, Where-in All the Men Perished but Himself. With an Account How He Was at Last as Strangely Deliver'd by Pyrates. Written by Himself.*

In *Lord of the Flies*, a group of British schoolboys is marooned on an island. They quickly abandon the social norms and conventions of British society and, led by former choirboy Jack Merridew, engage in ritual torture and human sacrifice. Robinson Crusoe, in contrast, is a British sailor who is similarly shipwrecked. But unlike Merridew, Crusoe recreates in the wilderness a model of his homeland (complete with his famous manservant, Friday) and defeats a tribe of native cannibals in battle before being rescued.

Leaving aside the obvious political overtones of these works (both imperialist and anti-imperialist), these novels both explore the stability of enculturation in the face of new social and material conditions. That is, they ask if once we have become enculturated, practices can be reenacted in another setting, or whether they can only be expressed within the original cultural surround. Once we have learned to function in a particular context, can we recreate the conditions we need to continue using those practices elsewhere? Or when we leave the supporting structures of the original cultural context, do we lose the ability to enact the practices that came with it? Are we, in the end, more like Crusoe or Merridew?

The answer is, of course, both – and neither. Or rather, we are sometimes one and sometimes the other. Developing a theory that explains under what conditions we are like the British sailor Crusoe or the British schoolboy Merridew is central to understanding the nature of learning and thus of learning in games and other technological environments.

Communities of Dysentery

To illustrate why *Robinson Crusoe* is so important to the science of learning, permit me to use one more piece of personal experience, this time from being a Peace Corps volunteer in a country that I shall call "Nepal."[5]

In the United States, all the water that comes from a tap (in a sink, drinking fountain, or bathtub, for example) has been treated to remove parasites such as amoebae, bacteria, and other threats to human health and digestion. In Nepal, quite the reverse is true: There is, for all intents and purposes, no treated drinking water anywhere. As a result, part of the intensive training in Nepali culture given to Peace Corps volunteers includes water purification practices that are the norm neither in the United States nor in Nepal.

Acquiring those practices means acquiring a new Discourse, in the sense that Gee (2001) describes: a new way of "talking, listening, writing, reading, acting, interacting, believing, valuing, and feeling (and using various objects, symbols, images, tools, and technologies)" (p. 719). Thus, for example, it requires developing new skills, such as learning how to ask that food be served on a plate that has been dried with a towel or learning the proper way to use iodine to purify a bottle of water.[6] It means developing a fairly elaborate repertoire of cultural knowledge, including when fruit or eggs might be safe to eat and under what conditions the rag being used to wipe the plate might be more contaminated than the water itself. It means acquiring the values that let you protect your personal hygiene in a way that is culturally sensitive. It means developing a new decision-making process regarding food and drink, a new set of concerns and criteria: a more complex calculus of hunger and thirst than either Americans or Nepalese practice. And the cumulative acquisition of this Discourse requires developing a new identity that is neither quite American nor quite Nepali. Anyone who doubts that Peace Corps volunteers have a shared culture in this regard need only listen to the endless and intimate discussions volunteers have of the state of their intestines whenever they gather.

In this sense, acquiring the Peace Corp volunteers' Discourse of water purification in Nepal means becoming part of a *community of practice*. Lave and Wenger (1991) describe a *community of practice* as a group of individuals who share a repertoire of knowledge about and ways of addressing similar (often shared) problems and purposes. A community of practice shares a common body of knowledge and set of skills but also a system of values that determines when and how those skills and that knowledge should be employed and a set of processes through which such decisions are made. And, of course, such a community also has a shared identity that is manifest in both overt markers (such as the carrying of a water bottle or wearing of a bicycle helmet) and the shared enactment of the skills, values, and decision-making processes. In fact, acquiring any Discourse involves becoming part of a community of practice, in the sense that a Discourse is the manifestation of a culture – a way of acting and being in the world – and a community is a group of people with a shared culture (Rohde & Shaffer, 2004).

I raise the Peace Corps' attempt to bring volunteers into a community of practice regarding water purification because it illustrates the dilemma of learning environments more generally. Volunteers go through a scaffolded process of learning to purify water. They are, quite literally, newcomers, who move from easier and more peripheral participation in the practice, such as treating water with iodine, to more central and challenging ones: determining what food is safe to eat under which conditions, for example, or securing a clean plate from which to eat. By the end of training, all the volunteers are more or less a part of this community of shared practices. Then volunteers head to their posts, where for the most part they are the only member of that shared community for miles around. They are surrounded by a different culture with very different practices regarding the cleanliness of water.[7]

While I was in Nepal, an informal sampling of my fellow volunteers showed that some continued to treat their water at post, and some did not. And some of those who did not treat their water when they were at post continued to treat their water when they were around other volunteers in Kathmandu.[8] Some volunteers, in other words, enacted the practices of the community of volunteers without the original cultural surround, whereas others adopted the practices of their new surrounding context. Some were Crusoe and some were Merridew – and in saying this I want to be clear that I mean in no way to cast aspersions on Nepali culture because Americans do not ordinarily purify their own water individually either. Rather the question is about the persistence of the use of a particular configuration of skills, knowledge, values, and decision-making processes – and thus also the display of identity – from one community when the original setting of practice is altered.

In what follows I will argue that one productive way to think about conditions under which enculturation persists across context is by looking at the extent to which a person has become proficient in a Discourse within its original context. That is, we can understand the extent to which learning transfers by analyzing participation in (and thus enculturation into) a community of practice.

One Productive Way, Part I: Framing a Discourse

I want to draw particular attention to one key phrase in the preceding paragraph: *one productive way*. Quite specifically, I want to point out that I am offering this idea – that we can examine the extent to which a person has become enculturated into a community of practice and use it to understand whether that person can mobilize the practices from that community in new situations – not as "the" solution to the problem of transfer but as an example of an approach to the study of learning that draws on both individual and sociocultural perspectives. The approach I outline here, in effect, describes two theoretical constructs, each of which I have written about in more detail elsewhere, and brings them together to suggest a way of conceptualizing (and describing) the broader class of theories that the field of learning needs to develop.

The first and more fundamental construct is an *epistemic frame*, which I have written about elsewhere as "the combination – linked and interrelated – of values, knowledge, skills, epistemology, and identity" that people have as part of a particular community of practice (Shaffer, 2007, p. 160). The term draws on Papert's (1980) use of the concept of *epistemology* as a *particular way of thinking* and on Dewey's (1933) idea that *knowing is doing* to define epistemology as a community's norms for making decisions and justifying actions. The concept of a *frame* comes from Goffman (1974; see also Tannen, 1993), who argued that any activity is interpreted in terms of a frame: the organizational rules and premises, partly existing in the minds of participants and partly in the structure of the activity itself, that shape the perceptions of those involved. That is, a frame is something that is simultaneously individual and social: a set of norms and practices through which experiences are interpreted.

The terminology of epistemic frame is useful because one can think of such frames like a pair of glasses that colors the world in particular ways. They highlight some things as important and relevant and hide or elide other aspects of experience; in this sense, they are a description of Goodwin's (1994) concept of *professional vision*. And, of course, putting on such a frame marks one as the kind of person who sees the world in a particular way. At the same time, it is useful to describe such frames as "epistemic" because they constitute a way of knowing and suggest that the practices of one community are no more or less fundamental than those of another. Thus there is no reason, a priori, to privilege the educational value of Discourses of school subjects over extant practices in the world – or over the practices that are employed in a game. All communities have ways of knowing, and the relevant question is: How useful are those practices to solve problems and attain goals that matter to someone or to some group of people?

The concepts of epistemic frame and Discourse obviously share a lot in common, in the sense that "the combination – linked and interrelated – of values, knowledge, skills, epistemology, and identity" that people have as part of a particular community of practice can be seen as a more specific description of a way of "talking, listening, writing, reading, acting, interacting, believing, valuing, and feeling (and using various objects, symbols, images, tools, and technologies)." In this sense, it can be quite useful to think of an epistemic frame as the grammar of a Discourse: a more formal description of the configuration of elements of a Discourse exhibited by members of a particular community. However, there are at least four properties of an epistemic frame that are distinct from the more general notion of a Discourse – although in making this comparison, I want to emphasize that one is not necessarily better than the other; rather, their different features are useful for different kinds of analyses.

Three of these distinctions are important to note but not necessarily central to the utility of epistemic frames as a theoretical construct. First, describing the epistemic frame of a community requires specifying some set of elements of the Discourse of the community as being critical to the community's way of seeing and acting in the world. These are usually described as skills, knowledge, identity, values, and/or epistemology, but those categories are clearly guidelines rather than a rigid formula. There may be settings in which only some of these elements are significant or analytical circumstances where only some can be observed. The choice and definition of frame elements can come a priori from some theoretical or empirical analysis – that is, it can be an etic structure imposed on the data by the researcher – but more often (and more effectively) they arise from some ethnographic or other grounded examination of the community in action. In the same vein, the claim could never be that this listing of discourse elements is exhaustive, only that it is sufficient for the analysis at hand. Further, these discourse elements are often speech acts but need not be limited to verbal utterances. As in a Discourse, doing is a form of speaking – that is, trafficking in meaningful symbols – just as speaking is a form of doing.

A second distinction between an epistemic frame and a Discourse is that an epistemic frame is always and explicitly a construct that is both internal and external: that is, a property of the community and of an individual to the extent that an individual has appropriated or internalized the Discourse of the community. And finally, epistemic frames take epistemology as a central analytical focus rather than identity, which is the organizing structure of a Discourse.

I suggest that these first three distinctions are worth noting but are not central because, in fact, these are shared properties of both a Discourse and an epistemic frame, and the differences here are matters of emphasis rather than inclusion or exclusion. Like an epistemic frame, a Discourse similarly is both a property of a community and something that can be appropriated by an individual. A Discourse naturally includes both forms of epistemology and of identity. And any Discourse analysis requires focusing on some key discourse practices and not others. In practice, these elements of the two constructs are highlighted differently, but this is a pragmatic rather than an ontological distinction. Pragmatic differences in emphasis can be important and often sufficient to merit the introduction of a new theoretical construct. In this case, however, there is a more important distinction that marks epistemic frames as a distinct hypothesis about the nature of learning and enculturation.

The critical distinction of epistemic frame theory is its explicit – indeed, central – focus on the *linkages between frame elements*.

One Productive Way, Part II: Forming a Frame

What it means for two frame elements – that is, two discourse markers within a Discourse or two sign tokens within a symbolic system – to be "linked" depends, of course, on what the frame elements are. To take a simple example, the "skill of asking for a dry plate in Nepali" is linked to "knowledge of when the towel that will be used to wipe the plate is likely to be dirtier than the water it is wiping off" in the sense that experts only use the skill after taking this particular piece of knowledge into account. Thus we might describe the nature of the linkage as "the knowledge mediating the application of the skill." On the other hand, the decision to politely refuse a cup of tea served by a government official because the glass was not dried first could easily require caring about the cultural sensitivities of the moment, the ability to explain the decision clearly but respectfully, and the willingness to assert one's identity as an quasi-outsider; that is, the decision-making process would depend on holding a particular value, having the skill to act in accord with it, and holding a particular view of oneself.

I will come back to the nature of the links in a moment. But first I would like to focus on the question of linkage itself. Strictly speaking, because discourse is a cultural artifact, elements of discourse always invoke some combination of skills, knowledge, values, and decision-making processes – as well as the identity or identities associated with them. That is, anything we say or do marks us as the kind of person who makes some set of assumptions, interprets a situation in particular ways, and decides on certain kinds of actions. The process of discourse analysis, writ large, is an attempt to understand how some action (or sequence of actions) is interpreted by the participants in their original context (Wood & Kroger, 2000). This necessarily means identifying the ways of knowing, doing, thinking, and being that the action signifies. Put another way, in practice, discourse elements are always interpreted in terms of a larger Discourse or Discourses. Any display of skills invokes a particular identity. Any interpretation of a situation through the lens of a particular value requires knowledge of the context and its relevant features. Any decision is conditioned on the skills, knowledge, values, and identity of the community.

Thus one might argue that it is impossible, in principle, to distinguish frame elements in isolation. Indeed, what would it mean to use a particular skill "on its own," independent of any relevant knowledge, values, or identity? But this is the wrong question because although skills are always linked to some form of knowledge, values, identity, and epistemology (and each of the other elements are, in turn, associated with all the others), they are *not always linked to the same ones* or in the same ways. The purpose in marking certain frame elements as significant to a community of practice is to understand *how* they become linked in the ways characteristic of expertise within the community. Put another way, if we assume a priori that using some skill from a community is an assertion of identity in that community (for example), we are assuming the very thing that from the perspective of learning we are trying to find out: that is, how someone comes to see that skill as part of a particular identity in the first place.

The careful reader – and particularly the careful reader familiar with Discourse analysis – will no doubt recognize at this point that the concept of links in an epistemic frame plays an analogous role to the idea of *cultural models* in a Discourse (D'Andrade & Strauss, 1992; Gee, 1999; Holland & Quinn, 1987). Cultural models are memories of prototypical events in a Discourse, which could be real events experienced by an individual or stories told by or about events in the experience of members of the community. These prototypical event memories create images of expected patterns of behavior within the community. That is, they do the work of linking elements of the epistemic frame of the Discourse to one another in particular configurations: they show someone what choices are appropriate within the context of the community. In so doing, they provide a mechanism by which the norms of the community are enacted by individuals – and also a hypothesis about how the process of enculturation unfolds. Indeed, much of the work of Discourse analysis is the examination of moment-by-moment interactions to understand the cultural models at work and thus the structure of the Discourses being employed. Cultural models are a "tool of inquiry" that guides the asking (and answering) of important questions about the nature of action in a community.

In a similar way, we can conceive of the identification of frame elements and the structure of the links between them as a tool of inquiry. The concept of an epistemic frame is agnostic as to the mechanisms by which those links are created within individuals or within a community. Some are surely encoded in prototypical stories (Nelson, 1996), others in direct event memories (Donald, 1991; Dreyfus & Dreyfus, 1986), and some are reduced to heuristic "rules of thumb" or sayings or maxims. Some are enshrined in written or unwritten rules (Pinker, 1997). Some are maintained in the structure of the physical environment within which a community operates (Pea, 1993). But whatever the mechanism by which links between frame elements are created or maintained, modeling the structure of those links is a useful tool of sociological and psychological inquiry – and thus an important tool in the kit of the science of learning.

In saying that the structure of links in an epistemic frame models the structure of a Discourse, I want to emphasize the word *model*. I am not suggesting that a set of actual links exists, either within the mind of an individual or within the Discourse community, physically or even psychologically.[9] The organization of links in an epistemic frame is a tool by which the cumulative structure of the norms of a Discourse can be described. That is, it is a technique for providing a *mechanic grip* on what Pickering (1995) referred to as "the mangle of practice." Epistemic frames are a framework for describing the complex unfolding of events in the real world.

We can create a model of the epistemic frame of the Discourse (or more properly, of some community of practice that operates with a Discourse), but we also can create a model of the epistemic frame of any individual within that community. And the similarity between the two provides a tool with which learning as enculturation can be analyzed.

One Productive Way, Part III: Fitting a Frame

The second already-existing theoretical construct that I want to introduce here builds on the first. *Epistemic network analysis* (Shaffer, et al., 2009), or ENA, is a technique for quantifying – and thus analyzing – an epistemic frame. The central insight of ENA borrows, broadly speaking, from Minsky's (1988) notion of a *society of mind*: that is, of the mind as a set of interacting agents. Metaphorically, we can think of the different elements of an epistemic frame (the skills, knowledge, identities, values, and episte-mology of some community of practice) as agents in their own right that are connected to one another through different patterns of association. The pattern of their interaction thus can be mapped using existing tools from social network analysis. Social network analysis, at its core, involves coding events or objects as nodes and mapping the linkages among nodes to build social networks that can be analyzed mathematically or sometimes conceptually (Latour, 1987). As one account of ENA (Shaffer et al., 2009, pp. 40–1) explains:

> [U]sing social network analysis we might examine the relationships among a group of people meeting for the first time at a cocktail party. To do so, we might take a photograph of the party at appropriate intervals – perhaps every time the music changes, every time someone orders a drink, or at a fixed time interval, depending on the nature of the party and our hypoth-eses about the people and relationships involved and the social forces at work. If we make the assumption that people who spend more time in the same conversational group develop a closer relationship over time, we can quantify the social network being developed at the party by summing, for each pair of party-goers, the number of times they are recorded in the same conversational group during the party. Once quantified in this way, social network analysis provides a wide range of analytical tools for inves-tigating the properties and processes at work in the social relationships of the party.
>
> If we think of the "party" not as a collection of individuals in a room, but rather as a collection of elements from the epistemic frame…then we can use the same analytical tools to conduct epistemic network analysis.

I want to draw out two important points from this brief summary of the relationship between social network analysis and ENA.[10]

The first is rather evident but nonetheless significant: Social net-work analysis is a simplification of the complex dynamics of a social sit-uation. As in any analysis of data, it is based on an assertion about the relationship between the observed data and some phenomenon of interest. In the hypothetical case earlier, there is an inference made that "being in the same conversational group" tells us something about a developing relationship. It is possible to posit more complex inferences (perhaps based on more complex observations), including all manner of possible relationships between people using social network analysis. The subsequent mathematics may become more complex (depending on the relationships hypothesized), but the principle remains the same: As in any model, social network analysis simplifies the observed situation, and the test of whether the simplification is appropriate lies in the nature of the question being asked and the subsequent results obtained.

In a similar way, then, ENA is a simplified representation of the structure of the practices of a community – although one has to quickly admit that a cultural model (and any other model, qualitative or quantitative) is as well. I will provide an example of ENA being used on real data in a moment, but most ENA analyses use a relatively small number of frame elements (six to twenty) and take "co-occurrence in discourse" as a proxy for "linkage." This is a simplification, but one of practical convenience, not theoretical necessity. The same technique could account for more elements, different kinds of linkages (including directional links), and more complex decision rules for determining linkage.

The second issue to draw out is actually a point of omission: namely, that the preceding account makes no more mention of an epistemic frame being the property of a single individual than a social network is – although, of course, an individual has collections of both epistemic frames and social networks.[11] In fact, the preceding description does not even suggest that an epistemic frame is uniquely the property of people, in the sense that the artifacts with which people interact similarly could provide links between frame elements. In this sense, a theory of epistemic frames mimics Pasks' (1975) conversation theory or a theory of distributed mind (Shaffer & Clinton, 2006), where persons and machines contribute to the co-creation of systems of meaning. This is a central point, in the sense that one can use ENA to describe, quantify, and compare the epistemic frame exhibited by various combinations of actors in the system (including individuals and groups of persons and technologies).

What's in the Game?

By way of example, I'd like to present empirical work that, again, has been reported in more detail elsewhere (Hatfield & Shaffer, 2006, 2008; Shaffer,

2007): this time, a study by my colleague David Hatfield on an educational game he developed with Alecia Magnifico. In the game, called *science.net*, players become science journalists and produce an online science news-magazine. *Science.net* is an example of an *epistemic game*, in the sense that it is a game designed to develop the epistemic frame of a particular socially valued community of practice (Shaffer, 2007). It recreates in game form what cub reporters experience in their professional training.

This particular claim – that the game recreates what cub reporters experience in their professional training – provides an excellent example of the kind of analysis I have been describing. It asserts that the practices in one community (the game) model the practices in another (the professional practicum through which journalists are trained). If ENA can be used to empirically test Hatfield's claim about the structure of the game, then it provides a theoretically grounded metric for comparing Discourses – and thus a means to assess enculturation.

The computer game *science.net* was designed based on two ethnographic studies of journalism capstone courses in which undergraduate journalism students were apprenticed into the community of practice in a class designed to mimic key practices of a real newsroom. One of those key practices was *copyediting*: line-by-line corrections to a news story that are copious, detailed, and blunt. The copyedits in *science.net* – a game designed for middle school students – were somewhat less blunt, but they were supposed to retain the other salient features of the original. Graduate students working on the project (none of whom were themselves journalists) were trained to give feedback in the game, and Hatfield's question was whether these mentors in the game setting were modeling the same practices as the journalists who were mentors in the professional training.

To assess whether the mentors in the game and in the journalism practicum on which it was modeled were engaging in the same practices, Hatfield created a coding scheme from the ethnographic data, cataloging some eighteen skills, forms of knowledge, values, identity markers, and epistemological stances: everything from "knowledge of the reader" to the "skill of narrative storytelling," the "value of making a difference," and the "epistemology of accuracy."[12] Each of the copyedits from each of the stories filed was coded as to whether the mentor referenced each of the eighteen frame elements, as in the example in Figure 23.1.

Hatfield then used ENA to construct a model of the epistemic frame the journalist was enacting. He treated the individual copyedits across all stories as if they were snapshots of people (i.e., frame elements) interacting at a party (i.e., being linked in discourse) to model the *enacted epistemic*

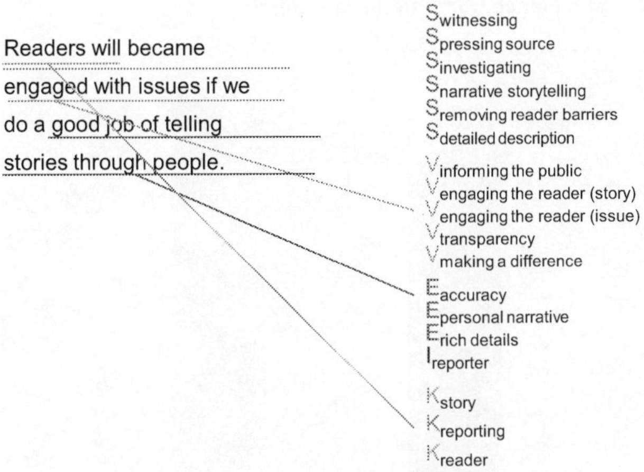

Figure 23.1. A copyedit created by a professional journalist and coded using elements of the epistemic frame of a journalism practicum.

frame of the journalist: that is, to create a model of the journalist's epistemic frame as reflected in the copyedits he or she made. In this model of the Discourse of journalism, copyediting served as a *reference frame* because it was a model of the practices (or part of the practices) that the game *science. net* was trying to replicate.[13]

Hatfield then used the same coding scheme on all the copyedits from the game *science.net*, and as a point of comparison, also on copyedits made on papers in a graduate psychology course, which were of similar style and form to the journalism edits. He then computed the epistemic frame for each of the stories in each of the venues: journalism practicum (JP), *science. net* game (G), and psychology course (PC). Using a technique called *relative centrality distance* (which is described in more detail in his work), he computed the "distance" between the reference frame and each story in the data set.

I do something of an injustice to Hatfield's study in describing it so briefly here, but suffice it to say that he triangulated his findings using both further qualitative investigation of the different stories and further quantitative analysis of the frames he constructed, which both confirmed his initial findings and led to some refinements in the methods for computing the distances between frames. The overall result, though, was clear and straightforward and can be seen in Figure 23.2, which shows that the distances from the reference frame to the frames from the game stories (G) were not significantly different from the distances from the reference

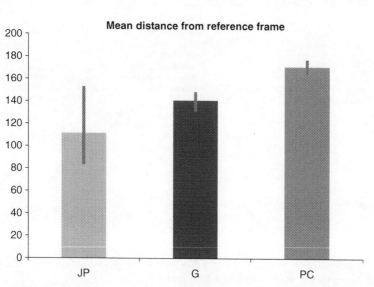

Figure 23.2. Graph showing mean distance from reference frame for stories in three conditions: journalism practicum (JP), game (G), and psychology course (PC). Smaller distance shows stronger overlap.

frame to the stories in the journalism practicum (JP). The papers in the psychology course (PC), on the other hand, were significantly further away from the reference frame.

The differences are even more dramatic when the frames are actually visualized, as in this projection from the high-dimensional space in which frames are analyzed into a 2D plane, where the blue network represents the journalism practicum, the green the game, and the red the psychology course (Figure 23.3).

In both cases, the results are the same. The model suggests that the copyediting practices used by mentors in the game *science.net* working with middle-school-aged players reflected the same practices used in the training of journalists during one capstone course. In other words, Hatfield used ENA to show that the epistemic game *science.net* was...well, epistemic.

Another colleague, Elizabeth Bagley, has taken a similar approach to looking at the epistemic game *Urban Science*, which recreates the training practices of urban planners (Bagley & Shaffer, 2009, 2010). Like Hatfield, she studied the training of professionals to model a reference frame for the game, this time from the practice of planning rather than journalism. In her study (again, reported in more detail elsewhere), she used ENA to show how, from one week to the next during the practicum, the enacted frame of

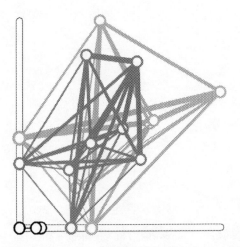

Figure 23.3. A projection of the links between frame elements in a journalism practicum (light gray), the game *science.net* (medium gray), and a psychology course (black).

novice planners converged with the frame being modeled by their mentor. That is, the Discourse of the novices became more like the Discourse of the profession. ENA, then, and with it the concept of epistemic frames, appears to be a useful tool in assessing learning as the reflection of an individual's enculturation in a community of practice.

ENA and Crusoe

To explain how ENA might provide such a model, let us imagine, for a moment, superimposing two epistemic networks, one on another. Like social networks, epistemic networks can be visualized in a number of ways, including as a *network graph*, similar to those in Figure 23.3, where frame elements are represented by nodes and links are represented by lines, with strength of association between two elements represented by the length and/or thickness of the line that connects their associated nodes in the graph. Networks also can be represented by adjacency matrices, where each cell in the matrix quantifies the association between two elements, or even as points in a very high-dimensional space, where points in the same neighborhood represent networks of similar configuration.

There are thus several ways of imagining the superposition of networks, and perhaps Figure 23.4 is as good as any.

Let us assume, again for the sake of simplicity, that the full set of nodes and links in Figure 23.4 is the reference frame for some community of

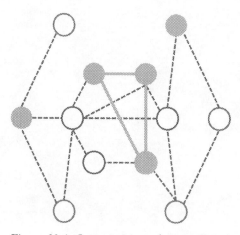

Figure 23.4. Superposition of two epistemic networks. The set of all nodes is a reference frame from some community of practice. The orange (*solid*) nodes and orange (*solid*) lines represent the epistemic frame of a novice at some point in time.

practice; that is, it is the set of frame elements and links between them that experts in the community exhibit when taking action. A novice's epistemic frame might be represented by the set of orange (solid) nodes and links: It is a subset of the reference frame, including only some of the nodes and links from the original. There also could be extraneous or overweighted links, although this diagram does not show that case.

The key point is that the orange frame alone does not appear to be "stable." Key connecting nodes and links that are part of the reference frame are missing. Some of the frame elements that are present (the node in the upper right, for example) are not connected to other elements. Thus it is easy to believe that our orange novice would not be able to enact practices of the community in an unfamiliar setting with much success. Too many of the conditions for successful practice are missing in his or her epistemic network. He or she is not sufficiently enculturated because he or she has not (yet) internalized enough of the frame of the community. On the other hand, some links are in place, so with appropriate support from the setting – whether from peers, mentors, or from the material conditions of practice – it appears that the orange novice could participate in the practices of the community, even if perhaps at this stage still only peripherally.

As the orange novice progressed through his or her enculturation, more of the skills, knowledge, values, epistemology, and identity of the community would become part of his or her epistemic frame. If the reproductive practices of the community were effective, the appropriate kinds of links would be formed between them. At some point the configuration would become stable, in the sense that it would be able to operate with minimal support from the setting in which our orange (now) expert finds himself or herself. If we take the liberty of describing the reference frame at work here as the Peace Corps volunteers' Discourse of water purification in Nepal, we might expect that the orange links and nodes represent the epistemic frame of a volunteer who treated his or her water when around other volunteers in Kathmandu but not when he or she was alone at post. If the reference frame is, in some broad sense, "British culture," our orange novice might be Jack Merridew.

MSA and Games

There is, of course, much to be said (some of which, as earlier, already has been said elsewhere) about the details of coding, constructing, quantifying, analyzing, and visualizing epistemic frames using ENA. But I began this meditation on the nature of learning in games with a claim that my intent was to describe a theory of learning that is simultaneously individual and situated and to suggest that it provides an example of the kind of theory that we need to develop to study learning in games. My argument thus is that the specific details of epistemic frames and ENA are less important (in this context) for their own sake than in the way that they exemplify a class of theory that I propose to call *models of situated action* (MSAs). MSAs are representations of participation in a practice that, like epistemic frames, are amenable to comparison between and across individuals, groups, and situations. They are postschism theories that are both symbolic and sociocultural.

The term *models of situated action* is meant to recognize that any such theory is necessarily a *model* of action, in the sense that it does not necessarily propose that a specific physical or psychological structure exists in the minds of individuals or in the world around them. Rather, it proposes that some construct is useful for analyzing situated action. Further, any such theory must make a link between individuals, groups of individuals, and the context around them; that is, it must be *situated* in the sense that it provides a formal language that accounts for the way in which individuals take certain actions in certain situations. And finally, any such theory must focus on *action* in the sense that it can provide not only descriptive but also predictive accounts of the discourse individuals and groups use (including, of course, but not limited to, particular speech acts). Put in simpler terms, any

MSA has to be the kind of theory that could account for which Americans will wear bicycle helmets in Amsterdam and which Peace Corps volunteers will treat their water at post in Nepal.

Thus epistemic frames are but one example of an MSA. Other researchers are similarly working on models – often, like ENA, quantitative and computational – of situated action. For example, Shute and her colleagues have been using Bayesian networks to model player choices in a game (Shute et al., 2009). Mislevy has proposed evidence centered assessment design as a framework for constructing, describing, and validating assessments of complex practices (Mislevy & Riconscente, 2006). Hickey has looked at models that link proximal situated data with distal standardized assessments to understand the efficacy of learning activities, particularly in the setting of educational games (Hickey, Ingram-Goble, & Jameson, 2009). Suthers and colleagues have looked at quantifying the distance between forms of discourse (Constantino-Gonzalez, Suthers, & Escamilla de los Santos, 2003). Each of these is a different quantitative and theoretical framework for looking at situated action. And each is thus, I claim, a kind of MSA.

Which brings us to a key question, for the future of learning and for this volume: Why are MSAs so important for understanding learning in games?

My answer starts with recognition that a game is fundamentally a culture (Gee, 2003; Shaffer, 2007; Steinkuehler, 2006). Playing a game – and certainly playing a game well – requires a certain way of thinking about and being in the world: a set of skills, knowledge, values, ways of making decisions, and ways of seeing oneself and being seen by others who "work" in the game. The players of any game form a community of practice, complete with newcomers and old-timers, with rites of passage and increasingly central participation. Thus one powerful way to analyze the experience of players of a game is through some model of enculturation – that is, using an MSA.

A second aspect of computer games that makes MSAs such useful conceptual tools is that, compared with other interactive settings, games record a relatively large subset of activity. No game can record everything that happens with, by, and to players because some actions that matter in the game always take place outside the computer system and even away from the game interface itself. For example, players talk with one another or with onlookers while playing, multiple players design or play the same character, and players talk about games at the schoolyard or water cooler. But these issues notwithstanding, games record an enormous amount of discourse in the form of players' choices, actions, and even (in good games) dialog with other players and nonplayer characters. There is, in fact, an overwhelming stream of cultural information available about players in a game – too much to be managed, in most cases, without some formal model of participation, that is, without an MSA.

Third, although some games are more "open-ended" than others – a multiplayer online role-playing game has more possible interactive contexts than a game such as *Tetris*, for example – the cultural context of a game (particularly a computer game) is bounded in predictable ways. That is, relative to social interactions writ large, the structure of the game situation constrains the set of discourse moves that players may undertake. The game provides a restricted semiotic system (Gee, 2003) that, while not finite, is more formally tractable than discourse in many interactive settings. The organization of the game into set levels, scenes, nonplayer characters, and other structural features – not to mention formal rules through which these game elements operate – provides a degree of standardization across contexts for different players. The game system consists of arenas in which particular kinds of discourse are likely to recur.

Games worlds thus are fundamentally cultural in nature. They provide a rich record of players' discourse. And they have the potential to provide standardized elements of situations in which players interact. All these features, in turn, suggest that MSAs are particularly powerful – and perhaps essential – tools for understanding learning in games. Contrariwise, games are also particularly powerful – and if not essential, certainly quite valuable – contexts in which to develop and understand MSAs and learning through enculturation in practices more generally.

Consider, for example, one of the players in Hatfield's *science.net* game. Let's call her Sarah. At any point in the game, we could, in theory, construct the epistemic frame of journalism that Sarah has enacted during the game; that is, we can quantify the structure of links between frame elements in Sarah's recorded discourse. We also could construct the frame enacted by the group or groups with which Sarah has worked. In fact, we could construct the frame enacted by all the elements of the game (including other players) that have been visible to Sarah during the game. This would constitute her *observed frame*, which would represent all the discourse within her *horizon of observation* in the game (Hutchins, 1995). As discussed earlier, we could, from studies of expert performance – either in real newsrooms, journalism practica, or by having journalists play the game – construct a *reference frame* (or reference frames) that represent an ideal set or sets of expert performance.

These frames would constitute an MSA, and using ENA, these different frames could be compared quantitatively. Thus we might ask, for example, whether during the game Sarah's frame converged with one of the reference frames of expert journalists. We could ask whether her frame was more likely to converge toward the reference frame if her observed frame also converged with the reference frame. That is, we could quantify one of the most elusive concepts in education, *opportunity to learn* (Darling-Hammond, 2006), by examining the progress of players relative to the qualities of the context in which they were embedded.

We could determine the trajectory over time of Sarah's frame development in the game and compare it with successful trajectories of experts, or of other players. We could determine whether certain learning progressions are more or less likely to lead to significant enculturation. We could determine which kinds of responses from mentors are most and least effective in promoting enculturation at different points in the game. We could even, with sufficient data, potentially replace the cognitive model in an automated tutoring system with an MSA to produce realistic mentoring in an ill-formed domain such as journalism (Shaffer, 2009).[14]

To the extent that any of these have been done, can be done, or will be done with ENA, they also could be done with any MSA that similarly provides a model of participation in a community of practice. In other words, MSAs provide a mechanism for assessing enculturation by determining the extent to which – and the particular ways in which – an individual has or has not adopted the discourse practices of a community: the community of players of a game or a community of practice in the world outside the game. MSAs do so by explicitly connecting events at the sociocultural level (participation in a Discourse) with events at the individual level (actions of a player). They do so by explicitly modeling the relationship between discourse markers (symbols) and the structure of a Discourse (practices).

Full Circle

This chapter began by asking how we might measure whether things players do in a game help them to do things in the world outside the game. I have argued for a view of transfer in which learning, even when occurring within a video game, is simultaneously a deeply individual and thoroughly cultural affair. It is situated learning that can best be conceptualized as models of situated action – if which I offer epistemic frames and epistemic network analysis as merely one example.

In this sense, an MSA is a theoretical construct that looks at learning – at transfer in the general sense of how one experience can affect another – from both a sociocultural and symbolic perspective. In so doing, an MSA is a model of the authentic practices of a community in action, providing an assessment of learning over time and in situ. A model of learning that has the potential to distinguish *Robinson Crusoe* from the *Lord of the Flies*. A model for the kind of learning that happens in games and that ideally happens in effective learning environments of any kind.

Acknowledgments

This work was funded in part by the Macarthur Foundation and the National Science Foundation through Grants REC-0347000, DUE-091934, DRL-0918409, and DRL-0946372. The opinions, findings, and conclusions do not reflect the views of the funding agencies, cooperating institutions, or other individuals. Thanks to these funders, and to David Hatfield, Elizabeth Bagley and the Epistemic Games Research Group, and to Jim Gee and Katie Clinton for their suggestions on the manuscript.

Notes

1   And, of course, reflexively, communities change through the participation of individuals.
2   This is, of course, quite transparently a fiction because anyone who knows me knows that in fact I was on sabbatical in the real European city called Amsterdam. I make the distinction between the Amsterdam in the Netherlands and the "Amsterdam" I discuss here because I am not presenting a rigorous empirical study of a particular city. Rather, I am making a point about the nature of culture and learning, which only requires that the details are illustrative. In this I am following Barthes, who in *Empire of Signs* (1982) writes in detail about the semiotics of Japanese culture but claims explicitly that he "can also – though in no way claiming to represent or analyze reality itself (these being the major gestures of Western discourse) – isolate somewhere in the world (*faraway*) a certain number of features (a term employed in linguistics), and out of these features deliberately form a system. It is this system which I shall call: Japan" (p. 3).
3   I refer to these physical features of the city and social norms as *habitus* because they are part of the taken-for-granted infrastructure of Dutch society that shapes the meaning of experience (Bourdieu, 1977).
4   The study is as yet unpublished, but the convenience sample consisted primarily of other parents at my children's school.
5   See note 1 for the relationship between the country I describe and the country of Nepal in Asia.

6   For those planning travel to Nepal, one way to ask for a dry plate is: *"Plet rumalle putchepaachi khaana raknus."* But although this phrase may seem simple, actually getting a dry plate requires a far more complex demonstration of skills, usually including various forms of gesture and mime. The concern about the dryness of the plate is that if the plate is only washed clean, drops of contaminated water may remain on it. By contrast, using iodine to purify water requires only waiting twenty minutes, but you also have to remember to turn the bottle over and let some of the iodized water run over the screwtop, or the water trapped there can still contain parasites.

7   In many places in Nepal, the main criterion for the purity of water is the speed with which it moves. That is, flowing water is cleaner than standing water, no matter what its original source. So water flowing in a strong stream or tap is regarded as clean.

8   And not surprisingly, while everyone got parasites sometimes, volunteers who did treat their water got fewer serious parasites and got parasites less often than those who did not.

9   And even if they did, we are not currently able to observe them directly. Any representation of a Discourse is always a model, although recent advances in neuroscience suggest that perhaps a model of neural functioning could be similarly conceptualized as a set of links.

10   A third point worth making, although not central to the argument here, is that early empirical work with ENA suggests that epistemic networks, in fact, have mathematical properties that differ somewhat from the networks analyzed by traditional social network analysis. (Social networks tend to contain large numbers of nodes with sparse connections. Epistemic networks tend to have fewer nodes and are more densely connected.) Thus, although the same principles apply, in practice the use of ENA requires slightly different algorithms.

11   To be completely fair, the original text at this point actually *does* refer to the frame elements as belonging to an individual. In the original presentation, this was for clarity of the description. Later in the same treatment of ENA, there is a discussion of quantifying the frames of collections of individuals.

12   There are, perhaps, those who might wonder why accuracy is coded as a form of epistemology and not a kind of value. In fact, it could be coded as either because, as above, the categories of skill, knowledge, and so forth are guidelines only. In the case of journalism, however, epistemology may be the better choice for accuracy in the sense that the practice of journalism is inextricably bound up with "scientific" concepts such as accuracy and verification (Kovach and Rosenstiel, 2001) or, as some suggest, the fundamental commandment of journalism is: "Thou shall not fabricate" (Gardner et al., 2001).

13   More details on the mathematics of ENA can be found in Shaffer and colleagues (2009). More details on Hatfield's specific methods can be found in Hatfield and Shaffer (2010).

14   I use the term *ill-formed domain* here because problems in journalism – as in many domains of complex practice – cannot be solved using a set of procedures specified in advance. (This is in contrast, for example, to work in a factory or a game like *tic-tac-toe*.) Well-formed domains can be represented

computationally using cognitive models, and automated tutoring systems have had some success in supporting learning in well-formed domains. The same cannot be said (yet) for ill-formed or open-ended problem spaces (Dreyfus & Dreyfus, 1986; Graesser et al., 2004).

References

Anderson, J. R. (1993). *Rules of the mind.* Hillsdale, NJ: Erlbaum.

Anderson, J. R., Reder, L. M., & Simon, H. A. (1996). Situated Learning and Education. *Educational Researcher,* 25(4), 5–11.

Bagley, E., & Shaffer, D. W. (2009). When People Get in the Way: Promoting Civic Thinking Through Epistemic Game Play. *International Journal of Gaming and Computer-Mediated Simulations,* 1(1), 36–52.

(2010). *The epistemography of urban and regional planning 912: Appropriation in the face of resistance.* Paper presented at the ICLS, Chicago, IL.

Bakhtin, M. M. (2002). *The dialogic imagination : four essays.* Austin, TX: University of Texas Press.

Barab, S. A., & Plucker, J. A. (2002). Smart People or Smart Contexts? Cognition, Ability, and Talent Development in an Age of Situated Approaches to Knowing and Learning. *Educational Psychologist,* 37(3), 165–182.

Barthes, R. (1982). *Empire of signs,* 1st American ed. New York: Hill and Wang.

Bourdieu, P. (1977). *Outline of a theory of practice.* Cambridge, England: Cambridge University Press.

Brown, J. S., Collins, A., & Duguid, P. (1989). Situated Cognition and the Culture of Learning *Educational Researcher,* 18(1), 32–42.

Chi, M. T. H. (1997). Quantifying Qualitative Analyses of Verbal Data: A Practical Guide. *Journal of the Learning Sciences,* 6(3), 271–315.

Constantino-Gonzalez, M. d. l. A., Suthers, D. D., & Escamilla de los Santos, J. G. (2003). Coaching Web-Based Collaborative Learning Based on Problem Solution Differences and Participation *International Journal of Artificial Intelligence in Education,* 13(2–4), 263–99.

D'Andrade, R., & Strauss, C. (eds.). (1992). *Human motives and cultural models.* Cambridge, England: Cambridge University Press.

Darling-Hammond, L. (2006). Securing the Right to Learn: Policy and Practice for Powerful Teaching and Learning. *Educational Researcher,* 35 (7), 13–24.

Defoe, D. (1996). *The life and strange surprizing adventures of Robinson Crusoe, of York, mariner who lived eight and twenty years all alone in an un-inhabited island on the coast of America, near the mouth of the great river of Oroonoque; having been cast on shore by shipwreck, wherein all the men perished but himself. With an account how he was at last as strangely deliver'd by pyrates.* Available from http://gateway.proquest. com/openurl?ctx_ver=Z39.88–2003&xri:pqil:res_ver=0.2&res_id=xri:ilcs-us&rft_id=xri:ilcs:ecf:Z000001109.

Dewey, J. (1933). *How we think, a restatement of the relation of reflective thinking to the educative process.* Reading, MA: D.C. Heath and Company.

(1938). *Experience and education.* New York: Collier Books.

Donald, M. (1991). *Origins of the modern mind: Three stages in the evolution of culture and cognition.* Cambridge, MA: Harvard University Press.

Dreyfus, H. L., & Dreyfus, S. E. (1986). *Mind over machine: The power of human intuition and expertise in the era of the computer.* New York: Free Press.

Gardner, H., Csikszentmihalyi, M., & Damon, W. (2001). *Good work: When excellence and ethics meet.* New York: Basic Books.

Gee, J. P. (1999). *An introduction to discourse analysis: Theory and method.* London: Routledge.

(2001). Reading as Situated Language: A Sociocognitive Perspective. *Journal of Adolescent & Adult Literacy*, 44(8), 714–25.

(2003). *What video games have to teach us about learning and literacy.* New York: Palgrave Macmillan.

Geertz, C. (1973). *The interpretation of cultures.* New York: Basic Books.

Goffman, E. (1974). *Frame analysis: An essay on the organization of experience.* New York: Harper & Row.

Golding, W. (1954). *Lord of the flies, a novel.* London: Faber and Faber.

Goodwin, C. (1994). Professional Vision. *American Anthropologist*, 96(3), 606–33.

Graesser, A. C., Lu, S., Jackson, G. T., Mitchell, H., Ventura, M., Olney, A., et al. (2004). AutoTutor: A Tutor with Dialogue in Natural Language. *Behavioral Research Methods, Instruments, and Computers*, 36, 180–193.

Greeno, J. G. (1997). On Claims That Answer the Wrong Questions. *Educational Researcher*, 26(1), 5–17.

Hatfield, D., & Shaffer, D. W. (2006). *Press play: Designing an epistemic game engine for journalism.* Paper presented at the ICLS, Bloomington, IN.

(2008). *Reflection in professional play.* Paper presented at the ICLS, Urecht, The Netherlands.

(2010). *The epistemography of journalism 335: Complexity in developing journalistic expertise.* Paper presented at the ICLS, Chicago, IL.

Hickey, D. T., Ingram-Goble A., & Jameson, E. (2009). Designing Assessments and Assessing Designs in Virtual Educational Environments. *Journal of Science Education Technology*, 30, 837–861.

Holland, D., & Quinn, N. (eds.). (1987). *Cultural models in language and thoughts.* New York: Cambridge University Press.

Hutchins, E. (1995). *Cognition in the wild.* Cambridge, MA: MIT Press.

(2008). The Role of Cultural Practices in the Emergence of Modern Human Intelligence. *Philosophical Transactions of the Royal Society*, 363(1499), 2011–19.

Kovach, B. & Rosentiel, T. (2001). *The elements of journalism: What newspeople should know and the public should expect.* New York: Random House.

Latour, B. (1987). *Science in action: How to follow scientists and engineers through society.* Cambridge, MA: Harvard University Press.

Lave, J., & Wenger, E. (1991). *Situated learning: Legitimate peripheral participation.* Cambridge, England: Cambridge University Press.

Minsky, M. L. (1988). *The society of mind.* New York: Simon and Schuster.

Mislevy, R. J., & Riconscente, M. M. (2006). Evidence-Centered Assessment Design: Layers, Concepts, and Terminology. In S. Downing & T. Haladyna (eds.), *Handbook of test development* (pp. 61–90). Mahwah, NJ: Erlbaum.

Nelson, K. (1996). *Language in cognitive development: Emergence of the mediated mind.* Cambridge, England: Cambridge University Press.

Packer, M. (2001). The Problem of Transfer, and the Sociocultural Critique of Schooling. *Journal of the Learning Sciences*, 10(4), 493–514.

Papert, S. (1980). *Mindstorms: Children, computers, and powerful ideas*. New York: Basic Books.

Pask, G. (1975). *Conversation, cognition and learning*. Amsterdam: Elsevier.

Pea, R. (1993). Practices of Distributed Intelligence and Designs for Education. In G. Salomon (ed.), *Distributed cognitions: Psychological and educational considerations*. Cambridge, England: Cambridge University Press.

Pickering, A. (1995). *The mangle of practice: Time, agency, and science*. Chicago: The University of Chicago Press.

Pinker, S. (1997). *How the mind works*. New York: Norton.

Rohde, M., & Shaffer, D. W. (2004). Us, Ourselves, and We: Thoughts About Social (Self-) Categorization. *Association for Computing Machinery (ACM) SigGROUP Bulletin*, 24(3), 19–24.

Sahlins, M. D. (2000). *Culture in practice: Selected essays*. New York: Zone Books.

Seel, N. M. (2001). Epistemology, Situated Cognition, and Mental Models: 'Like a Bridge Over Troubled Water.' *Instructional Science*, 29(4–5), 403–27.

Shaffer, D. W. (2007). *How computer games help children learn*. New York: Palgrave.

(2009). AutoMentor: Virtual Mentoring and Assessment in Computer Games for STEM Learning. University of Wisconsin-Madison: National Science Foundation.

Shaffer, D. W., & Clinton, K. A. (2006). Toolsforthought: Reexamining Thinking in the Digital Age. *Mind, Culture, and Activity*, 13(4), 283–300.

Shaffer, D. W., Hatfield, D., Svarovsky, G., Nash, P., Nulty, A., Bagley, E., et al. (2009). Epistemic Network Analysis: A Prototype for 21st Century Assessment of Learning. *International Journal of Learning and Media*, 1(2), 33–53.

Shute, V. J., Ventura, M., Bauer, M. I., & Zapata-Rivera, D. (2009). Melding the Power of Serious Games and Embedded Assessment to Monitor and Foster Learning: Flow and Grow. In U. Ritterfeld, M. Cody, & P. Vorderer (eds.), *Serious games: Mechanisms and effects* (pp. 295–321). Mahwah, NJ: Routledge, Taylor and Francis.

Steinkuehler, C. A. (2006). Massively Multiplayer Online Videogaming as Participation in a Discourse. *Mind, Culture, & Activity*, 13(1), 38–52.

Tannen, D. (1993). *Framing in discourse*. New York: Oxford University Press.

Wertsch, J. V. (1998). *Mind as action*. New York: Oxford University Press.

Wood, L. A., & Kroger, R. O. (2000). *Doing discourse analysis: Methods for studying action in talk and text*. Thousand Oaks, CA: Sage.

Afterword: Games and the Future of Education Research

Richard Halverson

The games, learning, and society community is positioned to spark a revolution in education research. Video games emerged in the 1980s and 1990s as a radically new form of entertainment technology. Within a single generation, arcade and text-based adventure games evolved into first-person shooters, simulations of world history, and million-player massively multiplayer online worlds. Games proliferated on fast Internet connections and on mobile devices. It has taken a while for research communities to catch up. At first, much of the popular rhetoric on gaming focused on the risks and potential damage of gaming. Commentators issued cautionary tales that focused on deviance, distraction, and the potential for sparking antisocial behaviors and corrupting youth. Only recently has scholarly discussion begun to turn a corner to consider gaming as a powerful catalyst for learning.

Recent education research on games and gaming has struggled with self-definition. The potential of games to produce learning is no longer in much doubt. No one who has ever played, for example, *Deus Ex*, *Civilization*, or the *Sims* would question the power of immersive games as learning environments. The game environments are not only brilliant at scaffolding increasingly sophisticated play, but they also provide easy access to the tantalizing experience of world immersion. The interactive nature of gaming allows some players to actively participate in the direction and outcomes of narratives and others to create elaborate rule-based systems with emergent properties. The education research community, however, has been slow to embrace the revolutionary potential of games for learning. Instead of focusing on the unique affordances of game design and game play, many games researchers instead have focused on defining games in terms of existing education research agendas. At the beginning of this collection, Kurt Squire cites the refrain demanded of games researchers: "Where is the evidence that games work?" This question haunts video games and learning research. *(How) Do games teach math? (How) Can games lead to careers in science? (How well) Can games teach students to read?* It turned out that, in most cases, games proved neither as efficient nor as effective in reproducing the kinds of results characteristic of other kinds of instructional interventions. Thus the value of gaming as a new form of learning was stunted by the lack of evidence that games work as well as traditional methods to deliver traditional content.

The question "Where is the evidence that games work?" follows from a social science theory of action that guides much contemporary research in education. This theory of action assumes that education is a matter of implementing interventions (e.g., curricula, programs, software, etc.) into learning contexts. The purpose of research is to test the quality of the interventions (e.g., the value and reliability of expected outcomes) and to develop procedures for appropriate implementation. Research methods describe the appropriate experimental and analytic procedures to ascertain the causal effects of interventions. Education research, in this context, considers games as generic interventions intended to teach specified content. Research methods can assess what students know prior to and after the treatment. Learning gains then can be compared with other interventions (e.g., computer adaptive learning, classroom instruction, etc.). Once adequate evidence is provided of intervention success, researchers then can move to the question of deployment at scale and design controls for the fidelity of local implementation to ensure that the results produced under controlled settings also would be seen "in the wild." If games researchers could effectively engage in this type of social science policy research, they would finally legitimate games as viable interventions for public investment.

Seen from the perspective of contemporary education research, commercial games and gaming generate plenty of buzz but little evidence of learning. Most immersive games fail miserably when considered as mere interventions – they are not interchangeable with other forms of learning interventions (e.g., textbooks or simulations), and they do not often produce clear outcomes that can be measured outside the experience of play. Of course, some games can be designed to fit into categories that make them conducive for social science research, but these seldom afford the kinds of immersive play characteristic of console and PC commercial games.

Presumably, answering the question with evidence of effectiveness would put to rest, once and for all, the public disquiet around using entertainment technologies for education. The connection of "evidence of learning" to "public legitimation" reveals that there are larger issues at work here. Evidence would provide an objective scientific warrant for game play, design, and learning to legitimate games for public investment in education. This use of science as a rhetorical tool for public persuasion is certainly not new. Education is, after all, a serious matter, worthy of public policy and tax funding, whereas entertainment is a leisure activity best left to the marketplace. Using toys for learning irritates the serious-minded proponents of education – how could games, of all things, fulfill our daunting expectations for schooling as the path to national destiny and the remedy for social ills? The burden is on games researchers to provide evidence that games produce the kinds of learning we value in schools. Then games can join the ranks of curricula that "work" and could become viable resources that would extend the contemporary practices of teaching and learning in and out of schools. The future of games research, it would seem, hinges on the ability to produce and disseminate sufficiently persuasive evidence that games lead to learning.

My Afterword for this ambitious, challenging, and visionary collection of games-based research is to describe how and why this social science approach to education research is a profound mismatch for games-based research. Rather than define games research in terms of intervention research, instead, I state that this volume argues for a powerful new vision of education research. The core of this new vision is contained in the insight that games provide access to participating in and creating new *worlds*. In a phenomenological sense, worlds are the *referential totalities* of tools, practices, traditions, and routines in which actors make meaning of actions and interactions. All action – and all learning – takes place in the context of a world. A world includes the know-how, tools, and contextual information necessary to orient both action and identity. Knowledge claims must be understood against the backdrop of a world context that make knowing possible.

In education, the world can be thought of as the learning environment, that is, the context in which learners can make meaning of new information in relation to existing practices and constructs. The conventional approach to policy-driven education research is to bracket the world out, so to speak, and to consider the ways in which new interventions produce desired results regardless of the context. Bracketing the world out means that issues of participating in alternative worlds and building new worlds seldom arise in the traditional intervention research process. Traditional research methods excel at determining whether users/learners get what designers have built but falter at understanding the agency of users/learners in constructing and engaging in worlds. Designing interventions that provide the kinds of learning that we currently expect for schools will result in the kinds of schools we currently have. If the future of learning requires us to understand how students navigate, modify, and create new worlds, then we must develop new approaches to research to lead the way.

The video games research described throughout this book illustrates new approaches for games research to revitalize education research. Games allow players to engage in new worlds. Video games provide access to the kinds of worlds in which players can take on identities and interact with the environment and with others. Game worlds display many of the features that shape everyday social interaction. Jim Gee and Betty Hayes use *(D)iscourse* to describe the rules of interaction and communication characteristics of the *Sims* game world; David Shaffer uses *epistemic frame* to describe the network of beliefs, norms, and heuristics that orient actors in a professional worlds. Immersive game play leads many players to what Sasha Barab and colleagues call *transactive engagement* that allows players to use tools and social interaction in the pursuit of learning goals. Engaging in new worlds, with different norms of communication and different stances on identity exploration, allows players to create the kinds of spaces necessary to reflect on practices in their "real" worlds. Games, however, go beyond the invitation to *engage* in new worlds – they also provide opportunities to *design* new worlds. This level of learner/player agency instantiates new forms of interaction and world making. As Tom Malaby notes, putting the world-making tools in the hands of users shifts the locus of control from participation to creation. Studying how interaction unfolds through play and design in these new worlds gives rise to the kinds of skills and knowledge that will shape learning in the next century.

In the following sections I will describe how games research will anticipate the next generation of education research in three areas: *play*, *learning*, and *design*. The play section focuses on the wide variety of ethnographic and descriptive research practices presented in this book that were used to capture how interaction unfolds in game worlds. The learning section addresses the new approaches offered to analyze the process and the outcomes of participation in game worlds. The design section describes the ways in which researchers understand the world-making and world-altering practices of game players. This Afterword concludes with reflections on what education might look like once we decide to shift our research perspective from "what works" to "what's happening" and "what's possible."

Play

Play describes how players actually engage in game worlds. Play characterizes how players negotiate rule-based worlds and how player engagement transcends the rule-based game world to evolve unanticipated forms of interaction. Research on play seeks to understand how players navigate the tensions between constraint and freedom. The value of play research comes from descriptions of how players engage with and transcend in game worlds. This careful, basic research helps us to understand the social, psychological, and cognitive capacities that players bring to bear in play and also highlights the sociocognitive practices that emerge as players carve narrative arcs through game worlds.

Video game play highlights the tension between constraint and freedom because games are *designed experiences* (Kurt Squire). Games result from the intentional decisions of designers, and game play thus can be seen as a kind of asynchronous communication as players discern, exploit, and transform the features of the play environment. Soren Johnson captures this negotiation of designer and player by asking, "Who decides what the game is about?" Designers of games such as *Spore* and *Peggle* may base play on organizing metaphors (in this case, evolution and Pachinko) that suggest play mechanics and achievement structures, but once circulated in the world, players turn these games into explorations of creativity and chaos theory. Soren further notes that the negotiation between game play and design, as with most other forms of communication, requires that trust be established between the designer and the player. Players need to be able to trust that the game world will respond in satisfying ways to play, and cheats become a kind of credit that designers extend to players to fill in gaps between the underlying design metaphor and the play experience.

Conceiving of play as negotiation between the player and the rules of the system reveals a number of compelling directions for research. Richard LeMarchand and Drew Davidson, for example, analyze the design experience to show how developers translate play expectations into play experience. Trina Choontanom and Bonnie Nardi show how theory-crafting communities allow players to recreate the mathematics designers use to allocate rewards and punishments in the course of game play. Theory crafting can be seen as an organized method developed by players to ferret out the designed features that guide game play. Doug Clark and Mario Martinez-Garza call attention to the imperfect nature of the communication between design and play. Designers might intend to spark play (and cognition) in one direction, but play simply may float past intended learning goals. Doug and Mario note that while "players may spend the vast majority of game-play time interacting with the core ideas as a means of navigating through the world," researchers cannot simply assume that exposure results in interaction with core ideas. Because "making the core ideas and relationships explicit rather than tacit is a much bigger challenge" in game play than in direct instruction, the communication gap present in play worlds presents a considerable challenge for creating games to teach specific lessons.

The negotiation between design and freedom discloses the spaces in which player-centric social worlds can emerge. These emergent worlds provide rich opportunities for players to engage in knowledge-building activities on at least two levels – first to collaboratively decipher and navigate challenges built into game environments and second to extend game play into new forms of interaction. Jim Gee and Betty Hayes' interest-based concept of *affinity spaces* describes the hybrid in-game and out-of-game communities players build to support knowledge making and sharing during play. Kurt Squire's discussion of Apolyton University illustrates how players adapt existing education practices to organize interactive online learning experiences. The Apolyton community co-opted the university metaphor to provide develop courses, forums, and lessons to create game-play expertise. Yasmin Kafai and Kylie Peppler describe how embedding game worlds in social spaces also can spark the kinds of social interactions that give rise to advanced technological fluencies among adolescents. Meaningful social knowledge building opens up as members encounter real challenges in game designs that call for collaborative solutions.

Game worlds provide ideal environments to study the interaction of intended and emergent aspects of play. Building a game world requires designers to explicitly code expectations for interaction into game features. The degree to which players faithfully implement, subvert, ignore, redesign, or cheat game features can be reliably described by researchers. Researchers can trace how occasions for emergent social interaction arise directly from flaws or challenges of game design and can follow how play helps to transform game play through the redesign and modification of salient game features. The digital context of video games affords a remarkable opportunity to track the decision paths that players follow. This opportunity to trace the process of learning demonstrates how gaming can extend the practices of education research. The need for traditional education researchers to document the results of interventions can lead to the dismissal of contextual information irrelevant to understanding learning.

Because of their ability to trace the paths players follow between intended and actual game play, game researchers can create models to describe how the process actually unfolds in complex domains.

Learning

The link between intervention and effect also characterizes how games researchers think about learning. Many of the studies presented here investigate how games (can) teach the kinds of knowledge, skills, and dispositions we want to result from schooling. Sasha Barab and his colleagues explicitly address the challenges of adapting game technologies to desired learning goals, such as persuasive writing, in the *Modern Prometheus* game world. Rebecca Black and Stephanie Reich describe the sophisticated literacy practices sparked by children's participation in *Webkinz World*; Bob Coulter and his colleagues explore how learning in augmented reality games can be analyzed in terms of National Research Council dimensions of informal learning. In the out of school context, Colleen Macklin and John Sharp describe how games can spark interest in social issues.

Education research on learning has been dominated by understanding that the relation of intervention to outcome creates a gap between the occasion for learning and its measurement that, as David Shaffer notes, puts a premium on the concept of transfer. Learning is what survives the intervention, and the quality of learning typically is measured according to the quantity and duration of survival. What separates games research from traditional intervention research is the careful attention to how the (virtual) world mediates the learning process. Each effort to document learning here shares a common commitment to map the rich experience that takes place in game worlds onto theories and measures of valued learning goals. Each reenacts the core education research commitment to link games (as interventions) with valued learning outcomes. Each uses frameworks such as sociocognitive theories, communities of practice, new media literacies, and informal science frameworks to resist the reduction of in-game experience to the constraints of norm-referenced, standards-based tests. Investigating game worlds as means to learning allows researchers to better understand the contextual influences on learning and can help designers to build more robust environments that lead toward specific learning outcomes. The study of transfer is not simply the ability to leap from one context to another. Rather, the contextual, data-rich nature of games research helps us to understand what mediates the ability to extend strategies from one domain to another.

Games help to redefine the nature of learning from outcome to process. The studies presented here show how games research helps to reconceptualize the gap between learning and measurement by tracing the connections of how games can best mediate activity toward existing learning goals and by exploring the new kinds of learning that unfold in game contexts. In the following sections I briefly address several of the contextual features raised by our authors that mediate the connection between game play and learning: the relation of identity and learning, the production process as evidence of learning, the conception of gaming as social learning, and games as a model for interactive assessment.

Identity

Game worlds highlight the tight connection between identity and learning. During short-term play, players experiment with virtual selves to navigate through the game world. Long term, players integrate games-based skills into game-related environments that can translate into possible identities. In one example, Rob LoPiccolo's suggests that games such as *Guitar Hero* "clu[e] people, particularly kids, into some of the fundamentals; here are the roles in the band, here's what a bass guitar part is like, and this is what a rhythm guitar part is like." Researchers can investigate whether features of in-game identity persist as out-of-game behaviors. Rob describes how "there are a lot of guitar and drum teachers in this country now who are seeing steady business because people started with *Guitar Hero* or *Rock Band* and then developed a taste for the real thing." Games such as *Guitar Hero* can provide opportunities to observe how players gain knowledge and skills by adopting identities in virtual worlds that can transform personal roles in out-of-game contexts.

Production

Games allow researchers to consider learning as a form of *production*. The knowledge and skills learned in games typically have direct implications for successful play. The perceived value of knowledge in a game context can help researchers to explore how learning environments lead players to build representations and models to guide play. Tom Malaby shows how navigation of in-game virtual spaces is itself a form of meaningful production, especially when in-game play involves customization and consultation. Theory crafting and soft modding provide examples of how production is an expression of knowing in game contexts. Erica Halverson's discussion of participatory media space design (described below) captures how knowing as production can reflect back on issues of design.

Social Learning

Games research demonstrates the *social* aspects of learning. Games research indicates a trajectory of increasing communicative involvement with opportunities for social learning. Jim Gee and Betty Hayes' affinity group model describes how play first sparks a need to know, then increases motivation to seek out knowledge from others, and finally creates motivation to participate in a knowledge-building community. The trajectory from individually guided learning to social interactive learning parallels the evolution of interest in affinity spaces. Games researchers have already traced this trajectory in a number of spaces (in this volume, we can see examples in *Quest Atlantis*, *Apolyton.com*, GlobalKids, and the *Sims*) that retain the unique research advantages of allowing for the comparison of intended and actual learning outcomes in game worlds.

Constance Steinkuehler and Yoonsin Oh, for example, trace the development apprenticeship relationships in the massively multiplayer gaming world. The interactive nature of the game world presses players to develop long-term collaborative teams as a condition for successful play. In game worlds where some players know much more than others, apprenticeship practices emerge as reasonable solutions to learning social practices through which relevant knowledge and skill are acquired. Constance and Yoonsin suggest that massively multiplayer online games provide a context in which apprenticeship relations emerge as a social accomplishment rather than an institutional imposition. It may well be that the scarcity of these kinds emergent learning relationships is at the heart of the learning challenge for contemporary high school students. If access to socially legitimate learning relationships is indeed a critical problem for teens, then games researchers who uncover how games lead players to participate in meaningful social learning can begin to play a role in the necessary work of high school redesign.

Assessment

Finally, games research can point to new forms of *assessment* for learning. Games research can directly address the gap between the occasion and measurement of learning. Dan Schwartz reminds us that "looking at the choices people make in a course of actions devoted to solving problems in a certain area is a much better assessment both of what they know and of how well prepared they are for future learning" (as quoted in Gee and Hayes, this volume). Scholars such as Robert Mislevy and Valerie Shute explore how performance-based assessments can be developed to supplement or even replace the contemporary correlation-centered assessment model. Games researchers can exploit the degree to which virtual game-based environments are designed to make contextual information, so often tacit in conventional learning environments, open to direct investigation. Game worlds include logs that record the frequency and duration of play, discussion boards that capture player knowledge construction and exchange interactions, modding and design tools that trace how players reconstructed play trajectories, and forums that track how audiences receive and rate game play. These forms of data access are simply not available to researchers in conventional learning environments and can trace a much more comprehensive path of how learners progress.

Access to these kinds of data on learning will continue to lead scholarship toward the grail of using performance-based assessment to measure learning. David Shaffer's epistemic network analysis (ENA), for example, points toward the future of performance-based assessments in virtual environments. ENA demonstrates how the performance of complex learning tasks in data-rich environments can help researchers to use social network analytics to trace growth at different rates across multiple dimensions and to compare learning to expert and novice models. Developing methods such as ENA will allow games researchers to finally provide scalable measures of learning that are true to the complexity of the contexts and processes of real-life learning.

Design

Game design is where game research has the greatest potential to transform education research. If education is concerned with the design of learning environments, then the game designers who have made the most significant and revolutionary exploration of the technologically mediated design space should lead the way. I would like to highlight two aspects of design raised by our authors: design *for* learning and design *by* learners. I think that both areas open up rich areas for investigation that will result in new forms of learning environments for all students.

Design for Learning

Design for learning addresses the principles we can derive (and communicate) for building game-based learning environments. Jim Gee's (2003) outline of principles for video game learning spaces describes the design space in which researchers work. Game designers have developed fully articulated models of scaffolding new users into compelling game worlds, have demonstrated how to adapt player choice into rich narrative environments, and have shown how to integrate just-in-time data into interfaces that guide users in complex tasks. Game designers also have shown how to balance social interaction and task completion so that players are sufficiently motivated to continue play while relying on one another for help. Nathan McKenzie's contribution illustrates the capacity of designers to generate almost limitless variations on genres that exhaust the design affordances of a given genre and point toward new forms of play. When these games are played, designers deepen their understanding of how to structure the game environment to motivate better play. Taking advantage of these powerful precedent designs for virtual learning environments should help educators to create more compelling designs for education.

The researchers in this volume provide several key insights to guide design for learning. Sasha Barab and colleagues, for example, emphasize that the learning environment must allow for transactive engagement by the learner with the game learning goals. Designers must connect "a sense of intentionality with user actions occurring in relation to a situationally meaningfully goal, legitimacy with academic content becoming conceptual tools for acting on the world, and consequentiality as user actions have effect on the virtual world." Doug Clark and Mario Martinez-Garza relate that "game play that…remain[s] in the player's 'thumbs' neither pushes players to articulate the components of their thinking…nor the overarching relationships and connections between the multiple relevant components relevant to the phenomenon at hand." Design for learning must engage players on two levels of representation: the play environment and the concepts to be learned.

Studying design for learning also requires researcher to investigate how designs fail to translate into intended courses of play. Designing game content can lead to interaction that bypasses the underlying concepts. Doug and Mario note how "few games provide structures for externalizing and reflecting on these cycles. More often, such articulation and reflection occur outside the game, through discussion among players or participation in online forums." Designers for learning must use the tools of game design, such as gradually introducing players to game features or designing challenges that call on players to use certain capabilities that problematize the game environment in order to create opportunities for players to reflect on their play. Bob Coulter and his colleagues discuss whether the opportunities for players to reflect on the relation between play representations and underlying concepts can be elicited within game contexts. "Traditional video game[s]...won't be able to activate a player's web of tacit and explicit local knowledge.... While virtual environments are certainly becoming much richer and more realistic, there is still an air of artificiality and, ultimately, of simplification. Even the most complex of virtual game spaces is limited to what the designer chose to place in the game, inevitably constraining choices to a set of pre-arranged options." Coulter and his colleagues suggest that another plane of interaction, such as an augmented reality plane, a forum for social interaction, or a classroom space, may be necessary to trigger interaction with underlying game concepts.

Design by Learners

Erica Halverson's discussion of participatory media space design provides an example of how the design for learning research agenda might unfold. Erica's work considers how media arts organizations organize production experiences for interested youth. She proposes three design principles necessary for student learning and for quality production: iterative production cycles of conceptualization, production, and distribution; assessment benchmarks embedded throughout the production process; and the arrangement of digital tools to facilitate communication and knowledge exchange. The principles that Halverson describes as guiding design *for* learning also apply to design *by* learners. Successful youth media arts and game-development organizations (e.g., GlobalKids, GameTech) understand that learning environments must allow learners to grapple with the hard problems of design. Learning through design is the foundation of the progressive and constructivist movements in education.

Successful game design introduces learner agency into the virtual world. Rather than passively working through problems and situations established by others, good game design allows learners to express hypotheses about possible interaction in worlds of their own. David Sirlin, for example, describes how the compelling game play of *Virtua Fighter* results from designer anticipation of the player-controlled fighting moves. Successful game design anticipates typical and advanced player interactions in ways that reflect the abilities of good teachers. Inviting players (i.e., peers, colleagues, and strangers) into created worlds facilitates a new level of feedback in which must players come to anticipate how worlds must look from the perspective of play.

Seeing the alteration of the game context as a form of design allows us to extend the concept of player agency. After all, the design of a compelling game world probably is the most advanced form of design and the most difficult for many players to undertake. Tom Malaby reminds us of the small adjustments players make to the world that, as de Certeau describes, are also forms of production and thus forms of design. Most acts of design involve the modification, rather than the recreation, of a world. Design activities span a continuum from changing the color of your pants when rolling a character, to soft modding and theory crafting, to modding and the manipulation of game-development engines. From an education perspective, each decision players make to modify their environment represents an idea to be tested in a game environment. Game design by players provides an entirely new dimension in which we can use the concepts and theories of hypothesis testing to capture how learning unfolds in the world(s).

Conclusion

What does the world of education research look like from the point of view of gaming? The chapters in this volume point toward an exciting new future for researchers interested in studying education. There is contemporary pressure for games researchers to organize their work in terms of existing policy-driven research traditions. This may help games researchers to satisfy the short-term goals of legitimacy (and funding), but it will not address the larger crisis in education research. The existing practices that dominate education research may successfully measure the outputs of interventions, but they have difficulty showing how learners navigate worlds. If we believe, as a society, that all the answers to our problems of teaching and learning have already been developed and that improvement is simply a matter of implementing the right interventions, then our current approaches to research are probably sufficient to the task. However, if we believe that the world is changing, that information technologies are transforming teaching and learning, and that the future designs for learning and by learners have yet to be developed, then we will need tools that allow for innovation, exploration, and experimentation. Games researchers can lead the way.

The games research presented here provides a genuine opportunity to reframe education research around the kinds of dynamic innovations that are reshaping the nature of teaching and learning in and out of schools. Games allow researchers and players to experiment with new worlds. Studying how players navigate, learn, and design these worlds provides unprecedented access to the core psychological and social practices of teaching and learning. Grasping the design principles that govern successful game play may enable education researchers and designers to build environments that result in improved outcomes on the learning goals we currently favor. More likely, games will enable us to envision entirely new ways of organizing and measuring learning. We may be able to create meaningful assessments of, for example, systems learning, and we may be able to measure learning in the solution of some of the chronic environmental and economic issues of our times. Games researchers who continue down the paths described in this volume will lead us in the description of emerging learning environments and the translation of design principles into new environments. As Sasha Barab and his colleagues note, the policy that led to the No Child Left Behind legislation has "done little to inspire curriculum that helps children see and desire futures that call on disciplinary content knowledge. An important focus of this [games research] work is to fill that gap, both positioning existing content in new learning platforms and expanding our understanding of what it means to be literate. All of this in a manner that creates a vision of the future that can begin today."

Index

*The Learning in Doing series was founded in 1987 by Roy Pea and John
Seely Brown.*